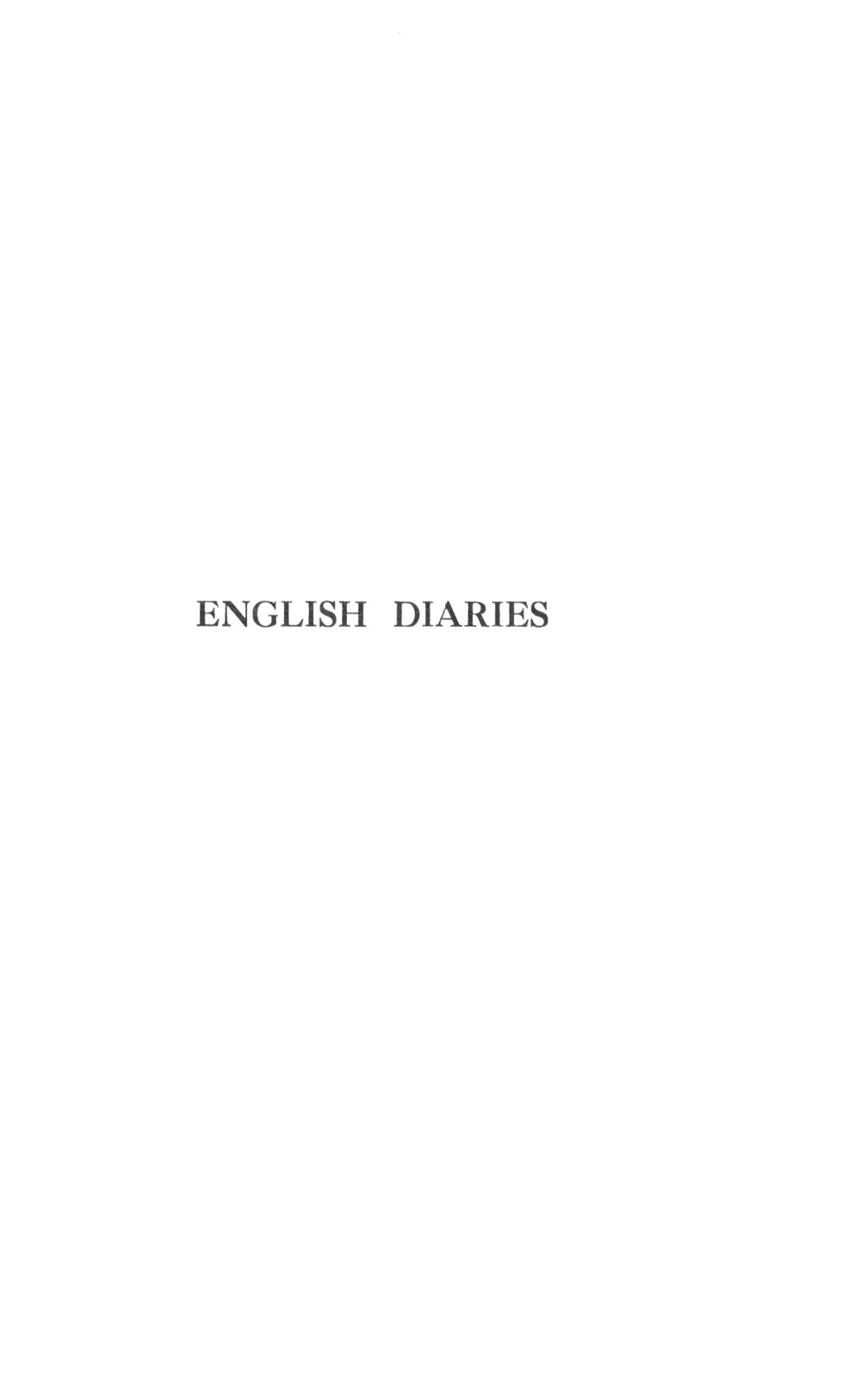

ENGLISH DIARIES

ENGLISH DIARIES

A REVIEW OF ENGLISH DIARIES FROM THE SIXTEENTH TO THE TWENTIETH CENTURY WITH AN INTRODUCTION ON DIARY WRITING

BY

ARTHUR PONSONBY

"No kind of reading is so delightful, so fascinating, as this minute history of a man's self."
MACAULAY

BOOKS FOR LIBRARIES PRESS
FREEPORT, NEW YORK

First Published 1923
Reprinted 1971

INTERNATIONAL STANDARD BOOK NUMBER:
0-8369-6623-6

LIBRARY OF CONGRESS CATALOG CARD NUMBER:
77-175708

PRINTED IN THE UNITED STATES OF AMERICA
BY
NEW WORLD BOOK MANUFACTURING CO., INC.
HALLANDALE, FLORIDA 33009

To
J. P.
AND
F. E, G. P.

PREFACE

I WAS attracted to the study of Diary writing, not by the well-known diaries which are a part of English history or literature, but by the fragments of journals of quite obscure people which are tucked away in the collections of archæological and other learned Societies or unprinted. They seemed to me so human in their interest that they were worthy of being better known. In fact, when embarking on my collection I was inclined at first to leave out the celebrated diarists. The dividing line, however, would have been too difficult to draw, and a book which was to be a study of diary-writing would have been incomplete if the best examples were omitted.

Once I began to collect I found the field opened out pretty widely. There were published diaries some of which had been forgotten, there were privately printed diaries, there were manuscript diaries in libraries or in private houses, and there were diaries absorbed by or scattered in biographies. I had to put a limit to the range of my net. Tempted as I was by the great foreign diarists, I soon saw there was obviously material enough at home. Even within the United Kingdom, if part of my object was to unearth what was little known, I found I should have to confine myself to England alone. This deprived me of some specially good diaries, such as Sir Walter Scott's, Carlyle's, Sir John Moore's, Swift's and John Mitchel's. But to reach the more obscure diarists in Scotland and Ireland special research on the spot would be necessary. In England alone I found indeed as much, if not more, than I could manage. The only other limitation I imposed on myself, and that very willingly, was that my diarists should not be living.

I have not set out to select the best diaries or even only good diaries. My object has been to give a full representation of all shades of diary-writing, long and short, historical, public and private, good, bad and indifferent.

In the reviews which follow the Introduction each diary is dealt with separately. After much consideration I found this a better way than grouping them. The diaries are treated more from the subjective point of view as illustrations of the method, manner, and character of their authors, than from the objective point of view, that is to say the consideration of the subjects about which they wrote. I have not attempted an impartial and colourless survey which would give every diary the same amount of attention, leaving the reader to form his own judgment. But I have criticised freely and expressed my own individual opinion and preferences at the risk of failing to secure in all cases a full measure of agreement from my readers. I have thought it well to insert a few biographical notes, specially in the case of more or less unknown people.

Privately printed and manuscript diaries have been kindly lent to me. Some of the diaries are no doubt rare and out of print, but many are available in any large public library. They are, however, not always easy to find, because diaries are not catalogued as diaries; some books which are called diaries are not diaries at all, and some diaries are hidden away in Lives.

In order to illustrate fully the different styles and methods, a fair number are included in the series. However, I may quite well have missed some diaries which are well worthy of attention.[1]

I do not think I need apologise for having devoted a volume to English Diaries. The study has been repaying, and the subject is one that has hitherto been insufficiently explored. A man who buys a dog immediately becomes interested in other people's dogs. On this analogy I hope anyhow the diary-keepers of to-day may like to know how others have kept diaries in days gone by.

I am indebted to the owners of several unpublished manuscript diaries which have been placed at my disposal. The passages quoted from them appear for the first time in print, and a note of acknowledgment is inserted in each particular case. I have received the kind consent of the publishers of the biographies for the reproduction of the diary entries which have been extracted from these books. My thanks are due to several friends who have helped to call my attention to certain diaries which I might otherwise have missed, and more especially to Mr. Charles Strachey, C.B., for his valuable assistance in revising the proofs. A. P.

SHULBREDE PRIORY,
SUSSEX.
1922.

---

[1] The Farington Diary and Sir Algernon West's Diaries appeared too late to be included; and Mr. Wilfred Blunt was still alive when the book was concluded.

CONTENTS

	PAGE
PREFACE	vii
INTRODUCTION—DIARY WRITING	1
CHRONOLOGICAL LIST OF DIARIES	45
SIXTEENTH-CENTURY DIARIES	55

SEVENTEENTH-CENTURY DIARIES :

SIR SIMONDS D'EWES	71
SIR HENRY SLINGSBY	76
SAMUEL PEPYS	82
JOHN EVELYN	96
HENRY TEONGE	107

SEVENTEENTH-CENTURY MINOR DIARIES . . 112

EIGHTEENTH-CENTURY DIARIES :

JOHN WESLEY	156
THE EARL OF EGMONT	164
FANNY BURNEY	171
WILLIAM WINDHAM	184

EIGHTEENTH-CENTURY MINOR DIARIES . . . 193

NINETEENTH-CENTURY DIARIES :

B. R. HAYDON	254
BYRON	264

NINETEENTH-CENTURY DIARIES—*cont.*:

CHARLES GREVILLE	272
WILLIAM COBBETT	280
QUEEN VICTORIA	288
CAROLINE FOX	300
GENERAL GORDON	306

NINETEENTH-CENTURY MINOR DIARIES . . . 314

TWENTIETH-CENTURY DIARIES 424

INDEX 445

ENGLISH DIARIES

INTRODUCTION ON DIARY WRITING

THERE is a very clear distinction between diary writing and other forms of writing. A consciousness of some literary capacity, however meagre it may be or however unjustified any such assumption may be, stands behind every other form of writing except letter writing. In diary writing no such consciousness need exist nor indeed is any literary capacity necessary. Diary writing is within the reach of every human being who can put pen to paper and no one is in a more advantageous position than anyone else for keeping a diary. People of all ages and degrees who may never have ventured to write a line for publication and may be quite incapable of any literary effort, are able to keep a diary the value of which need not in any way suffer from their literary incapacity. On the contrary, literary talent may be a barrier to complete sincerity. Diaries may or may not be called literature, some undoubtedly have literary value, but this has nothing whatever to do with their merit as diaries.[1] *Diary writing compared with other forms of writing*

A diary, that is to say the daily or periodic record of personal experiences and impressions, is of course a very different thing from history, although some of the older diaries have been of great use in furnishing the historian with facts and giving him examples of contemporary opinion. When Greville concludes one of his entries with "I am too sleepy now to go on with the subject," one feels immediately the wide distinction between the daily contemporary diarist-observer depending for present events *History*

---

[1] In the four-volume history of English literature edited by R. Garnett and E. Gosse only about a dozen of the diaries mentioned in this volume are referred to.

only on his own eyes and ears and memory and the historian making his balanced estimate of the past from the mass of documents with which he is surrounded. For a true judgment of the significance of public affairs one must of course await what Mr. George Trevelyan calls "the slow foot of history." But the incomplete and necessarily restricted comments of the eye-witness have a merit of their own although by themselves they cannot be regarded as history.

Autobiography   A diary differs from autobiography, as in the one we get the fresh relation of events at the moment, and in the other the events are moulded and trimmed into a unified whole more often than not with a view to publication, such for instance as George Fox's Journal, which is not a daily record but an autobiographical survey. Memoirs and Reminiscences are nearly always written for publication. Modelled though they may be on diary memoranda and dated periodically they are presented in narrative form, more easily read perhaps, with all the roughness and repetitions of diary writing eliminated but with a consequent loss of spontaneity and individuality. There are cases in which the dividing line between memoirs and diaries is difficult to draw. But as a general rule memoirs do not record the events of the day on that day.

Letters   Lastly, letter writing has little or no resemblance to diary writing. Letters may contain fresh impressions and personal confidences and confessions, they may be written in almost diary form, but the consciousness in the writer of an immediate recipient exercises a restraint on the author and produces a certain sort of self-consciousness which may be entirely absent from the pages of a diary. Moreover rarely if ever are they found in the regular and complete sequence of a diary. Every one writes letters but a very small percentage of them are readable to anyone but the recipient. Comparatively few people keep diaries, yet it would seem that a fairly large proportion of them have some sort of general human interest. Letters may be said to have two parents, the writer and the recipient. Diaries have only one. A diary can be written with no thought whatever of the discriminating eye of a publisher, of the critical eye of a reviewer, or even of the interested or bored eye of a reader. No pause is needed for modelling phrases, no attention need be given to form, even grammar can go to the winds, and above all there need be no explanations. All restraints can be lifted and in the open fields of fact and fancy the diarist can browse, repose or gallop along at his own sweet will.

We may claim, therefore, that diary writing is a unique form of writing. The literary, the learned and the great by no means necessarily excel in this particular art. It is confined to no one class, no one profession, no one age of life. Sovereigns, scholars, sportsmen, tradesmen, philosophers, old women, and children all write diaries.

There is no need to trace the genesis of diary writing far back into history. Although it is conceivable that documents of the nature of diaries existed in England before the sixteenth century and have been destroyed, there is no real evidence of the existence of what we now know as private diaries in the previous centuries. Instances can of course be found of more personal writing, of chronicles, of accounts, or of reflections. But these are not diaries. The idea of writing down daily thoughts and notes on passing events, especially when it takes a more or less introspective form, is of comparatively modern growth, and would seem to be the outcome of the increasing self-consciousness which intellectual development has produced in humanity. It is a result of psychological evolution, of expanding self-knowledge and subtler powers of analysis. As the centuries pass, the diary-habit seems to gain ground and will probably assume more generally an introspective form. The objective journals will continue, but the more acutely analytical diaries like Arthur Graeme West's (*The Diary of a Dead Officer*) and Barbellion's (*The Diary of a Disappointed Man*) in the twentieth century are likely to increase in number, more especially since the serious introduction of psycho-analysis. *Origin and progress of diary writing*

Some people may be reluctant to confess to their contemporaries that they are keeping a diary. That is why diaries are nearly all " private " in the lifetime of the author. Anyone suspected of careful diary-keeping would naturally be approached with some caution. If he be a Pepys, a Burney, or a Greville he would defeat his own object if the fact were generally known that he was taking notes; his friends and acquaintances would become reticent and shy in his presence. Anyone making inquiries about diary-keeping may quite well be met with a denial from an habitual diarist. So the practice goes on, so to speak, quietly and behind the scenes. The production of a diary in a law court is not an uncommon occurrence. A few people burst into print in their lifetime, but many diaries are discovered afterwards, sometimes long afterwards. A large number of people will be reluctant that anything they have written of a private character should ever reach the public eye, and they may take steps to prevent it. *Diaries kept private*

Biographies

A classic instance of a diary which was converted into a Biography—but an unusual case because it was the diary of the Biographer and not of the subject of the Biography—is Boswell's. It was a detailed objective record carefully kept for a specific purpose. Boswell was known even during a meal to take out his tablets and make notes and he often stayed up late at night entering every incident and word of his intercourse with Johnson. But when it came to the publication of his great book he abandoned the diary form except for the Tour to the Hebrides. Fragmentary extracts from diaries are sometimes quoted in biographies, as, for instance, in the Tennyson Memoir, merely to fill up gaps in the chronological sequence of events.

Classification of diaries

But taking the diaries that have remained more or less intact, they may be found to fall roughly into three classes : (i) the regular diary record with only occasional breaks, (ii) the periodic record written at intervals summing up several days, weeks, or even months. These two classes are often combined ; and (iii) the diary that is written up and edited by the author in later years (the dates often being retained) either with a view to publication or because he or she in retrospect considers a better composition may be produced by emendation and by the pruning away of indiscretions.

Daily writing

Daily writing differs considerably from writing even a few days later. The impulsive note of the moment catches a mood and picks up an impression which may in twenty-four hours evaporate and which in a week or month will have entirely disappeared. But it must be noted that daily dates do not always necessarily imply daily writing. The methodical daily writer, when he misses a day or two, writes up those days separately under their dates when he resumes his writing. A daily record is not by any means more accurate ; on the contrary the focus is too strong, the perspective too restricted and consequently the vision is warped. But accuracy is no particular asset in diary writing except from the point of historical research. Many daily diaries are rendered priceless as human documents by just the little petty trifling details which after a few hours' reflection the writer would have omitted.

Indiscretions

Indiscretions are sometimes the colour of a diary, and their removal seriously impairs the quality of the writing. Autobiographers, and more especially biographers, may find themselves compelled to cut away personalities from the more modern diaries in their fear of offending the susceptibilities of the living. That is why the older diaries, where no such scruples need exist, are often more real and more human. Biographers who are in possession of a diary will dismiss all passages which may not reflect credit on their subject. In such work the tendency to idealise prevails, reputations have to be kept up and heroes elevated on to pedestals. A diarist's undignified little details are discarded, but actuality and truth may suffer. No editor can be trusted not to spoil a diary.

Diaries definitely written for publication obviously differ very materially from private diaries. As Macaulay said, intention to publish "destroys the charm proper to diaries." But this point must be more fully considered when the question of motive on the part of the diarist is examined.

Broadly speaking another classification may be applied to diaries : (*a*) those which are of historical or archæological value on account of the subjects of which they treat and (*b*) those that are of psychological interest on account of the light they throw on the personality of the diarist. *[Historical and psychological interest]*

There are two words which if they were used strictly would help to draw the distinction between these two classes. The word *Journal* should be reserved for the purely objective historical or scientific records, and the word *Diary* for the personal memoranda, notes and expressions of opinion. Some it is true might fall across the division. But as it is, the words are used quite indiscriminately and give no guidance as to the nature of the record.

Political, historical and public chronicles such as Rugge's, Luttrell's, Lord Malmesbury's, Greville's, and Senior's, would come under the first heading, although some of them contain personal comments. In the second category the diaries may be found to be a good deal more interesting and arresting. A shop assistant (Strother) or a storekeeper (Thomas Turner) may claim more of our attention than one who has lived in the midst of exciting events and associated with important people. But the variety displayed in diary writing as regards method, regularity, and style is endless. In writing history, fiction, or even letters you may adapt your style to the model of some admired author. In diary writing this is much more difficult. If you are making daily entries the effort is too great ; you have no time to think, you do not want to think, you want to remember, you cannot consciously adopt any particular artifice ; you jot down the day's doings either briefly or burst out impulsively here and there into detail; and without being conscious of it, you yourself emerge and appear out of the sum total of those jottings, however brief they may be.

Motive   Why do people write diaries ? This question is not easy to answer in a sentence, for the motive seems to vary widely and is sometimes not apparent on the surface. It is not possible to generalise on the subject. Children are often encouraged to keep a diary or enjoined to keep one for disciplinary reasons, and the majority of them find the effort too great, and discontinue it when they grow up. Queen Victoria began at the age of 13, Elizabeth Fry before she was 16, and Fanny Burney at 15, if not earlier, Gladstone when he was at Eton, and all of them kept it up to the end of their lives. Edward VI wrote at about the age of 12 and an instance will be given of a child (Mary Browne), who wrote for a special period, and some examples of diaries begun but not continued are also included. Diaries begun about the age of 20 are common, but there are also many instances of regular diary writing begun at a later age. Pepys began at 27, Fynes Clinton at 28, Byron at 30, Windham at 34, Rutty at 56, Bubb Dodington at 58, and so far as continuance of writing is concerned there are the cases of Henry Crabb Robinson and Edward Pease, who were still keeping diaries when they were over 90.

Habit   The habit having been acquired, either in youth or later, a diarist may continue without having any clear notion with regard to the eventual fate of his diary. In fact, habit and nothing else may account for the writing of a good many diaries. Habit also will make a methodical man keep memoranda of his doings, notes and accounts for future reference, as Windham puts it, " to strengthen the powers of recollection." Daily single line notes have been entered by business men over long periods. A case is known of a very methodical diarist who before he wrote his record of the day re-read the entries of corresponding dates in former years. It is clear that the disciplinary effort of regular writing is pleasant ; and as time passes the growing volumes become a treasure.

Egotism   But beyond the child age and beyond bald business memoranda the question arises : Is egotism the mainspring of diary writing ? The answer to this is yes. But it does not carry us very far, because most people are egotists whether they are diary writers or not, and egotism except in excess ought not to be regarded as a fault. In some cases a diary may be a sort of safety valve for egotism and outwardly the diarist may not appear to be so egotistical as a more obvious egotist who wants to pour out his egotism on his friends, and not confine it to the pages of a private note-book. Indeed, a man may appear very reticent socially

DIARY WRITING

yet all the while he may be unburdening himself privately in the pages of a very full diary. A diarist is self-conscious and sometimes perhaps self-absorbed. A diary, however, may simply serve to enable the writer to take a detached point of view of himself which will be helpful. Egotism in its extreme sense cannot be said to be universally attributable to all known diarists. Vanity, however, in varying degrees, sometimes perhaps in an inordinate degree, can more accurately be recognised as the vice of many diarists.

The autobiographer is a notorious egotist and usually founds his books on a diary, but he has gone a long step further than the diarist. There are well-known instances of literary men who have wrapped autobiographical episodes in a more or less fictional setting in their endeavour to avoid the crudity of purely personal disclosures.

While it may be argued that the highest type of being, so selfless as never for a moment to consider that anything he thought or did was worth recording, would not keep a diary, he anyhow is a rarity ; and it is not selflessness which prevents most people from keeping a diary. In fact it is impossible to classify diarists as a type, for among them may be found all sorts and conditions from the loftiest to the most common, from the most original to the most conventional.

Nevertheless some rough analysis of motive in diary writing can be made. Having disposed of Habit, we come next to " the itch to record," which is an overflowing and exuberant desire for self-expression. People who witness important events, come in contact with celebrated people, or themselves have interesting and exciting experiences, have a natural desire to write about them, without any clearly formed intention as to what they will do with their notes, if they are not in the form of letters. Sometimes they may write definitely for eventual publication or sometimes for the information of their family. But the mere desire to write down their impressions is the instinct which impels them. So strong is this that some will write about public events which they have not witnessed and about which they express no opinion, knowing all the time that a far fuller account of them will be given in newspapers and other public records. Others may confine themselves to the recital of special personal experiences in a particular period without being regular diarists. This sort of record differs to some extent from a private diary, but we will consider it more fully when we reach the question of the various subjects dealt with in diaries.

The itch to record

Surveying Life

Without any excess of egotism and without vanity there are people with orderly minds who by means of private writing want to make a sort of survey of their position and of their opinions as well as of events which concern them. They have sentiment and feeling for the past, they are interested in the stages of life's journey and they do not want to leave unrecorded anything that has struck them deeply. They use their diary pages for clearing their minds, for threshing out human problems, for taking stock of the situation, for weighing the pros and cons when they find themselves confronted with dilemmas. They consider the practice useful. They may even derive from it the same sort of relief as others find in prayer. Some may write down actual prayers while others will as an equivalent brace themselves by a full contemplation of the facts they have to face set down in writing. Although diaries such as these may eventually find their way into print, publication is not present in the minds of the writers.

Self in old age, and posterity

Then there is the not uncommon desire to put down on paper an account of daily events and opinions on men and matters for perusal in later life. That is to say, some people feel sure that in their old age they will want to be reminded of past events and of their changing moods. They write for their future selves. They store, they collect, they are reluctant to lose any passing thoughts. Some again desire definitely to paint their own portrait for posterity, and as they write they are conscious of the eyes of future generations perusing their record though they may keep it locked up from the inspection of their contemporaries. Posterity will know less, will be more lenient, and may accept a man at his own valuation. As Greville says: "Some will pour forth upon paper and for the edification and amusement of posterity what they never would have revealed to living ear; but the majority of those who indulge in this occupation probably only tell what they desire to have known."

Consciousness of a reader

In this connection it may be said that it is almost impossible for anyone to write without imagining a reader, so to speak at the other end, however far off that other end may be—self in old age, family, a friend, the public or remote posterity. Some diarists face this question openly, many seem to write for self in old age, the most critical reader of all, although they do not realise that as they write; others write for a member of the family, others again for the public; but the majority leave the matter undecided or unrevealed. We cannot know, but we should be inclined to think that the case of a person keeping a

DIARY WRITING

regular diary with a definite intention throughout of destroying it before death must be rare, although no doubt many during their lifetime may have destroyed diaries that have been begun, or parts of diaries. Johnson, in talking to Boswell of the Journal the latter kept, said he " might surely have a friend who would burn it in case of his death." Testamentary injunctions on this point may have existed. But most diaries have been left or discovered with no sort of clue as to the intentions of the writer.

Mr. Parkinson, one of the editors of the Chetham Society's volumes, says on this question of consciousness of a reader : " It is not easy to call to mind a journal, private as it may profess to be, which has been undeniably written without some view to a possible reader. The writer, though in his dressing-gown and slippers, still seems to feel that some privileged friend may by some possible chance rush in upon his privacy, and so he arranges his undress with some (perhaps unconscious) view to such a casualty."

This question of a possible reader becomes psychologically very interesting when we come to the class of diaries containing disclosures which reflect no sort of credit on the writer. And this brings us to a distinct and not uncommon motive in diary writing which is the more or less morbid desire for self-analysis, self-dissection, introspection, and even self-revelation. It may take the form of private thoughts which the writer feels he cannot communicate to any friend ; it may take the form of confessions of faults and resolutions for self-correction ; it may be a private vent for complaint or for the commonest of all human failings, self-pity ; it may be a self-indulgent expansion of egotism, or an expected aid to self-discipline. It has been known even to take the form of unrestrained revelations on sexual matters with details which one would suppose the writer would shrink from allowing others to read. If sensuality looms large in the inner consciousness, the attempt of diarists to note it is anyhow a proof of their honesty. So strong is the impulse for ruthless self-dissection in some natures that they will deliberately lay bare their very souls with an almost reckless hope that posterity shall see them naked. But in the majority of cases the confessions are general and vague ; the actual reasons for self-condemnation are not specified. The diarist generalises on his weakness, his sin, his lapses without always recording the particular occasion or character of the faults in question. He is aware of his failure and wants to record his penitence, and by aid of his diary to make resolutions for improvement. It may be the consciousness of a

Introspective diaries

possible reader which restrains him from actually relating the fault in question. Penitence, however vague, will be counted to his credit, the description of the fault committed might lower him in the estimation of posterity. Introspective writers often seem to entertain " an inferiority complex " and to hope that by carefully recording their symptoms they may be able to make some helpful diagnosis.

We have our Haydons and Barbellions, but the most famous instances of introspective diaries are not British. There is something alien to the British temperament in Tolstoy, in Amiel, or in Marie Bashkirtseff who flourishes her dissecting knife and cries : " I not only say all the time what I think but I never contemplate hiding for an instant what might make me appear ridiculous or prove to my disadvantage. For the rest I think myself too admirable for censure." Reticence and reserve are national characteristics outwardly and probably inwardly too ; and among available English diaries there are none which extend the practice of self-dissection to such an extreme as the continental diarists. Most Englishmen think it bad form to be too expansive or to give themselves away. They conceive it improper to write down their innermost feelings, and they shun like the pest anything that approaches affectation.

Self-consciousness Although the honesty and sincerity of the introspective writers may be beyond question, they do not necessarily by their method give a faithful picture of themselves. Indeed it is not through their intentional and deliberate self-dissection that we really get to know people. Such method is too self-conscious and too artificial. A diarist reveals himself or gives himself away by casual and quite unpremeditated entries far more than by laborious self-analysis. Thomlinson's diary is a good instance of this.

We think we know ourselves better than others know us. But the truth is we only know the inside half, and it is doubtful whether any human being in varying moods can describe even that accurately. Moreover the little shop window we dress and expose to view is by no means all that others see of us. We may be very self-conscious about things which others hardly notice and throughout our lives we may be entirely unaware of some glaring peculiarity which continually strikes our neighbours. A pelican is not the least self-conscious about the size of his beak. A peacock may be self-conscious about his tail, but he thinks too that he has a beautiful voice. On the other hand, outsiders may believe that some person is quite oblivious of certain failings till

DIARY WRITING

it is discovered by his diary that he has been struggling with them all along.

We have said that the honesty and sincerity of indiscreet and unreticent writers are beyond question. This perhaps requires some qualification. Self-deception is very prevalent. There is a good deal of truth in Byron's remark in his diary, "I fear one lies more to one's self than to anyone else," or as Gladstone puts it, "I do not enter on interior matters. It is so easy to write, but to write honestly nearly impossible." The luxury of self-depreciation or self-justification which can be written without fear of contradiction or criticism from outsiders is very likely to upset anyone's judgment. Some people with an eye on posterity are apt to make themselves out worse than they are so that by self-disparagement they may eventually get credit for being better than they seemed. *Self-deception*

The introspective Diary, however, is specially interesting as it often discloses unsuspected features, and the light thrown on the writer's personality coming from within gives a different and new relief to the tissue of his character. On the subject of these more intimate diaries Henry Fynes Clinton, who kept one, makes the following observations: "I am not sure that the practice is beneficial. Many evil thoughts that would pass away from the mind are arrested in their passage, fixed in the attention and made permanent by the habit of noting them down. Many transient uneasinesses too are magnified in importance by being registered in the journal and a morbid sensibility generated; thus we become less satisfied with our condition and with those who surround us. Perhaps then it is safer to confine a journal to a mere *diary of facts*, but carefully to abstain from setting down opinions upon subjects that try the passions deeply. Let the transient thought *be* transient; let us forbear to give it a habitation and a name, form and substance, in our minds." *Use of introspective diaries*

Some diarists express a similar opinion, while others agree with J. A. Symonds' verdict, "ordinary log book a poor affair." As to whether the practice is beneficial to the writer or not we need express no opinion. The fact remains that in varying degrees it is fairly common with diary-writers; and readers have no reason to deplore it. A long subjective diary giving as it does the history of a personality is certainly more interesting to read than a long objective diary giving a bare record of facts.

It will be seen that there is a very wide difference between the motives of the two extremes: the impersonal memorandum-writers and morbid self-dissectors. The former often retain their habit over a number of years, whereas the latter generally cover short periods, although Heywood, Windham, Haydon, Fynes Clinton, and Barbellion are exceptions. There are diarists who write so much about themselves that one is sometimes surprised they do not write more. It seems there is always some limit; either reluctance or disinclination may prevent them from noting their most poignant personal experiences. Moreover, even regular diarists will hesitate to write down a passing impression or opinion coloured as it may be by momentary bias. They have sufficient foresight to realise that after reflection their view may alter and their considered opinion is likely to be quite different, but that owing to a certain inherent inconsequence and carelessness in diary-keeping, the hasty opinion may remain uncorrected and conceivably be read. Caution, however, is not as a rule a diarist's characteristic, and there are many who impulsively jot down the passing thought. It may be found that a diarist sometimes fails to note some preoccupation until events arise which force it to the front. He may then disclose how much the circumstances or impressions have been occupying his thoughts.

Non-diarists
To those who have never kept, and never intend to keep, any sort of diary—that is to say, the majority of people—the idea of deliberately sitting down, inscribing on paper and keeping a record of passing thoughts, and worse still of private sentiments and innermost feelings, is absolutely and entirely incomprehensible.

Here we come to the very clear and sharp dividing line between diarists and those whom we may call non-diarists. The interesting thing about it is that outwardly on the surface there is no sort of indication of the difference between the two. It is an interior matter of psychology. A diarist cannot be unfailingly detected by his appearance, manner, habit, or position, although owing to certain circumstances some may be suspected of keeping a diary. But unless the fact is unconcealed or well known, no one can divide, with anything like accuracy, even his intimate friends into those who keep diaries and those who do not.

Some attempt is being made here to explain why people keep diaries, and it must be simply the entire absence of any of the motives, incentives, and peculiarities of disposition enumerated, which gives us the negative explanation of why people do not keep diaries.

Short entries in diaries
Before dealing with the subjects which occur in diaries, it should be noted that every diarist has to exercise a certain discretion

DIARY WRITING

and to go through a process of sifting and selection. It is manifestly impossible to record *everything*, although at least one pathetic attempt has been made to do the impossible. The chronicling of every thought, word and deed from morning to night would be too great a tax on the memory and would occupy too much time and space. The diarist therefore chooses the incidents which at the moment he thinks matter—the governing facts of the day.

The single sentence or even a single word entries of regular diarists, except those which consist merely of a note of a birth, death, dinner, visit, journey, or some such ordinary occurrence, are often curiously characteristic. The following very brief entries extracted from diaries may be given as examples:

DR. DEE—I had a grudging of the ague.

THOMAS MARCHANT—We had a dish of green peas for dinner to-day.

THORESBY—This day as yesterday wholly spent in study.

PEPYS—Looking after my workmen, whose laziness do much trouble me.

HEYWOOD—I had gracious meltings of the heart in prayer. God helpt me in all the duties of the day, blessed be God.

BEPPY BYROM—Smoothing (i.e. ironing).

GALE—Having taken three pills I went to Peerless for a 1*d*. worth of warm ale.

WESLEY (at 22)—Resolved to reflect twice a day.

WINDHAM—Saw a tight battle at the corner of Russell Street.

FYNES CLINTON—Hodie Augustinum " De civitate Dei ! "

DR. RUTTY—A little swinish at dinner.

ELIZABETH FRY—A much better day though many faults.

HAYDON—Nothing but horror and idleness to reflect on for the last three weeks.

CAROLINE FOX—Plenty to do, and plenty to love and plenty to pity. No one need die of *ennui*.

BAKER—Prawns, shrimps, and cockles.

GEORGE ELIOT—Read Theocritus ; meditated on characters for Middlemarch.

COL. PONSONBY—Very hot, played at rackets, on guard at Bank.

ROSE—No material alteration in the King's health.

GLADSTONE—Wrote a brief abstract of the intended Bill ; wood cutting.

COBBETT—At Burghclere, one half the time writing and the other half hare-hunting.

LORD COLCHESTER—I carried up the Population Bill to the Lords.

MACAULAY—Wrote : this Glencoe business is infernal.

LORD MALMESBURY—Dinner at Zinzendorff's, first assembly at Count Finckenstein's.

BARBELLION—The immediate future horrifies me.

The regular diarist at his accustomed moment, probably the last thing at night, scribbles down the incidents of the day. If the day appears to him comparatively uneventful and he is in no mood for general reflections, or if he is hurried or tired, he will just register what appears to him the most salient impression—

enough for him to recall the day when he re-reads the entry, if he ever does, and sufficient to prevent a break in the continuity.

Subjects dealt with in diaries

The subjects dealt with in diaries may reveal motive; the manner of their treatment discloses the diarist's style and method. Topics of the most frequent occurrence may be considered seriatim.

Health

The regular diarist will invariably enlarge on the state of his health. Nothing could be more natural. If you write on the day even a bilious attack or a bad cold matters considerably and looms large. If you write two or three days later the memory of the minor ailments has vanished. Operations and prolonged illness will be noted by anyone who is keeping a faithful account of his days, because they are impediments to action and alter the whole routine of life. Morbid instances can be found of people who literally watch the state of their health, and the fact that they suffer no doubt gives the clue to their morbidity. John Baker is an extreme instance, but Dr. Dee, Pepys, Rutty, Newcombe, Byron, George Eliot, J. A. Symonds, Barbellion, and many others give a good many particulars with regard to their health. In the earlier diaries both the diseases and the cures are, to say the least of them, curious. Timothy Burrell has "flatulent spasms" from eating new cheese after getting his feet wet, and Ashmole hangs three spiders round his neck, which cures his ague. But in the later diaries, too, health remarks are very common. Even Greville, in what is almost an official chronicle, invariably notes his attacks of the gout. A carefully-kept analysis of symptoms may have considerable value from the medical point of view.

The weather

The weather comes under much the same category as health. A fine day or a rainy day affects the mood of the sensitive daily writer, and certain temperaments are undoubtedly very susceptible to the cheering influence of sunshine and the depressing effects of an overcast sky. That it rained to-day is an important matter *to-day*, as it may have entirely altered the course of our pursuits. Next Tuesday we shall not remember whether it rained or not. Daily diarists therefore often note the weather regularly. Haydon's father, whose diary was destroyed, hardly made an entry without registering the state of the wind. In naval diaries of course the weather stands out as a special feature. Some periodic diarists note storms, hurricanes, frost, heat, or drought, more especially if they are personally affected by them. Even in very scrappy diaries earthquakes, comets, and floods are described.

DIARY WRITING

Food figures very prominently in many diaries. A good dinner is noted by people who might never be suspected of having noticed the food at all. The good meal leaves a deeper impression than might be supposed. There are more remarks about food in regular diaries than in occasional diaries. Sometimes it is elaborated into a special feature of the diary, as, for instance, Teonge's tremendous dinners and Lady Nugent's Jamaica banquets, and we have an instance in which over-eating is a special vice to be corrected. There are many diaries, however, in which food is never mentioned at all. *Food*

Drink occurs more often than food. The immediate effects of excess naturally colour the outlook of the daily diary writer. In the seventeenth and eighteenth centuries drink is very prominent as drunkenness was very common. It becomes the cause of the diarist's hilarity or depression, sometimes of his illness, and in more than one diary resolutions against over-indulgence are conscientiously noted. Turner's constant and it is to be feared fruitless endeavours to overcome his excesses occupy a large part of his extraordinary but very amusing diary. Mrs. Browne's companions on board ship were certainly not a sober company. *Drink*

In the earlier diaries we get more domestic details than in the later ones, where original manuscripts are not at our disposal and where the editor's blue pencil has been more rigorously used. The relations of husband and wife and of parents and children occur in the fuller and more intimate diaries. Pepys' relations with his wife are almost the most amusing part of his diary. Adam Eyre objects to his wife brawling; Turner's two wives Peggy and Molly are realistically represented; Burrell has an affection of the stomach owing to his irritation with his sister; Baker's devotion to " Uxor " is very pathetic, Egmont's eulogy of his wife comes almost as a surprise in his voluminous official diary. Mary Shelley's brief reference to the death of her child is tragic. *Domestic details*

Servant troubles are frequently noted, sometimes by writers for whom such trivial mundane affairs might be supposed to have no sort of importance. Dr. Dee says his wife is " desperately angry " with her maids; Slingsby gives elaborate details about his cook, his gardener and other servants; the learned Ashmole has trouble with his man Hobbs; Timothy Burrell is impatient when his servant puts too much salt in his broth; Adam Eyre whips Jane; Newcombe complains of " the villainous carriage " of his servants, and Elizabeth Fry is depressed at their ingratitude. Servants, indeed, like ill-health and the weather, can upset the day's routine.

It would be interesting if a diary could reveal their side of the story. But so far a domestic servant's diary is not available. Besides the noting of family and domestic affairs there are instances of diarists who register the most trivial details. A case is known of a man who wrote down the number of cigarettes he smoked each day.

Religion   No subject occurs more frequently than religion in some shape or form. Accounts of sermons, theological discussion, the reading of religious books, philosophic meditations, self-examination, devotional practices and private prayer may be found in abundance in many diaries. Sermons are given sometimes very fully. Manningham reports them almost verbatim. Thanksgiving and supplication to God, whether expressed in a sentence or in a page, may be discovered in almost any regularly kept diary. In fact it may be said that a temperament addicted to religious meditation or speculation is just the sort of temperament that produces a diary. As Elizabeth Fry puts it, " that is the advantage of a true journal, it leads the mind to look inwards." In the seventeenth century and later the keeping of a register of facts and feelings was regarded as part of the religious exercise of pious people. The seventeenth-century diaries given here consist very largely of those of divines. But apart from these, declarations of faith in supernatural intervention and expressions of humility or of gratitude to the Deity find their way into the great majority of private diaries, no matter what the profession or character of the diarist may be. In some diaries which contain a great deal of religious matter, a sanctimonious, not to say self-righteous, touch may occasionally be detected, and the common tendency of mistaking dependence on a supernatural power for spiritual excellence. These diarists do not show any real perspicacity in self-knowledge or self-analysis because they generally take refuge in writing down more or less conventional religious formulæ of self-disparagement. There may also be found in some cases a scarcely-concealed conviction that the prayer and moralising will at some future date be edifying reading for others. Undoubtedly a certain natural relief results to the diarist from written expressions of repentance and self-administered homilies, as when Henry Newcombe has " a deale of sweet discourse " about the " baseness " of his heart, " rivers of tears " issue from Thoresby's eyes, and Henry Martyn loathes himself for his " secret abominations." We, as readers, in perusing such diaries find that our glance wanders perhaps rather maliciously over the page in search of the lapses rather than of the conquests. There is colour in faults, but not always in righteousness. The truth is that self-disparagement in excess, even when practised privately, is a form of self-indulgence and does not ring quite true. Both the exultant righteousness and the exaggerated self-abasement in some religious diaries are not convincing; and insincerity is a fatal fault in a diary. But, on the other hand, a really pathetic and even tragic note may be found in some expressions of regret, self-blame and despair, even though they be expressed in a single sentence.

Many people take the opportunity of excursions or travel to write very full descriptions of the sights they see. Lakes and mountains, cathedrals and monuments, inspire travellers with a desire to write. But it must be frankly confessed that unless the writer is endowed with considerable literary talent this section of their diary is likely to prove extremely dull. Nothing indeed shows up a writer's literary incapacity more than his attempts to expatiate on the wonders of nature and art; and his or her (for women are more especially fond of this form of writing) unrestrained enthusiasm in no way makes these passages more tolerable. Only a few instances will be found of diarists who succeed in this line. Even in biographies the chapters on travel are seldom readable. Surveyors' topographical records of their journeys such as the *Itinerary* of John Leland in the sixteenth century cannot be classed as diaries. *[margin: Scenery and travel]*

When a diarist meets a celebrity he will unfailingly make a note of it. When anyone constantly meets celebrities it becomes a reason for keeping a diary. It certainly must have been the main motive in the case of Crabb Robinson. Contact with sovereigns and royalties frequently produces diary writing. Quite a considerable number of diaries deal with the sayings, doings, habits and appearance of royalty. For instance, the sections of her diary noted by Emma Sophia Lady Brownlow in her *Reminiscences of a Septuagenarian* (1867), which is not included in the collection, deal exclusively with minor royalties in Holland. Of course this sort of thing may be well done or badly done. Occasionally we get a vivid and intimate sidelight such as Dee's and Manningham's references to Queen Elizabeth; Pepys on Charles II; Lake's account of the marriage of William and Mary, on which occasion Charles II behaved in a highly characteristic way; Bubb Dodington's intercourse with Frederick Prince of Wales and his wife, and Egmont's character sketch of that Prince; Fanny Burney's conversations with George III and Queen Charlotte; Lady Charlotte Bury's striking portrait of Queen Caroline; and Lady Malcolm's description of Napoleon. George IV's " undignified *[margin: Royalties, celebrities and social life]* practices, at which," Greville tells us, " grave men were shocked," form the subject-matter of many diaries. George calling for brandy when he first meets Caroline of Brunswick was an astonishing scene of which Lord Malmesbury was the sole witness. But often we may get just the bald mention of the presence of royalty, or a list of names of eminent people seen or met. In any case the vision of or casual intercourse with kings, queens, princes, dukes, ministers, poets, authors, painters, and actresses prompts a diarist to go home and write it all down. He feels he is contributing to history. It is certainly true and after all quite natural that every diarist who came within eyeshot or earshot of Dr. Johnson and the Duke of Wellington at once made a special note of it.

Accounts of balls, dinner-parties, country-house parties, ceremonies, pageants, and social functions of every description occur in a multitude of diaries. In fact some diaries may be found to be composed of very little else. It requires an exceptionally skilful pen to make anything of this kind interesting or amusing, especially if it is of fairly recent date. From the class of mind that thinks it worth while to register nothing but bald social notes it is useless to expect any gleams of perception or indeed anything of interest. Celebrities seem often to be mentioned, not because the writers want to draw a portrait of them, but because they want to increase their own importance by showing they were on intimate terms or even acquainted with the great. Indeed keepers of social diaries are apt to give rather a false idea of their own importance. A reader gets the impression that they only dine with authors and great statesmen and consort with notables. They seem to echo the author of *Vanity Fair* in saying, " I declare I swell with pride as these august names are transcribed by my pen." Unless an eye is kept on the dates the dull days that are omitted are not noticed. We very seldom get " dined with Mrs. Jones " or a character sketch of John Smith, and it must be acknowleged that the unceasing presence of the great is very fatiguing. In the more genuine full diary, minor matters are just as carefully noted, as for instance when Egmont writes, " This day old Mrs. Minshull and Mr. Javaegam dined with us." It is in the category of Social Diaries that more might probably be found than are included in this collection. Miss Mary Bagot's early nineteenth-century diaries quoted in *Links with the Past*, by Mrs. Charles Bagot (1901), have not been included, as there would seem to be a sufficient number of examples of social diaries in that period. Playgoing is a very favourite topic with some

DIARY WRITING

diarists, notably Pepys, Windham, Crabb Robinson, Henry Greville, and concerts and opera are often described.

Lists of books read or purchased and comments and opinions on books are of common occurrence. We get an insight into the diarist's tastes, but searching criticism, even where there is literary appreciation, is rare. Fynes Clinton gives a curiously elaborate analysis of the books he studies, and of course books figure prominently in Macaulay's Diary and Mary Shelley's. There is one case of a soldier's diary (Sir Gerald Graham) in which the books he is reading are the only subject he mentions outside his strictly professional military pursuits. Thomas Green's diary is exceptional, being almost entirely confined to literary criticism. Books

Lists of deaths, births, and marriages are common. A few diaries are exclusively occupied with them. John Hobson shows a morbid love of recording deaths. Accounts of expenditure are often noted in diaries, or anyhow the mention of prices. Giles Moore writes almost exclusively in the language of accounts, and Stapley notes punctiliously the exact spot where payments were made. How personal character as well as information as to prices can appear in a list of payments, is illustrated in the page of accounts kept by one of the Ladies of Llangollen. A good many old account books are available which cannot be reckoned as diaries, although by their weekly and sometimes daily entries they come very near to some of the brief diary memoranda. Mention may be made here of two of these. Records and accounts

There are the household books of the 3rd and 4th Earls of Derby kept between 1561 and 1589.[1] The writer of the first one is unknown. William Harington, the steward or secretary, kept the later one. These books give the most exact and minute account of everything connected with their Lordship's household. They contain bills for all provisions, food and wine, bills of fare, items of wages paid, long lists of servants with orders and regulations for the household; also a carefully kept daily record of all guests who came to stay or who dined, and sometimes the name of the preacher. They give in fact a complete picture of a large Elizabethan establishment, and incidentally much information with regard to prices.

The other instance is the household account book of Sarah Fell of Swarthmore Hall,[2] kept between 1673 and 1678, which is strictly an account book and not a diary. In it we see not only

---

[1] Chetham Society: *Stanley Papers*.
[2] *Household Accounts of Sarah Fell of Swarthmore Hall*, ed. by Norman Penney, 1920.

the liberal provision that was made for the household, but we can note prices, wages and taxes, and various entries give us a glimpse into the fortunes of the family. There is a note of her going to prison in 1676. The tobacco that is bought is used for washing sheep as well as for smoking, " tobacco pipes " are purchased for Sister Susannah, but we can hardly believe she used them herself. References to dress show that a " muffe " was bought for Sarah, a " black allamonde rounde whiske " for Sister Rachel, " a little pocket looking-glass " for Susannah, and " a vizard maske for myselfe 1s. 4d." We also find an echo of the inevitable servant trouble, " Ann Standish's wages for the year is £1 17s. 6d., but she paid 8s. for a silver spoon lost and 6d. for a pot broken." In fact, an analysis of these carefully kept accounts yields a good deal of history.

Another business register and record of payments which has not been included in this collection is Philip Henslowe's so-called Diary. It consists of memoranda of receipts and payment connected with the plays produced between 1592 and 1603 in the theatres of which he was proprietor. While it contains much valuable information from the point of view of literary archæology. it cannot by any stretch of the definition be classed as a diary. There is a business record of the same description by Thomas Osborne, Duke of Leeds, kept between 1705 and 1712. The dated entries are not daily but very frequent. They are written on long narrow sheets in a rough but clear handwriting, and concern his property, his will, the transfer of stock, mortgages, deaths, family illnesses and dates of parliamentary events. Only once does he express anything like an opinion in an indignant reference to the Act of Toleration.

No special mention is made of the diary of John Worthington who was master of Jesus College, Cambridge, in the middle of the seventeenth century. It is nothing more than an enlarged engagement book, although he puts in a few notices about his health. Dowsing's journal, though it can hardly be regarded as a private diary, has been included owing to the unique character of his business.

Clothes   One might think that as food and drink are so often referred to, clothes would be also, but this is not the case. Pepys' very elaborate description of his own costume and his wife's stands more or less alone. There are casual references like Giles Moore's scarlet waistcoats, etc., the stockings Burrell purchases for his daughter ; and the Ladies of Llangollen's riding habits. Queen Victoria discusses her clothes with Lord Melbourne, and Fanny

DIARY WRITING

Burney talks of Queen Charlotte's clothes, if not her own. But even daily diarists seldom dwell on the subject.

Thrilling adventures, hairbreadth escapes (Thoresby's dangerous ride, Evelyn's adventure with the cut-throats, Crabb Robinson's encounter with a thief in the Strand, Caroline Fox's escape from a bull), fires, floods, etc., are related even in meagre diaries. The immediate vivid recollection of the event written down perhaps while the diarist is still affected by the experience sometimes give the descriptions a striking realism even with diarists whose powers of expression appear normally rather restricted. *Accidents*

Notable public events, a king's death, the outbreak of war, civil commotion, a murder or a trial are noted by many diarists even though they may be far removed from the scene. References to political and public affairs in the diary of some obscure person in the provinces, although they may be just perfunctory statements, help to link him to the centre of national life and remind one of the historical period in which he lived. Of course there are full diary records of such events which, like Egmont's or Greville's, become the foundation material for history, the author having had exceptional opportunities for observation. Admiral Cockburn's diary of the voyage to St. Helena is an instance of a short one. Labouchere's Diary of a Besieged Resident in Paris in 1871, though written daily, is not a diary, but articles for a newspaper. They were reprinted from the *Daily News*. The social political diaries like Henry Greville's and Raikes' deal largely with public events, and there are two diaries of Speakers which are reserved principally for parliamentary business. *Public, political and social events*

A good many diaries are confined exclusively to the recital of public events, whether national or local, without any personal colour at all. Instances are given, but it is not worth while to examine them all. Nicholas Brown's diary published in the Surtees Society's collection, although it covers a long period (1767 to 1796), is devoid of any but local interest. The diary of Walter Younger (1604–1628), M.P. for Honiton, except for notes on the weather and the crops, is simply a register of public affairs.

If a census of diary keepers could be made it would probably be found that divines and soldiers headed the list. Many a man in war time will keep a diary though he has never done so before and does not do so again. War is of such crucial importance while it lasts and so filled with exciting and nerve-racking experiences that a participant very naturally wants to make some immediate record of it, however brief. Unfortunately it is a case in which the events to be recorded are too vast for any recorder. *War*

The individuality of the writer often, though not always, becomes submerged, and in any event he is confined to noting the particular incidents in his particular corner. While the sum total of such experiences becomes of great value to the military historian, they are in themselves, except for hairbreadth escapes and dangerous adventures, seldom worthy of special notice. There is a sameness about military movements, preparations, tactics and organisation which no pen can relieve. In the rare cases where a writer describes his own sensations, or can give a really graphic picture of scenes and incidents, we get a welcome personal note and the individuality of the diarist emerges. But naturally enough the number of troops he has, the amount of ammunition, the prospects of reinforcements, the reported movements of the enemy and the state of the weather are of overmastering importance on the day he writes. But that importance fades quickly. The consequence is that military diaries (many more of which might be cited than are mentioned in this collection) are on the whole not among the most interesting. General Gordon's Khartoum diary is a notable exception.

But in British soldiers' diaries there is a special characteristic which would not be found in the diaries of soldiers of other nations. They write with extreme reticence about dangers and horrors, and they never betray themselves by any display of emotion. Even important engagements are very baldly described. Typical diaries of this description are referred to in the reviews. An instance may be quoted here of an officer in the South African War, who was present at the battles of Modder River and Magersfontein. In his diary entry he describes a day's fishing, going into detail as to the flies he used and the sort of rod and gut suitable for South African rivers. He notes that he wants a pony for coursing hares and thinks he will find a suitable one at a Dutch farmer's. Then he adds: "We have had two big battles."

But in many soldiers' diaries during the war will be found the recurrence of the three same moods : eagerness to be in action, impatience at the delays and periods of waiting, followed by a longing for the end.

Sport and games

Diarists pretty frequently mention their hunting, fishing and shooting exploits, and cricket matches are described. But there are diaries kept exclusively for a record of sport. The second Earl of Malmesbury, for instance, kept a journal of his sporting life (1801–1840) in which he entered the quantity of powder and shot he used, the game he killed each day, the time he was out, the distance he walked, and the weather. Hunting diaries are very common. In the history of any Hunt will be found extracts from a number of hunting diaries. In addition to William Goodall's diary which is reviewed, we may mention H. B. Yerburgh's *Leaves from a Hunting Diary in Essex*; Edwin Stevens's, the huntsman of the Warwickshire Hunt, whose regular entries cover a number of years in the 'forties; Lord Willoughby de Broke's diary, and Sir Charles Mordaunt's, with their long, regular and elaborate entries dealing with runs with the hounds. There may be mentioned, too, the diary of the Rev. W. S. Millar in the eighteen sixties, who shows a very keen enjoyment of the sport and is thoroughly pleased with his own exploits. " Rode the Squire, who carried me splendidly, jumping South Newington brook in capital style "— " the most satisfactory kill I have seen this season," etc. This diary of a sporting parson forms an amusing contrast to the many diaries of his fellow-divines which are mentioned here, occupied largely as they are with prayer and self-condemnation. The *Extracts from the Diary of a Huntsman*, by Thomas Smith, is not a diary, but descriptions of runs and hunting adventures, with advice about keeping hounds. Some of the many hunting diaries are literally voluminous, others just brief notes, but all are totally devoid of any remarks not concerned with the actual sport itself. They are, however, real diaries written probably on the very evening of the events recorded. When H. B. Yerburgh writes, " Let me jot it down this Monday evening while memory runs hot within me and ere its colour fades away," he is exercising the method of a true diarist. The curious thing is that these diaries, not only in the similarity of their style, but in the extremely limited range of the subject—the line of country, the fox's course, the conduct of the hounds and of the horses, accounts of accidents, and sometimes a list of people present—are practically unreadable even for other hunting men. The keen enjoyment produces an " itch to record," and these sportsmen write for themselves in their old age so that in the evening of life they can be reminded of these great moments and enjoy once more in imagination the famous runs.

Apart from soldiers, sailors and explorers, it is curious how often diaries avoid any but the briefest mention of the professional work of the author. It would seem as if he turned away from his daily professional duties deliberately in order to expand the more private side of his nature in his diary. But there are many too who note the progress and development of their professional work and are obviously absorbed in it, like Gladstone, for instance, who notes little else.

Professional work

Anecdotes and quotations

While a good anecdote, a joke or a verse may be inserted in many diaries, there are some which seem to be solely kept for collecting and storing such material. Manningham with his anecdotes, and John Rous with his satirical poems, are instances of diaries which come very near to being commonplace books, but they contain other material as well. Miss Frances Wynne's ten volumes, selections from which were published in 1864 under the title of *Diaries of a Lady of Quality*, are not, as the editor remarks, what is commonly understood or described by the name of diary, but a store of extracts from other people's letters and reminiscences of striking events. They are not included in this collection, although reference is made to Sir M. Grant Duff's large assortment of anecdotes which were produced in diary form.

Gossip and scandal

There are a fair number of collectors of gossip and scandal either in the form of anecdote, rumour or revelation. They seem confident that their notes will be interesting and important in the future, perhaps after they are dead, although some are tempted to let it all out before they die. But contrary to their belief a collection of *on dits*—" so-and-so told me privately," " I could hardly believe it, but . . .," " I actually heard to-day that . . ." —makes the dreariest possible reading—more especially when they are stale and a little tarnished from the passage of time. Their only interest lies in the disclosure they give of the type of mind of the writer. However, a sudden little bit of unexpected scandal, a malicious hint or a sly hit, can give a welcome spark and flicker to a low-burning flame.

Many regular diarists take the occasion of their birthday or of the end of the year to make a sort of survey of their lives, review their work and pursuits, or indulge in religious or philosophic reflections, and several write up their early life before they began diary writing. In these practices we can see clearly the self-regardant nature of the diarist.

Diaries not written for publication

The above subjects have been mentioned as being common to most diaries. But each diary contains something individual, and even in the baldest record phrases and comments will occur which disclose to the reader the idiosyncrasies of the writer. Diaries manifestly not written for publication, while their literary value may often be negligible, are as human documents of peculiar interest. Very often too a diary is all that exists to tell us the story of some otherwise quite unknown person. There is a fascination here in unearthing the unexplored which we do not get in the case of prominent people about whom much else is known beyond what is contained in their diaries. A very poor diary may be printed if its author becomes famous, while a very much better diary may never see the light if its author was publicly a person of no particular account.

In all diaries that have been printed—and the great majority of those collected here have been—a certain amount of trimming has taken place. Indiscretions, intimacies, or indecencies, have been cut out. The more modern they are the more this has been done. No one can be expected to go and examine the original manuscripts even if it were always possible, with a view to ferreting out the passages omitted. But undoubtedly something has been lost. In some cases a slightly different impression of the diarist, whether better or worse, might be given by a perusal of the manuscript intact. Stars, blanks, initials and dashes are often very annoying and tantalizing to the reader.

Various devices are used by diarists to ensure secrecy. Many seem to fear the accidental discovery of their volume. Cypher is by no means uncommon for special entries and the use of it is a clear proof that the diarist is only writing for himself. Pepys wrote his diary throughout in shorthand, fearing a possible reader. Byrom did the same, but in his case it was because he was the inventor of a system of shorthand. Foreign languages are also used occasionally. Baker introduces a good many French, Latin and Italian words and phrases, Burrell conceals his remarks about his family and his diseases in Latin, Dr. Dee and Fynes Clinton frequently break into Latin, and Dugard's whole diary is written in Latin. Diarists may not fear posterity, but practically all of them shrink from the prying eye of their own contemporaries. *Devices to ensure secrecy*

Only a few diaries here mentioned were illustrated. Burrell seems to have used little sketches as figures to catch his eye in looking back over his accounts; the illustrations of the child Mary Browne are the chief features of her diary; General Gordon, in addition to maps and plans, draws one or two amusing caricatures; some drawings from her sketch-books are inserted in Queen Victoria's early diary and in the *Leaves from the Highlands* she makes a few sketches. One of the private manuscript diaries mentioned contained many drawings and caricatures by the author; and Hannington, the missionary, illustrates African scenes. *Illustrated diaries*

Dull and almost colourless records are common enough, even in cases where the diarist has had specially favourable opportunities of seeing interesting people and participating in notable events. He may be embarrassed by the abundance of his material, he may be confused as to what to select, or he may be deficient in powers of observation and description. A sentence of criticism or of *Dull diaries* frank personal opinion may convey a scene or present a personality better than pages of description. In a diary the writer counts much more than the subject. A prominent London man of society may not give us such a good diary as an obscure provincial schoolmaster. Indeed it may be said that the nineteenth-century social diaries are among the most difficult to read. But in the dullest diary it is well to be on the look-out for sudden indiscretions or betrayals of feeling.

Eccentricity Diarists are not in themselves eccentric any more than those who do not keep diaries, although people who are mentally unbalanced often indulge in the practice. But the unexpected and latent eccentricity which exists in many people may find an outlet in diary writing. Even the most apparently conventional people are sometimes given to strange peculiarities of thought and habit. But Dr. Rutty's diary has a degree of sustained eccentricity which is unparalleled. John More shows signs of being rather odd, and the diary of the Ladies of Llangollen is certainly original.

Old diaries Many old diaries become interesting merely on account of their age, as illustrations of manners and customs which have disappeared, or as providing archæological information with regard to places or people. We can appreciate more fully through diary reading the extraordinary mortality among children in the seventeenth century than we can through the bare recital of statistical facts. We can also gather in the same early period something of the astonishing precocity of the very young. There are remarkable instances of this in Evelyn's diary and also in Slingsby's.

Old diaries, by their references to habits and fashions and through the amusement derived from their archaic language and spelling, give ordinary commonplace events a quality they would not otherwise possess. A scrappy memorandum of the pursuits and purchases of a country gentleman in the early seventeenth century is entertaining, whereas the equivalent written at the end of the nineteenth century would be unreadable. The latter, however, in three hundred years' time will derive in its turn new value from its age.

Explorers The diaries of explorers are not included in this collection because they come under a different category of writing. A soldier may or may not keep a diary. If he does, even though he deals with little else than military matters, it is the " itch to record " which impels him to write. However technical his diary may be, nevertheless it is a diary very much in the same sense as any other diary. A staff diary only recording official military matters would not be a diary in the sense we are using it here any more than the log-book of a ship. An explorer only uses the daily entry as a convenient means of giving a scientifically exact account of the enterprises on which he is engaged. It is the recognised method of recording scientific observations and collecting data in research. As this class of diary is not included for review, a word may be said about them here because, however scrupulously specialised the entries may be, the personality of the writer still emerges. Three diaries of this description may be mentioned as typical of this class of record: Captain Cook's, Darwin's, and Captain Scott's.

There are two published diaries of Captain Cook's. They are a good deal more than ship's log-books. The first concerns his first voyage round the world between 1768 and 1771, and the second his last voyage in 1776 up to his death in 1779. While the entries consist for the most part of nautical observations, he gives very full descriptions of places and interesting details with regard to native races. It is no ordinary dull recital of fact. One feels behind the carefully collected observations an outstanding personality, a man of humane instincts, fine judgment, and skilful management. Very occasionally he allows himself an expression of opinion like the following: *Captain Cook*

> Such are the tempers and disposition of seamen in general that whatever you give them out of the common way—altho' it be ever so much for their good—it will not go down and you will hear nothing but murmurings against the man who first invented it; but the moment they see their superiors set a value upon it, it becomes the finest stuff in the world and the inventor an honest fellow. Wind easterly.

But the long and often elaborate notes of the great navigator's explorations are part of the literature of scientific research, not a personal diary.

Darwin's Journal of Researches during the voyage of the *Beagle* is another instance of a record of scientific research in diary form. But it is no dry technical treatise. By writing quite naturally without omitting the enthusiasms of a young man filled with wonder, devoured by curiosity and absorbed in the work of investigation, he produced a book which brought within the range of the layman the researches of a scientific expert, and thus what might have been a dry and difficult dissertation becomes coloured with the spirit of adventure and invested with the charm of personality. The Journal covers almost five years, 1831 to 1836, and many quotations might be given to show that not only could he write and describe, but that he combined the æsthetic sensibilities of an artist with the curiosity and analytical *Darwin* concentration of a man of science. The marvels of the forests of South America evoke from him unrestrained enthusiasm. He says in one place : " It is not possible to give an adequate idea of the higher feelings of wonder, astonishment and devotion which fill and elevate the mind." The most unscientific reader may be carried away by perusing his accounts of adventures with native tribes, and even when he particularises and elaborates his descriptions of fauna and flora he uses the simplest language. However, it cannot be called a personal diary, as he notes nothing about himself or his relations with his comrades.

Captain Scott

Captain Scott's diary of the Antarctic Expedition, 1910–1912, has attracted more than scientific interest owing to the tragic termination of the expedition so far as he and some of his companions were concerned. Although his journal gives all the detailed observations necessary to illustrate the object of the expedition, it is often written in natural and almost colloquial language. The last entry, now famous, is not only personal but of so poignantly a dramatic character that it may be quoted. It is one of the few diary entries written by a man in the immediate face of death. It will be remembered that he and his comrades, though only eleven miles from the depôt, were unable to leave their hut owing to the continuous " whirling drifts " of snow. He scribbled while he still had the strength, no prayers and supplications, no self-blame or recrimination, no posturing philosophy, no melodramatic finale, but the following simple words :

> I do not think we can hope for any better things now. We shall stick it out to the end, but we are getting weaker of course, and the end cannot be far. It seems a pity, but I do not think I can write more.
>
> R. SCOTT
>
> For God's sake look after our people.

Many other explorers' diaries might be mentioned, but these three will suffice as examples.

Characteristics of diarists

To return to the more personal diaries which are being considered here, it might be supposed that very busy people do not keep diaries. But diary writing does not depend on time, but on inclination. It requires a certain effort before the habit can be acquired, and many people find this effort beyond them, not exactly from laziness, but from a feeling either that it is not worth while or that their lives are not sufficiently interesting to warrant any record being kept. Anyhow, time has nothing to do with it. A man who may be engrossed in his business or

DIARY WRITING

profession will find time even for a daily record, while a man of leisure may not take the trouble to write at all.

Diarists are interested in themselves, they are watching themselves journeying along the road of life. It may be claimed for them that they are not of a vegetating apathetic disposition. They are awake, alert, and alive to all that concerns them, and this degree of egotism will make the busiest of them find time and opportunity for writing notes.

There are some noticeable differences between the diaries of women and the diaries of men. Women, if they write at all, write a great deal. Instances of women who have kept daily to periodic brief notes, if they exist, must be rare; the idea of noting regularly insignificant details of daily life does not seem to appeal to the female mind. They prefer the memoir or letter form, which gives them more scope. Women are sometimes prolific letter writers. This may prevent them from expanding themselves in a diary. But if their desire for self-expression were deprived of this outlet it is not unlikely it would overflow into the pages of a diary. Lady Mary Coke tried to combine the two, with the result that she cannot be said to have been successful in either. Practically all the diaries of women mentioned in these volumes are the diaries of well-known and more or less eminent women, with the exception of Mrs. Browne's entertaining little record, whereas it has been easy to collect the diaries of many absolutely unknown men. *[margin: Women diarists]*

Generally speaking, women seem to be more cautious and less prone to give themselves away. The examples discovered of English women diarists show that they are less morbid and introspective and fonder of objective narrative. Women often excel in the particular line they set themselves. Their powers of narrative are sometimes specially good. The diaries of Fanny Kemble and Lady Nugent are both entertaining, though comparatively little known. Celia Fiennes stands by herself in the seventeenth century, and Lady Cowper amongst others in the eighteenth century, as women whose distinctive characters are displayed by their spontaneous writing. Queen Victoria must be judged more by the early diaries and by the knowledge that many volumes of a similar character exist than by the *Leaves from the Highlands*. The women social diarists, like the men, are less interesting. Rapture, enthusiasm, and we must say, too, gush, abound in some women's diaries. Indeed Fanny Burney herself, who may be claimed by many as the best English woman diarist, is by no means immune from criticism on this score.

For many reasons we should be inclined to give the palm among women to Caroline Fox. The comparatively small number of female diarists that are discoverable may be taken as an indication, not so much that women were formerly less addicted to diary writing than men, but that women's education in the past was largely neglected. As the centuries pass, however, the number of women diarists seems to increase, and in the nineteenth century there were undoubtedly a large number, although many of these diaries are not available.

Objective and subjective diaries There are two ways of estimating a diary: according to the light it throws on the incidents recorded, or the light it throws on the character of the writer. Most diaries have been examined and judged from the former point of view; footnotes, amplifications and even new material for history have been discovered in old diaries. New facts and incidents have been found in the lives of well-known people, and fresh revelations have been made with regard to their characters. Domestic details, expressions of private feelings, and all the more intimate particulars are dismissed as negligible. It may often be found in the printed editions of diaries that editors extract only those portions which deal with events of public, historic or local importance, and a note will be found declaring that the rest is omitted because it was only of a private character. Many a diary has been emasculated in this way. If, however, we examine diaries from the subjective point of view of the diarist, the so-called private part becomes every bit as important as the rest. Every detail helps to acquaint us with the author, his method of writing, his manner of living, his hopes and aspirations and his inmost thoughts. In the following review of diaries the human side rather than the historical side, the psychological interest rather than the objective interest, is dwelt upon. There are several cases in which the events described overshadow other considerations, and the author can only be reached through his style and comments. But in many other cases the events are of little consequence, and we therefore get a clearer view of the diarist.

Should private diaries be read? It may be asked whether reading diaries not intended for publication is not prying into private affairs, spying out chambers of the soul we have no business to enter, peeping behind the curtain, or, as Lord Morley puts it, " violating the sanctuary." Are we justified in exposing to the public eye intimate revelations and secret thoughts and confidences jotted down in unguarded moments of self-expansion ? Is nothing to be held sacred and inviolable ? Are the last garments which conceal nakedness to be torn off by our eagerness to analyse and dissect beings who have passed away and therefore cannot protest? Whatever may be the reply to these questions from the ethical point of view, scruples and misgivings come too late now. The thing has been done. Private diaries not intended for publication and others about which there is doubt have been unearthed, deciphered, printed and published. If the writers did not wish this they should have taken precautions and left injunctions for the destruction of their diaries. Their wishes would have been respected. There are several known instances where "locked books" and diaries were kept and instructions left for their destruction. But in no instance in the diaries considered in this volume was there any such instruction. On the contrary, we are disposed to think that the absence of any specific injunction implied on the part of the diarist a perhaps unexpressed but nevertheless not unabsent expectation that what he or she wrote might one day be read.

Anyhow we are the gainers. In no case do we think less of a diarist for what he wrote down, though we may be surprised at his candour. We ourselves are all guilty of unprintable and unpublishable feelings, and this ought to prevent us from condemning anyone whose feelings of this sort have found their way on to a printed page not at his own instigation.

In every case a diary amplifies what we know of its writer, if we know anything at all. In some cases a new and different, possibly a less favourable, light is thrown on the character of the diarist. Windham and Manning are examples of this. The former is almost unrecognisable when the self which is revealed is compared with the man as he was known. In the latter the inner workings of a complex nature which we catch sight of alter the general estimate of him that was accepted for public consumption. Some deplore such diary revelations as detracting from the high opinion of the figures of romance which history from outside presents. But surely it is more interesting to know the *real* man. If the discovery of their faults and weaknesses makes us lower their pedestals, anyhow we are taking them out of the realm of romance into the realm of reality, and our opinion need not be lowered. We get nearer to them by means of their own explanation, and we need only reflect that other great heroes who are still aloft would be found to be just as faulty had we the same opportunity of scrutinising them through the pages of a full diary.

Diarists explain themselves

Diarists cannot help explaining themselves—unintentionally

perhaps and incompletely. Nevertheless an explanation is there. Not only to the general public in the case of published diaries may this be important, but in the case of private and unpublished diaries the closer knowledge may prove to be of considerable consequence. For instance, a young man who lost his father and had known very little about him, one day came across his father's diary and read it. In a letter to his uncle he said : " I was surprised how little I knew him really and what a fine character he must have had at the bottom. It gave me a feeling of affection for him that I had never had before. I think I understand his difficulties and peculiar mentality. I could sympathise with him." So intimate a revelation would not have been possible even through letters. Knowledge of this kind goes very far to dispel misunderstandings and erroneous judgments, because it produces the most valuable of all relationships, which is sympathy.

Reflections of human nature In diaries human nature—our own nature—is revealed to us in a way unattainable in any other form of writing. The lineaments of character penetrate freely. We recognise the joys, the little vanities, the disappointments, the exaggerated ambitions, the broken resolutions. We can enter into the trivial pleasures and petty miseries of daily life—the rainy day, the blunt razor, the new suit, the domestic quarrel, the bad night, the twinge of toothache, the fall from a horse, the newly purchased book, the good meal, the over-sharp criticism, the irritating relation, the child's maladies, the exasperating servant. We know them all. We have experienced many of them ourselves. Through these casual notes we are brought into a sort of familiar relationship and fellow-feeling with the writer which philosophic discourses or even collected correspondence cannot produce in quite the same way. We find in them a reality and a life which the more artistic and skilful compositions of fiction cannot reach. The diarist is endeared to us for the strongest of all possible reasons—that he is so like us. His diary may be fatuous, it may be ridiculous, it may be insignificant, it may be dull, but if he is not furbishing up a memoir for public consumption it will, with all its defects, be human. It is this distinctive humanity which differentiates diary writing from other forms of literature.

Elements necessary for a good diary There may be some difficulty in determining what constitutes a good diary—good that is to say from the point of view of a reader who is a stranger. It may fulfil the intention of the writer, and be to him or her a useful book of reference, or give information to the family. But we must look at it from the point of view of the general reader. Regularity and fulness are not sufficient by themselves. Instances will be given of regular diaries extending over long periods which are neither particularly edifying nor entertaining. There are good and bad diaries which are long and regular; there are good and bad diaries which are short and scrappy. Entries made on the day have an unquestionable advantage over entries made as summaries of a period after delay and reflection. The entry made on the day has the peculiar freshness, the spontaneous note of individuality which cannot be secured otherwise. It is the snapshot, rough, unpremeditated—ill-composed and out of focus perhaps—but catching the fleeting expression which the carefully arranged and more finished studio photograph misses. But the imprint of a passing impression fades very rapidly from the sensitive plate of our memory. Caroline Fox, resuming her journal after an illness, writes: " I write all this now because my feelings are already fading into commonplace, and I would fain fix some little scrap of my experience." Even the writer with little natural power of literary expression may scribble down a phrase at the moment which no amount of studied ingenuity on the part of a literary author could equal. This spontaneity is a form of sincerity which may be claimed as the one indispensable quality for a good diary. If too the writer has not publication definitely in view; if, so far as it is possible, he is just talking to himself, this spontaneity will be all the more evident. This in itself makes the style—not the balanced phrasing of a literary style, but the *mot juste* forced on the diarist by his close proximity to the incident or impression he records. Powers of observation would seem to be an indispensable part of the equipment of a good diarist, and by no means all diarists have those powers even though they may have good memories, which is quite another thing. Perception, which is the faculty of detaching the significant from the things observed, is a rare talent. The diarist who possesses it will never fail to keep alert a reader of his record.

Egotism improves a diary. But the egotist must have some method or else he will not keep it up. Haydon kept it up to the end. Byron, otherwise an admirable diary-writer, could not persist for more than a few months. The writer who is more concerned with what he is recording than with himself or than with his opinion and attitude towards his subject may be a superior person, but he is unlikely to be a good diarist. It would be going too far to say that the good quality of a diary is in inverse ratio to the importance of the events related. But it is certainly true that the diarist who sets himself the task of chronicling important public affairs must either be a literary artist, or must have a specially favourable point of vantage as an observer, if he is going to attract attention to his record. Some succeed, but many more fail.

Misconception as to capacity for keeping a diary

"You ought to keep a diary" is a remark which may be often heard addressed to people who live within the range of great events and mix with the high and mighty. "I do not keep a diary" is also a common reply of people who go on to explain that they do not meet interesting people or live within the orbit of public affairs. Both these remarks show an entirely wrong conception of diary writing. Roughly speaking, the majority of diaries of eminent people or participants in occurrences of historical moment are less good than the diaries of those who live out of the beaten track in comparative obscurity. It is the life inside and the personality of the writer, not the circumstances outside, which help to give the particular quality to a diary which cannot be found in other methods of writing. The world of events is better dealt with by history and memoirs, but the private and inner life can only be occasionally snatched in its vital reality by the observant or introspective writer of a daily record who by the advantage of an inner view of his subject can perhaps commit to paper an exact reflection of human experience. And even without being introspective or self-analytical, the writer of a record of quiet days among unknown people can give an atmosphere to his story which the bewildered recorder of great proceedings may be unable to impart to his. The great fallacy that the quality of a diary depends on the circumstances in which a person is placed will be dispelled by a perusal of the extracts given in these pages.

Trivialities

Both in the larger and in the minor diaries trivialities seem at times to count more than the weightier events. We prefer Pepys when he is singing with Mercer in the coach while his wife is shopping rather than when he is telling us about the exploits of the navy; we pause longer over Sir Simonds d'Ewes' quarrels with Mr. Danford than over his political dissertations; Slingsby is interesting on the Civil War, but one cannot help specially sympathising with him in his embarrassment with the variety of doctors who attend his wife. General Dyott and his inconvenient cousin Miss Bakewell amuse us, while his intercourse with his "uncommonly gracious" royal acquaintances palls. Newcombe's piety may be impressive, but his failure to leave off smoking is a relief. Elias Ashmole was a great antiquary, but we are in-

DIARY WRITING

terested to know that he fell ill from drinking water after venison. Lady Nugent gives a good description of Jamaica, but we are also amused to know that her husband's predecessor had dirty nails.

All this does not mean that diary readers are frivolous-minded, but that diary writers are at their best when they are just scribbling down with effortless frankness the little incidents which they are honest enough to record as having caught their attention at the moment: little incidents which may indeed be of greater personal importance to them than their participations in the larger concerns, the great flow of public life, or the profound speculations on religion in which individual contributions must at most be very insignificant.

And there is this further consideration: political, court, military and diplomatic incidents fade very quickly and become stale; unless they are related by a man of consequence who speaks authoritatively we are not impressed. Raikes's gossip about Paris under Louis Philippe was no doubt quite amusing to read a year or two after he wrote, but his diary will find very few readers to-day. Personal episodes and individual reflections, on the other hand, retain their freshness and appeal to us just as much after the passage of centuries. The case of Wilberforce is an example in which it is the personal rather than the business and social entries that give the diary special value. We are looking for the human being—that is the truth of it—not the sovereign, the bishop, the general, the author, but the *man* and *woman* ; and in their diaries they can give us the best chance of finding them. *[Public events and private episodes]*

It may be said then that daily writing, powers of observation and of perception, honesty so far as it is possible, a fair quantum of egotism, no immediate thought of publication, no pretentious attitudinising and no hesitation to put down the things that ruffle and the things that please in the twelve hours that have passed—a certain amount of recklessness in fact—will help to make a good diary. If these elements are combined with the pen of a Pepys, a Fielding, a Fanny Burney, a Byron, a Haydon, or a Barbellion, the result will be an arresting human document. And even when there can be no claim to special literary talent as in such cases as Teonge, Baker, Gale, Strother, Lady Nugent, etc., an intimate insight into human character is provided which could not be gained in any other way. The diary which fulfils all the above conditions and which may without dispute be accorded the highest place among English diaries is undoubtedly *[Composition of a good diary]* that of Pepys. It is dealt with in its place with as much fulness as space will allow, although insufficiently to bring all its merits to light. Much has been written about Pepys, and the diary is accessible in many editions, so that it has not been thought necessary to give him in these pages the larger proportion of attention which is his due.

But while the elements which seem to make a good diary can be enumerated, it is really useless to lay down rules and regulations or prescriptions for diary writing. For a diary may be found to contravene most of them and yet be very readable. If a man sets out to conform to rules or to adopt a style which is not absolutely natural to him, if he writes with intention and becomes self-conscious about his writing, it will mean that he has his eye on a possible reader: the thought of eventual publication will obtrude and pure spontaneity will inevitably vanish. The only safe advice is—follow no rule, write as you like. The only rule is that there is no rule. Indeed, for some almost inexplicable reason one diary may absorb a reader to the extent of his not wanting to miss a single entry; while in another he may find difficulty in reading two consecutive pages. It is not the style or the subject, it is the personality behind which counts, and that personality must be free, without intention and without premeditation, to make use of whatever form or method it desires. The personality may strike one as pleasant or unpleasant; this in no way affects the quality of the diary.

Long diaries

Fulness and length, that is to say long continuance, are no particular assets. It might be interesting to know which is the longest English diary. But without an examination of all the manuscripts there is no means of deciding the question. In some cases parts of a manuscript are missing; and length of time does not necessarily indicate length of diary. However, the honour would probably fall to one of the following: Greville (40 years), Crabb Robinson (56 years), Thoresby (57 years), Haydon (60 years), Wesley (66 years), Queen Victoria (68 years), or Egmont, who only wrote for about 18 years, but at immense length.

Criticism of diary writing

There may be superior persons who condemn diaries as frivolous and negligible unless they deal with historical incidents. People who attach more importance to the actual than to the human may agree. But every event, every historical fact, is composed in its essence of purely human elements. Anything, therefore, which contributes to a knowledge of humanity, not only prominent humanity, but humble humanity, ought not to be ignored by historians, or indeed by philosophers and psychologists.

Apart from this wholesale condemnation of the practice it may be questionable whether diary writing, or anyhow some forms of it, is not rather a snare, an encouragement to the revolving of wheels that do not bite. Curiously enough the most uncompromising condemnation of it comes from one of the most celebrated diarists. Amiel writes : " A private journal is a friend to idleness. It frees us from the necessity of looking all round a subject, it puts up with every kind of repetition, it accompanies all the caprices and meandering of inner life and proposes to itself no definite end . . . a journal takes the place of a confidant that is a friend or wife, it becomes a substitute for production, it is a grief-cheating device, a mode of escape and withdrawal. But though it takes the place of everything, properly speaking it represents nothing at all."

Few people dream of attempting to keep the sort of diary which Amiel continued to keep in spite of this outburst. Whatever may be the effect on diarists their productions anyhow supply us with a form of writing we should be very sorry to be deprived of.

History and literature are apt to represent people more as actors than human beings. They become figures of romance rather outside the human range. But we find ourselves drawn to people at once when we discover they are just like ourselves and did actually by their own testimony given in their own words—and not in the great language of history—lose their temper, enjoy their dinner, quarrel with their families, catch cold, be elated by worldly joys, and dejected by the perplexities of human existence. Sovereigns, statesmen, saints, poets, generals and scholars are brought down to our own level, and as Moore says, " we rejoice in the discovery so consoling to human pride that even the mightiest in their moments of ease and weakness resemble ourselves." *Distinctive features*

It must be admitted that the diary form of writing is awkward and not always easy to read. As a vehicle for conveying precise information it is cumbrous and diffuse. Repetitions, abbreviations, lists of names of people, bald registering of the dates of movements, of births and deaths, the occasional dropping and picking up of threads, unnecessary prolixity, puzzling laconism, and little mysteries of which there is no explanation, are constant obstacles to the easy run which a reader wants. There is indeed no form, no order, no attempt at construction—often no begin- *The diary form* ning, no culmination, and only a broken ending. In rare cases only is there any attempt at literary style or finish. The more or less complete diaries are a minority, and Haydon's last entry is unique. For the most part the diaries are fragmentary—shreds torn from a bit of cloth which itself was not cut or trimmed into shape. It may be that these drawbacks prevent diaries from being popular reading. Yet the appearance of a contemporary diary always has a certain *succès de scandale*. The diary form is often imitated in fiction and some sham diaries have had a considerable vogue: notably the diary of Lady Willoughby, a fictitious seventeenth-century diary which appeared in the early nineteenth century, the very successful and not entirely fictitious *Pages from a Private Diary*, which was published not long ago, and *The Diary of a Nobody*, which has become almost a classic.

The broken diary form of periodic dated entries has been adopted in notebooks which are not in themselves diaries, such for instance as Samuel Butler's notebooks and Jowett's memoranda. Its adoption is an indication of spontaneity and for the noting of personal impressions and reflections of the moment can be very effective. Nevertheless the diary form seems more suitable for occasional than consecutive reading. Biographers meet the difficulty by taking bits of diary as illustrations and fitting them in here and there to complete the life story. But most diarists have not acquired fame enough to justify their biographies being written at all. In these cases the fragmentary entries are all we have; and if the reluctance to read the clumsy little notes can be overcome, it is astonishing how much human interest may be discovered in them, and how distinctly one is able to form an estimate of the character of the writer. They also have the advantage that there has been no thought of publication.

Variety and contrasts

To collect together people as diarists is no arbitrary grouping any more than to collect poets or dramatists. All who write diaries take themselves more or less seriously, and have in common a desire to register and record the incidents connected with their own lives and sometimes to note thoughts and opinions. Whether it be from habit, egotism, vanity, or self-discipline, they are by this practice connected together by a very tangible link. It is interesting therefore to note the variety that exists within this classification; and, more than variety, the astonishing contrasts. Take, for instance, two lifelong and regular diarists, Haydon and Wesley, both vain and both religious. Different as were the careers of the unsuccessful artist and the eminently successful divine, the dramatic and highly coloured narrative of the one and the methodical register of the other form an even greater contrast. Or take Captain Lloyd, who was killed in the Boer War, and Arthur Graeme West, who was killed in the Great War, both British officers, the official records of whose careers would not be found to be very different, both the product of more or less the same age, and the same system of education. The bald, almost professional notes of the one and the elaborate self-analysis of the other present perhaps as great a contrast as any two diaries in the collection. Read General Dyott on the Florentine gallery, and then turn to a page of J. A. Symonds on the same subject, and they were both of them lifelong diarists. Elizabeth Fry and Frances Lady Shelley were writing their diaries at the same time, but their outlook on life could hardly have been more divergent. George Eliot, a famous novelist, gives us very dry notes and rather depressing reflections; Lady Charlotte Bury, a very obscure novelist, fills her pages with sentimental rapture and gossip. Henry Newcombe and Henry Teonge lived about the same time in the seventeenth century and both were ministers of religion. Newcombe's severe religious self-discipline and pious phraseology has little resemblance to Teonge's free and easy enjoyment of life expressed in language that has to be expurgated. A famous early nineteenth-century huntsman and a parliamentary visitor for the destruction of Church ornaments under the Commonwealth both keep a diary for the exclusive record of their professional work. The Rev. Henry Martyn keeps the diary of a rigid and penitent ascetic; the Rev. W. S. Millar keeps a hunting diary. We gather into the same fold Gladstone, the great statesman concerned with events of high national import, and Turner, the storekeeper, who recounts his village orgies; we can have side by side the royal gossip of a lady-in-waiting and the metaphysical introspection of a museum assistant, the experiences of a not very high-minded village schoolmaster naturally told, and the scholarly reflections of an Eton master rather sententiously expressed; and no two individuals could be further removed from one another in character, temperament, and experience than our two monarch diarists.

Another sort of contrast is afforded by diaries which deal with the same subject, not because of the difference in the style, method, or personality of the writers, but because of the widely separated periods in which they lived. The account of warfare given by Coningsby, the officer who accompanied an expeditionary force to France in the days of Queen Elizabeth, compared with the account of warfare given by Gordon-Lennox, who accompanied the expeditionary force to France in 1914, may give food for reflection to those who believe in "the progress of civilisation."

Differences of disposition in diarists of the same profession

Whether by contrast or by resemblance diaries show us that people of the same class, age, and even profession, may differ fundamentally in their outlook on life, and also that although their lot may be cast in very different spheres and although they may live separated by centuries, they may yet have in common just that degree of self-consciousness and vanity which impels them to watch and note their daily experiences.

Diaries destroyed

No conjecture can be made of what proportion of educated people have kept diaries, on account of the large number which must have been destroyed. In the days of the monasteries it is not improbable that some of those who led the contemplative life noted with regularity the thoughts and impressions which occurred to them in the routine of the cloister. Yet only the Chronicle of Jocelin of Brakelond, which is not a diary, brings us into any close relation with monastic life. This is not surprising when we know how the libraries and archives of abbeys and monasteries were treated at the dissolution. The wholesale destruction was carried out on a grand scale, although grocers may have rescued a few sheets for their parcels. Old papers in the lumber rooms of country houses were regarded as rubbish till comparatively recent years, and it is only in exceptional cases that much has been preserved. Even now people are apt to destroy the diaries of their grandparents, under the impression that they can be of no interest as they only deal with domestic incidents of obscure lives.

Nevertheless, unknown manuscript diaries may be peppered about the country in numbers which we cannot guess at. Their whereabouts is beyond the reach of the antiquary and catalogue maker and we have here to rest satisfied with the very few examples of these private manuscripts which have come within range. Perhaps these diaries still under lock and key, some not having yet the value given by antiquity, others not considered worth printing, form the majority of existing diaries. There is no means of knowing. But taking these into account, as well as a considerable number which must have been destroyed along with letters, accounts, deeds, and other manuscript records, it may safely be asserted that a comparatively small minority of people have been and are now diarists.

Diarists a minority

An inquiry with regard to diary keeping made of a hundred educated people chosen at random has produced the following result.

The hundred consisted of fifty-six males and forty-four females, sixty-five of them over 30, thirty-five under 30.

Twenty-four (twelve males and twelve females) keep diaries. Seventy-six (forty-four males and thirty-two females) do not keep diaries. Those who do not keep diaries include twenty-six (eleven males and fifteen females) who either in their childhood or on a special occasion have kept diaries which have been discontinued.

The twenty-four diarists included sixteen persons over 30; eight under. The seventy-six non-diarists forty-nine over 30; twenty-seven under.

The number is too small to serve as a basis for any enlightening deductions, but it is probably fairly representative. Something like 20 to 25 per cent. of educated people may be reckoned as keeping diaries of some sort. In the table females show proportionately a slight preponderance over males. This may be true now, though in the earlier centuries they were undoubtedly in a small minority. The figures do not seem to show that the younger generation are either more or less inclined to keep diaries than the elder. There may be a tendency to consider that diary writing is an occupation for the leisured class. But as we have already pointed out, spare time has nothing whatever to do with it. What is true is that owing to a defective or rather non-existent educational system in the past the great mass of the people were either prevented from being able to write at all or found writing a considerable effort. Once writing becomes as easy for one person as another and real education spreads over the whole community the number of diarists will increase actually in numbers; but proportionately, owing to diary writing being a matter of temperament, the percentage is likely to remain about the same.

The diaries collected here have been arranged more or less in chronological order. Their classification according to subject or the profession of the writer would have been too awkward and many could not have been fitted into any particular category. The method of detaching each one separately appeared to be the best way of illustrating their individual characteristics. Extracts of special passages often give a good idea of the diarist and his method and opinions, but there are many cases where something is lost because a still fuller revelation of character and circumstances would certainly be gained by the consecutive reading of daily entries even though many of them might be, comparatively speaking, dull. Peculiarities and characteristics can

Arrangement of diaries reviewed

be illustrated by extracts, but the perusal of the whole diary and if possible the handling of the original manuscript would assist very much the realisation of the actual atmosphere.

Some one hundred and twenty diaries are reviewed and a score or so of others have been examined. While no doubt the Friends' Library and the United Service Institution contain the manuscripts of some others, there is good reason to believe that the collection of another hundred diaries would be attended with difficulty without access to the archives of country houses or without the key of the cupboards where old family papers are reposing on dusty shelves. Some doubt may be expressed as to whether the right proportion of notice has been given to all the various and widely differing diaries in the collection. The unquestionable importance of the subjects dealt with in some of them might seem to warrant their fuller treatment. Byron did not write for more than a few months and perhaps ought hardly to be called a diarist, but his method and matter seem to justify longer quotations being made from his record than from far fuller and more regular diaries. But throughout, not the subject, but the quality of the diaries is the matter under consideration. The decision as to their relative value becomes therefore a matter of opinion which while it may seem arbitrary can best be arrived at by a perusal of them all.

Surveying the series from Edward VI to Barbellion, we can note the growth of elaboration, the expansion of more philosophic self-analysis and greater sophistication. But it would be very far from true to say that our later diaries are superior to our earlier ones.

Diary writing should be encouraged

In conclusion it may be assumed with general agreement that diary writing is a practice that should be encouraged. People need only consult their own convenience and mood, they need obey no rules, they may follow their own inclination to write regularly, irregularly, fully, or briefly. They may publish or not as they wish. But let them realise that no special talent, and more particularly no high position or favourable circumstance, will necessarily make their diary important or interesting. In fact, its interest or importance is not a matter that need concern them. They may or may not find it useful for reference, but let them never think that the personal jottings of any human being are entirely futile.

We may go so far as to deplore that there are not more diaries in existence. In spite of their necessary limitations, their inaccuracies and their bias, they would add considerably to the sum total of

DIARY WRITING

human knowledge. Towards the end of the nineteenth century the practice of diary writing was undoubtedly very much favoured, although many of the diaries of that period have not yet emerged from their cupboards. The appearance of Marie Bashkirtseff's journal encouraged many people to make a similar attempt. In earlier and more leisurely days, too, when people wrote long letters and authors rewrote and rewrote their books, opportunity was found for diary writing. In the more mechanical age in which we now live excessive pressure caused by the mania for movement and the frenzied eagerness for varied sensations make accomplishment of every sort more difficult, and render moments for reflection much more rare. People are not busier, but they hear and see too much and they are more quickly tired, and it may be surmised that apart from diaries produced by the war, there are rather fewer diarists relatively speaking. The lack of reticence on the part of the younger generation may be a defect, but if they wrote diaries it would become a quality. It is to be feared, however, that their egotism takes a cruder and more external form.

If nevertheless there are indeed more diary writers to-day it will be an advantage for posterity. Notwithstanding all the immense store of facts we are compiling by means of newspapers, books, registers and official records with regard to the history of our own times, the privately written comments of an individual spontaneously scribbled and so reproducing the mood, the atmosphere, and, so to speak, the particular aroma of the moment, are priceless and can be regarded as the spice of history. Diaries link up the reader of to-day with the writer of the past with intimate threads and exhibit as nothing else can the unbroken consecutive flow of human endeavour, failure and hope.

LIST OF DIARIES

ARRANGED IN CHRONOLOGICAL ORDER

SIXTEENTH CENTURY

Name of Diarist.	Occupation.	Date of Diary.	Source.	Page.
Edward VI	King	1549–1552	*Literary Remains of Edward VI*, ed. by J. G. Nichols, 1857. Clarendon Historical Reprints, 1884	55
Henry Machyn	Undertaker	1550–1563	Camden Society, vol. 42	58
Dr. John Dee	Astrologer and mathematician	1554–1601	Camden Society, vol. 19	61
Sir Francis Walsingham	Statesman	1570–1583	Camden Miscellanies, 1871	66
Sir Thomas Coningsby	Soldier	1591	Camden Miscellanies, 1847	68

SEVENTEENTH CENTURY

Name of Diarist.	Occupation.	Date of Diary.	Source.	Page.
Sir Simonds d'Ewes	Barrister, Member of Parliament and antiquary	1619–1636	*Autobiography of Sir Simonds d'Ewes*, ed. by J. O. Halliwell, 1845	71
Sir Henry Slingsby	Member of Parliament and soldier	1638–1648	*The Diary of Sir Henry Slingsby*, ed. by the Rev. D. Parsons, 1836	76
Samuel Pepys	Clerk of the Acts, Clerk of the Privy Seal and Secretary to the Admiralty	1660–1669	*Pepys' Diary*, ed. by H. B. Wheatley. *Samuel Pepys*, by Percy Lubbock, 1909, R. L. Stevenson's essay, etc.	82
John Evelyn	Country gentleman and author	1640–1706	*The Diary of John Evelyn*, ed. by Austin Dobson, 1906, 3 vols.	96
Henry Teonge	Naval chaplain	1675–1676 1678–1679	*Teonge's Diary*, 1825	107

45

MINOR DIARIES

Name of Diarist.	Occupation.	Date of Diary.	Source.	Page.
John Manningham	Barrister . .	1602–1603	Camden Society, 1868, Brit. Mus. Harleian MS. 5353	112
Elias Ashmole .	Antiquary . .	1641–1687	*Diary and Letters of Elias Ashmole*, 1717	114
John Rouse . .	Clergyman . .	1625–1642	Camden Society, 66	116
Sir William Brereton	Country gentleman and traveller	1634	Surtees Society, vol. 124	118
John Aston . .	Courtier . .	1639	Surtees Society, vol. 118	119
William Dowsing	Iconoclast . .	1643–1644	*The Journal of William Dowsing*, 1st Ed. 1786, 2nd Ed. 1818	120
Adam Eyre . .	Country gentleman	1646–1648	Surtees Society, vol. 65	122
Giles Moore . .	Clergyman . .	1655–1679	Sussex Archæological Collections, vol. I	125
Henry Newcombe	Presbyterian minister	1661–1663	Cheetham Society, vol. XVIII	128
Oliver Heywood .	Nonconformist divine	1666–1702	*Oliver Heywood's Diaries*, ed. by J. Horsfall Turner, 4 vols., 1881	131
Ralph Thoresby .	Antiquary . .	1667–1724	*Diary of Ralph Thoresby*, ed. by Jos. Hunter, 2 vols., 1830	134
Sir Walter Calverley	Country gentleman	1670–1718	Surtees Society, vol. 77	136
Dr. Edward Lake	Chaplain and archdeacon	1677–1678	Camden Miscellanies, vol. I	138
Abraham de la Pryme	Clergyman and antiquary	1680–1704	Surtees Society, 1870	140
Timothy Burrell	Barrister . .	1686–1717	Sussex Archæological Collect., vol. III	142
Thomas Cartwright	Bishop . .	1686–1687	Camden Society, vol. 22	144
John More . .	Clergyman . .	1694–1700	Brit. Mus. Add. MS. 28,041	147
Celia Fiennes .	—	1695–1697	*Through England on a Sidesaddle in the Time of William and Mary*, 1888	148
T. Rugge . . N. Luttrell .	} Annalists . .	1659–1724	{ Brit. Mus. Add. MS. 10,116 and 10,447	. 152

LIST OF DIARIES 47

Short Notices

Name of Diarist.	Occupation.	Date of Diary.	Source.	Page.
William Ayshcombe	—	1608–1633	Historical Manuscripts Commission, Report 10, Appendix VI	153
T. Dugard	Clergyman	1632–1643	Brit. Mus. Add. MS. 23,146	154
John Manners, Earl of Rutland	Courtier	1639	Historical Manuscripts Commission, Report 12, Appendix IV	154
Jacob Bee	Tradesman	1681–1706	Surtees Society, vol. 118	154
Richard Stapley	Country gentleman	1682–1710	Sussex Archæological Collections, vol. II	155
John Bufton	—	1699	Essex Archæological Transactions, vol. I	155

EIGHTEENTH CENTURY

Name of Diarist.	Occupation.	Date of Diary.	Source.	Page.
John Wesley	Divine	1725–1791	The Journal of John Wesley, Standard Edn., 8 vols., 1910, John Wesley's Journal, abridged; pref. by A. Birrell	156
Viscount Percival, Earl of Egmont	Member of Parliament	1728–1733	Diary of Viscount Percival, Earl of Egmont, Historical Manuscripts Commission, Vol. I, 1920	164
Fanny Burney (Madame d'Arblay)	Novelist	1768–1819	Early Diaries of Frances Burney, 2 vols., 1889. Diary and Letters of Madame d'Arblay, ed. by Austin Dobson, 1904	171
William Windham	Statesman	1784–1810	The Diary of William Windham, ed. by Mrs. Baring, 1866	184

ENGLISH DIARIES

MINOR DIARIES

Name of Diarist.	Occupation.	Date of Diary.	Source.	Page.
Mary, Countess Cowper	Lady in waiting	1714–1720	*Diary of Mary, Countess Cowper*, 1804	193
Thomas Marchant	Yeoman farmer	1714–1728	Sussex Archæological Collection, vol. XXV	196
John Thomlinson	Clergyman	1717–1722	Surtees Society, vol. 118	197
John Byrom	Poet and theologian	1722–1744	Cheetham Society, vols. XXXII, XXXIV, XL and XLIV	200
Elizabeth Byrom	—	1745–1746	Cheetham Society, vol. XLIV	203
John Hobson	Country gentleman	1725–1734	Surtees Society, vol. 65	205
Walter Gale	Schoolmaster	1749–1759	Sussex Archæological Collections, vol. IX	206
George Bubb Dodington (Lord Melcombe)	Member of Parliament	1749–1761	*The Diary of G. Bubb Dodington*, ed. by Henry P. Wyndham, 1785	208
John Baker	Solicitor	1750–1779	Sussex Archæological Collections, vol. LII. MS. at Newbuildings, Sussex	212
John Rutty	Doctor	1753–1774	*A Spiritual Diary*, by John Rutty, M.D., 2 vols., 1776	215
Mrs. Browne	—	1754–1757	Original MS. in the possession of Mr. S. A. Courtauld	220
Henry Fielding	Novelist	1754	*The Journal of a Voyage to Lisbon* by H. Fielding, ed. by Austin Dobson, 1892	224
Thomas Turner	Tradesman	1754–1765	Sussex Archæological Collections, vol. XI	227
John Dawson	Captain of militia	1761	Surtees Society, vol. 124	231
Lady Mary Coke	—	1766–1791	*The Journal of Lady Mary Coke*, 5 vols., privately printed	233

LIST OF DIARIES

Minor Diaries—*continued*.

Name of Diarist.	Occupation.	Date of Diary.	Source.	Page.
James Harris, Earl of Malmesbury	Diplomatist	1767–1820	*Diaries and Correspondence of the 1st Earl of Malmesbury*, ed. by his grandson, 4 vols., 1844	234
Thomas Gray	Poet	1769	*Tour in the Lake District.* Works of Thomas Gray, ed. by E. Gosse, vol. I, 1884	236
Strother	Shop assistant	1784–1785	*Strother's Diary*, ed. by Cæsar Caine, Brit. Mus. Eg. 2479	237
The Ladies of Llangollen	—	1785–1788	*Lady Eleanor Butler's Diary*, original MS. in the possession of the Marquis of Ormonde. *The Swan and Her Friends*, by E. V. Lucas, Chap. XIII	241
Elizabeth, Lady Holland	—	1791–1811	*The Journal of Elizabeth, Lady Holland*, ed. by the Earl of Ilchester, 2 vols., 1909	246
Thomas Green	Critic	1796–1811	*The Diary of a Lover of Literature*, 1803, and *Gentleman's Magazine*, 1834–1838	249

Short Notices

Sir George Rooke	Admiral	1700–1703	Navy Records Society, 1897	251
Peter Oliver	Doctor	1781–1821	Brit. Museum Eg. MS. 2674	252
Thomas Gyll	Lawyer and antiquary	1748–1778	Surtees Society, vol. 118	252
Mrs. Powys	—	1756–1808	*Passages from the Diaries of Mrs. Powys*, ed. by Emily Climenson, 1899	252

4

ENGLISH DIARIES

NINETEENTH CENTURY

Name of Diarist.	Occupation.	Date of Diary.	Source.	Page.
B. R. Haydon	Painter	1786–1846	*Life of B. R. Haydon*, ed. by Tom Taylor, 3 vols., 1853	254
Lord Byron	Poet	1813–1814 1816 1821	*Life of Byron*, by Tom Moore, 1832	264
Charles Greville	Clerk of the Council	1814–1860	*The Greville Memoirs*, ed. by H. Reeve, 8 vols., 1875, 1885, 1887. Miscellanies of the Philobiblion Society, IX, 1865	272
William Cobbett	Politician and author	1821–1832	*Cobbett's Rural Rides*, ed. by Pitt Cobbett, 1893	280
Victoria	Queen	1832–1840 1848–1882	*The Girlhood of Queen Victoria*, ed. by Viscount Esher, 1912. *Leaves from a Journal of our Life in the Highlands*, 1862. *More Leaves*, 1883	288
Caroline Fox	—	1834–1871	*Journals and Letters of Caroline Fox*, ed. by H. N. Pym, 1882	300
General Gordon	Soldier	1884	*Journals of General Gordon at Khartoum*, ed. by A. E. Hake, 1885	306

Minor Diaries

General Dyott	Soldier	1781–1845	*Dyott's Diary*, ed. by R. W. Jefferey, 1907	.314
Frances, Lady Shelley	—	1787–1813	*The Diary of Frances, Lady Shelley*, ed. by R. Edgcumbe, 1912	318
Charles Abbot, Lord Colchester	Speaker of the House of Commons	1795–1829	*Diary and Correspondence of Charles Abbot, Lord Colchester*, 3 vols., 1861	320

LIST OF DIARIES

MINOR DIARIES—*continued.*

Name of Diarist.	Occupation.	Date of Diary.	Source.	Page.
Elizabeth Fry	—	1797–1845	*Memoir of the Life of Elizabeth Fry*, ed. by her two daughters, 2 vols., 1847	321
George Rose	Member of Parliament	1800–1811	*George Rose, Diaries and Correspondence*, ed. by L. V. Harcourt, 1860	327
Lady Nugent	—	1801–1814	*Lady Nugent's Diary, Jamaica One Hundred Years Ago*, ed. by F. Cundell, 1907	328
Sir George Jackson	Diplomatist	1801–1816	*Diaries and Letters of Sir G. Jackson*, ed. by Lady Jackson, 4 vols., 1872	331
Henry Martyn	Missionary	1803–1812	*Journals and Letters of the Rev. H. Martyn*, ed. by Rev. S. Wilberforce, 1839	332
Thomas Creevey	Member of Parliament	1809–1818	*The Creevey Papers*, ed. by Sir Herbert Maxwell, 1903	335
Lady Charlotte Bury	Lady in waiting and novelist	1810–1820	*The Diary of a Lady in Waiting*, ed. by A. Francis Steuart, 1908	337
Lieutenant Swabey	Soldier	1811–1813	*Lt. Swabey's Diary*, ed. by Colonel F. A. Whingates, 1895 (Royal United Service Institution Library)	342
Henry Crabb Robinson	Barrister	1811–1867	*Diary and Correspondence of Henry Crabb Robinson*, ed. by T. Sadler, 3 vols., 1869	344
Mary Shelley	—	1814–1840	*Life and Letters of Mary Wollstonecraft Shelley*, by Mrs. Julian Marshall, 1889	349
Sir George Cockburn	Admiral	1815	*Napoleon's Last Voyage*, 1888	352

ENGLISH DIARIES

Minor Diaries—*continued.*

Name of Diarist.	Occupation.	Date of Diary.	Source.	Page.
Lady Malcolm .	—	1816	*A Diary of St. Helena*, ed by Sir A. Wilson, 1899	354
Henry Matthews	Lawyer . .	1817–1819	*The Diary of an Invalid*, by Henry Matthews, 1819	355
Henry Fynes Clinton	Member of Parliament	1819–1852	*Literary Remains of Henry Fynes Clinton*, ed. by C. J. Fynes Clinton, 1854	357
Mary Browne .	—	1821	*The Diary of a Girl in France in 1821*, 1905	362
Richard Hurrell Froude	Clergyman .	1826–1828	*Remains of Richard Hurrell Froude*, 2 vols., 1837	363
W. E. Gladstone	Statesman .	1826–1896	*Life of Gladstone*, J. Morley, 3 vols., 1903.	364
Thomas Raikes .	Clubman . .	1831–1847	*A Portion of the Journal of Thomas Raikes*, 3 vols., 1856	369
Fanny Kemble (Mrs. Butler)	Actress. . .	1832–1833	*Journal by Frances Anne Butler*, 2 vols., 1835	371
Henry Greville .	Diplomatist and courtier	1832–1872	*Leaves from the Diary of Henry Greville*, ed. by the Countess of Strafford, 1883–1893–4, 6 vols.	374
Edward Pease .	Railway projector	1838–1857	*The Diaries of Edward Pease*, ed. by Alfred Pease, 1907	376
William Goodall	Huntsman .	1843–1859	*The History of the Belvoir Hunt*, by Dale	379
H. E. Manning .	Cardinal . .	1844–1890	*Life of Cardinal Manning*, by E. S. Purcell, 2 vols., 1896	380
Samuel Wilberforce	Bishop . .	1830–1873	*Life of Samuel Wilberforce*, by A. R. Ashwell, 3 vols., 1880	385

LIST OF DIARIES

Minor Diaries—continued.

Name of Diarist.	Occupation.	Date of Diary.	Source.	Page.
Lord Macaulay	Historian . .	1838–1859	Life and Letters of Lord Macaulay, G. Trevelyan, 2 vols. 1876	389
George Howard, Earl of Carlisle	Statesman .	1843–1864	Extracts from Journals of the Earl of Carlisle (privately printed)	393
Nassau Senior .	Economist .	1848–1858	Journals of Visits to Ireland, 1852–1862; to France and Italy, 1848–1852; to Turkey and Greece, 1857–8	396
Colonel A. Ponsonby	Soldier . .	1849–1868	Original manuscript in the possession of Maj.-General J. Ponsonby	397
Lieut.-General Sir Charles Windham	Soldier . .	1854–1855	Crimean Diary and Letters of Gen. Sir C. Windham, ed. by Maj. H. Pearse, 1897	400
George Eliot .	Novelist . .	1855–1877	George Eliot's Life, by G. W. Cross, 1884, 2 vols.	403
John Addington Symonds	Author . .	1860–1888	John Addington Symonds, by Horatio Browne, 2 vols.1895	407
Sir G. Graham .	Soldier . .	1860 1882 1885	Lt.-Gen. Sir Gerald Graham, by Col. R. H. Vetch, 1901	411
William Cory .	Poet and schoolmaster	1863–1873	Letters and Journals of W. Cory, arranged by F. Warre Cornish,1897	412
James Hannington	Bishop . .	1863–1885	James Hannington, by E. C. Dawson, 1887	416
Captain Eyre Lloyd	Soldier . .	1899–1901	Boer War Diary of Capt. T. H. Eyre Lloyd, privately printed, 1905	418

ENGLISH DIARIES

SHORT NOTICES

Name of Diarist.	Occupation.	Date of Diary.	Source.	Page.
Miss Berry	—	1783–1848	*Journals and Correspondence of Miss Berry*, ed. by Lady T. Lewis, 3 vols., 1865	420
Joseph Hunter	Antiquary	1806	Brit. Museum Add. MS. 24,441	421
The Marquis of Hastings	Governor-General of India	1813–1818	*The Private Journals of the Marquess of Hastings*, ed by the Marchioness of Bute, 1858	421
Thomas Grey	—	1826	Original MS.	422
Sir Mountstuart Grant-Duff	Member of Parliament, Governor of Madras	1851–1901	*Diaries of Sir M. Grant - Duff*, 14 vols.	422
J. E. Denison, Viscount Ossington	Speaker of the House of Commons	1857–1872	*The Diary of John Evelyn Denison*, 1900	423
TWENTIETH CENTURY					
Lord Bernard Gordon-Lennox	Soldier	1914	Original MS. in the possession of the Duke of Richmond and Gordon	424
Arthur Graeme West	Soldier	1915–1917	*The Diary of a Dead Officer*, 1920	428
W. N. P. Barbellion	Museum Assistant	1903–1919	*The Journal of a Disappointed Man*, 1919. *A Last Diary*, 1921	432

An alphabetical list of all diaries mentioned in the volume will be found in the Index.

In the diary extracts quoted in the reviews round brackets denote parentheses written by the diarists themselves, and square brackets explanations and notes which have been inserted.

SIXTEENTH CENTURY

EDWARD VI

ONLY two diaries of English sovereigns are available; and no two other diaries in this collection can present a greater contrast. In due course we shall deal with the diary of the Queen who lived till she was 82. We now must examine the diary of the King who died when he was 16.

Although the diary is all in Edward's handwriting, the fact that this sedate, concise and dignified epitome of events should have been recorded by a boy who was under 12 years old when he began to write it naturally led to some doubt being cast on its absolute authenticity. Mr. J. G. Nichols, who was responsible for the full annotated edition of the diary which appeared in 1857, agrees with Burnet, the seventeenth-century historian, that, apart from the introductory summary, it was not written from dictation, but was entirely his own. Some inaccuracies with regard to dates seem to support this opinion. Hallam also comes to the same conclusion, although he would like it not to be genuine because of the off-hand way in which Edward refers to the execution of his uncles and the treatment of his sister. " But," he concludes, "he had, I suspect, too much Tudor blood." We have also to bear in mind that there is plenty of contemporary evidence of the boy King's extraordinary erudition.

So we may take it that this pithy and restrained recital of events was written by a boy between the ages of 11 and 14. The diary does not contain any definite expression of opinion or any personal jottings, nevertheless in its style the compendious and succinct narrative of events is by no means colourless or impersonal.

There is an introductory record of events from his birth (1537) to his accession; the burial of Henry VIII, his own coronation, the war with Scotland, the war with France, and the suppression of Kett's rebellion. In March, 1549, the actual diary begins with frequent brief and sometimes almost daily entries. He records his movements, official appointments, royal proclamations, foreign events, diplomatic negotiations, trials, and executions and his pastimes. The elaboration of the tilting jousts and bear-bating is the only boyish feature in the diary. While there is nothing in the nature of comment on events, there is a conscientious exactness and curiously mature and distinctly regal tone in the entries which is significant. (" Me " is always written with a capital M.)

The following extracts have been taken from the Clarendon Historical Society's reprint in which the original spelling has been modernized. We will take first his intercourse and negotiation with the French Ambassadors.

1549. May 25. The Ambassadors came to the Court where they saw Me take the oath for the Acceptation of the Treaty and afterwards dined with Me ; and after dinner saw a Pastime of ten against ten at the Ridg whereof on the one side were the Duke of Suffolk, the Vicedam, the Lord Lisle, and seven other gentlemen apparell'd in yellow. On the other the Lord Strange, Monsieur Henandoy and eight other in blue.

May 29. The Ambassadors had a fair supper made them by the Duke of Somerset and afterwards went into the Thames and saw both the Bear hunted in the River and also Wildfire cast out of Boats and many pretty conceits.

In July in the following year he records with great clearness a conversation he has with the French Ambassador in an " Inner Chamber," and ends up :

I assured him That I thank him for his order and also his Love, etc., and I should show like love in all points. For Rumours, they were not always to be believed and that I did sometimes provide for the worst but never did any harm upon their hearing. For Ministers, I said I would rather appease these controversies by words than do anything by force.

July 26. Monsieur le Mareschale dined with Me. After dinner saw the strength of the English archers. After he had done so at his departure I gave him a Diamond from my finger worth by estimation £150 both for Pains and also for My memory. Then he took his leave.

After a careful summary of a long diplomatic communication to the Emperor, he adds, " The reasonings be in my desk."

Edward's unrelenting adherence to Protestantism is apparent in many of the entries, but in none more than those which relate to his sister Mary.

March 18. The Lady Mary my sister came to me to Westminster where after Salutations she was called with my Council into a Chamber ; where was declared how long I had suffered her Mass in hope of her reconciliation and how now being no hope which I perceived by her Letters, except I saw some short amendment I could not bear it. She answered That her Soul was God's and her Faith she would not change nor dissemble her Opinion with contrary doings. It was said I constrained not her Faith but willed her not as a King to Rule but as a subject to obey ; and that her example might breed too much inconvenience.

April 10. Mr. Wotton had his Instructions made to do withal to the Emperor to be as Ambassador Legier in Mr. Morison's place as to declare this Resolution that if the Emperor would suffer my Ambassador with him to use his service then I would his ; if he would not suffer Mine I would not suffer his. Likewise my sister was my Subject and should use my Service appointed by Act of Parliament.

June 22. The Lady Mary sent Letters to the Council marvelling at the Imprisonment of Dr. Mallet her Chaplain for saying of Mass before her houshold seeing it was promised the Emperors Ambassadour she should not be molested in Religion but that she and her Houshold should have the Mass said before them continually.

Aug. 29. Certain Pinaces were prepared to see that there should be no conveyance over sea of the Lady Mary secretly done. Also appointed that the Lord Chancellor, Lord Chamberlain, the Vice Chamberlain and the Secretary Petre should see by all means they could whether she used the Mass ; and if she did that the Laws should be executed on her chaplains. Also that when I came from this Progress to Hampton Court or Westminster both my sisters should be with Me till further Orders were taken for this purpose.

No regrets are expressed with regard to the trial and execution of Somerset, and when anyone is " condemned to the Fire " he notes it without comment. His supposed compassion for Joan of Kent is not expressed in the diary, in which her fate is simply related in the following words :

May 2. Joan Boacher otherwise called Joan of Kent was burnt for holding that Christ was not Incarnate of the Virgin Mary ; being condemned the year before but kept in hope of Conversion and the 30th of April the Bishop of London and the Bishop of Ely were to persuade her but she withstood them and reviled the Preacher that preached at her Death.

He gives an interesting description of the funeral of Martin Bucer, the well-known Protestant divine, whose body in Queen Mary's reign was exhumed and burnt.

1550. Feb. 28. The learned man Bucerus died at Cambridge who was two days after buried in St. Mary's Church at Cambridge ; All the whole University with the whole town bringing him to the Grave to the number of 3,000 persons. Also there was an oration of Mr. Haddon made very eloquently at his death and a sermon of (Dr. Parker) after that Master Redman made a third sermon ; which three sermons made the People wonderfully to lament his Death. Last of all all the learned men of the University made their epitaphs in his praise laying them on his grave.

58   ENGLISH DIARIES

He notes his illness in April, 1551. " I fell sick of the measles and small pox." The diary concludes some time before his death.

It was used by Sir John Heywood in the first history of Edward VI's reign, which appeared shortly after the King's death. The original manuscript formed part of the Cottonian Library now in the British Museum.

HENRY MACHYN

THE diary of Henry Machyn extends over a period of thirteen years from 1550 to 1563. He was an undertaker or furnisher of funeral trappings resident in London. The diary is largely taken up with elaborate accounts of funerals, but he also describes pageants, revels, processions, proclamations, trials and punishments. The latter occur with very great frequency during Queen Mary's reign. Of himself and his opinions he says practically nothing. On the few occasions when he mentions himself he refers to himself in the third person. Living as he did in the reigns of Edward VI, Mary and Elizabeth, he witnessed extreme religious changes. His sympathies were evidently inclined to the old form of worship which in its elaborate ceremonial gave a better chance to the craft by which he gained his livelihood. He mentions the preachers at St. Paul's Cross and at the Court, and elsewhere, and once or twice he comments on the weather. The entries are not regular but frequent, and the diary is as impersonal as a diary can be. The spelling is so bad as at times to be unintelligible; the extracts will, therefore, be transcribed into modern spelling. But an instance of Machyn's own spelling may first be given. The entry records the arraignment of Sir Thomas Arundell in the reign of Edward VI.

The XXVII day of Januarii was reyned Sir Thomas Arundell knyght and so the quest cold nott fynd ym tyll the morow after and so he whent to the Towre agayn and then the quest wher shutt up tyll the morrow with-owt mett or drynke or candylle or fyre and on the morow he cam a-gayne and the quest quytt ym of tresun and cast hym of felony to be hangyd.

The very full descriptions of funerals are filled with technical terms and heraldic expressions. This being his main interest, they recur on very many pages throughout the diary. It will suffice to give one example.

Edward VI Funeral.

1553. The VIII day of August was buried the noble King Edward VI ; and at his burying was the greatest mourning (mone) made for him of his death as ever was heard or seen both of all sorts of people weeping and lamenting ; and first of all went a great company of children in their surplices and clerks singing and then his father's bedeman and then ii heralds and then a standard with a dragon and then a great number of his servants in black and then another standard with a white greyhound and then after a great number of his officers and after them comes more heralds and then a standard with the head officer of his house ; and then heralds, Norroy bore the helmet and the crest on horseback and then his great banner of arms in embroidery and with divers other banners and then came riding Master Clarenceaux with his target with his garter and his sword gorgeously and rich, and after Garter with his coat armour in embroidery and then more heralds of arms ; and then came the chariot with great horses draped with velvet to the ground and every horse having a man on his back in black and every one bearing a banner roll of divers kings arms and with scutcheons on their horses and then the chariot covered with cloth of gold and on the chariot lay a picture lying " recheussly " with a crown of gold and a great collar and his sceptre in his hand lying in his robes and the garter about his leg and a coat in embroidery of gold ; about the corpse were borne four banners, a banner of the order another of the red rose another of Queen Jane another of the queen's mother. After him went a goodly horse covered with cloth of gold unto the ground and the master of the horse with a man of arms in armour which was offered both the man and the horse. There was set up a goodly hearse in Westminster Abbey with banner rolls and pensells and hung with velvet about.

A couple of instances may be given of other events. The visit of " the old Quyne of Schottes " to London in 1551 :

Then came the Queen of Scots and all our ladies and her gentlewomen and our gentlewomen to the number of 100 ; and there was sent her many great gifts by the mayor and aldermen as beefs, muttons, veals, swines, bread, wild foul, wine, beer, spices and all things and quails, sturgeon, wood, and coals and salmons by divers men.

A May game in 1555 :

The same day was a good May game at Westminster as has been seen with giants, morris pikes, guns and drums and devils and three morris dances and bagpipes and viols and many disguised and the lord and the lady of the May rode gorgeously with minstrels divers playing.

The punishments he records occur in the earlier part of the diary with great frequency. But even executions he only describes from the ceremonial point of view. Latimer's and Ridley's burning is noted, but with no further comment than " they were some time great preachers as ever was ; and at their burning did preach doctor Smyth." In one entry in 1554 he records the hanging and quartering of no less than fifty-seven people in different parts of London. Almost consecutive extracts may be given showing how common these excessive punishments were in Queen Mary's reign.

> 1555. The 6th day of July rode to Tyburn to be hanged 3 men and one drawn upon a hurdle.
>
> The 8th day of July were 3 more delivered out of Newgate and sent into the country to be burned for heretics.
>
> The 12th day of July was burned at Canterbury 4 men for heresy 2 priests and 2 laymen.
>
> The 20th day of July was carried to the Tower in the morning early 4 men.
>
> The 2nd day of August was a shoemaker burned at St. Edmundsbury for heresy.
>
> The 8th day of August between 4 and 5 in the morning was a prisoner delivered unto the sheriff of Middlesex to be carried to Uxbridge to be burned.

Machyn belonged to the Merchant Taylors and he mentions the Company several times. He notes very often the names of preachers, but makes no remarks about the sermons. All proclamations are duly set down.

The only personal references to himself are : Two occasions on which he mentions his birthday, not however on the same date, nor does the age tally. Such trivialities were beneath the notice of one who was occupied with hearses and scutcheons and banners and mantles. On the 16th of May, 1554, he makes himself out to be 56, and on May 20th, 1562, he says he is 63 ; on another occasion he records the birth of "a whenche," afterwards christened Katherine, who was probably a grandchild ; and further the occasion on which he had to sit on the stool of penance for having spread defamatory reports concerning Veron, the French Protestant Minister.

> 1561. The 23 day of November did preach at Paul's cross Renagir, it was St. Clement's day, did sit all the sermon time "monser Henry de Machyn" for 2 words the which was told him that Veron the Frenchman the preacher was taken with a wench, by the reporting by one William Laurans . . . the which the same Harry [i.e. Machyn himself] knelt down before Master Veron and the bishop and they would not forgive him for all his friends that he had worshipful.

He gives an account of an amusing but scandalous incident dated April 8th, 1554.

> On the same day somebody unknown hanged a cat on the gallows beside the cross in Cheap, habited in a garment like to that the priest wore that

said mass ; she had a shaven crown and in her fore feet held a piece of paper made round representing the wafer.

A few days later (and as this is our last extract we will relapse into Machyn's own spelling):

was a proclamasyon was mad that what so mever he wher that cold bryng forth hym that dyd hang the catt on the galaus he shuld have xx marke for ys labur.

Machyn writes " welwet " and " wacabond," early examples of cockney pronunciation which remind one of Sam Weller.

The diary is of historical and antiquarian interest because of its age and the rareness of such complete descriptions of pageants of that time. A diary, however, on the same subjects to-day would be unreadable.

The manuscript was one of the volumes which suffered from the fire of the Cottonian Library, but it was not destroyed. In 1848 it was printed and published with notes by the Camden Society.

JOHN DEE

JOHN DEE was a magician, a necromancer and astrologer, who was consulted by queens and princes and the nobility. Before examining his diary some brief account of his strange career may be given. He was born in 1527 ; he took up mathematics and astronomy at Cambridge, working at times with only four hours' sleep, and was elected a Fellow of Trinity College. He also studied abroad in France and Holland, and became celebrated as a learned mathematician. He was assigned a pension by Edward VI in 1551, but on the accession of Mary he was accused of using enchantments against the Queen's life, placed in confinement, and only obtained his liberty after four years. He was always in favour with Queen Elizabeth from the time that he was asked by Lord Dudley to name a propitious day for her coronation. His home was at Mortlake, where the Queen on more than one occasion visited him. He travelled abroad to present a copy of one of his books to the Emperor Maximilian, and later again to consult with German physicians and astrologers in regard to the illness of the Queen. Edward Kelly, an apothecary who had been convicted of forgery and lost both his ears in the pillory, became Dee's friend, and together they performed various incantations and maintained a frequent imaginary intercourse with spirits. They travelled together and stayed with Albert Laski, a Polish nobleman who visited Dee when he was in England. But Dee quarrelled with his companion and returned home. During his absence the mob, believing him to be a wizard, had broken into his house and destroyed furniture, books and chemical apparatus. In 1595 he became warden of Manchester College, where he stayed nine years. He died at Mortlake in 1604, at the age of 81, in the greatest poverty. We have the following description of him from Aubrey, which seems to fit in with the part he played : " of very fair clear sanguine complexion, with a long beard as white as milk—a very handsome man tall and slender. He wore a gown like an artists gowne with hanging sleeves."

His diary covers the period from 1577 to 1600, although also from 1554 to 1577 there are a few entries each year consisting of notes of nativities inserted by him at various times when he was consulted as an astrologer. For instance :

1560. July 8. Margaret Russell Countess of Cumberland hora 2 min 9 Exoniœ mane.

1563. March 23. Mr. William Fennar a meridie inter horam undecimam et duodecimam nocte.

The diary does not provide the amount of occult material that we should expect, as it is taken up with lists of visitors, business about his property, weather reports, accounts, the borrowing of money and a great deal about his changes of servants and the wages he paid them. The servant problem, acute in all ages, was no doubt specially anxious for a man who was suspected of being a magician.

I did before Barthilmew Hikman pay Letice her full yere's wages ending the 7th day of Aprill : her wages being four nobles an apron a payr of hose and shoes.

I discharged Letice of my service and payd all duetyes untyll this day. I gave her for a month over 2s. 6d. and for to spend on the way I gave her 2s. 6d.

Anne Powell cam to my service ; she is to have four nobles by the year a payr of hose and shoes.

Jane (his wife) most desperately angry in respect her maydes.

He has frequent visits from celebrated people :

The Erle of Lecester, Mr. Philip Sydney, Mr. Dyer came to my house.

The Countess of Kent and the Countess of Cumberland visited me in the afternoon. The Lord Willoughby dyned with me.

The Lady Walsingham cam suddenly into my house very freely.

The Lord Albert Laski cam to me and lay at my howse all night.

The Erle of Derby with Lady Gerard Sir — Molyneux and his lady dawghter to the Lady Gerrard, Master Hawghton and others cam suddenly uppon me after three of the clok. I made them a skoler's collation and it was taken in good part.

He also dines with Sir Walter Raleigh, the Archbishop and other great people. No doubt he was the fashionable rage at one time owing to the Queen having patronized him. It is known that in 1577 his services were hurriedly demanded in order to prevent the mischief to Her Majesty's person apprehended from a waxen image of her with a pin stuck through its breast found in Lincoln's Inn Fields. We will give a selection of entries concerning his meetings with Queen Elizabeth.

1578. I spake with the Quene hora quinta : I spake with Mr. Secretary Walsingham.

The Queen's Majestie had conference with me at Richmond inter 9 et 11.

1580. The Queen's Majestie cam from Rychemond in her coach, the higher way of Mortlake felde and when she cam right against the church she turned down toward my house : and when she was against my garden in the felde she stode there a good while and then cam ynto the street at the great gate of the felde where she espied me at my doore making obeysains to her Majestie : she beckend her hand for me ; I cam to her coach side, she speedily pulled off her glove and gave me her hand to kiss and to be short asked me to resort to her court and to give her to wete when I cam ther : hor. 6¼ a meridie.

The Quene's Majestie to my great comfort (hora quinta) cam with her trayn from the court and at my dore graciously calling me to her, on horsebak, exhorted me briefly to take my mother's death patiently.

1583. The Quene lying at Richmond went to Mr. Secretary Walsingham to dynner ; she coming by my dore gratiously called me to her and so I went to her horse side as far as where Mr. Hudson dwelt [the following referring to the Duc d'Anjou is in Greek characters which Dee uses occasionally for the more secret entries] *Her Majestie asked me oboscurely of Monsieur's state dixi biothanatos erit.* The Quene went from Richmond toward Grenwich and at her going on horsbak being new up she called for me by Mr. Rawley his putting her in mynde and she sayd " quod defertur non aufertur " and gave me her right hand to kisse.

1590. The Quene's Majestie being at Richmond graciously sent for me. I cam to her at three quarters of the clok afternone and she sayd she wold send me something to kepe Christmas with.

The Quene's Majestie called for me at my dore circa 3½ a meridie as she passed by and I met at Estshene gate when she graciously, putting down her mask, did say with merry chere " I thank the Dee there was never promisse made but it was broken or kept." I understode her Majesty to mean of the hundred angels (coins) she promised to send me this day.

1594. Between 6 and 7 after none the Quene sent for me to her in the privy garden at Grenwich when I delivered in writing the hevonly admonition and Her Majestie tok it thankfully. Onely the Lady Warwyk and Sir Robert Cecil his lady wer in the garden with Her Majestie.

But royal favour, as he learned, is capricious, for Dee died in great poverty.

Controversies and disputes figure frequently in the diary. There is Emery's " most unhonest, hypocriticall and devilish dealings and devises agaynst me " ; there is Roger Cook's " unseemly dealing " ; there is " the knavery " of Vincent Murfyn against whom he gets £100 damages ; there are " the nowghty dealings " of one Barnabas, a dispute with the Bishop of Leightyn, and eventually he fell out with his fellow astrologer Edward Kelly. But they were close friends for some years and Kelly's name occurs very frequently.

Mr. E. K. at nine of the clock afternone sent for me to his laboratory over the gate to se how he distilled sericon.

Mr. E. K. did disclose some accounted me frendes how untrue they were [in Greek characters].

Mr. K. put the glass in dung.

E. K. did open the great secret to me, God be thanked.

Vidi divinam aquam demonstratione magnifici domini et amici mei incomparabilis D. Ed Kelei ante meridiem tertia hora.

I gave Mr. Ed Kelly my glass so highly and long esteemed of our Quene and the Emperor Randolph the second.

Mr. Edward Kelly gave me the water earth and all.

I delivered to Mr. Kelly the powder, the bokes, the glas and the bone.

After they parted Dee corresponds with him and refers to him as Sir Edward Kelly. A few extracts must be given of the more mysterious references to rappings, spirits and dreams.

It was the 8th day being Wednesday hora noctis 10, 11, the strange noyse in my chamber of knocking and the voyce ten times repeted, somewhat like the shriek of an owle, but more longly drawn and more softly as it were in my chamber. All the night very strange knocking and rapping in my chamber.

Barnabas Saul lying in the hall was strangely troubled by a spiritual creature about midnight.

Robert Gardner declared unto me hora $4\frac{1}{2}$ a certeyn great philosophical secret, as he termed it, of a spirituall creatuer, and was this day willed to come to me and declare it which was solemnly done and with common prayer.

Robert Wood visitted with spiritual creatures had comfort by conference.

My dream of being naked and my skyn all overwrought with work like some kinde of tuft mockado with crosses blew and red ; and on my left arme about the arme in a wreath this word I red—*sine me nihil potestis facere.*

Saturday night I dremed that I was deade and afterwards my bowels wer taken out I walked and talked with diverse and among others with the Lord Threserer who was cam to my howse to burn my bokes when I was dead and thought he loked sourly on me.

My terrible dream that Mr. Kelly would by force bereave me of my bokes, toward day break.

This night I had the vision and shew of many bokes in my dreame and among the rest was one great volume thik in large quarto new printed on the first page whereof as a title in great letters printed *" Notus in Judaea Deus."* Many other bokes methought I saw new printed of very strange arguments.

[In Greek characters.] This night my wife dreamed that one cam to her and touched her saying Mistres Dee you are conceived of child whose name must be Zacharias be of good chere he sal do well as this doth.

We also get this account of a curious ceremony :

Ann my nurse had long byn tempted by a wicked spirit but this day it was evident how she was possessed of him . . . at night I anoynted (in the name of Jesus) Ann Frank her brest with holy oyle. In the morning she required to be anoynted and I did very devowtly prepare myself and pray for vertue and powr and Christ his blessing of the oyle to the expulsion of the wycked : and then twyse anoynted the 'wycked one did resest a while.

He records quite a trivial incident, evidently attaching to it some occult significance :

The spider at ten of the clok at night suddenly on my desk and suddenly gon ; a most rare one in bygnes and length of feet. I was in a great study at my desk.

His marriage with his second wife, Jane Fromonds, is briefly noted in Latin. There are references to her and frequently these words occur in Greek character, " Jane had them," but it cannot be said what " them " refers to. His children are also mentioned, specially Arthur, who on one occasion was wounded " on his hed by his own wanton throwing of a brik bat upright and not well avoyding the fall of it agayn " ; and Theodor, who " had a sore fall on his mowth at mid-day."

Dr. Dee was naturally concerned about his own health and there are many references to it and to the remedies he took :

My mervaglous horsnes and in manner spechelesnes toke me, being nothing at all otherwise sick.

I was very sick upon two or thre sage leaves eten in the morning; better suddenly at night; when I cast them up I was well.

I had on the Sunday afternoon the cramp most extremely in the very centre of the calves of both my legs and in the place where I had the suddeyn grief on Bartilmew even last I had payn, so intollerable as if the vaynes or artheries wold have broken by extreme stretching or how else I cannot tell. The payn lasted about half a quater of an hour. I took my purgation of six grayns.

A great fit of the stone in my left kydney; all day I could do but three or four drops of water but I drunk a draught of white wyne and salet oyle and after that crab's eyes in powder with the bone in the carps head and abowt four of the clok I did eat tosted cake buttered and with sugar and nutmeg on it and drunk two great draughts of ale with it and I voyded within an howr much water and a stone as big as an Alexander seed. God be thanked.

In the morning began my hed to ake and be hevy more than of late and had some wambling in my stomach. I had broken my fast with sugar sopps.

Much more is known of Dr. Dee than what is contained in this diary. He wrote nearly eighty different works, but most of them were not printed. He was very much interested in the reform of the Calendar and refers to it several times in his diary. In his *Compendious Rehearsal* he gives a full account of his career, but this was written for the official eye. As will be seen, he was religious but intensely superstitious, and he had an intellectual and scientific mind which was obscured by his belief in the occult.

The diary was discovered in the library of the Ashmolean Museum at Oxford written in a small illegible hand on the margins of old almanacs. It was printed, together with the catalogue he made of his Library Manuscripts, by the Camden Society (edited by J. O. Halliwell) in 1842.

SIR FRANCIS WALSINGHAM

THE high offices held by Sir Francis Walsingham under Queen Elizabeth and the important negotiations with which he was entrusted would lead one to suppose that, if he kept a diary at all, it would be one of particular interest. It is a disappointment, therefore, that the Journal which exists consists of nothing more than notices of his movements, the Queen's movements when he is in England, and occasionally of other events, with memoranda for each day of all letters received and sent.

A peculiar feature of the diary is that, although the entries are in the first person, the manuscript is not in Walsingham's own hand but in that of his secretary.

The diary begins in December, 1570, when Walsingham, who had been already sent as ambassador to France to assist in negotiating an accord between Charles IX and the Huguenots, had been again dispatched thither as resident ambassador, and part of his instructions was to prepare the way for the marriage of the Queen with the Duke of Anjou. This is interesting, but all we get in the Journal is:

I went to the Palais and there had audience at Queen Mother's handes.

I went to Gallion and there had audience of Queen Mother and Monsieur

or equally brief entries of the same description.

The last entries are dated April, 1583, but there are several breaks, one of nearly two years between 1578 and 1580. It is unnecessary to quote the entries as they are seldom more than one line and they tell us practically nothing of what Walsingham was doing and absolutely nothing of what Walsingham was like.

The very first entry is in peculiar grammar:

Sunday Dec. 3. That the Queene of Scotes shoulde be verie sycke.

But on Monday Walsingham corrected his secretary and no doubt instructed him that he did not want the diary kept in the *oratio obliqua*.

Great events are suggested, but never related:

I wente unto the Courte and had conference with my Lord of Lecestre and Mr. Secretarie about a matter of great importance.

This is how he records a journey:

Monday 8. I departed from Abbeville and came to bed at Piquenel.

Tuesday 9. I departed from Piquenel and came to bed at Amiens.

And so on till he gets to Paris.

Apart from his official duties, the only entry which suggests anything in the least domestic seems to refer to the engagement of a coachman.

Oct. 21. Entertaynment of a new cochier.

Just to illustrate the brief memorandum style of the diary, some consecutive entries may be given in February, 1581.

Thursday 1. The Court removed to Rochester. Monsieur departed.
Friday 2. I went to Rochester.
Saturday 3. Hir Majestie removed to Sittingbourne. I went to Mr. Cromar's to bed.
Monday 5. Hir Majestie removed to Cantorbury. I went to Cantorbury to bed.
Wednesday 7. Monsieur departed from Cantorbury to imbarke at Sandwich. I wayted on him some part of the way and returned to Cantorbury.

Luckily there is a great deal more known about Sir Francis Walsingham than can be gathered from these meagre diaries His correspondence during his embassies in France was published *in extenso* by Sir Dudley Digges in 1655, under the title *The Compleat Ambassador*.

The diary was published by the Camden Society in 1871.

SIR THOMAS CONINGSBY

THIS is the earliest of the soldiers' diaries which are included in this collection. It is only a fragment covering, with some breaks, the few weeks from August 13 to December 24, 1591. Like the majority of soldiers' diaries, it is concerned exclusively with military operations and contains no personal references. Sir Thomas Coningsby wrote definitely for the information of some particular person whom he addresses once or twice. His notes are full and graphic; his style is so natural, easy and unstilted that it makes one regret that the fragment is so brief.

The Siege of Rouen with which the diary deals is well known in the history of France as one of the incidents of the wars of the League. The city was seized and garrisoned by that party in the year 1590. Henry IV invested it on November 11, 1591, and the siege was raised on the approach of the Duke of Parma in the following April. Queen Elizabeth was prevailed upon to send forces in aid of the protestant King of France, as she then had reason to esteem him. It was with this expeditionary force under the Earl of Essex that Sir Thomas Coningsby served.

The diary is headed:

A Jornall of Cheife Thinges happened in our Jorney from Deape the 13 of Auguste untyll [blank]

The first entry begins:

Upon Satterdaie binge the 13 of Auguste my lord having intelligence that those of Roan mente to give him a camisado [surprise] in the nighte, in his army provided all things necessarie to welcome them, together with a determynation that if they came not that nyghte then the next morninge he would have surprysed some of them in some of their own holdes and fortresses nere adjoynynge.

They leave Dieppe and proceed on their march

in a very hot daie wonderfullie dusted and pestered with flies.

They are as hospitably received in the French villages as the expeditionary force 323 years later :

We found the villages and howses utterlie abandoned but yet mylke, syder, freshe water and bread almost in everie house readye sett to relieve our soldiers.

Some of Sir Thomas's descriptions of adventures and engagements with the enemy may be given.

Having scarcely ended our soldierly repaste there came four harquelatieres who advertysed that they had discovered the enemye comynge out of a wood nere unto us ; and being sente backe to take some better understanding of them in going to the rising of a lytel hill they were encountered by seven harquelatiers of th' ennemy, who shrowded themselves behind a wyndmyll and assalting ours slewe ii of them and hurt the third.

My lord only accompanyed with two gentlemen wente to the King's quarter where after dynner th' ennemye sallyed out on every syde and were verie braggante and upon the castle syde made skyrmysh with our French there. The King, my lord and his grand esquire lay upon an immynente place all on a cloake and beheld it. Upon our quarter they sallyed out upon our neighbor Mounte Morancy's men who indevored to take a church nere unto the verie gate and possessed themselves of it. Whereupon they made their sally and inforced their horse and foote to abandon the place with more than a lytle haste.

Although I saie it, our forwardnes doth make the French wonder to see ours of the beste sorte eyther well mounted or placed in the head of the troupes of pykes, to aunswere all alarme and to make the proudest ronne when any offer to charge them.

We might see many of their horse drove downe and th' ennemye withdraw within the covert of the towne ; and there we might behold many a horse well spurred and many a sword jollyly glystering in the sunn on both sydes.

This daie a page commynge into the king's quarter with a letter from Villiers to some men aboute the king, was reprehended, and he ymmediatly put the letters into his mouth to have eaten them and had so doan but that one caught him by the throate and made spytt them out ; but they were so marred that noething could be read at all ; he hath bene tortured and confessed some things for the king's torne in this buysines.

This daie being a great myst, th' ennemye had laid soundrie ambuscadoes for us, and with all invention of villanous railing they thoughte to have drawn us out of our trenches to skyrmysh but ours foreseeing the padd in the strawe have deferred to aunswer their words tyll we be strong ynough to breake their heads.

But Coningsby makes notes about the lighter moments of recreation as well as about the fighting.

The next daie being well loged, my lord invited for solace monsieur Revience lieutenant governor of Picardye where a great nomber of ladies were gathered together not without dauncing and musicke.

This eveninge being the 22 of Auguste the kinge with his nobles would neades leap where our lord generall did overleape them all.

The 19 and 20 October we passed in making goode cheare, coursing in the fields, ryding of horses playing at ballone and the lyke.

The 22 daie we passed with playinge at tennys in the forenoone and a playinge at ballon in th' afternoone with the lieuetenant-gouvernor of Deape and the victorie fell on our syde.

Sir Roger and I were invyted to certaine French gentlemen where we dranke carowses; and what eyther with the cold of the long expectation in the mornynge or overmuch wyne at dynner th' one syde of my head ake 2 daies after.

The diary closes on December 24 and was transmitted to his friend for whom it was written, whom he addresses in one passage: " I pray you use it (the information) with your wonted dyscretion; for I would not wryte thus much but to you."

Probably Coningsby went on writing: unfortunately nothing further is in existence. It is to be regretted that we have not his account of the first demonstration made by the Englishmen before Rouen in which the Earl of Essex had not only the misfortune to lose his brother but also to incur the censure of his detractors at home and the displeasure of his royal mistress.

Sir Thomas Coningsby was elected to Parliament for the city of Hereford in 1593, and also became sheriff of the county. He died in 1625.

The journal was published in 1847 in the first volume of the *Camden Miscellanies*.

SEVENTEENTH CENTURY

SIR SIMONDS D'EWES

BORN in Coxden, in Dorsetshire, in 1602, Simonds d'Ewes was educated at St. John's College, Cambridge, and called to the Bar. He became High Sheriff for Suffolk in 1639 and was elected member of Parliament for Sudbury in 1640. In 1641 he was created a Baronet by Charles I, but on the outbreak of the Civil War he adhered to Parliament. In 1648 he was turned out of Parliament by the army as one of those who were thought to retain some regard for the person of the King. He then gave himself up to literary and, more especially, antiquarian studies and died in 1650.

Between 1619 and 1636 he kept a diary, and for a few years again at a later date. This diary he wrote up and left in the form of an autobiographical note. It therefore comes very near the limit where diary becomes autobiography, but after a prefatory chapter or two he retains the diary form, often copying several pages from the original diary. Although repetitions and the awkwardness of diary style may have been avoided by this revision, it is doubtful whether he improved his original notes, because the final result is heavy and often tedious and lacks the freshness and spontaneity of momentary writing.

The heaviness is added to by the fact that Sir Simonds was deeply religious, and took himself very seriously. He comes dangerously near being a prig.

The diary deals largely with historical events and is of value to historians as the careful opinion of a contemporary observer. His estimate of James I is on the whole favourable, owing to the fact that he compares him with his successor. He gives a characteristic picture of the King going down to open Parliament in 1621.

> First he spoke often and lovingly to the people standing thick and threefold on all sides to behold him, " God bless ye ! God bless ye ! " contrary to his

former hasty and passionate custom which often in his sudden distemper would bid a p—— or a plague on such as flocked to see him. Secondly, though the windows were filled with many great ladies as he rode along yet that he spake to none of them but to the Marquis of Buckingham's mother and wife : that he spake particularly and bowed to the Count of Gondomar the Spanish Ambassador ; and fourthly looking up to one window as he passed, full of gentlewomen or ladies, all in yellow bands, he cried out aloud " A p—— take yo ! are ye there ? " at which being much ashamed they all withdrew themselves suddenly from the window.

D'Ewes expressed special admiration for Prince Henry, Charles I's elder brother, " a prince rather addicted to martial studies and exercises than to golf, tennis or other boy's play." His bias against Bacon is very marked : " his vices were so stupendous and great as they utterly obscured and out-poised his virtues." He gives a charming description of Henrietta Maria :

On Thursday I went to Whitehall purposely to see the Queen which I did fully all the time she sat at dinner and perceived her to be a most absolute delicate lady after I had exactly surveyed all the features of her face much enlivened by her radiant and sparkling black eye. Besides, her deportment amongst her women was so sweet and humble and her speech and looks to her other servants so mild and gracious as I could not abstain from divers deep-pitched sighs to consider that she wanted the knowledge of the true religion.

His puritanical religious views gradually estrange him from the Court in Charles's reign and his disapproval of Buckingham makes him go the length of not only defending but almost excusing Felton. He regards Laud " a little, low, red-faced man of mean parentage," with the strongest misgivings, greatly preferring a virtuous Papist to the men " who call themselves Protestants as Bishop Laud and Bishop Wren and their wicked adherents." Needless to say he condemns Ship-money and prays daily that the Sovereign may abolish " this lamentable and fatal taxation."

Much of his time is taken up with antiquarian research. Not only does he transcribe all the Journals of Parliament of Queen Elizabeth's reign, but he is perpetually examining Escheat Rolls, Communia Rolls, Plea Rolls and all kinds of registers and deeds. Hours upon hours he spends in this way. The vast histories he projected, however, never materialised, and indeed he evidently had little power of exposition or narrative. Many of the fruits of his industry in the shape of transcripts from ancient records are contained in the Harleian Collection in the British Museum.

D'Ewes, however, does not only deal with public affairs, and we can discover a good deal about the man in the more domestic pages of the diary even in its amended form.

He is very proud of his pedigree. " I ever accounted it a great outward blessing to be well descended," and he spends much time in tracing his family history and that of his wife. Cambridge did not suit him.

> The main thing which made me even weary of the College was that swearing, drinking, rioting and hatred of all piety and virtue under false and adulterated nicknames did abound there and in all the university.

He is in every way exemplary, or anyhow says he is:

> My love to the study of the law began now to increase very much, being resonably well able to command what I read and finding daily use for it, I exceedingly desired knowledge.

When the Prince Elector comes over Sir Simonds visits him and modestly writes:

> I gave him such solid and faithful advice for the recovery of his lost country and dominions as he highly approved and might I believe ere this have been resettled in them had it laid in his own power to have put my advice into execution.

In fact, on one occasion he is obliged to admit that "self-conceit and pride of heart" were faults "to both of which I was naturally prone and inclined."

To his "dear and tender mother," who died when he was a boy, he had been passionately devoted, but with his father he was apt to have rather acrimonious disputes. First over his desire to have a private chamber of his own for a study, which desire "by reason of my father's unreasonable and ever-to-be-condoled tenacity and love of money" was thwarted at first. Later over his allowance:

> Coming to my father on Saturday Oct. 6 to receive and demand that small stipend he allowed me he denied me part of it upon some pretended defalcations. This so amazed me being unprovided of most necessaries and considering also that he kept from me an estate of five or six thousand pounds of mine own that I unawares expressed my grief unto him somewhat unadvisedly, at which he grew so extremely offended with me as he was never before that time nor after it so as I spake but once with him for about the space of five weeks ensuing although I resided near him all that time.

Again, after his marriage, when his father wanted part of the jointure to his wife to be released owing to the fact that she had no children, there is a sharp dispute between them. When his father dies he becomes more charitably disposed towards him, but he cannot resist some comment on his failings:

> I have much confidence also that he did seriously set himself during all that time (when he was ill) to search and try his own heart, which had been

too much set upon the business and profits of his present life and to prepare his way by a lively faith and a true repentance.

Sir Simonds married Anne Clapton. Love and courtship do not enter into the proceedings, which were arranged by contract between the two fathers. We do not learn anything about his wife's character, though he frequently expresses devotion to her. He earnestly desired a male heir, but although she had a number of children they none of them survived. He recites the ever-recurring death of these infants with great resignation, attributing it all to God's will. By Elizabeth Willoughby, his second wife, he had a son who survived him.

He was very strict in his religious practices. Constantly we read: " I spent the day in a private religious fast and humiliation," or " Saturday I devoted to a family humiliation and religious fasting with my wife and most of our people." It was his religion indeed that was the motive power behind his politics. As a young man he was once assailed by serious doubts and " fell into a strong and dangerous temptation." The occasion of this was the death of a friend. His reflections on it made him fall upon " two dangerous rocks of atheism." He argues the whole problem at length and finally concludes :

I found that those unruly thoughts of atheism were the devils engines and the fruits of infidelity not to be dallied withall or disputed, but to be avoided prayed against and resisted by a strong and lively faith.

And for the rest of his life his rigid orthodoxy and puritanical strictness never leaves him.

However, with his own parson in Suffolk, Mr. Danford, he has the most embittered relations. We are never told quite plainly what the cause of controversy is and we cannot help feeling some sympathy with Mr. Danford, who was brought into such close contact with the self-righteous and sanctimonious baronet.

Mr. Danford practised daily new and malicious devices to vex us so as we feared we should at last be driven for very peace and quiet's sake to forsake our mansion house and dwelling. . . . Loath I am to mention his malicious practices but that the necessity of setting down a full and true relation of the good and evil events and passages of mine own life enforceth me to it.

I might have bestowed more time on my precious studies had I not been interrupted by Mr. Danford's wicked malice. . . . For though he had forborne to catechise in the afternoons upon Sundays merely out of his spleen to me and had sometimes leavened his forenoon sermons with some malicious sprinklings—yet did he never break out into an open invective and a profanation of the church and pulpit with downright railing till Sunday April 13 of which wicked discourse unworthy the name of a sermon, I then took notes.

He complains to Dr. Corbett, Bishop of Norwich, who however seems to have taken Mr. Danford's side and the " malicious practices " continue, so that he removes his wife, when she is about to have a child, to his stepmother's house, " so as I might not be vexed with his cross and mischievous oppositions." We find, however, Mr. Danford being called in at a later date to christen one of his dying infants, and it is to be hoped that on that occasion anyhow there were no " malicious sprinklings."

Sir Simonds' own health did not trouble him to any extent. He only records one occasion on which a series of " aguish fist " made him very ill. His wife's many confinements and her eventual death, which he attributes to the negligence of his stepmother, Lady Denton, caused him great anxiety. Religion and study throughout are his solace and comfort in the terribly solemn business of living.

Sir Simonds did not write with a view to publication. But considering himself a person of no small importance, he desired that this account of his life should be handed down to his descendants as a memorial of their illustrious ancestor.

The diary, together with his will and family letters, edited by J. O. Halliwell, was published in 1845.

SIR HENRY SLINGSBY

IF special notice is taken of this diary, which only covers ten years very cursorily, it is not because of the circumstances which made Sir Henry Slingsby an eye-witness of and participant in the defeat of Charles I's armies, nor because of his own tragic fate some years later, but because the diary itself is a document which discloses an attractive personality and which in its literary style and lively presentation of domestic as well as public events seems to claim a more than usual amount of attention.

Sir Henry Slingsby was born in 1601; he married Barbara Bellasyse, daughter of Viscount Falconbridge, in 1631. He sat in Parliament for Knaresborough and was one of the fifty-nine members who voted against the Bill for the attainder of Strafford. He adopted the King's cause against Parliament; was with Charles at York, fought at Marston Moor, was present at Naseby, and at the surrender of Newark. In 1655 he was implicated in a Royalist plot at Hull. He was taken to London, tried, convicted, and condemned to be hanged, drawn and quartered. The sentence was altered to one of execution and he was beheaded on Tower Hill in 1658. Sir Henry lived in a time of public calamity, his natural preference would have been for the tranquil employments of a country life. He shows a high degree of learning, and often quotes passages and takes illustrations from the classics.

The diary begins in 1638 and continues for ten years. Charles I's execution is mentioned in one of the last entries. Sometimes he seems to write on the day, but more often he summarises periods. In diary writing he took Montaigne as a model. He describes Montaigne's Day Book or memorial of household affairs and adds:

> Hereupon I follow'd the advise of Michael de Montaigne to sett down in this Book such accidents as befell me not that I make my study of it but rather a recreation at vacant times without observing any time, method, or order in my wrighting or rather scribbling.

Like the great majority of diarists, Slingsby is far more effective when he is describing domestic matters than when he deals with military engagements and the political turmoil of the Civil War. He has a happy knack of describing people. He records the death from falling chimneys during a gale of Edward Osborn, a nephew of his wife's :

> He was but of a slender body and indifferently shot out in height, his limbs small but sinewy, his hair of a light colour and long and curled, his disposition gentle and sober, of a good meine and carriage of body, loving and affable to everyone and thus was he taken away before he had experience of the vanities and vices of the Times.

Here is his account of Francis Oddy, a most useful man in Sir Henry's household, who acted as upholsterer, " to furnish the Lodgin rooms and dress them up," and also as caterer :

> He is of very low stature, his head little, and his hair cut short, his face lean and full of wrinkles, his complection such that it shows he hath endured all wethers : his disposition not suitable with the rest of his fellow servants which both either by diligence breed envy or else thro' plain dealing Stir up variance : and having a working head is in continual debate.

We learn a good deal about his servants, he takes a great interest in them. He has sixteen men servants and eight women servants. When his cook, George Taylor, marries, he writes some reflections on his experience of cooks :

> This cook hath been the freest from disorder of 5 several Cooks which I have had since I became a housekeeper ; some of which hath been without all measure disorder'd. When they have sometimes stolen abroad I should not hear of them for 3 or 4 days together : yet commonly I never part'd with any of them till I made them as glad to be gone as I would have them. I never grew passionate with them nor threatened them much if I found them serviceable otherwise but still sought to win them from the habits of drinking, by fair means, willing to accept their future promise of amendment. . . . I required not of them so much their dressing the meat having a woman servant that took into her custody all the provision and delivered it out : so that I need not fear the cook embezeling, especially if he be a married man as this cook Samuell was ; and for their curiosity in the art of cooking I do not much value, not have we much use for it in our country housekeeping unless sometimes when we have a meeting of friends and then only to comply with the fashion of the times, to show myself answerable to what is expected, and not out of any love unto excessive feasting which now a days is very much practised.

There is also a note about his gardener :

> The last of October dy'd my Guardener Peter Clark after 12 or 14 years service to my father and me ; he was for no curiosity in Guardening, but

exceeding laborious in grafting, setting and sewing : which extream labour shortened his days ; he languish'd many years and so handl'd as he was nor could any judge what he ail'd ; sometimes he would say he was bewitch'd and at other times that he had a great worm in his gutts that did knaw and torment him which made me when he dy'd send for a chirurgeon from York to embowell him ; but no such thing appeared.

Slingsby is affectionate about his wife, who unfortunately is a great sufferer and gets little or no relief from the various doctors he employs ; he says of her :

She is by nature timorous and compassionate which makes her full of prayer on the behalf of others. I have sometimes been awakened in the night when I have heard her praying to herself as she never mist that duty in the day time.

He is called home and finds her very ill :

It did at first puzell the Physitians to understand what she ail'd ; that thought it had been the cholick, then the Cardiaca Passio, then the Jaundice, then the Spleen.

One doctor after another visits her : Dr. Parker who gives her a vomit, Dr. Micklethwate who declares it is jaundice, Dr. Frires who is a specialist for spleen, and prescribes very elaborate medicines, including hot beer at meals, which are all carefully set down. The latter he describes thus :

This man is of great fame for his skill and cures which he doth not a little brag of who tells you of his £50 and £100 cures.

Later on he goes to another and still greater man, a consultant, Sir Theodore Mayerne.

He seldom went to any, for he was corpulent and unwieldy ; and then again he was rich and the King's physician and a Knight which made him more costly to deal withall.

Yet another doctor he tries, but again in vain, and his wife dies " after she had endur'd a world of misery." He writes of her with charming affection and without a trace of sentimentality :

The loss of her by death is beyond expression both to her children and all that knew her ; but chiefly to myself who hath enjoy'd happy days in the company and society which now I find a want of ; she was a woman of very sweet disposition, pleasant and affable ; and when anything moved her to anger or that she conceived any injury done to her she would easily forgive and be the first that would offer termes of reconsilement ; and though she was passionate it was not lasting but soon passed over.

He hesitates to go to his home, Redhouse at Scaglethorp, after her death :

> I had not been yet at my own house, not abiding to come where I should find a miss of my dear wife and where every room will call her to my memory and renew my grief I therefore staid at Alne at my sister Bethell's house until I had better digest'd my grief.

It was while he was here that he received his commission to command the " trainbands of the City of York." But before we come to his public experiences his references to his son Thomas may be quoted. He was evidently a believer in early education. Before the child was four years old he could " tell the Latin words for the parts of his body and of his cloaths," but Sir Henry adds when he is engaging a tutor :

> I find him duller to learn this year than last (he was not yet five) which would discourage one but that I think the cause to be his too much minding Play which takes off his mind from his books ; therefore they do ill that do foment and cherish that humour in a child and by inventing new sports increase his desire to play which causeth a great aversion to their book ; and their mind being at first season'd with vanity will not easily loose the relish of it.

The next year he buys him a suit of clothes,

> being the first breeches and doublet that he ever had and made by my tailor Mr. Miller ; it was too soon for him to wear them being but 5 years old, but that his mother had a desire to see him in them, how proper a man he would be.

Slingsby has a way of branching off into general reflections and aphorisms after he has recorded some particular event. On the subject of ambition and ostentation he says :

> We judge our actions lost if they be not set out to show like Mountebanks that show the operation of their skill upon scaffolds in view of all passengers that more notice may be taken of them ; so ambitious are we of renown that goodness, moderation, equity, constancy and such qualities are little set by.

He deplores the morals of the age in which he lives :

> The approbation of others in so corrupt an age is an uncertain foundation to build vertuous actions upon ; that which is commendable is not always learnt by example of the most part. God keep every man from being an honest man according to the description is now a days made of it ; that which was account'd vice is now grown in fashion and nothing count'd vice.

And this on war :

> There is no stability in anything of this world ; when things are once advanced to such a height, it is not to be expected they will there settle but rather return to the same degree they were. But all is lost if warr continue

among us ; one year's continuance shall make a greater desolation than 20 years shall recover.

Yet warlike operations were to occupy so much of his time. He partakes in them out of a sense of duty and loyalty to the King, but in the middle of them he confesses, " My own disposition is to love quietness," and occasionally he snatches a day at home. His descriptions of the engagements were evidently written some time afterwards. They are often difficult to follow, and though detailed are not very illuminating.

In marching about the accommodation was not always of the best :

> At old Radnor the King lay in a poor low Chamber and my Ld of Linsey and others by the Kitching fire on hay ; no better were we accomodat'd for victuals ; which makes me remember this passage ; when the King was at his supper eating a pullet and a piece of cheese the room without was full but the mens' stomachs empty for want of meat ; the good wife troubl'd with continual calling upon her for victuals and having it seems but the one cheese comes into the room where the King was and very soberly ask if the King had done with the cheese for the Gentlemen without desired it.

There are one or two little sketches of Charles :

> He kept his hours most exactly both for his exercises and for his dispatches as also his hours for admitting all sorts to come to speak with him. You might know where he would be at any hour from his rising which was very early to his walk he took in the garden and so to Chapple and dinner ; so after dinner if he went not abroad he had his hours for wrighting and discourcing, or chess playing or Tennis.

> Here I do wonder at the admirable temper of the King whose constancy was such that no perils never so unavoidable could move him to astonishment ; but that, still he set the same face and settl'd countenance upon what adverse fortune soever befell him : and neither was exalt'd in prosperity nor deject'd in adversity ; which was the more admirable in him seeing that he had no other to have recourse unto for councill and assistance but must bear the whole burden upon his shoulders.

Slingsby makes a flying visit home disguised and at night time : " scarce any in my own house knowing that I was there." The record of fighting is of course one of continual disaster. The last entries are very scrappy. There is a note on the King's execution :

> But not withstanding all his prayers and intreaties they would not release him : and while I remained concealed in my house I could hear of his going to Holmby, to the Isle of Wight and to Whitehall at last ; where he end'd his good life upon the 30 of January 1648–9. I hear *heu me ; quid heu me ? humana perpessi sumus*. Thus I end'd these commentaries or book of remembrance beginning in the year 1638 and ending in the year 1648.

He then adds some notes about his garden and about the " great flouds as seldome hath been known."

When he was in prison in 1658 Sir Henry Slingsby wrote *A Father's Legacy to his Sons*, which was a sort of moral and philosophic injunction. Clarendon says he was " in the first rank of the gentlemen of Yorkshire " and " was a gentleman of a good understanding but of a very melancholic nature." " When he was brought to die he spent very little time in discourse : but told them ' he was to die for being an honest man of which he was very glad.' "

Extracts from the diary were published by Sir Walter Scott in 1806. A more or less complete edition of it, edited by the Rev. D. Parsons, was published in 1836.

SAMUEL PEPYS

BY general consent the diary of Samuel Pepys may be awarded the first place among English diaries. It fulfills all the conditions of what a diary should be. It is written with scrupulous regularity daily and is therefore quite spontaneous. Detailed narrative of public events, intimate domestic incidents and candid self-revelation all find a place in it. Such are the powers of narration and observation of the writer that it may certainly be said that any page from Pepys occurring in anyone else's diary would be worth quoting in full.

We are concerned with Pepys as a diarist, not with his official or political career. But it will be well to give a brief outline of his life.

Samuel Pepys was born in 1633. His father, John Pepys, was a London tailor, who subsequently inherited an estate at Brampton, near Huntingdon. Samuel, the fifth child of a large family, was educated at Magdalene College, Cambridge. All we hear of his university career is that on October 22, 1653, he was publicly admonished with another undergraduate for having been "scandalously overserved with drink." In 1655 he married Elizabeth Marchant, daughter of a French Huguenot exile. He started his official career as secretary to his cousin, Edward Montague, afterwards Earl of Sandwich, through whose influence he was appointed " clerk of the acts " in the Navy Office and afterwards clerk of the Privy Seal. In 1668 he delivered a speech at the Bar of the House of Commons in defence of the Navy, which had been violently attacked after the war with Holland. This gave him the ambition of becoming a member of Parliament. After an interval during which he became secretary of the Admiralty, Pepys was elected in 1679 member for Harwich. He had been unjustly suspected of popery and was also accused of betraying naval secrets to the French. This arose out of his friendship with the Duke of York (James II). In 1684 he was elected president of the Royal Society, which he had joined in 1664. On the accession of James II he became virtually Minister for the Navy.

The revolution of 1688 ended his career. Except for a brief period of imprisonment in 1690 on the charge of Jacobite intrigue, he spent the rest of his life in retirement, corresponding with his friends and arranging his valuable library. He died on May 25, 1703, at his house at Clapham.

Such a career as this, though quite successful, would not bring any man's name to the front, and the name of Pepys would only have been known to the more industrious students of history who were investigating the condition of the Navy in Stuart times. It is safe to say that for over a hundred years after his death his name was absolutely unknown except to those who came across the various portraits made of him. He was painted by Savill, Hales, Lely and Kneller. There is a uniform similarity of type in the portraits of periwigged gentlemen of that period, and admirable as the representations of Pepys by these distinguished painters may be, they are as nothing compared to the detailed finished and living picture he gives of himself.

The diary, written between 1660 and 1669, was first partially published in 1825. The fuller edition did not appear till 1848. The six manuscript volumes had remained in the interval since their author's death undisturbed in the library at Magdalene College with Pepys' other books. The diary was very neatly written in cipher or shorthand (Sheltons' system, published in 1641) and was further complicated by the use of foreign languages and varieties of his own invention. It was deciphered by John Smith, rector of Baldock, in Hertfordshire, between 1819 and 1822, and after its publication the unique fame of Samuel Pepys was established for all time.

General considerations as to motive in keeping a diary have already been discussed. In the case of Pepys the motive is by no means clear. That he intended it to be kept secret from his contemporaries and specially from his wife, is obvious enough, not only because of his use of cipher, but because he only once divulged the fact that he was keeping a diary to a friend (Sir William Coventry) and he regretted it afterwards, " it not being necessary nor may be convenient to have it known." But how about posterity? Dr. R. Garnett says: " He certainly did not intend or expect his Diary to be read."[1] This seems almost impossible. The diary writer whose intentions were as decided as this would leave direction for the destruction of his diary on his death. Pepys never did this, and when arranging and burning old papers he explains that he went through them all " that I

---

[1] Preface to Everyman's Library Edition of the Diary.

may have nothing by me but what is worth keeping and fit to be seen if I should miscarry."

R. L. Stevenson suggests that he was writing for himself in his old age. "The appeal to Samuel Pepys years hence is unmistakable."[1] Against this we would set the fact that the diary shows no signs whatever of having been read over by him subsequently. Except for one unimportant addition of the dates of death to a list of names (written in longhand as all names were), there is not a single correction, addition or alteration. No, it seems clear that Pepys had not the failing common to many diarists of reading over their past effusions, though this may be also attributed to his failing eyesight. Moreover, reading shorthand comfortably is a different matter from writing it, and its casual perusal would in any case have been a labour. The idea that Pepys was engaged in building up posthumous fame may also be dismissed. He could not have regarded with equanimity the disclosure of his indiscretions, weaknesses, petty faults, and doubtful and sometimes positively disreputable behaviour. He had, we feel sure, no sort of idea of the value of what he had written. The habit of daily diary writing had grown on him and he wrote primarily for his own satisfaction; although no doubt he was unconsciously aware that the position in which he was placed in constant contact with eminent people made his experiences worth recording. Gradually the diary became a friend, a confidant, and indeed a treasure. He filled three thousand pages and never missed a day, with the exception of one fortnight in 1668. He only left off writing because of the trouble with his eyesight. But the six volumes could not have been forgotten. There they were in the library which he was always arranging and rearranging with the minutest care. Mr. Percy Lubbock seems really to get nearest to the possible solution when he suggests that Pepys in his old age was always considering the question, should he destroy it, should he revise it, should he use the material for a book; and finally died before he had decided on the answer.[2]

A word about his style. As to whether it was literary or not is beside the question. He was certainly not a scholar like Slingsby, d'Ewes and Evelyn. The advantage of a literary style in diary writing is a very minor consideration. One of the indispensable essentials is the faithful disclosure of individuality; and no diary ever written more completely portrays the character

---

[1] *Men and Books.*
[2] *Pepys* (Literary Lives Series), by Percy Lubbock.

of the writer. He does not write, he talks or rather chats. The absurdly trivial details most carefully recorded give the atmosphere and finish of a Dutch picture. There is a consequent loss of relative values. For no one with their eye or, as in the case of Pepys, a magnifying glass concentrated on the present, day by day, can distinguish the importance or unimportance of passing events. Anyhow we would not miss his telling us that the candle was going out, " which makes me write thus slobberingly," nor the hundred details about his clothes, his food and his servants; nor when he fetches his watch from the watchmaker :

> But Lord to see how much of my old folly and childishness hangs on me still that I cannot forbear carrying my watch in my hand in the coach all this afternoon and seeing what o'clock it is one hundred times.

Nor his first shave with a razor :

> This morning I begun a practice which I find by the ease I do it with that I shall continue it saving me money and time ; that is to trimme myself with a razor, which pleases me mightily.

The secret of his genius was his zest for living. He was an amateur in the highest sense of the word. Not only did the arts appeal to him so that he was able to give a good critical opinion about painting and specially about music, but his intense interest in life carried him much further, and politics, the drama, theology, mechanics, gardening, hydrostatics, astronomy as well as riding, dancing, games, dressing, eating and drinking, all claim his rapt attention. To his friends and acquaintances he must have appeared specially sympathetic. He was not, however, a wit, nor a raconteur or a great talker. Such people are far too egotistical to be observant. John Evelyn, his fellow-diarist, mentions him when he dies as his " particular friend," and describes him as " a very worthy industrious and curious person none in England exceeding him in knowledge of the navy . . . he was universally beloved, hospitable, generous, learned in many things, skilled in music, a very great cherisher of learned men of whom he had the conversation." The word " curious," here meaning eager for knowledge, is the exact right adjective.

We picture Pepys in company watching, listening, observing, making mental notes, encouraging others to give him material for the faithful record which in a few hours he was going to write down. He was all eyes and ears, and whether it was at a council meeting, a court of justice, a church service, a play, a dinner, a dance, or a ride, he was collecting impressions and hoarding up gossip.

The production of his diary in an expurgated form has been necessary owing to the coarseness and realistic detail of some passages in the original manuscript. The result of this is to give us a Pepys of greater refinement and modesty than was actually the case. Pepys was not a model man. Far from it. He was a mass of faults, petty, frivolous, venal, sensual, often drunken and sometimes brutal. In fact, the unpublished passages rather destroy some of the illusions we get in the published editions. But whatever his faults and vices were he admits and records them all. He regrets many of them. He is often humble, but his repentances are never morbid.

His natural " mirth " saved him from over-indulgence in self-depreciation and helped him too in sorrow and danger and in discomfort. Crowded in a most uncomfortable way in a cabin on board ship, instead of complaining, he writes:

But, Lord, the mirth which it caused to me to be waked in the night by this snoring round about me; I did laugh till I was ready to burst.

To a man of this temperament much can be forgiven. He never allowed tragic incidents of which he was a witness to depress him unduly, and as soon as there was an opportunity for mirth he took advantage of it. So that as he looked back these were the times that coloured his life most : " Thus ends this year with great mirth to me and my wife."

Pepys was industrious in his official duties, took them seriously and performed them efficiently. The keeping of the diary is itself a testimony to his industrious persistence. He was very orderly in his household arrangements and liked everything to be " neat." He was a *bon viveur* and a materialist without any great refinement, yet he had artistic perceptions far above the average ; while he was absurdly punctilious in one direction he could be frivolously and childishly bohemian in another: without special erudition he was naturally critical, and while in many ways a snob he hated snobbishness.

But reflections on his character, style, and career are better illustrated by extracts from the diary than by inferences. The great difficulty in this, however, is that there is such a vast amount of quotable material, and extracts must spoil one of the chief features of the diary, which is the fulness of the consecutive record. Unlike some diarists, Pepys does not set out with the intention of laying bare by self-revelation and self-analysis the light and shade of his character. But the faithful and minute recital of his every-day pursuits gives us the portrait even better than any self-conscious dissection of himself would have done. Compared to some other diarists, Pepys' entries with regard to his ailments are comparatively rare. The anniversary of the operation when he was successfully " cut for the stone " was always celebrated by a family dinner on " the day of my solemnity for my cutting of the stone." On these occasions the stone, which was carefully preserved in a case, was exhibited to his friends. It was even lent for inspection more than once in order to encourage some sufferer to undergo the operation. His failing eyesight, which was eventually the cause of his giving up diary writing, is naturally spoken of more and more towards the end. Otherwise, except for occasional excesses, he seems to have enjoyed good health. He was an early riser. " Up betimes " is a frequent introduction to the day's entry, and sometimes " up mighty betimes," though there were occasions when he lay in bed till late in the day. Of course if he has a bilious attack or a cold he tells us :

> About the middle of the night I was very ill—I think with eating and drinking too much—and so I was forced to call the mayde who pleased my wife and I in her running up and down so innocently in her smock.

> Home to supper having a great cold, got on Sunday last, by sitting too long with my head bare for Mercer [his wife's maid] to comb and wash my eares.

As an epicure and hedonist Pepys thoroughly enjoyed his food. He shows this as much by his reference to his relish of certain dishes as by his indignation at bad food. On one of the celebrations of his operation for the stone he says :

> Very merry at before and after dinner and the more for that my dinner was great and most neatly dressed by our own only maid. We had a fricassee of rabbits and chickens, a leg of mutton boiled, three carps in a dish, a great dish of a side of lamb, a dish of roasted pigeons, a dish of four lobsters, three tarts, lamprey pie (a most rare pie) a dish of anchovies, good wine of several sorts, and all things mighty noble and to my great content.

But sometimes he complains :

> Dined at the Duke of Albermarle's and a bad and dirty, nasty dinner.

> He [Sir W. Hickes] did give us the meanest dinner of beef shoulder and umbles of venison . . . and a few pigeons and all in the meanest manner that ever I did see to the basest degree.

Pepys drank ; but who did not in Restoration days ? He does not by any means become a slave to the habit, but rather notes its injurious effects on his health and finally makes a resolution to abstain.

> Finding my head grow weak now a days I come to drink wine and therefore hope I shall leave it off of myself which I pray God I could do.
>
> What at dinner and supper I drink I know not how, of my own accord, so much wine that I was even almost foxed and my head aked all night ; so home and to bed without prayers, which I never did yet since I come to the house of a Sunday night ; I being now so out of order that I durst not read prayers for fear of being perceived by my servants in what case I was.

After the vow there seems to have been an improvement :

> There (at the Guildhall) wine was offered and they drunk, I only drinking some hypocras which do not break my vowe it being to the best of my present judgment only a mixed compound drink and not any wine.

His clothes interested him even more than food or drink and the references to them are innumerable. A few only can be given.

> This morning my brother's man brought me a new black baize waistcoate faced with silk, which I put on, from this day laying by half shirts for this Winter. He brought me also my new gown of purple shagg ; also as a gift from my brother, a velvet hat very fine to ride in and the fashion which pleases me.
>
> My tailor brings me home my fine new coloured cloth suit my cloak lined with plush—as good a suit as ever I wore in my life and mighty neat to my great content.

He tells us a great deal about his servants. Some pleased him, others made him impatient and angry. On one occasion he is brutal enough to kick his maid, and on another occasion he loses his temper with the boy.

> I sent my boy home for some papers when he staying longer than I would have him I became angry and boxed my boy when he come that I do hurt my thumb so much that I was not able to stir all the day after and in great pain.

Nothing in the diary is exposed in a more vivid and natural way than the relationship between Pepys and his wife. His pride and affection alternate with his impatience and irritability, and his changing moods are recorded with unfailing candour. Her untidiness exasperated him frequently and she dressed badly. Although he spent a great deal on his own clothes, he was often very niggardly in this respect towards her. She had ample cause for complaint in his infidelities and his incurable flirtatiousness, but so deep was their underlying affection that it stood the strain of what proved sometimes to be rather severe wear and tear. A succession of extracts from the diary will give the picture.

I was angry with my wife for her things lying about and in my passion kicked the little fine basket which I bought her in Holland and broke it which troubled me after I had done it.

Somewhat vexed at my wife's neglect in leaving of her scarfe, waistcoate and nightdressings in the coach to-day that brought us from Westminster though I confess she did give them to me to look after.

A little angry with my wife for minding nothing now but the dancing master, having him come twice a day which is folly.

My Lord [Lord Sandwich] replied thus : " Sir John, what do you think of your neighbour's wife ? " looking upon me. " Do you not think that he hath a great beauty to his wife ? " " Upon my word he hath." Which I was not a little proud of.

By and by comes my wife by coach well home, and having got a good fowl ready for supper against her coming, we ate heartily and so with great content and ease to our own bed, there nothing appearing so to our con*t*ent as to be at our own home, after being abroad awhile.

Lay long in bed talking with pleasure with my poor wife, how she used to make coal fires and wash my foul clothes with her own hand for me, poor wretch ! in our little room at my Lord Sandwich's : for which I ought for ever to love and admire her and do ; and persuade myself she would do the same thing again if God should reduce us to it.

My wife having dressed herself in a silly dress of a blue petticoat uppermost and a white satin waistcoat and white hood . . . did, together with my being hungry which always makes me peevish, make me angry.

My wife dressed this day in fair hair did make me so mad that I spoke not one word to her though I was ready to burst with anger.

Anon comes down my wife dressed in her second mourning with her black moyre waistcoat and short petticoat laced with silver lace so basely that I could not endure to see her . . . so that I was horrid angry and would not go to our intended meeting which vexed me to the blood.

Somewhat out of humour all day reflecting on my wife's neglect of things and impertinent humour got by this liberty of being from me which she is never to be trusted with : for she is a fool.

So home to dinner with my wife very pleasant and pleased with one another's company and in our general enjoyment one of another, better we think than most other couples do.

Away home when I told my wife where I had been. But she was as mad as a devil and nothing but ill words between us all the evening while we sat at cards, even to gross ill words, which I was troubled for.

My wife extraordinary fine to-day in her flower tabby suit bought a year and more ago before my mother's death put her into mourning and so not worn till this day; and everybody in love with it; and indeed she is very fine and handsome in it.

> My wife fell into her blubbering . . . and then all come out that I loved pleasure and denied her any . . . I said nothing but with very mild words and few suffered her humour to spend till we begun to be very quiet and I think all will be over and friends.
>
> This evening I observed my wife mighty dull and I myself was not mighty fond because of some hard words she did give me at noon out of jealousy of my being abroad this morning . . . but I to bed thinking but she would come after me . . . after an hour or two she silent and I now and then praying her to come to bed she fell out into a fury that I was a rogue and false to her. I did, as I might truly, deny it and was mightily troubled but all would not serve. At last about one o'clock she came to my side of the bed and drew my curtain open and with tongs red hot at the ends made as if she did design to pinch me with them at which in dismay I rose up and with a few words she laid them down and did little by little very sillily let all the discourse fall and about two, but with much seeming difficulty come to bed and there lay well all night and long in bed talking together with much pleasure.

Pepys's susceptibility to female beauty which so often caused his wife anguish was incorrigible. He never fails to express his admiration of Lady Castlemaine after he has seen her, and afterwards of Mrs. Stewart, Nell Gwyn and many others both high and low. He describes it as " a strange slavery that I stand in to beauty, that I value nothing near it."

Even in church he was distracted by his amorous passions:

> Stood by a pretty modest maid whom I did labour to take by the hand; but she would not but got further and further from me; and at last, I could perceive her to take pins out of her pocket to prick me if I should touch her again, which seeing I did forbear and was glad I did spy her design. And then I fell to gaze on another pretty maid in a pew close to me and she on me; and I did go about to take her by the hand which she suffered a little and then withdrew. So the sermon ended and church broke up and my amours ended also.

He was a great church-goer (from social rather than religious motives) and invariably notes the sermon with some comment, such as " a sorry silly sermon," " heard a man play the fool," " an unnecessary sermon," " full of action but very decent and good." But his two mastering passions were music and the drama. The vow he made with regard to drink included also play-going, but in respect to the latter it entirely broke down and he remained an inveterate play-goer.

> Troubled in mind that I cannot bring myself to mind my business but to be so much in love of plays.

Sat by Colonel Reames who understands and loves a play as well as I do and I love him for it.

The plays he saw were innumerable and of every description. He is critical both about the play and the acting:

To the Duke of Yorks playhouse and there saw "Mustapha" which the more I see the more I like and is a most admirable poem and bravely acted; only both Betterton and Harris could not contain from laughing in the midst of a most serious part from the ridiculous mistake of one of the men upon the stage: which I did not like.

The play was a new play and infinitely full the King and all the court there. It is "the Storme" a play of Fletchers': which is but so-so methinks.

He was no admirer of Shakespeare. *Romeo and Juliet*, " a play of itself the worst that ever I heard." *Midsummer Night's Dream*, " which I had never seen before nor shall ever again for it is the most insipid ridiculous play that ever I saw in my life." *The Merry Wives of Windsor*, " which did not please me at all in no part of it." *The Taming of the Shrew*, " a silly play and an old one."

He generally sat in the pit (the stalls) and spent several shillings on oranges. Of course he went behind the scenes frequently as he had many friends among the actresses.

Here is the best description of the other side of the curtain:

To the King's house: and there going in met with Knipp and she took us up into the tireing rooms; and to the womens' shift where Nell was dressing herself and was all unready, and is very pretty, prettier than I thought. And into the scene room and there sat down and she gave us fruit. . . . But Lord to see how they were both painted would make a man mad and did make me loath them; and what base company of men comes among them and how lewdly they talk! And how poor the men are in clothes and yet what a show they make on the stage by candle light is very observable. But to see how Nell cursed for having so few people in the pit was pretty; the other house carrying away all the people at the new play and is said nowadays to have generally most company as being better players. By and by into the pit and there saw the play which is pretty good.

But acting and even beautiful women were secondary with Pepys compared to his love of music. For not only was he rapturously fond of listening to it, but he played several instruments, he sang and he composed. So much so that in after life there are notes in his letters saying it is " still my utmost luxury " and referring no doubt to his growing blindness " music was never of more use to me than it is now." The references to music are far too numerous to be sufficiently quoted to show what a large part of his time was occupied with it. But as some of the most charming passages in the diary have music as their background, a few examples must be given :

> Coming in, I find my wife plainly dissatisfied with me that I can spend so much time with Mercer teaching her to sing and could not take the pains with her which I acknowledge, but it is because that the girl do take musique mighty readily and she do not and musique is the thing of the world that I love most.
>
> To the King's House to see " the virgin Martyr " . . . that which did please me beyond anything in the whole world was the wind-musique when the angel comes down, which is so sweet that it ravished me and indeed in a word did wrap up my soul so that it made me really sick, just as I have formerly been when in love with my wife ; that neither then nor all the evening going home and at home, I was able to think of anything but remained all night transported so as I could not believe that ever any music hath that real command over the soul of a man as this did upon me ; and makes me resolve to practice wind-musique and to make my wife do the like.
>
> I played also, which I have not done this long time before upon any instrument and at last broke up and I to my office a little while being fearful of being too much taken with musique for fear of returning to my old dotage thereon and so neglect my business as I used to do.
>
> I by water at night late to Sir G. Carteret's but there being no one to carry me I was fain to call a skuller that had a gentleman already in it, and he proved a man of love to musique and he and I sung together the way down with great pleasure and an incident extraordinary to be met with.
>
> [Even as he walked along] . . . humming to myself (which now a days is my constant practice since I began to learn to sing) the trillo and find by use that it do come upon me.
>
> [While Hales paints his wife's portrait] while he painted, Knipp, Mercer and I sang.
>
> Wife did a little business while Mercer and I staid in the coach and in a quarter of an hour I taught her the whole Larke's song perfectly so excellent an ear she hath.

Reluctantly indeed must we pass on from these and many other quotations showing him playing his many instruments, teaching his wife, criticising and appreciating the music he hears, and composing his songs, the chief one of which was " Beauty Retire."

Pepys was a courtier. His business brought him into close contact with the King, the Duke of York, and what he calls " very high company." While he thoroughly enjoys the pomp and circumstances of Court life, he fully realises the dissolute character of Charles II's entourage. He cannot refrain from admiring the King's various mistresses, but he deplores the general tone of the Court and foresees trouble : " every day things look worse and worse. God fit us for the worst." While he himself is mightily pleased at a word from the King, the sycophancy and adulation of courtiers sicken him.

He was an embarrassingly close observer of Lady Castlemaine whenever he saw her :

> One thing of familiarity I observed in my Lady Castlemaine : she called to one of her women for a little patch off of her face and put it into her mouth and wetted it and so clapped it upon her own by the side of her mouth, I suppose she feeling a pimple rising there.

The constant references to the King's amours are not very edifying, nor indeed interesting. He pictures the King in Council making inane remarks or playing with his dog instead of listening to the business, and at the tennis court :

> but to see how the King's play was extolled without any cause at all was a loathsome sight though sometimes indeed he did play very well and deserved to be commended ; but such open flattery is beastly.

Pepys was quite shrewd enough to see that the Court were riding for a fall. He disapproved strongly of the Duke of York's advice to the King to rule without a parliament, and he sums up the situation when Parliament is dissolved in 1667 :

> Thus they are dismissed again to their general great distaste, I believe the greatest that ever Parliament was, to see themselves so fooled and the nation in certain condition of ruin while the King, they see, is only governed by his lust, and women, and rogues about him.

The best epitome of the situation that any historian could make.

Pepys was a zealous official and there are many entries with regard to his work, the naval policy of the day and the war with Holland. His general estimate of the Duke of York in connection with the Navy is favourable. But he is often in despair at the state of affairs :

> All the morning I was much troubled to think what the end of our great sluggishness will be, for we do nothing in this office like people able to carry on a war.

His great opportunity came when he was called to the Bar of the House of Commons, and there made his celebrated defence of naval administration before a very hostile House.

> I began our defence most acceptably and smoothly and continued at it without any hesitation or losse but with full scope and all my reason free about me as if it had been at my own table.

The speech was a huge success.

All the world that was within hearing did congratulate me and cry up my speech as the best thing they ever heard.
The King said " Mr. Pepys I am very glad of your success yesterday."

No wonder we read later :

and my great design if I continue in the Navy is to get myself to be a Parliament man.

During the terrible days of the Plague, Pepys remained at his post and gives descriptions of the gruesome scenes and his constant sight of corpses in the streets. Of the fire, too, he was also an eye-witness :

Staid till it was dark almost and saw the fire grow ; and as it grew darker appeared more and more ; and in corners and upon steeples and between churches and houses as far as we could see up the hill of the City in a most horrid, malicious, bloody flame not like the fine flame of an ordinary fire . . . we saw the fire as only one entire arch of fire from this to the other side of the bridge and in a bow up the hill for an arch of above a mile long ; it made me weep to see it.

Pepys' capacity for being interested and entertained by experiences of widely different characters might be illustrated by his delightful description on the one hand of the Shepherd on the Downs, and on the other hand of the gambling scene at the " Groome Porters." But justice cannot be done to either without very long extracts.

In quest of experiences indeed he once goes into very low company and ends his account of it :

But Lord ! What loose company was this that I was in to-night, though full of wit and worth a man's being in for once to know the nature of it, and their manner of talk and lives.

This is Pepys' secret, nothing was above or beneath him. To the appeal of human nature in all its various disguises he was ever ready to respond—only solitude to him was intolerable. His extreme sociability helped him.

Dined alone ; sad for want of company and know not how to eat alone.

His passing comments and characterisation in a line or two on people he meets are often inimitable :

Aunt James ; a poor, religious, well meaning, good soul talking of nothing but God Almighty and that with so much innocence that mightily pleased me.

Dr. Tom Pepys is dead for which I am but little sorry not only because he would have been troublesome to us, but a shame to his family and profession —he was such a coxcomb.

SAMUEL PEPYS

Lady Crewe; the same weak silly lady as ever asking saintly questions.

Mr. Case: a dull fellow in his talk and all in the Presbyterian manner; a great deal of noise and a kind of religious tone, but very dull.

Mrs. Horsfield; one of the veriest citizen's wives in the world, so full of little silly talk and now and then a little slyly indecent.

Nothing has been said of the books he read, bought, collected, and had bound. It was yet another hobby of his and the one to which in his old age he devoted much attention, with the result that his collection is handed down to us in the Pepysian library at Cambridge. He must have spent a great sum on books, though he was by nature extremely careful about his money.

Every year he gives us a note of his balance, which gradually grows as his position improves. Throughout he maintains his loyalty and gratitude to his original patron, Lord Sandwich, to whom when his lordship was out of favour he writes an admirable letter of respectful advice.

Although the diary is regularly kept, the entries vary in length. The political situation or some particularly entertaining experience sometimes occupies several pages. But the briefest one line entry somehow gives one a faithful reflection of mood as well as of event; for instance, " April 4. Home, and being washing-day, dined upon cold meat," or to take an example of his more compressed style, packing all the events of the day into a few lines:

April 10. Friday. All the morning at office. At noon with W. Penn to Duke of York and attended Council. So to Duck Lane and then kissed bookseller's wife, and bought Legend. So home, coach. Sailor. Mrs. Hannam dead. News of peace. Conning my gamut.

No doubt the Pepys of the later years became more discreet, more important, and probably less frivolous. But we must part from him, not because we lose interest in him, but simply because he ceases to be a diarist.

JOHN EVELYN

EVELYN'S diary covers more than half a century, 1640–1706. There is a natural inclination to draw a comparison between the journals of Evelyn and Pepys. But although the two diarists were contemporaries and friends, and although they came across many common acquaintances in their official and Court experiences, they did not live in the same stratum of society, and their method, their motive, their point of view, their manner and their characters were so completely different that except for the fact that they refer to the same people and the same events, the two celebrated journals that have been handed down to us have very little resemblance, and they seem to call for different moods in the reader. Pepys covers a period of a little over eight years, Evelyn a period of sixty-six years, but Pepys' diary is longer than Evelyn's. Pepys wrote daily, Evelyn wrote intermittently. Pepys left his diary untouched, Evelyn's is written up at subsequent dates, so much so that it comes very near to being memoirs. Unlike Pepys, Evelyn indulges in no introspection, and except for his tastes and his political views we do not get in the pages of his diary any intimate revelation of his character. In fact, we have to go to Pepys for a view of him which mitigates the rather severe and sedate impression which his own writing seems to suggest. Just as Evelyn's estimate of Pepys portrays a more dignified figure than we might otherwise have expected, so in Pepys' estimate of Evelyn we get a more human picture than Evelyn himself gives us. Pepys refers to him as " a very fine gentleman " and " a most excellent humoured man " and tells the following anecdote :

> The receipt of this news [a successful engagement against the Dutch] did put us all into such an extasy of joy that it inspired into Sir J. Minns and Mr. Evelyn such a spirit of mirth that in all my life I never met with so merry a two hours as our company this night was. Among other humours, Mr. Evelyn repeating of some verses made up of nothing but the various acceptations of *may* and *can* and doing it so aptly upon occasion of something of that nature and so fast did make us all die almost with laughing and did so stop

the mouth of Sir J. Minns in the middle of all his mirth, and in a thing agreeing with his own manner of genius, that I never saw any man so outdone in all my life ; and Sir J. Minns's mirth too to see himself outdone was the crown of all our mirth.

Pepys also describes a visit to Evelyn, who, after showing him his art treasures,

read to me very much also of his discourse he hath been many years and now is about, about Gardenage ; which will be a most noble and pleasant piece. He read me part of a play or two of his making, very good, but not as he conceits them, I think, to be. . . . In fine a most excellent person he is and must be allowed a little for a little conceitedness ; but he may well be so being a man so much above others. He read me through, with too much gusto, some little poems of his own that were not transcendant, yet one or two very pretty epigrams.

They remained close friends for many years, and Evelyn records a visit to Pepys in 1700, when he himself was 80 and Pepys 67.

I went to visit Mr. Pepys at Clapham where he has a very noble and wonderfully well furnished house especially with Indian and Chinese curiosities, the offices and gardens well accommodated for pleasure and retirement.

John Evelyn was born at Wotton House, near Dorking, in 1620. He was educated at Balliol College, Oxford, and admitted to the Middle Temple. In 1652 he settled at Sayes Court, at Deptford. He enjoyed unbroken Court favour but he never held any important official post. In a minor capacity he did much useful and laborious work as commissioner for improving the streets and buildings of London, for examining into the affairs of charitable foundations, as commissioner of the Mint and of foreign plantations. He was one of the founders, and afterwards Secretary of the Royal Society, but refused the position of President which was offered to him and later he was Treasurer of Greenwich Hospital. In 1694 he left Sayes Court to live at Wotton with his brother, whom he succeeded in 1699. Evelyn was a country gentleman of means, a patron of art, and a writer of many books on horticulture, science, and politics, the most important of which was *Sylva*, a work on arboriculture and a plea for afforestation. He died at the age of 86. Living as he did from the Civil War till after James II's flight, he was the witness of many remarkable events.

He must have begun diary writing in 1640 or even before, and he kept it up till within a month of his death. In writing up the diary he gives an autobiographical note of his early life, and many entries are clearly inserted some time after the events recorded as there are several confusions in the dates. It is probable that he wrote memoranda at the time, and then transcribed and amplified them subsequently. Mr. Austin Dobson in his preface to the diary says that the diary was " obviously never intended for publication. . . ." Evelyn was quietly, briefly and methodically noting what seemed to him worthy of remembrance.

Although from the psychological point of view we are not admitted to any very close inspection of Evelyn's inner character, nevertheless we get the general impression from his opinions, tastes and occupations of a very high-minded, cultivated and refined man of domestic habits, without perhaps much sparkle or wit, but shrewdly observant and with considerable literary aptitude and a great deal of scientific knowledge.

In his earlier years he travels a great deal, making a " Grand Tour " in France, Italy and Flanders. He gives his impressions at great length, but as we have already noted, travellers' experiences and description of foreign scenery and monuments are seldom interesting reading. Between his journeys he is in London, not apparently engaged in any occupation.

> Jan. 19. I went to London where I stayed till March 5 studying a little but dancing and fooling more.

At the age of 32 he describes an exciting and dangerous adventure he has with two cut-throats, who set on him three miles from Bromley, robbed him and tied him up to a tree.

> Left in this manner grievously was I tormented with flies, ants and the sun, nor was my anxiety little how I should get loose in that solitary place where I could neither hear nor see any creature but my poor horse and a few sheep straggling in the copse.

However, with great efforts, he manages to loosen his hands and get free and he afterwards recovers the rings, buckles, and onyx seal of which he had been robbed.

From the earliest times Evelyn shows a particular appreciation of works of art and throughout the diary he refers constantly to pictures, prints and all manner of *objets d'art* which he comes across, so that rare perspectives, miniatures, landscapes, antiquities, *relievos*, collections of *taille douces*, vases of porcelain, brasses, cabinets of *maroquin*, tapestries, medals, intaglios, etc., etc., figure very frequently in his diary. The following entry characteristic of his artistic tastes may be given :

> Came old Jerome Lanière of Greenwich a man skilled in painting and music and another rare musician called Mell. I went to see his collection of pictures especially those of Julio Romano which sure had been the King's and an

Egyptian figure etc. There were also excellent things of Polydore Guido, Raphael, and Tintoretto. Lanière had been a domestic of Queen Elizabeth and showed me her head, an intaglio in rare sardonyx cut by a famous Italian which he assured me was exceeding like her.

Evelyn's greatest artistic achievement we may safely say was his discovery of Grinling Gibbons, the great carver in wood. We will let him tell the story in his own words :

1670-1. Jan. 18. This day I first acquainted his Majesty with that incomparable young man, Gibbons, whom I had lately met with in an obscure place by mere accident as I was walking near a poor solitary thatched house in a field in our parish near Sayes Court. I found him shut in ; but looking in at the window I perceived him carving that large cartoon or crucifix of Tintoretto. . . . I asked if I might enter ; he opened the door civilly to me and I saw him about such a work as for the curiosity of handling, drawing and studious exactness I never had before seen in all my travels. I questioned him why he worked in such an obscure and lonesome place ; he told me it was that he might apply himself to his profession without interruption and wondered not a little how I found him out. (Gibbons tells him he would like to sell that piece for £100.) In good earnest the very frame was worth the money there being nothing in nature so tender and delicate as the flowers and festoons about it and yet the work was very strong. . . . I found he was likewise musical and very civil and sober and discreet in his discourse.

Charles II comes round to Sir Richard Browne's (Evelyn's father-in-law) chamber to see the carving.

No sooner was he entered and cast his eye on the work but he was astonished at the curiosity of it and having considered it a long time and discoursed to Mr. Gibbons whom I had brought to kiss his hand he commanded that it should be immediately carried to the Queen's side to show her. It was carried up into her bedchamber when she and the King looked on and admired it again ; the King being called away left us with the Queen believing she would have bought it, it being a crucifix ; but when His Majesty was gone a French peddling woman one Madame de Boord who used to bring petticoats and fans and baubles out of France to the ladies, began to find fault with several things in the work which she understood no more than an ass or a monkey, so as in a kind of indignation I caused the person who brought it to carry it back to the chamber finding the Queen so much governed by an ignorant Frenchwoman and this incomparable artist had his labour only for his pains which not a little displeased me.

Nevertheless, Gibbons' reputation grew and Evelyn tells us seventeen years later in the next reign that in the Queen's apartment in Whitehall, " the carving about the chimney piece by Gibbons is incomparable."

In addition to art, Evelyn's interests were of the most varied description. We find him discoursing at considerable length on all sorts of mechanical devices, strange clocks, an engine for weaving silk stockings, a diving bell, musical instruments, glass works, paper mills, fireworks, rattle snakes, a whale, a rhinoceros, a fire eater, a knife swallower, and a hairy woman. But first and foremost came his love of gardens and his intense interest not only in his own, but in the many he inspects. It is impossible to give a large selection of his charming descriptions as they are generally long and elaborate. A few must suffice :

> *Marden.* . . . It is in such a solitude among hills as being not above sixteen miles from London seems almost incredible, the ways up to it are so winding and intricate. The gardens are large and well walled and the husbandry part made very convenient and perfectly understood. . . . Innumerable are the plantations of trees especially walnuts. The orangery and gardens are very curious. . . . This place is exceeding sharp in Winter by reason of the serpentining of the hills and it wants running water ; but the solitude much pleased me. All the ground is so full of wild thyme, marjoram and other sweet plants that it cannot be overstocked with bees ; I think he had near forty hives of that industrious insect.
>
> *Windsor.* . . The Castle itself is large in circumference ; but the rooms melancholy and of ancient magnificence. The keep or mount hath besides its incomparable prospect, a very profound well ; and the terrace towards Eton with park, meandering Thames, and sweet meadows yield one of the most delightful prospects.
>
> *Swallowfield* . . . the gardens and waters as elegant as it is possible to make a flat by art and industry and no mean expense, my lady [Lady Clarendon] being so extraordinarily skilled in the flowery part and my lord in diligence of planting ; so that I have hardly seen a seat which shows more tokens of it than what is to be found here not only in the delicious and rarest fruits of a garden, but in those innumerable timber trees in the ground about the seat to the greatest ornament and benefit of the place. . . . The garden is so beset with all manner of sweet shrubs that it perfumes the air. The distribution also of the quarters walks and parterres is excellent. . . . There is also a certain sweet willow and other exotics ; also a very fine bowling green meadow pasture and wood ; in a word all that can render a country seat delightful.

Politically Evelyn was a staunch Royalist, but his opinions did not carry him to any heroic length.

After the trial of Strafford and the severance from its shoulders of " the wisest head in England " he discreetly withdraws himself for a season, " from this ill face of things at home " and during the Commonwealth and the Protectorate, although he clung consistently to the traditions of the Church, he was far too cautious to allow his resistance to take any active form. After the Restoration he is in high favour at Court, and he always refers to " the Usurper Oliver " and his followers in terms of the greatest disparagement. On the return of Charles, of whom he had seen a good deal during his exile, Evelyn goes with the Sussex gentlemen to present an Address :

I kissed His Majesty's hand who was pleased to own me more particularly by calling me his old acquaintance and speaking very graciously to me.

Charles consults him about the smoke nuisance, which even in those days was being tackled and about which Evelyn wrote his *Fumifugium* which he dedicated to the King. He has conversations with him about bees, gardens, arboriculture and new designs for rebuilding Whitehall. The King also commissions him to write on the Dutch war,

enjoining me to make it a *little keen* for that the Hollanders had very unhandsomely abused him in their pictures, books and libels.

Of the strange royal ceremony of touching for the evil there is a full description :

1660. His Majesty began first to touch for the evil according to custom thus ; His Majesty sitting under his state in the Banqueting-house the chirurgeons cause the sick to be brought or led up to the throne, where they kneeling, the King strokes their faces or cheeks with both his hands at once at which instant a chaplain in his formalities says " He put his hands upon them and he healed them." When they have all been touched they come up again in the same order and the other chaplain kneeling and having angel gold [a coin with the figure of an angel on it] strung on white ribbon on his arm delivers them one by one to His Majesty who puts them about the necks of the touched as they pass whilst the first chaplain repeats " This is the true light that came into the world."

Charles is said to have " touched " nearly a hundred thousand people during his reign.

Pageants and ceremonies and attendance at Court, however, were not greatly to Evelyn's liking, for he says :

I came home to be private a little not at all affecting the life and hurry of Court.

He gives us the following description of the Queen :

She was yet of the handsomest countenance of all the rest and though low of stature, prettily shaped, languishing and excellent eyes, her teeth wronging her mouth by sticking a little too far out ; for the rest lovely enough.

Evelyn is by no means blind to the dissolute character of the Court and makes many references to the King's mistresses, especially Louise de Kéroualle (Duchess of Portsmouth) with her " childish simple and baby face." His final estimate of Charles is worth quoting in full :

He was a prince of many virtues and of many imperfections ; debonair, easy of access, not bloody nor cruel ; his countenance fierce, his voice great, proper of person, every motion became him ; a lover of the sea and skilful in shipping ; not affecting other studies, yet he had a laboratory and knew of many empirical medicines and the easier mechanical mathematics; he loved planting and building and brought in a politer way of living which passed to luxury and intolerable expense. He had a particular talent in telling a story and facetious passages which he had innumerable. . . . He took delight in having a number of little spaniels follow him and lie in his bedchamber where he often suffered the bitches to puppy and give suck, which rendered it very offensive and indeed made the whole court nasty and stinking. He would doubtless have been an excellent prince had he been less addicted to women who made him uneasy and always in want to supply their unmeasurable profusion . . . his too easy nature resigned him to be managed by crafty men and some abandoned and profane wretches who corrupted his otherwise sufficient parts, disciplined as he had been by many afflictions during his banishment which gave him much experience and knowledge of men and things; but those wicked creatures took him from off all application becoming so great a King. . . . He was ever kind to me and very generous upon all occasions and therefore I cannot without ingratitude but deplore his loss.

Evelyn gives a very full account of the document which Pepys had been shown by James II, proving that Charles II " both was and died a Roman Catholic." Evelyn as a loyal Protestant was deeply shocked.

I was,—he says—heartily sorry to see all this though it was no other than was to be suspected by his late Majesty's too great indifference, neglect, and course of life. . . . God was incensed to make his reign very troublesome and unprosperous by wars, plagues, fires, loss of reputation by an universal neglect of the public for the love of a voluptuous and sensual life which a vicious Court had brought into credit.

He makes a very wrong estimate of James II's character when he says:

By what I observed in this journey is that infinite industry, sedulity, gravity and great understanding and experience of affairs in His Majesty that I cannot but predict much happiness to the nation as to its political government.

However, he is soon disillusioned and accepts the advent of William III, who with his "thoughtful countenance is wonderful serious and silent and seems to treat all persons alike gravely and to be very intent on affairs." Princess Anne he only refers to as making "so little figure."

There are many interesting character sketches and personal descriptions in the diary. He visits Sir Thomas Browne, whose house and garden he describes as " a paradise," and in addition to courtiers and statesmen he is friends with artists, men of letters and antiquaries such as Kneller (who paints his portrait), Christopher Wren, Ashmole, Camden and Dugdale.

Evelyn lived through a time of such stirring incidents that his diary is a very important supplement to the history of the Stuart period. But in our extracts we can only cull here and there some of his most characteristic passages.

It is curious to note that less than a week before the outbreak of the Great Fire of London he was engaged in surveying St. Paul's Cathedral and making recommendations for strengthening and restoring the structure. This was on August 27, 1666, and on September 3, the day after the outbreak, he describes it :

> The conflagration was so universal and the people so astonished that from the beginning I know not by what despondency or fate they hardly stirred to quench it ; so that there was nothing heard or seen but crying out and lamentation, running about like distracted creatures without at all attempting to save even their goods ; such a strange consternation there was upon them so as it burned both in breadth and length the churches, public halls, Exchange, hospitals, monuments and ornaments ; leaping after a prodigious manner from house to house and street to street at great distances one from the other. . . . God grant mine eyes may never behold the like who now saw above 10,000 houses all in one flame ! The noise and cracking and thunder of impetuous flames, the shrieking of women and children, the hurry of the people, the fall of towers, houses, and churches was like a hideous storm . . . the stones of Paul's flew like grenados the melting lead running down the streets in a stream and the very pavements glowing with fiery redness so as no horse nor man was able to tread on them.

Two years earlier, but entered curiously enough on the wrong date, he gives an account of Oliver Cromwell's funeral :

> Saw the superb funeral of the Protector. He was carried from Somerset House in a velvet bed of state drawn by six horses. . . . Oliver lying in effigy in royal robes and crowned with a crown, sceptre and globe like a King. . . . In this equipage they proceeded to Westminster ; but it was the joyfullest funeral I ever saw ; for there were none that cried but dogs which the soldiers hooted away with a barbarous noise drinking and taking tobacco in the streets as they went.

Here is the earliest description of the Grenadier Guards :

> 1678. Now were brought into service a new sort of soldiers called Grenadiers who were dexterous in flinging hand grenadoes, everyone having a pouch full ; they had furred caps with coped crowns like Janizaries which made them look very fierce and some had long hoods hanging down behind as we picture fools. Their clothing being likewise piebald, yellow and red.

We get some view of the domestic side of Evelyn's life from his references to his home and his wife and children. During the Great Frost of 1684, he describes the first fair on the Thames and the coaches plying from Westminster to the Temple on the ice, but he hurries home to see the effects on his own garden :

> I went to Sayes Court to see how the frost had dealt with my garden when I found many of the greens and rare plants utterly destroyed. The oranges

and myrtles very sick, the rosemary and laurels dead to all appearance, but the cypress likely to endure it.

After a hurricane, too, he notes how his own trees have suffered, and one feels that his garden which he began with such thought and care to set out as early as 1653 was the real background of his life.

In 1698 Sayes Court was occupied for a time by Peter the Great, who was the King's guest. Evelyn goes down to Deptford " to see how miserably the Czar had left my house after three months making it his Court." One of the amusements of " his Zarish Majesty " was to be driven furiously in a wheel-barrow through the magnificent holly hedge, which was 400 feet long, 9 feet high and 5 feet in diameter.

In 1647 Evelyn married a daughter of Sir Richard Browne. She was his companion all his life through and survived him three years. However, we hear very little about her, as he did not use his diary as a record of intimate relationships. He notes the death of his children, and in two instances breaks out into pathetic lamentations over his loss. His son Richard, who died in 1657 at the age of 5, seems to have been a most remarkable prodigy. His father gives a long account of his wonderful talents :

> At two years and a half old he could perfectly read any of the English, Latin, French or gothic letters pronouncing the first three languages exactly. He had before the fifth year, or in that year not only skill to read most written hands but to decline all the nouns, conjugate the verbs regular and most of the irregular ; learned out *Puerilis*, got by heart almost the entire vocabulary of Latin and French primitives and verbs . . . began to write legibly and had a strong passion for Greek. The number of verses he could recite was prodigious . . . he had a wonderful disposition to mathematics having by heart divers propositions of Euclid . . . he had learned all his catechism early and understood the historical part of the Bible and New Testament to a wonder. . . . He had learned by heart divers sentences in Latin and Greek which on occasion he would produce even to wonder. He was all life all prettiness far from morose, sullen or childish in anything he said or did.

After a touching account of the little boy's death, he exclaims :

> Here ends the joy of my life, and for which I go ever mourning to the grave.

Three weeks later he loses his youngest son, but resigns himself to the will of God. In 1685 his daughter Mary was carried off by the small-pox at the age of 19. She, too, was very talented and intellectually proficient, and when she sang " it was as charming to the eye as to the ear." The rapturous account of her is perhaps the longest entry in the diary, and her death was the bitterest loss he suffered in his life. At the conclusion he says :

> This is the little history and imperfect character of my dear child, whose piety, virtue, and incomparable endowments deserve a monument more durable than brass and marble. Precious is the memorial of the just. Much I could enlarge on every period of this hasty account but that I ease and discharge my overcoming passion for the present, so many things worthy an excellent Christian and dutiful child crowding upon me. Never can I say enough, oh dear, my dear child, whose memory is so precious to me.

He had six sons, none of whom survived him, only one of them, John, reaching manhood. Of his three daughters one outlived her father.

Evelyn comments very rarely on his own health. When his birthday comes round he gives heartfelt thanks to God for his protection. He is of an orthodox religious nature, and while his loyalty to the Crown makes him often appear too much to act the part of a courtier, he not only refuses honours for himself but occasional comments show that he was well aware of the low and corrupt tone of Whitehall. For instance, he exclaims :

> I now observed how the women began to paint themselves, formerly a most ignominious thing and used only by prostitutes.

His occasional resolutions to survey his life, make " an accurate scrutiny " of his actions and give himself up " more entirely to God," his affection for his children, his deep compassion for the wounded sailor who undergoes the amputation of a leg, his detestation of the " butcherly dog fighting and bull baiting " from which he turns away " weary of the rude and dirty pastime," taken together with his appreciation of nobility of character and his love of beauty—all point to a sensitively refined nature. It is with somewhat of a shock, therefore, that we find him on one or two occasions as callous and indifferent to scenes of horror as any common person of his age. A more hideous and brutal torture than that which he describes with elaborate detail as having been undergone by a prisoner at the Châtelet cannot be conceived. But he spares us nothing of the gruesome cruelty of the scene, merely remarking at the end that the spectacle was " so uncomfortable " that he did not want to see it repeated with a second malefactor. His political bias carries him the length of being able to pass " the quarters " of some of the regicides who had been executed, "mangled and cut, and reeking as they were brought from the gallows in baskets on the hurdle " with only the exclamation, " Oh, the miraculous providence of God ! "

Of course there were many hideous sights for the passer-by in London of those days and to see " a miserable creature burning " in Smithfield was nothing strange. Nevertheless, John Evelyn appears so far in advance of his day in so many ways that the occasional reminder of what he, like everyone else, considered quite commonplace occurrences comes as a surprise.

The diary remained in two manuscript volumes until 1818, when with the permission of the Evelyn family a selection was printed, and fuller editions were issued in subsequent years.

HENRY TEONGE

TEONGE came from Spernall, in Warwickshire, and was at one time rector of Alcester, near by. Circumstances seem to have arisen which made him desire to absent himself from his parish. Accordingly at the age of 54 he became chaplain on "His Majesty's Frigott *Assistance*," and his first voyage occupied from May, 1675, to November, 1676. After staying some months in London he returned to Spernall, where his son had been undertaking the rector's duties. But the original cause of his absence appears to have remained in full force. He says: "Though I was glad to see my relations and olde acquaintance yet I lived very uneasy being dayly dunnd by som or other or else for feare of land pyrates which I hated worse than Turkes." Consequently he set out on a second voyage on board the *Bristol* and afterwards the *Royal Oak*, which lasted from March 31, 1678, to June 28, 1679. During these two voyages he kept a diary, in which he records the fortunes of the ship and in very picturesque language describes the new and curious sights he saw. He enjoys himself thoroughly, "no life at the shoare being comparable to this at sea." He is always " merry " and " without the least care, sorrow or trouble."

On his first voyage he joined Sir John Narborough's expedition against the corsairs of the Barbary States, and whether in storm or in calm, in active service or merely sightseeing, his cheerful disposition never leaves him and there is " nothing but merryment." Every Sunday he is by way of preaching or conducting a service, though at times he writes: " no prayers to-day by reason of business." He sometimes gives the text of his sermon, but theological and indeed moral questions do not seem to trouble him at all. He bursts into verse on many occasions, but his poems are not of a high order and his ballads about Chloris, Amynta, Phyllis and Amaryllis are not worth quoting. He writes a poem to his wife beginning:

> O ! Ginnee was a bonny lasse
> Which makes the world to woonder
> How ever it should com to passe
> That wee did part a sunder.

He gives an acrostic as a new year's gift to the captain, and he is always ready with a Latin epitaph if one of the crew dies.

" Boules of punch " occur very frequently : and the feasting was often on a tremendous scale :

> Nov. 9. Wee had a princelike dinner ; and every health that wee dranke, every man broake the glass he drank in ; so that before night wee had destroyd a whole chest of pure Venice glasse.

The consul at Assera gave them " a treate," " such a on as I never saw before." He gives a careful plan of the thirty-six dishes which were placed on the table : " Turkeys, geese, venison pasty, a pyramid of marchpane, a dish of harticocks, sausages, biscotts, etc., etc." But later a Mr. Brown gives a feast which " did far exceede the Consull's feast." " There were above a hundred princely disshes, besyds cheese and other small dishes of rare kinds of sweete meats."

Even " a brave gale " does not destroy his appetite :

> More myrth at dinner this day than ever since we cam on board. The wind blew very hard and we had to dinner a rump of Xante beife a little salted and well rosted. When it was brought in to the cabin and set on the table (that is, on the floore for it could not stand on the table for the ship's tossing) . . . wee all sat closse round about the beife, some securing themselves from slurring by setting their feete against the table which was fast tyd downe. The Lieutenant set his feete against the bedd and the Captain set his back against a chayre. Severall tumbles we had, wee and our plates, and our knives slurrd oft together. Our liquer was white rubola, admirable good. Wee had also a couple of fatt pullets ; and whilst wee were eating of them a sea cam and forced into the cabin through the chinks of a port hole, which by looking behind me I just discovered when the water was coming under mee. I soone got up, and no whitt wett ; but all the rest were well washed and got up as fast as they could and laughed on at the other.

Of the various places in the Mediterranean at which they stopped he gives picturesque descriptions, entering into historical details. He finds the Maltese " extremely courteouse " and when the knights came on board " I had much discourse, I being the only entertainer because I could speak Latine ; for which I was highly esteemed and much invited on shoare again."

A description of an Arabian lady at Antioch is a good instance of the chaplain's graphic style :

This Arabian Lady was tall and very slender very sworfy of complexion and very thinn faced ; having nothing on but a thinn loose garment a kinde of gyrdle about her middle and the garment open before. She had a ringe in her left nostrill which hung downe below her nether lipp ; at each eare a round globe as bigg as a tennis ball, shining like gold, and hanging almost as low as her brest. . . . She had also gold chaines about her wrists and the smalls of her naked legs. Her nayles of her fingers were coloured almost redd and her lips coloured as blew as indigo ; and so also was her belly from the navill to her hammes, painted blew like branches of trees or strawberry leaves. Nor was she cautious but rather ambitious to shew you this sight ; as the only raryty of their sex or country. The rest of the women were all alike for their painting in all places but farr fowler.

Christmas Day is a great opportunity for merriment :

Christmas day wee keepe thus. At 4 in the morning our trumpeters all doe flatt their trumpetts and begin at our Captain's cabin and thence to all the officers and gentlemens' cabins ; playing a levite at each cabin doore and bidding good morrow wishing a merry Christmas. After they goe to their stations on the poope and sound 3 levitts in honour of the morning. At 10 wee goe to prayers and sermon ; text Zacc. ix. 9. Our Captaine had all his officers and gentlemen to dinner with him where we had excellent fayre ; a ribb of beife, plumb pudding, mince pyes, etc. and plenty of good wines of severall sorts ; dranke healths to the King to our wives and friends and ended the day with much civill myrth.

On January 30 they are obliged for once in a way to be less merry.

This day being the day of our King's marterdome wee shew all the signes of morning as possible wee can viz our jacks and flaggs only halfe staff high . . . ringing the bells on the trumpet very dolefully . . . and so we ended the day mornfully ; which made the Maltese much woonder till they understood the reason of it.

The expedition was successful. Sir John Narborough negotiated with the Dey of Tripoli and concluded a treaty with him. All the stages in the negotiations are carefully noted by the diarist. The ship suffered a good deal especially from gales on the voyage home. He concludes on November 17 with the words :

Wee are payed off at Dedford ; where wee leave the rottenest frigot that ever cam to England.

Before embarking on his second voyage he stays in London a few days and has a sight of the King.

This morning our noble Captaine made my son Thomas a waterman and tooke him and myself with him to Whitehall where our Captain cam to mee and told mee I should kisse His Majesty's hand. He had no sooner sayd so but the King cam out ; my Capt. presented me to the King saying An't please your Majesty this gentleman is an old cavalier and my chaplen. I kneeled downe he gave me his hand. I kist it and said Pray God blesse your Majesty! He answered God blesse you boath together! twice and walked alonge the Gallery his wonted large pace.

They sailed along the coast of Portugal and Spain. Near Majorca there was a sudden alarm owing to an unknown but "lusty ship coming up with us." He himself goes up to the poop with his staff gun. But after shots had been fired the ship turns out to be a French vessel and a friend. But he relates an amusing incident during the encounter:

> The best passage was that wee had a Fryar with us, whoe, having been drinking wine was grone a little valiant, and he had got a musket in his hand, and a coller of bandeliares about him; and to see him stand in his white coate, ball'd pate, his muskett in his hand, and the 12 Apostles rattling about him, was a sight which caused much laughter.

The Friar remains with them and on Sunday attends divine service. He sits by the Chaplain " all the while very devoutly." The mortality in the crew was fearful, as many as sixty-six dying before they returned. Every few days he seems to be occupied with burying one of the crew, till at last the captain falls ill and dies. Teonge immediately goes to his cabin and composes a Latin " distich," an immense epitaph and a poem in English. He confesses for once we have had " a voyage of trouble." But he soon recovers and, after the appointment of the new captain, he writes:

> Wee are more merry than I thought wee should have beene; our new Captaine is wondrous free, not only of his excellent wine but also of his owne good and free company among us. Wee had a pigg to dinner this day worth 8s. in England.

On one occasion he has a rival in Lord Mordant, an eccentric character who afterwards saw a good deal of naval service. He was son of Lord Avanloe and at this time was only about twenty years old. Teonge's treatment of him is most entertaining:

> Lord Mordant taking occasion by my not being very well would have preacht and askt the Captain's leave last night and to that intent sate uptill 4 in the morning to compose his speech and intended to have Mr. Norwood to sing the Psalme. All this I myselfe heard in agitation; and resolving to prevent him I got up in the morning before I should have done had I had respect to my owne health and cam into the greate cabin where I found the zealous Lord with out Captaine whom I did so handle in a smart and short discourse that he went out of the cabin in greate wrath. In the afternoon he set on of the carpentar's crewe to worke about his cabin; and I being acquainted with it, did by my Captaine's order discharge the woorke man and he left working; at which the Reverent Lord was so vexed that he borrowed a hammar and busyed himselfe all that day in nayling up hangings: but being done on the Sabaoth day and also when there was no necessity I hope

the woorke will not be long lived. From that day he loved neyther mee nor the Captaine ; No prayers, for discontent.

One cannot help being rather sorry for the noble Lord who spent all night preparing his sermon.

This time on Christmas Day they had not " so greate a dinner as was intended." But they do not seem to have done so badly:

> Wee had to dinner an excellent rice pudding in a great charger, a speccial peice of Martinmas English beife, a neat's tongue, good cabbage, a charger full of excellent fresh fish fryde, a douzen of wood cocks in a pye, a couple of good henns roasted, 3 sorts of cheese ; and last of all a greate charger full of blew figgs, almonds and raysings ; and wine and punch gallore and a dozen of English pippens.

Our genial diarist returns to Spernall after being paid off, and the bald mention of his death in the register on March 21, 1690, is all that is to be found of his subsequent history. It is to be hoped that he succeeded this time in saving enough to keep him out of debt and trouble, as after his first voyage, although he " gott a good summ of monys," he " spent greate part of it."

The diary, though filled with detail of his ship's progress, nevertheless presents in its natural and vivid style a delightful portrait of the good-natured and observant author, without a trace of self-consciousness, and gives a very good picture of naval life in the time of Charles II.

The manuscript was in the possession of a Warwickshire family for more than a century. It was offered accidentally to a publisher for sale and was eventually printed in 1825. As may be imagined, a certain amount of expurgation was necessary before publication.

SEVENTEENTH CENTURY

MINOR DIARIES

JOHN MANNINGHAM

ALTHOUGH it contains a few memoranda and personal matters of a true diary kind, Manningham's diary is more of a note-book in which he noted down a collection of anecdotes, poems, epitaphs, gossip and jokes. It also includes very long accounts of sermons. As will be seen, references to sermons is a common feature in many diaries, but no other diarist gives them at such length. He must have been able to write some sort of shorthand, which was probably part of his legal training. Manningham was a barrister of the Middle Temple. He lived at Bradbourn, in Kent; the date of his birth is not known, but he was entered of the Middle Temple in 1597. His will was proved in 1622. His diary covers the period from March, 1601–02, to April, 1603.

In the anecdotes and gossip he gives his authority, " cosen told me," " my cosen's wife said," " Mr. Hall nar : ," or simply the name of the author of the saying. He always records his movements and journeys, but he gives no domestic details or account of his daily occupations, though some of his memoranda are of a homely character, as, for instance :

> My cosen shee told him that Joane Bachellor upon Thursday last had sent hir some fishe which she sent back again. Whereupon he said she was of an ill nature that could not forgive. And this shee tooke in such snuffe that she could not afford him a good look all that day but blubberd.

Little epigrams of his own are scattered throughout the book :

> Every man semes to serve himselfe.

> Suspicion is noe proofe nor jealousy an equall judge.

> A nobleman on horsebacks with a rable of footmen about him is but like a huntsman with a kennell of hounds after him.

One fee is too good for a bad lawyer and two fees too little for a good one.

There are references to the manners and fashions of the day. We learn that " a certain kind of compound called Laudanum " had been recently introduced; that " the play of shuttlecocke is become soe much in request at Court that the making of shuttlecockes is almost growne a trade in London," that scholars returning from Italy adopted the " new fashioned salutacions belowe the knee "; and there is a good description of a popular preacher, " a black fellow with a sour look but a good spirit, bold and sometimes bluntly witty." The incidents noted are for the most part trivial, such as :

> This afternoon a serving man, one of the Earl of Northumberland, fought with swaggering Eps and ran him through the ear.

> I heard my cosen Wingat is married to a riche widdowe in Kent.

We must give the now famous but not at all creditable reference to Shakespeare among Manningham's anecdotes :

> Upon a tyme when Burbidge played Richard III there was a citizen grone soe farr in liking with him that before shee went from the play shee appointed him to come that night unto hir by the name of Richard the Third. Shakespeare overhearing their conclusion went before was intertained and at his game ere Burbidge came. Then message being brought that Burbidge was at the dore, Shakespeare caused returne to be made that William the Conqueror was before Richard the Third. Shakespeare's name William. (Mr. Touse ?)

This certainly is a curious way of referring to the actor who, we are told, was known at that time as the author of several plays, including *Twelfth Night*, the performance of which Manningham himself attended, according to a note in his diary a few weeks before.

We are greatly indebted to Manningham for one of the fullest accounts that exist of the last hours of Queen Elizabeth. Dr. Parry, the Queen's chaplain, was a friend of Manningham's. At this time he was Prebendary of York, later he became Bishop of Gloucester and Worcester. He is frequently mentioned in the diary. In April, 1602, our diarist writes :

> Her Majestie merrily told Dr. Parry that shee would not heare him on Good Friday :
> " Thou wilt speake against me, I am sure " quoth shee ; Yet shee heard him.

On March 23, 1602–03, having heard Dr. Parry preach at Richmond, he dines with him.

> I dyned with Dr. Parry in the Privy Chamber and understood by him, the Bishop of Chichester, the Deane of Windsor etc that hir Majestie hath bin by fitts troubled with melancholy some three or four monthes but for this fortnight extreme oppressed with it, in soe much that shee refused to eate anie thing to receive any phisike or admit any rest in bedd till within these two or three dayes. Shee hath bin in a manner speechless for two dayes, verry pensive and silent, since Shrovetide sitting sometymes with hir eye fixed upon one object many howres togither, yet shee alwayes had hir perfect senses and memory and yesterday signified by the lifting up of hir hand and eyes to heaven a syne which Dr. Parry entreated of hir, that shee beleeved that fayth which shee had caused to be professed and looked faythfully to be saved by Christe's merits and mercy only and noe other means. She took great delight in hearing prayers, would often at the name of Jesus lift up her hands and eyes to heaven. Shee would not heare the Archbishop speake of hope of hir longer lyfe, but when he prayed or spake of Heaven and these joyes, shee would hug his hand. It seems she might have lived yf she would have used meanes ; but shee would not be persuaded and princes must not be forced. Hir physicians said shee had a body of a firme and perfect constitucion likely to have lived many yeares. A royall Majestie is noe priviledge against death.

And on the following day :

> This morning about three o'clock hir Majestie departed this lyfe, mildly like a lamb, easily like a ripe apple from the tree, *cum leve quadam febre absque gemitu.* Dr. Parry told me that he was present and sent his prayers before hir soule ; and I doubt not but shee is amongst the royall saints in Heaven in eternall joyes.

He gives an account of the accession of James I with this comment :

> I thinke the sorrowe for hir Majestie's departure was soe deep in many hearts they could not soe suddenly showe anie great joy, though it could not be lesse then exceeding greate for the succession of soe worthy a King.

The diary is contained in a small volume of 133 leaves, measuring not quite 6 inches by 4. The original manuscript is in the British Museum. It was reproduced by the Camden Society in 1868.

ELIAS ASHMOLE

THE old building in Broad Street, Oxford, known as the Ashmolean Museum, which used to contain the collection of curiosities left to the University by Elias Ashmole, the herald and antiquary, has helped to immortalise his name. Born in 1617, he started life as a solicitor, and subsequently held a variety of offices, such as Commissioner of Excise, Comptroller of the Ordnance, and Windsor Herald. His interest in astrology gave place in his later life to a study of heraldry and antiquarian research. He was offered the post of Garter King-at-Arms, but he refused it in favour of Sir William Dugdale.

His diary begins by a recital of the chief events in his life from his birth, but it must have been in or about 1641 that he began making the actual entries, which are not by any means regular and are very brief. They are chiefly of a private and personal character. He supplies some domestic details and he makes very frequent notes on the state of his health. His first wife dies in 1641, when he makes the following remarks :

> She was a virtuous, modest, careful, and loving wife ; her affection was exceeding great towards me as was mine to her which caused us to live so happily together. Nor was I less beloved and esteemed by both her Father and Mother inasmuch as at her Funeral her mother sitting near the corps with Tears professed to the Baron of Kinderton's lady who after told it to me and others present that she knew not whether she loved me or her only son better.

In 1649 he marries Lady Mainwaring, who was some twenty years his senior and had been married three times previously. Her son apparently disapproved of the match, as a year or so before the marriage he broke into Ashmole's chamber and attacked him because he thought " I would marry his mother." The marriage was not a success, for, in 1655, Lady Mainwaring petitioned for a separation and Ashmole notes in his diary:

> The cause between me and my wife was heard where Mr. Serjeant Maynard observed to the court that there were 800 sheets of depositions on my wife's part and not one word proved against me of using her ill nor ever giving her a bad or provoking word.

In January, 1668, he mentions Lady Mainwaring's death, and in November of the same year he marries Elizabeth Dugdale, the daughter of Sir William Dugdale, whom he had accompanied on his visitation through England.

In 1647 he rejoices because

> it pleased God to put me in mind that I was now placed in the condition I always desired which was that I might be enabled to live to myself and studies without being forced to take pains for a livelihood in the world.

Not only does he regularly attend " the Astrologers feast," but he seems to have been close friends with an alchemist whom he refers to as " my father Backhouse."

> This morning my father Backhouse opened himself very freely touching the great secret.

And later:

> My father Backhouse lying sick . . . not knowing whether he should live or dye about eleven of the clock told me in Syllables the true matter of the Philosopher's stone which he bequeathed to me as a legacy.

We have notes on his occupations, how he learns seal engraving, casting in sand, goldsmith's work and Hebrew, how he is commanded by the King to make a description of medals, how Joan Morgan his maid died of the small pox, when he discharged his man Hobs, etc., etc. But by far the most frequent references in the diary are to his own ailments, his constant toothache, and his attacks of gout, and also to some of the very strange remedies to which he had recourse. A few illustrations may be given:

> A boyle broke out of my throat under my right ear.

> About this time the left side of my neck began to break forth occasioned by shaving my beard with a bad razor.

> This night about one of the clock I fell ill of a surfeit occasioned by drinking water after venison. I was greatly oppressed in my stomach and next day Mr. Saunders the Astrologian sent me a piece of Briony root to hold in my hand and within a quarter of an hour my stomach was freed of that great oppression.

> I took early in the morning a good dose of Elixir and hung three spiders about my neck and they drove my ague away. *Deo gratias.*

> I rubbed the skin near my rump whereupon it began to be very sore.

This unfortunate occurrence produces nearly a dozen almost daily entries with regard to his symptoms. When he hurts his right foot he applies " a black snail " to it (presumably a leech, although he mentions them separately).

The last entry is dated October 9, 1687. He died in 1692.

The diary, which certainly throws some light on Ashmole's personality, was published, together with some of his letters, in a little volume in 1717.

JOHN ROUS

WHILE he lived out of the world in the small village of Santon Downham, in Suffolk, John Rous, a country parson, took a very close interest in public affairs, and his diary, which extends intermittently from 1625 to 1642, is filled almost exclusively with proclamations, petitions, trials and military and foreign events. He seems to be aware that there are other sources from which information on public events can be obtained when he writes :

> The many occurrences about Parliament business the differences between the King's Majestie and them; their Petitions, his answers (supposed or otherwise) the affairs of Ireland etc are extant in multitudes of books and papers (unto which God in mercy put an end).

There is an occasion when he records a discussion with his neighbours at Brandon with regard to the Rochelle Expedition in 1627. One of them

> fell in general to speak distrustfully of the voyage and then of our war with France which he would make our King the cause of.

Rous indignantly takes the high patriotic line against these " pro-French " anti-patriots, considering it

> foul for any man to lay blame upon our own King and State. I told them I would always speak the best of what our King and State did and think the best too till I had good grounds.

Rous, who was an upholder of the doctrine of " my country right or wrong," then proceeds to enlarge on the mischief and discontent caused by those who spoke disparagingly of State business.

Rous lived for many years with his father, who held the parsonage of Weeting. He married twice and had several children, but in his diary he never says a word about his family or himself. He comments on the crops, prices and the weather, and notes crimes and executions within the district.

Some of the public events he describes at great length, such as the murder of Buckingham. Once or twice he suddenly inserts quite irrelevantly some trivial incident. Between an entry giving the protest of the House of Commons on a very eventful occasion in May, 1629, and another with regard to the proclamation of peace with France, we find an account of a crow building its nest in the sail of a windmill. In the same year he describes a man who ate two toads on being offered a groat to do it. " When both were down his stomach held them and he had his groate."

A particular feature of this diary is the skits and satirical verses which he collects and other miscellaneous documents, some of which have not been discovered in any other source. He does not always approve of the rhymes as he heads one series :

> I hate these following railing rimes
> Yet keepe them for president of the times.

Many of them are interesting and amusing, but as they have nothing whatever to do with diary writing we must pass them by.
The diary was published by the Camden Society in 1856.

SIR WILLIAM BRERETON

SIR WILLIAM BRERETON, of Handforth, Cheshire, born about 1604, kept a diary of his travels in 1634 when he went to Holland, and again in the following year when he passed through the north of England and Scotland. There is no personal note in the diary, it is purely descriptive. But it is worthy of notice, as the writer is very observant and his style is picturesque. He enters into minute detail with regard to all he sees and hears, the daily entries sometimes occupying several pages. Architecture, agriculture and the weather attract him chiefly, and he sometimes makes a passing comment on the inns he stops at:

> We lodged att the Crowne; were well used; 8d ordinarie; and 5d our servants and great entertainment and good lodging. A respective hoast and honest reckoning.

Medical details seem to be an indispensable part of many early diaries. Sir William Brereton, however, does not enlarge on his own health, but he notes the following recipe:

> The Bishop assured mee that faire spring water in the morning receaved into your mouth and there kept untill itt bee lukewarme and then swallowed is an excellent medicine to cure the cholick and stone and that hee himself had been hereby cured.

He gives a detailed account of " a most daintie new saltwork " lately erected at Newcastle. But he is not above gossip and gives a very full description of the charge brought against Ralph Lambton of murdering his two wives.

In Scotland he is occasionally struck by the beauty of the scenery. But in describing the Scots he seems to lose all his usual restraint and lets himself go in unmeasured language.

> The sluttishness and nastiness of this people is such that I cannott ommitt the particularizing thereof though I have more than sufficiently often touched upon the same. Their houses and halls and kitchens have such a noysome tast and savour and that soe strong as itt doth offend you, soe soone as you come within their walls, yea sometimes when I have light from my horse, I have felt the distate of itt before I have come into the house : yea, I never came to my own lodging in Edinborough, or went out butt I was constrained

to hold my nose or to use warme-wood or some such sented plant : Their pewter I am confident is never scowred : they are afraid it should too much weare and consume thereby : only sometimes and that but seldome they doe sleightly rubb them over with a fillthy dish clowte dipped in most sluttish greasy water. . . . To come into their kitchen and to see them dress their meate and to behold the sinke (which is more offensive than any jakes) will be a sufficient supper and will take off the edge of your stomack.

The writer of this diary of travels was educated at Brasenose College, Oxford; he was created a baronet in 1622 and was a Knight of the Shire for Chester. He took a prominent part on the side of the Parliament in the Civil War.

The journal is written in a clear, regular and very close handwriting. The MS. belonged originally to Dr. Percy, Bishop of Dromore. Sir Walter Scott was much interested in it and went so far as to offer his services should it be published. It eventually passed into the hands of the Grey-Egertons of Oalton. It was not printed until 1844, when Mr. Edward Hawkins, Keeper of the Antiquities in the British Museum, edited it for the Chetham Society.

Sections of the journal have appeared in the *Surtees Society's Collections, Imprints and Reprints* by Richardson, and *Early Travellers in Scotland* by Hume Browne.

JOHN ASTON

CHARLES I, on his expedition through York, Durham and Northumberland in the first Bishop's war of 1639, took with him John Aston, of Aston, in Cheshire, as " Privy Chamber man extraordinary." Aston kept a diary from April 1 to June 29 which is of historical interest as giving the first-hand observations of an eye-witness on the progress of the King's army. Apart from this it has no personal or intimate features. When he sets out, he says :

I had a cuirassier's armes for my selfe, close caske, gorget, back and breast culet, pouldrons, vambrance, left hand gauntlet, and cuisses and a case of pistolls and great saddle.

He describes in detail towns, cathedrals, buildings and particulars with regard to the movements of the army and the quartering of the troops. The King's lodgings and goings and comings are mentioned without any account of conversations or personal remarks.

One quotation may be given to illustrate Aston's general style in recording the incidents of camp life :

> The 5th of June being Wednesday the order being not settled for our watching, wee were commanded to attend and then divided the squadron and cast lots which part should watch that night. It fell to my squadron where I was to bee dismissed, soe I was ryding home about 6 o'clock and there was presently a generall alarme through the campe. The Scots were discreid from our quarter pitched on a hill nearer Dunce, soe all the souldiers stood to their armes ; but about 9 a clock the King and the army were better quieted soe there was noe command layed upon us to attend only my selfe was inforced to be there all night in Mr. Hinton's tent because I could not get out of the army. Some thought the King knew of their intention to come thither long before, but would suffer it to come as a soddaine alaram to the campe to try their courage and affeccons which as the same polliticians sayed his majestie began now to distrust, but theise were clergy. I know not how well the King was satisfied but hee was inquisitive and curious as might bee and come to the bulwarke with his perspective and there stood viewing and counting the tents a long while and was followed with his nobles and courtiers as all amazed and wondring at the approach of the Scots, the King having sent them word they should not come within 10 miles of the campe.

Aston was not really a diary writer. It was simply the importance of the occasion which made him think it worth while to keep a record of his three months with the King's army.

The manuscript of the diary is in the British Museum and has been reproduced in the Surtees Society's publications.

WILLIAM DOWSING

ALTHOUGH not strictly speaking a private diary, William Dowsing's Journal, both in matter and manner, is a unique document. He is described as " Parliamentary Visitor appointed under a warrant from the Earl of Manchester for demolishing the superstitious pictures and ornaments of churches etc within the county of Suffolk in the years 1643–1644." In August, 1641, an order was published by the House of Commons " for the taking away of all scandalous pictures out of Churches etc.," and Manchester received his commission as General of the associated Eastern Counties in 1642. A good deal of destruction of this kind had gone on since the Reformation, but in the seventeenth century it was done more systematically.

Dowsing confines his Journal to dated entries devoted only to the registering of the amount of destruction he carries out in each place he visits, and it is obvious that he has a certain satisfaction

WILLIAM DOWSING

in the work he is engaged on. The entries are more or less alike, but a series taken from different parts of the Journal may be given to show his style and method :

> Sudbury. Peter's Parish. We brake down a Picture of God the Father, 2 Crucifix's, and Pictures of Christ about an hundred in all ; and gave order to take down a Cross on the Steeple ; and diverse Angels, 20 at least on the Roof of the Church.
>
> Sudbury. We brake down 10 mighty great angels in glass in all 80.
>
> Haver. We brake down about an hundred superstitious Pictures of God and Christ ; and diverse others very superstitious ; and 200 had been broke down before I came. We took away two popish Inscriptions with *ora pro nobis* and we beat down a great stoneing Cross on the top of the Church.

Sometimes the " we " is exchanged for " I," showing his pride in the part he personally took in the work.

> Clare. We brake down 1000 Pictures superstitious ; I brake down 200 ; 3 of God the Father and 3 of Christ and the Holy Lamb, and 3 of the Holy Ghost lika a Dove with Wings ; and the 12 Apostles were carved in Wood on the top of the Roof which we gave order to take down ; and 20 cherubims to be taken down ; and the Sun and Moon in the East Windows, by the King's Arms, to be taken down.
>
> Copdock. I brake down 150 superstitious pictures 2 of God the Father and 2 Crucifixes ; did deface a cross on the Font and gave order to take down a stoneing cross on the Chancel and to levell the Steps ; and took a Brass Inscription with *ora pro nobis* and *cujus animae propitietur Deus.*
>
> Bramford. A cross to be taken off the steple : we brake down 841 superstitious Pictures, and gave order to take down the steps and gave a fortnight's time.
>
> We were at the Lady Bruce's House and in her Chappel ; there was a Picture of God the Father, of the Trinity, of Christ and the Holy Ghost, the Cloven Tongues ; which we gave order to take down and the Lady promised to do it.

Window-breaking must have been his chief occupation, but on one occasion " we could not reach them nor would they help us to raise the ladders." He breaks up organs, pots for holy water, covers for fonts and wooden images. Sometimes he gives orders for the local authorities to carry out the work, as, for instance :

> Dunwich. St. Peter's Church. 63 Cherubims, 80 at least of JESUS written in Capital Letters on the Roof and 40 superstitious Pictures and a cross on the top of the Steeple. All was promised by the Churchwardens to be done.

He visits Ufford in January and comes round again in August to see if his orders have been carried out. But he finds that the Churchwardens that were enjoined these things above three months afore had not done them in May and I sent one of them to see it done, but they would not let him have the key.

New churchwardens are appointed and

Samuel Canham of the same Town said " I sent men to rifle the Church ", and Will Brown old Churchwarden said " I went about to pull down the Church and had carried away part of the Church."

Not content with the damage he does he also exacts a fee of 6s. 8d. which he notes down at the end of many of his entries. Occasionally he has difficulty, for there occurs " he refused to pay the 6s 8d." He evidently worked hard himself: " 2 crucifixes which I brake of part," " Organs, which I brake," etc. When he was employed in Cambridgeshire an eye-witness described him as having " battered and beaten downe all our painted glass."

Incidentally in this shocking tale of destruction one learns how richly decorated the churches were. There are only two or three occasions on which he notes " nothing to reform."

A visitor to some of our Cathedrals to-day when he gazes at nineteenth-century stained glass may regret that the Government does not employ a judicious Dowsing.

The Journal was originally published in 1786.

ADAM EYRE

BORN at Haslehead, in Yorkshire, in 1614, Adam Eyre served in the army during the Civil War under Lord Fairfax. While in the army he kept a journal which unfortunately is lost. At the close of the war he settled down at Haslehead, where he spent his time in rural occupations, taking an active part in the management of the affairs of the parish. For two years, 1646–1648, he kept a diary in which he made daily entries with great regularity. He calls it " A Dyurnall or catalogue of all my actions and expenses from the 1st of January 1646."

A large part of the diary is taken up with records of payments and expenses, his comings and goings, his rides and his intercourse with his neighbours. The entries are often quite perfunctory and of little interest. But sometimes he enters into greater detail, as, for instance :

I stayed at home all day and in the afternoon cut a corne which putt me to extraordinary trouble.

He records the fact that he took to smoking :

This day I took a pipe of tobacco and resolved to take every morning one and every night one but no more.

He attends a football match :

I went to Bordhill to see a match played at the foot ball between Peniston and Thurlston but the crowd hindered the sports so that nothing was done.

Eyre was evidently a reader and lent and borrowed books and occasionally bought them. The following are mentioned : Sir Walter Raleigh's *History of the World* ; Bateman upon Bartholomew ; Crisp's *Sermons* ; Saltmarshes' *Smoke in the Temple* ; Mr. Dell's *Sermons* ; a *Discourse on the Council of Basel* ; *The Personal Reign of Christ upon Earth*, by Archer ; *England's Propheticall Merlin and the Starry Messenger*, by Lylle (W. Lilly, the astrologer).

His reading perplexed him, for he writes: " had varyous thoughts by reason of the varyety of mens' opinions I find in reading." Though Adam Eyre probably only intended his diary to be a bald record of events, gradually he begins to make it his confidant. We can see by his reading that he is of a religious disposition, and he had just the degree of morbidity which makes a diarist expose himself as if in a confessional. There is no happy note in the writing, and his wife appears to have been a sore trial to him, so that he finds himself in his frequent moods of depression obliged to write about her. The only word of anything approaching appreciation of her is " my wife was very extravagant in her old humorous way."

The first outburst occurs six months after he had begun his diary :

June 8. This morne my wife began after her old manner to braule and revile mee for wishing her only to weare such apparell as was decent and comly and accused mee of treading on her sore foote with curses and othes ; which to my knowledge I touched not, nevertheless she continued in that extacy til noone.

A few days later: " This night my wife was worse in words than ever." In the autumn : " This day was my wife very angry and I stayed at home all day."

At the beginning of the next year a little more light is thrown on the domestic differences which seems to show the fault was not all on one side:

> Jan. 1. This morne I used some words of persuasion to my wife to forbeare to tell mee of what is past and promised her to become a good husband to her for ye tyme to come and she promised me likewise shee would doe what I wished her in anything save in setting her hand to papers; and I promised her never to wish her therunto.

This may have been a reconciliation, for no further mention of Mrs. Eyre occurs.

Whether it was infidelity, drink or something else which threw Adam Eyre from time to time into a paroxysm of depression and self-condemnation does not appear.

There is far less record of drinking than is usual in the diaries of this period. In fact only once does he write: " God forgive mee I drunk too much." Nevertheless the depression takes hold of him, as when he says: " This day I was very much perplexed with worldly cares and labored under a sore temptation all day," and on some occasions he breaks into an unintelligible cypher.

As time goes on he seeks consolation in his religion and entry of the day ends up with a prayer. Remorse overtook him after punishing Jane (the maid):

> Oct. 9. This night I whipped Jane for her foolishness as yesterday I had done for her sloathfulness; and hence am I induced to bewayle my sinfull life for my failings in the presence of God Almighty are questionless greater than hers are to mee; wherefore unless Thou, my most mercifull God, be mercifull unto mee what shall become of mee?

> Dec. 7. Let not my present dull and indisposedness avert Thy favors from me.

> Dec. 9. I must needs confess I am weake indeede but Hee is stil my defence.

> Jan. 8. (1648). This day I have been very much troubled with worldly cares but Thou O God whose I am deliver mee I pray thee from the guilt thereof.

On January 11 there is a very long outpouring of penitence which contains the following:

> I very well remember I never made vow in all my life, but, through weaknesse and the power of darknesse overruling mee, I have most shamefully broken so that I am in a most miserable condition by nature, neither have I any power of myselfe to think one good thought so miserable am I.

The next day again he complains of " yeeldding to the corruptions of myne own depraved imagination," and occupies many lines in the entry for that day in a prayer to God. But after writing a few days later, " when I came home, I was very angry and caryed myselfe unsivilly," he hardly refers to his failings again.

Before journeying to London he makes a sort of provisional will. He writes a " little booke " containing the particulars of his time in London, but this is missing.

The diary ends on January 26, 1848–9, and he sets out for London the following day, so that he would arrive there the night before the execution of Charles I, of which probably he was an eye-witness.

It would seem likely that this rather morbid man with his pathetic attempts at self-correction continued to confide in the pages of his diary. But nothing further from his pen exists.

GILES MOORE

GILES MOORE, who was rector of Horsted Keynes, Sussex, from 1655 to 1679, kept a journal which can hardly be called a diary, as it is far more like an account book, though he never adds up totals or makes any general survey of his financial position. Yet in the language of accounts he records all his doings. Besides his actual purchases, it would seem that marriage, death, illness, journeys, and indeed every incident in his life presented itself to him from the point of view of cost. But this very habit gives a clue to his character, and his purchases also throw light on what manner of man he was. There is an extraordinarily comic effect in a page of events presented in this peculiar style. Occasionally he allows himself a little more freedom and gives a description or expresses an opinion without immediate reference to cost. He is of a complaining disposition and resents unnecessary or excessive payments.

He puts the following lines as a heading :

Indicat hic liber de me tibi plurima lector ! Omnia quae merè mundana ac vana fuere. Wee reckon our expenses but not our sins ; wee account what wee expend but not wee offend.

Here are a few typical entries :

For 3 yards and ¾ of scarlet serge of which I made the library cupboard carpet besydes my wastcoate made thereof 15s. J. Daves brought me from Grinsted 4 stone of beefe which at 22d the stone and 2 lb of sewet at 4d came to 8s. I payed for barbouring for 6 moneths 7s 6d and for being blooded though I was so cold that I bled but one ounce 1s.

I bought my wyfe a fat hog to spend in my family for which I paid the sum of 30s the 2 flitches of bacon when dried weighed 64 lb. I gave her to buy a qr of lamb 3s 6d.

For 2 qts of sack in two bottles at the Widdow Newports 4s. For a pint of sack at the Inn at Lindfield 1s for a quart of claret 1s. I bought of a traveller 4 Venesionne glasses 2 of one sort and 2 of another 2s.

1 gave the howling boys 6d (it was the custom to wassail the orchards).

As to clothes, he appears to purchase a great variety :

I bought two payre of gloves for which I payed 2s 3d the payre I had them faced with my own fringe which cost mee 1s 4d.

I bought a levitical girdle containing 4 oz of silke. 10s & ½ a yd of velvet ; two worsted canonical girdles 5s.

I bought 2 yards and ½ of Devonshire red bazes to make me a waistcoat for which I paid 7s 4d and I bought a payre of silk stockings for which I paid £1 : 1 ; for silken tops 6s 6d and for a payer of black worsted stockings I gave 5s.

I bought of my countryman Mr. Cooke a shaggy demicastor hat of the fashion for which I payed 16s 6d.

With his scarlet waistcoat, silk stockings, fringed gloves, levitical girdle and shaggy demicastor hat the reverend gentleman must have been a very picturesque sight.

When ill he describes his symptoms. He takes " physicke " and is " mightily sicke " and ends up with an entry of the exact sum he pays the doctor, the nurse, and the curate who took his duty. On another occasion he consults Mr. Riche, chirurgeon, and gives him

for advising about the turning about of my neck £1. For 2 dozen of pills 3s and for a pint of sack 1s. His direction is that I am to take 3 pills over night and anything warm in the morning once in two dayes and if I am no better 1 am to use a large blyster behind the shoulder blade ; to do it againe in a fortnight and then afterwards to shave my head.

Two or three times he expresses annoyance in his accounts. He has to pay a considerable sum for repairing the chancel, " all of which was occasioned by and through the defaulte and neglect of Mistresse Sapphira Lightmaker in not keeping up her chancel." He also pays for the mending of a bridge " for whiche shee would not allow me one penney when I moved her unto it, no, not one farthing ! though shee stripped a good part of my church to lay her leads."

GILES MOORE

We can picture the interview. The Rev. Giles Moore as red as his waistcoat, and Sapphira Lightmaker simply laughing at him. Her very name suggests it.

Giles Moore has a god-daughter Mat. We get little glimpses of her through the accounts.

> I carried Mat up to London buying for her a new riding suite for which I payed 28s.

> I gave Mat 1s to play withall and I gave her 2s towards a payr of stockings which she is to knit for herselfe. I also gave her 1s which she is to spend at dancings.

> I sent for Mat's board for 6 weeks at Mistress Chalmers during which time shee made mee shirts and bands £1 : 10 and I gave her to buy a hood at the faire 5s.

He projects a marriage for her and writes to a neighbouring rector a cautious letter in which there is actually no mention of any payment. In this amusing epistle he says :

> I do not so little value you, nor your son, but that if the young man could fancy her for a wyfe this advowson and that well stocked . . . together also with library when I leave this world, I should not (with her consent thereto given) which shee hath no reason to deny, judge her amisse bestowed.

Nothing came of this matchmaking, however, and two years later Mat married Mr. Citizen. But the marriage only produces from the pen of our diarist an entry of the amount he spent on sack and " meate extraordinary," and a day or two later further details as to the exact amount he " layed out upon Mat." He had words with Mr. Citizen in the following year and calls him " knave " for not paying up money which was due, adding the comment " *Avaritia cum fraude conjuncta*." When he visits his god-daughter later he gives her 1s. " and her mayd 6d."

He takes several journeys to the Isle of Wight, to Chichester and to London, but it is always the same thing : we only get an account of his expenses and his purchases. Life for Giles Moore was purely economic. Money might not always pass, sometimes there was barter, as, for instance :

> I sent to Mr. Hely a ribspare and hoggs puddings for which hee returned me a box of pills and sermons.

Or a prettier one :

> I sent Mistresse Michelborne a galon of rose water and 1 quart of damasks, shee sending me back by the messenger 3 dozen of pigeons.

He makes one exception in what we may call his accountant's

style. He records with great detail the illness and death of his brother at West Cowes. Of course he finds a good deal to say with regard to the will and the legacies, but he also follows the course of illness, which has ups and downs. His brother one day seems to have taken the law into his own hands and attempted a very drastic form of remedy for anyone in the " anguish and misery " of a high fever. Being left alone for a moment " hee came forth speedily and leaped into a well which was ten feete deep in water, out of which he was quickly taken and put into a warme bed." It is not surprising that the following week he died, the burial only calling forth from our diarist a list of the payments he had to make.

The last entry is dated August 3, 1679, and Giles Moore died on October 3.

The manuscript was in the possession of the incumbent of Horsted Keynes, and from it extracts were printed in the Sussex Archæological Collections in 1853.

HENRY NEWCOMBE

THE only portion that remains of the very full diary which Newcombe kept throughout the greater part of his life is the section which covers the period from September 30, 1661, to September 29, 1663. He was a Presbyterian minister, educated at Cambridge, ordained in 1648, rector of Gawsworth 1650, and subsequently in Manchester. He died in 1695. The diary is a daily record dealing with his duties, his movements and his sermons, but it contains also domestic details, self-examination, resolutions and meditations on life. Although he is very strict in his manner of living, he is not above a game of bowls, shovel-board or billiards, and even reading comedies. But his extreme piety is the keynote of the journal. In the following quotations the constant abbreviations he uses have been written out in full.

Preaching.

It was sacrament day and I preached on 1 Cor. XI. 25. The Lord assisted mee much on that subject and I hope it made the sacrament more lively and refreshing. This remembering of Christ livelyly and effectually is of great use to a poore soule.

In the afternoone I preached at Haslenden on 1 Pet. IV. 3. Mary went with me to the towne. And at night wee had much pleasant discourse yet vergeinge to a good purpose about the vanity of the world etc. And after supper we had repetition and prayer. And so indeed had a Sabbath past expectation.

He notes down very frequently his resolutions in a sort of list:

1. The Lord helpe mee in secret dutys. 2. To be of a quicker and tender conscience. 3. Atheisme. Sure the worke of my conscience of late may doe something against that distemper. 4. What not a word for God upon occasion! 5. O what a thing will it be to be in heaven. 6. The Lord arme mee with patience.

1. Pride and vaineglory. 2. Slothfulness. 3. An unwillingness to secret dutys. 4. Want of spirituality. 5. Impatience. 6. Distrust.

Alas I must endeavour to walke closer with God or I cannot keepe cart on wheeles.

I was weary this night and upon that account very short and poore in dutys but I must beware that wearyness of body betray mee not as it hath done to slightynes in my course and to expose mee to a sharpe affliction for the quickening of mee, for that usually is the end of all such bouts with me.

But one resolution he finds considerable difficulty in observing. It is with regard to smoking.

My base heart is but too much concerned with this tobacco.

How tobacco doth too much fill my thoughts and selfe denial about such a stinkinge thing might do well.

I resolve to let this tobacco alone and to studdy to forget it for it doth mee no good.

This base tobacco. Take it before secret dutys then it prevents them, put it off and then my base heart would count of it all the time of duty.

I doe see my slavery with this tobacco. When it can hasten a duty to be at it and when I know it it doth not benefit mee but allmost allways makes mee sicke it is high time to dismisse it. But sometimes to deny it when it is so desired were but a small degree of self denial.

It is curious that he should have been so fond of smoking if it almost always made him ill. There is a vein of melancholy and self-reproach constantly recurring in all he writes. This is typical:

O my soule where have I beene all this while. So dead in dutys. So endles in my studdys. So unprofitable in company. So unedifying in my family. So negligent of meditation. So formall in preachinge. O my soule where hast thou beene? The Lord put some life into mee.

But he rather revelled in self-disparagement, even with his friends:

> Mr. Bagshawe came to mee at my returne and sate with me 2 houres. A deale of sweet discourse wee had about the baseness of both our hearts.

He often mentions the health of his children and his wife, who was a sister of Ashmole's first wife.

> The Lord hath restored my childe. But my great security hath moved the Lord to lay my wife somewhat low this day by distemper and great paine upon her.
>
> I got home about 2 and found my wife pretty hearty, havinge taken physicke this day and it workinge very easyly with her. A great mercy.
>
> What a deale of patience is requisite to beare any converse with our little children. How peevish and foolish are they! and what fits doth our heavenly Father beare with us in!

The inevitable servant troubles are of course noted:

> The villanous carriage of the servants that were all out at that time of the night on Saturday night.
>
> Mary quarrelled with her mistress and is to goe away. The Lord provide us with good servants.

He is critical, not to say a little pharisaical, sometimes with regard to company:

> We had a deal of company; and saw the free grace of God that wee are not given up to the same extreme vanitys and follys that others are. Alas how are some empty frothy ones of the gentry to be pittyed!
>
> After supper wee were at Lawrence Gardner's till pretty late. Very merry and cheerefull with our neighbours. I would thinke of beinge a little savory in our merth and to part so if it might be.

But we can hardly believe there was much mirth, savoury or unsavoury, when Newcombe was present.

There are notes on his own health; he has "collicks" and "sweats finely upon takeinge a rosemary posset," but he is chiefly concerned in meditation on purely religious theses in which he generally finds "much savour and sweetness." We may quote rather a shrewd observation on the subject of a mountebank:

> I went out, whether wisely or no, with my wife to see the mountebank on the stage. The fellow that acted the foole made many really fooles under that looked and laughed at him. He but acted foole and got money, they were real fooles and gave their money.

There is something original and telling in Newcombe's style. Even his references to the weather are picturesque, as, for in-

stance, " had a very sad dash of raine cominge over the hills."
He talks of " ells of time," " tough debates " : a difficult business
is " a tickle," and when an event does not come off he writes
" it misst." But the diary is only a fragment ; he wrote as well
an " Abstract " or sort of autobiography telling his adventures
from his early life onward. By the Abstract his whole career
can be traced and his political opinions during times of revolution
and change are related.

Newcombe's career is fully set out in the preface to the printed
edition of the diary which was published by the Cheetham Society
in 1849.

OLIVER HEYWOOD

IN the seventy-two years of his life (1630–1702) Oliver Heywood, the Presbyterian divine of Northowian, Yorkshire, made the most careful and elaborate record of his religious experiences. Not content with keeping an ordinary diary, he wrote his autobiography, long accounts of the members of his family with a genealogy, an " Event Book " giving " covenants, experiences, self-reflections," " combats with sin," and " groaning of the soul," a long register of " Returns of Prayer," and many other observations and memoranda. All these are carefully written down in a cramped hand in small notebooks, and we get a very complete inside picture of a conscientious, self-absorbed man exercising ceaseless discipline on himself in his spiritual life, displaying wonderful powers of concentration in religious matters, noting the hand of God in every incident that occurs, occupied in study, and more especially in preaching, courageously combating the obstacles and disabilities which Nonconformists encountered in those days, and taking himself very seriously. But of course the picture is incomplete ; the detail given from within only concerns preaching, prayer, visiting the sick, and study, with occasional references to his health and his family, and full as it is, is very dull and monotonous reading. From without we have no picture in words as to how Oliver Heywood impressed his contemporaries ; we only have a print showing a rather stout, self-satisfied looking ecclesiastic with ringlets and a double chin. His preaching record shows him to have been a man of immense energy, and when he is suspended from ministering in the diocese of York after the passing of the Act of Uniformity, when he is apprehended, or when he encounters all sorts of difficulties, he continues undismayed preaching and preaching, if not in a church then in his own house, or, after the Five Mile Act had become law, as an itinerant evangelist.

The diaries are incomplete, but they cover the greater part of the period between 1666 up to his death. A few typical entries may be given :

> I preacht to a pretty ful congregation at the house of Jeffery Beck the Lord made it a refreshing night to many soules though our adversarys watcht and gnasht their teeth when they saw so many coming together.
>
> There was a numerous congregation from all parts and I had great liberty of speech in preaching and praying but not such melting of heart as sometimes I have enjoyed.
>
> When I was in the pulpit singing a psalm comes up Mr. Broadhead vicar of Batley passing among the croud up the alley and got with much adoe to the clark bade him tell Mr. Heywood to come down and let him have his own pulpit and then hasted away he left his goune at an house took horse and went to Batley told Justice Copley what a multitude there was at Morley hearing a Non-conformist he took no notice of it, but let us alone and so through god's mercy we enjoyed the day quietly and it was a good day blessed be god.
>
> Went to George Horsmans house at little Woodhouse there preacht and before I had done was apprehended by constables carryed to the Mayor who sent me to the common prison.

However, he is released, and four days later is preaching again. Shortly afterwards he is served with a warrant " to make distresse upon my goods " in payment of a fine under the Conventicle Act.

A few of the references to his wife and family may be quoted :

> As the Lord had blessed me abroad so my poor family at home, they have been in health my sons have been very towardly, plyed their book, read chapters, learned chatichismes, got some chapters and psalmes without book, John repeated the 12th, Eliezor the 10th of Revelations last night in bed—blessed be god.
>
> On Saturday morning my sons having not made their latin in expectation to goe to Halifax were loath to goe to schoole yet I threatened them, they went crying, my bowels workt and I sent to call them back and I went into my study and fel on my knees and found sweet meltings—if god set in a little they will occasion much good.
>
> Aug. 24 (1671) called black Bartholomew day I resolved to keep a fast and because I came home but last night and could get no more company I kept it with my family, the forenoon we spent in prayer beginning at youngest Eliezer prayed first very sensibly, tho short, John prayed both a long time and exceeding pertinently and affectionately weeping much. I admired at it, god helped my maid, my wife and myself wonderfully—oh what a melting duty and day was it !

Food he never mentions, nor any trivial mundane matters, but two examples may be given of references to his own health.

> I tossed all the night in bed and could not sleep one wink by reason of toothach yet was pretty wel the day after then I saw the mercy of sleep and felt my unfitnes for holy thoughts in pain for if I could have got my thoughts on any good subject I should soon have slept.

> I preacht twice tho I was little fit but god graciously helped and hearts were much inlayed by the advantage of my distemper but it increased tormenting pain in my head. On Monday I was blooded, on Thursday morning I had a violent fit of tormenting pain al over my body which lasted for 10 houres I was set upon a rack but god was mercifull to this poore worme so that I had no more fits but from thence forth the Lord recovered me. . . .

He is very successful with his prayers for the sick and those who are in trouble : " a boysterous gentleman now under troubles of mind " is " wonderfuly affected by my company and discourse." But the main composition of the diary is the praying and preaching and journeying from one place to another. In addition to " melting," he has frequently " comfortable enlargement and assistance," and on one occasion " such a measure of affection, flood of teares, and large elocution as I can never remember." As time goes on the actual diary entries become very brief, the event book containing more of his prayers, supplications, self-examination and resolutions. After 1677 the diary entries are daily, but seldom more than one or two sentences. Such as :

> Saturday I stayed at home studyed god helpt and oh wt meltings of heart had I in prayer with my wife ! blessed be god.

> Lord's day I preached at Flockton oh what a good day was it ! god enlarged my heart in prayer wonderfully.

In the last four years, in addition to notes on prayer and preaching, he gives the names of his visitors and those whom he meets. He begins noting his last illness : " I was but ill," " I was very wrong," " had much adoe to get up into my chamber," and the last entry is written five days before his death.

The volumes in which the diaries, etc., were published in 1883 contain also registers and other lists compiled by Oliver Heywood, and are, therefore, of considerable antiquarian interest. He was the author of a number of religious books,

RALPH THORESBY

THE habit of keeping a diary was taught to Ralph Thoresby by his father. "I would have you," wrote John Thoresby, "in a little book, which you may either buy or make of two or three sheets of paper, make a little journal of anything remarkable every day principally as to yourself. . . . I have thought this a good method for one to keep a good tolerable decorum in actions because he is accountable to himself as well as to God, which we are too apt to forget."

Consequently, out of respectful devotion to his father, Ralph began, at the age of 20, in 1667, to keep a regular daily journal, "chiefly designed for my daily direction and reproof," and he retained the habit till within two months of his death in 1724.

Thoresby was an antiquary; he wrote a large work on the topography of Leeds, his native town, as well as a book on Leeds churches. He received a commercial education partly in Holland, but his mercantile concerns were not very successful. He was deeply religious. In 1683 he was prosecuted as a Nonconformist, but in 1699, after getting on intimate terms with the Bishop of Carlisle and the Archbishop of York, he abandoned his connection with the Dissenters. There is a great deal of prayer and penitence in the diary, but his archæological and genealogical studies, his interest in architecture, antiquities, manuscripts, coins, etc., gradually absorbed his time and attention, and towards the latter part of his life, while the prayers and petitions continue, they become less frequent and a little more perfunctory. In 1697 he was elected a Fellow of the Royal Society, and he had close relations with such men as Camden, Rymer, Sloane, Le Neve, and he also knew Evelyn.

Thoresby was intensely industrious, through many years of his life rising in the morning at five or even earlier. His diary is filled mainly with his religious reflections, his antiquarian pursuits, his travels, and occasional references to his health. He just mentions his wife and children, but abstains from giving any domestic details. He epitomises sometimes at great length sermons he hears, and self-reproach is the keynote of his private religious meditations. His penitence, however, is of a general character; he does not particularise with regard to his shortcomings. Here are some characteristic sentences extracted from various parts of the diary :

Went to bed with wet cheeks.

Spent too much of the day in frivolous visits. I doubt my affections are too much bent upon books.

By reason of the quivering and dithering of my body and the depravedness of my heart I could not understand anything to purpose.

Rivers of tears issued from my eyes.

Spent most of the evening too freely in company. Alas! that I have lived so long and done so little to any good purpose.

Lord, discover my naughty heart more and more to me.

I, an useless unprofitable cumber-ground. Much broken in spirit for fear of a snare.

There is no self-righteousness in his self-depreciation. He has a high standard and is genuinely penitent when he falls short of it. His manner of life is consistently studious and austere.

He tells us of seventeen particular studies of the Bible he made during his life, with various notes, paraphrases, analyses, and annotations, and in addition to this he read it through six times by itself.

When he is unable to go to church he reads "six of Blair's sermons." When setting out for a journey he asks certain devout gentlemen to pray for him, for he says, "it is a good provision against dangers to have a stock of prayers going forward for us." Thoresby evidently believed in the quantitative as well as the qualitative efficacy of religious devotions.

As time passes the entries become filled with his studies and his literary and archæological work and his collections of coins, etc.

When he journeys he makes careful note of churches and buildings and describes the places he sees in detail. An extract from his description of a dangerous ride near Teviotdale may be given:

Our danger here was most dreadful and I think inconceivable to any that were not present; we were upon the side of a most terrible high hill in the middle whereof was a track for the horse to go in which we hoped to find broader that we might have liberty to turn the horse; but instead of that it became so narrow that there was an impossibility to get further. . . . We had above us a hill so desperately steep that our aching hearts durst not attempt the scaling of it, it being much steeper than the roofs of many houses; but the hill below was still more ghastly, as steep for a long way as the walls of a house: and the track we had to ride in was now become so narrow that my horses hinder foot slipped off. . . . To add to our torments there was a river run all along close to the foot of the precipice which we expected every moment to be plunged into and into eternity. In this extremity ther was no way but by catching hold of the boughs of a tree, to throw myself off on the wrong side of the horse, and to climb up the hill.

It may be doubted whether the following example of juvenile smoking can be equalled:

> Evening with brother at Garraway's coffee house : was surprised to see his sickly child of three years old fill its pipe of tobacco and smoke it as *audfarandly* as a man of three score after that a second and third pipe without the least concern as it is said to have done above a year ago.

The parent of the " movies " it appears existed as early as 1679.

> I afterwards called to see the moving Pictures ; a curious piece of art ; the landscape looks as an ordinary picture till the clockwork behind the curtain be set at work, and then the ships move and sail distinctly upon the sea till out of sight ; a coach comes out of the town, the motion of the horses and wheels are very distinct and a gentleman in the coach that salutes the company : a hunter also and his dogs keep their course till out of sight.

Thoresby came of a short-lived family, and when his birthday comes round he often reflects on the short space of time he has before him. . . . But he lived to the age of 67, and managed to fill his life very full with reading, writing and research. He founded a museum in Leeds, in which all his manuscripts and papers, as well as his collection of antiquities and coins, were housed. In 1764 the collection was dispersed. The diary was found later lying neglected in a garret. It was rescued, but found to be incomplete, the records of several years being lost. Mr. Joseph Hunter, who edited and published the diary in two volumes in 1830, believed that if the manuscripts were complete we should find that there was not a single day in Thoresby's life for which he had not accounted.

SIR WALTER CALVERLEY

A NOTEBOOK, which is just as much or just as little a diary as several quoted in these pages, was kept by Sir Walter Calverley, who resided at Esholt, in Yorkshire. He made irregular entries, beginning with notes concerning the earliest part of his life, " 15 Jan. 1669–70 I Walter Calverley was borne," down to 1718. Two early experiences give one hope that the diarist was a humorist :

8. Oct. 1671. I fell into a tube of water and had like to have been drowned.
10 or 20 June 1672. I fell into a panfull of milk and was taken out for dead.

But unfortunately no spark of humour or indeed personal opinion occurs again throughout the pages, which consist merely of a recital, often very elaborate, of business matters, deaths, accidents, visits, with an occasional reference to cock-fighting. Sir Walter was evidently a very active and influential man. He entertains largely and seems to have been lavish with his gifts of food, etc. It was the custom at funerals to present the mourners with " white scarffes and gloves." He must have made a large collection of these, judging by the number of funerals he attended. The expenses at a funeral were considerable. At his sister's funeral :

> The gentlemen at the funerall had gloves and scarfes which were above 60 and all the rest gloves which perhaps might be about 70 or 80 besides gentlemens' men etc. And there was £5 given out to be distributed to the poor . . . to have 3d a piece, but they finding them very numerous gave them but 2d a piece and in so doing distributed all that and 10s more. So that there were towards 700 poor persons that had deals.

In 1706 he marries Julia, daughter of Sir William Blackett, of Wallington. Sir Walter's account of his marriage is purely from the point of view of settlements and expenses.

In 1715, the year of the Jacobite rebellion, his father-in-law Sir William Blackett's loyalty was strongly suspected. Sir Walter gives an account of a visit he paid to Sir Walter Hawkesworth. Sir W. Blackett had also been invited, and although " his charriot and 6 and two saddle horses and servants " arrived he himself did not turn up. But " a messenger " appeared on the scene who searched the house, cross-questioned Calverley and was mystified at not finding Blackett there.

Later Sir Walter has a controversy with Sir William Lowther over this business, and Lowther " fell into a great fury " on the question of the payment of the police who were searching for Sir William's horses. " By his behaviour one would have taken him to be a mad man." Before he went away " he took a glass of wine and drunk *confusion to the Pretender and all his adherents.*"

For harbouring Sir William Blackett, however, Lord Burlington " thought fit to discharge me (Sir Walter) from acting as deputy-lieutenant." He was reappointed in 1730.

He gives in the diary an instance of his wife's industry :

> 27. Nov. 1716. My wife finished the sowed work in the drawing-room it

having been three years and a half in doing. The greatest part of it has been done with her own hands. It consists of ten pannells.

These beautiful panels of embroidery bearing this date decorate a bedroom at Wallington, where Sir George Trevelyan, Bart., now resides.

Except for the incident of the supposed Jacobite plot, there is nothing in the notebook which is of interest otherwise than from the family and local point of view.

DR. EDWARD LAKE

ALTHOUGH it only covers the few weeks between October, 1677, and April, 1678, the diary of Edward Lake is an interesting footnote to history and has a distinctly Pepysian tone in its record of royal gossip.

Lake was a scholar of Wadham College, Oxford, but took his degree at Cambridge. In 1676 he obtained the Archdeaconry of Exeter. At Court he held the position of chaplain and tutor to the Princesses Mary and Anne, daughters of the Duke of York (afterwards James II).

We will first quote from his entries with regard to the marriage of Mary with the Prince of Orange (afterwards William III):

Oct. 21. The Duke of York din'd at Whitehall : after dinner return'd to Saint James', took Lady Mary into her closet and told her of the marriage designed between her and the Prince of Orange ; whereupon her highness wept all that afternoon and the following day.

Nov. 4. At nine o'clock at night the marriage was solemnized in her highness's bedchamber. The King [Charles II] who gave her away was very pleasant all the while ; for he desir'd that the Bishop of London would make haste lest his sister bee delivered of a son and so the marriage be disappointed ; and when the prince endowed her with all his worldly goods, hee willed to put all up in her pockett, for 'twas clear gains. At eleven o'clock they went to bed, and his majesty came and drew the curtains and said to the prince " Now nephew to your worke ! Hey ! St. George for England ! "

Nov. 5. The prince by his favourite Lord Benthein [? Bentinck] presented her highnesse with jewells to the value of £40,000.

Nov. 9. I went to her highnesse to take leave of the princesse who designed for Holland with her husband the Friday after. I perceived her eyes full of tears, herself very disconsolate, not only for her sister's illness but also for some discontent occasioned by the prince's urging her to remove her lodgings to Whitehall which the princesse would by no means bee persuaded.

DR. EDWARD LAKE

After making a speech to her and asking her to recommend him to the King he adds :

In fine, I wish'd her all prosperity that God would bless her and show her favour in the sight of strange people among whom she went ; wherewith I kneeled down and kissed her gown. Her highnesse gave mee thanks for all my kindnesses and assured mee shee would do all shee could for mee but was able to say no more for weeping and so turned her back and went into her closet.

Nov. 16. The wind being easterly their highnesses were still detain'd at St. James's. This day the court began to whisper the prince's sullennesse or clownishnesse, that hee took no notice of his princesse at the playe and balle nor came to see her at St. James' the day preceding this design'd for their departure.

Nov. 19. This morning about 9 o'clock their highnesses accompany'd with his majesty and royal highness and took barges at Whitehall with several other persons of quality. The princess wept grievously all the morning requested the Duchesse of Monmouth to come often to her sister to accompany her to the chapple the first time shee was able to appear there and to think often on her ; she left two letters to be delivered to her sister as soon as she was recovered.

The Queen observing her highnesse to weep as shee took leave of her Majesty would have comforted her with the consideration of her own condition when shee came to England and had never till then seen the King ; to whom her highnesse presently replied " But madam you came into England ; but I am going out of England."

Jan. 9. I was very sorry to understand that the Princess of Orange since her being in Holland did sometimes play at cards upon Sunday which would doubtless give offence to that people. I remember that about two years since being with her highness in her closett, shee required my opinion of it. I told her I could not say 'twas a sin to do so, but 'twas not expedient and for fear of giving offence I advised her highness not to do it nor did shee play upon Sundays while she continued here in England.

Dr. Lake was disappointed at not being made chaplain to the Princess in Holland. Dr. Hooper was given the post,

whilst Dr. Doughty and myself who had been her highness's chaplains and tutors many years were for some (I know not what) reasons laid aside, which occasioned great discourses both in the court and in the city.

In the meanwhile his other pupil, the Princess Anne, was suffering from the smallpox :

Her highnesse the Lady Ann (whom God preserve) having been 5 days sick appeared to have the smallpox ; whereupon I was commanded not to go into her chamber and read prayers, because of my attendance on the princess and the other children which very much troubled me and the more because her nurse was a very busy, zealous Roman Catholick and would probably discompose her if shee had an opportunity.

> I returned to Lady Anne at 7 o'clock and found her as I left her; the pox were very small and not many.
>
> Lady Anne went forth of her chamber to see the duchesse in her lodgings, the servants all rejoicing to see her highnesse so perfectly recover'd. The Duke visited her everyday of her sicknesse and commanded that her sister's departure should be conceal'd from her; wherefore there was a feigned message sent every morning from the princesse to her highnesse to know how she did.

There are other entries showing the devotion of the two sisters to one another and the apparent tragedy of Mary's marriage with William.

Lake discourses at some length on ecclesiastical appointments, more especially Sancroft's elevation to the Archbishopric of Canterbury. He also gives a little parliamentary news and some anecdotes about Charles I, one of which may be quoted:

> I waited on the Bishop of St. David's with whom I found the Bishop of Exeter who discoursing of and lamenting the debaucherys of the nation and particularly of the court, imputed them much to the untimely death of the old King who was always very severe in the education of his present majesty: in so much that at St. Mary's in Oxford hee did once hitt him on the head with his staffe when he did observe him to laugh (at sermon time) upon the ladys who sate against him.

The only domestic event he records is his wife's miscarriage.

The latter part of the diary is occupied with accounts of journeys in his archdeaconry.

Few as the pages of the diary are, we get a picture of a shrewd, observant man who was evidently ambitious to penetrate into the higher circles of government.

The diary was published in the first volume of the Camden Miscellanies.

ABRAHAM DE LA PRYME

IT is a pity that Abraham de la Pryme did not keep a regular diary, because he was evidently very observant and his style is picturesque. But *Ephemeris Vitae, or a Diary of my Own Life; containing an account, likewise, of the most observable and remarkable things I have taken notice of from my youth up hitherto*, written in two folio volumes, contains very little personal diary matter, and consists chiefly of records of public affairs, a great number of anecdotes, and detailed notes on archæological and topographical subjects which he studied as an antiquary.

ABRAHAM DE LA PRYME

De la Pryme was born "to all the miseries of life," he tells us, in 1671. He says in this diary, which he began writing when he was about 12 years old, "My father can speak Dutch and my mother French but I nothing but English." He was educated at St. John's College, Cambridge, and while there he relates the story of the burning of a valuable manuscript of

> one Mr. Newton (whom I have very oft seen) fellow of Trinity College, that is mighty famous for his learning being a most excellent mathematician philosopher, divine etc.

This was the famous Sir Isaac Newton. We get another reference to him in 1694, when Abraham de la Pryme gives a long account of the excitement caused by a haunted house which was supposed to contain a "devilish disturber."

> On Monday night likewise there being a great number of people at the door there chanced to come by Mr. Newton fellow of Trinity College; a very learned man and perceiving our fellows to have gone in and seeing several scholars about the door "Oh ! yee fools" says he, "will you never have any witt, know yee not that all such things are meer cheats and impostures ? Fy, fy ! go home for shame " so he left them scorning to go in.

De la Pryme in his youth was attracted by the occult.

> I and my companions yester night try'd again what we could do but nothing would appear *quamvis omnia sacra rite peracta fuerunt ; iterum iterumque adjuravimus*.

But he is dissuaded from such practices :

> He (Mr. Bohun) persuaded me exceedingly to desist from all magical studdys and lays a company of most black sins to my charge which he sayd I committed by darring to search in such forbidden things.

He wrote a history of Hatfield, in Yorkshire. In 1698 he was appointed curate in Hull, where again he compiled a local history. But such was the labour attending his studies that he confesses in the diary " that he began to grow somewhat weary thereof."

In 1701 he was given the living of Thorne, and was elected a Fellow of the Royal Society. He died in 1704. Some of his anecdotes are amusing and told at great length, and he makes natural history notes and records of weather phenomena. The volumes also contain copies of his letter to Sir Hans Sloane and others on antiquarian and scientific subjects. The entries are irregular and sometimes undated and he does not deal with any domestic events. An instance may be given of the forcible manner in which he expressed his opinion when referring to more public topics.

Of the House of Commons in 1697 he writes:

> The House of Commons are commonly a company of irreligious wretches who cares not what they do nor what becomes of the Church and religious things if they can but get their hawkes, hounds aud whores and the sacred possessions of the Church. It is plainly visible that the nation would be happier if there was no House of Commons but only a House of Lords. . . .

The diary, together with a memoir of the family, was published by the Surtees Society in 1870.

TIMOTHY BURRELL

THE small account book or diary of Timothy Burrell, covering the years 1686 to 1717, is noteworthy because of the little drawings with which he illustrates some of the entries. Burrell was born in 1643. He was educated at Trinity College, Cambridge, and was called to the Bar. He retired from practice and lived at Ockenden, in Sussex, where he died in 1717.

Although for the most part the diary consists mainly of a record of payments for provisions, wages, charities, funeral charges, and taxes, his personality peeps out here and there in comments and in the tags of Latin and Greek from Virgil, Seneca, Homer, etc., which he inserts from time to time. But the little pictures, which are well drawn, are more especially characteristic and amusing. For instance, if he buys " a charriott " he draws a picture of it with the four wheels very far from the body; if he pays wages for mowing and haymaking he draws a rake and a hayfork; when he buys hops he draws a sack; when he purchases hats " for my fellows' liveries " he depicts two little high-crowned, broad-brimmed hats with large feathers; there is a drawing, too, of the " pales by the orchard pond " for which he paid a man 10d. per rod, " which was a little too much for he worked two days but gently," the repair of his fowling-piece or his wheelbarrow is illustrated, also the church to which he gave money for certain repairs; when he pays May Slater her wages he gives a little sketch of her, when his daughter begins to dance he draws a guitar, and when he gives her " scarlet stockings " and " pink scarlet stockings " a small stockinged leg appears next the entry; coats, horses, carts, brooms, cows, mugs, fish, bees, also appear frequently; the window-tax is represented by a small window; the fattening of hogs is always illustrated, in fact a fortnight before he died at the age of 75 there is still a rough attempt to draw a hog. The pictures perhaps helped him to turn up particular entries easily. On one occasion his illustration seems to convey more meaning than can be gathered from the text.

Sep. 14. Goldsmith departed my service by consent this day on Oct. 24, he repented and returned half starved.

This is illustrated on one side by a long churchwarden pipe walking away on two little legs, and the other side two pipes joined together. Perhaps Goldsmith returned with a wife. On the front page of the diary he gives a sketch of his house with the fields round it.

The accounts themselves are of no special interest. But sometimes the entry contains a comment, as, for instance:

Paid John Coachman for a whip to spoil my horses 1/6d.

Ap. 7. bought a cheese weighing 18 lbs for $2\frac{3}{4}$d the lb. It was all eaten in the kitchen by the 18th.

His daughter's birth is recorded by a Latin verse, a line from Lucian in Greek and the picture of a tree. He loses his wife on the same day, but we only get the record of the funeral.

Burrell was evidently very well off and was generous in his charities, giving on one occasion a good deal to the poor " as long as the dearth of provisions continues." One of the features of the diary is the enormous list every year of the presents he received at Christmas, amounting in 1711 to seventy, but falling off very much towards the end. All his neighbours, rich and poor, seem to have presented him with something. The gifts include geese, lobsters, oranges, venison, claret, oysters, capons, woodcock, pigs, butter, " a bottle of usquebagh," and in 1700, for the first time, tea. On one occasion a map is given and " a silver tepot and porridge spoon " for his daughter.

After 1700 the entries are frequently in Latin and become more personal. The translation of one or two may be given:

Sep. 1702. My sister was impertinent to me, but I kept my temper pretty well.

My sister quarrelled with me and was insolent to me and I was somewhat, not to say too much, irritated with her; the consequence was that for two days my stomach was at intervals seriously affected. I took Tipping's mixture and doses of hiera picra.

> I was rather too impatient with my servant for having put too much salt in my broth.

And medical details with regard to his health became more frequent (also in Latin):

> Yesterday having wetted my feet by walking out in the dew and having eaten a small piece of new cheese, I have been to-day tortured with flatulent spasms. By taking two doses of hiera picra the pains in my stomach abated. Thanks to the great God for this his mercy towards me.

In 1710 there is a very carefully drawn hand pointing to certain dates on which he took special medicines.

Every Christmas he entertains largely, gives a list of his guest and a bill of fare. Thirty or more of his friends often sat down to this repast.

The immensely long bills of fare show heavy meals in which "plumm pottage" figures very prominently.

In his old age we can notice a general decline of good cheer and happiness. His last Christmas dinner is in 1713. He only receives seven presents in 1715, and in July of that year he writes:

> I gave over housekeeping and my son in law Trevor began to keep house the day and year above written.

After this there are very few entries. The son-in-law's housekeeping does not seem to have been a happy arrangement, and Burrell loses his daughter.

In spite of the brevity and baldness of the entries in this diary we get the outline sketch of a very pleasant, generous, hospitable, and cultivated old gentleman.

The manuscript, in the possession of a member of the family, was edited by R. W. Blencowe and reproduced in the Sussex Archæological Collections in 1850.

BISHOP CARTWRIGHT

THOMAS CARTWRIGHT was born in 1634, in Northampton. His parents were Presbyterians, and he was sent to Oxford for his education. After holding various livings he came into high court favour after the Restoration, was made Dean of Ripon in 1675, and in 1686 he was given the see of Chester, keeping at the same time the vicarage of Barking and the rectory of Wigan, in Lancashire. Desiring translation to a better bishopric he kept in close touch with James II, who made him an Ecclesiastical Commissioner and appointed him one of the three delegates to go to Oxford and determine the affairs of Magdalen College, where a scandal had arisen owing to the refusal of the Fellows to accept a President nominated by the King. Cartwright was a good preacher, but his devotion to James and his favour to Roman Catholics brought him into disrepute.

On the arrival of William III Cartwright fled to France, where he remained with James. He followed his master to Ireland, and died in Dublin in 1689.

His diary for the years 1686-7, written carelessly but regularly in a small octavo volume bound in black leather, was discovered early in the nineteenth century in a bookseller's shop in Northampton.

Unfortunately the diary is little more than a memorandum book giving lists of the people who dined with him and to whom he wrote letters, lists of the clergy he ordained, and records of services and confirmations. His opinions and ambitions emerge here and there even in these few pages. We see how closely he was in attendance on the King by his very frequent presence at the King's levee (not the function of to-day, but the early morning conference with the sovereign, which took place on one occasion as early as six o'clock).

> I was at the King's levee and kissed hands and had leave to return into the North with a gracious promise that he would never forget me nor my services and that I should find his favour in all places and upon all occasions.

> (The King) declared that such men as myself who had always stuck to him, should never want his favour; and that he would take an effectual course to make others weary of their obstinacy. And I advised him to begin with his own household which he promised to do.

> Kissed the Queen's hand in her bed chamber where she told me she nor the King would never forget my service to them before they were so nor should I ever want a friend so long as she lived.

> I was at the King's levee who went a hunting.

> I was at His Majesty's levee from whence I attended him into the choir where he healed 350 persons.

> I was at his Majesty's levee. . . . After that he had mass in the presence chamber where he eat. From thence I attended him into the choir where he healed 450 people.

We find one occasion on which he gives actual assistance to Roman Catholics.

> I sent for Captain Fielding the Recorder and others, to find out a convenient place by his Majesty's command in the castle or elsewhere for the Roman Catholic devotions.

He has Roman Catholic priests to dine with him as well as prominent Catholic gentry.

To us to-day the Bishop seems in this connection only to have been broad-minded, but bearing in mind the acute political nature of these religious differences in James II's reign, we can see that he was open to grave suspicions.

The diary covers the period of Cartwright's induction and enthronement at Chester, and the ceremonies are fully described. On his way to Chester he is entertained at Bolton by the Marquess of Winchester.

> I was received by the noble Marquess with all kindness imaginable at dinners from one at noon till one in the morning.

It appears that a twelve hours' dinner was a common occurrence at Bolton in these days. This mode of living is said to have been affected by Lord Winchester in order that he might be thought unfit for public affairs at a time when things were going in a manner of which he did not approve.

The Bishop has a serious dispute with the cathedral precentor.

> I admonished Mr. Ottway the precentor of his neglecting services and anthems and his teaching of the quire; and he refused to amend and be the packhorse as he called it to the quire and choristers. I told him I should take care to provide a better in his room and one that would attend God's service better and pay more respect to his superiors in behaving himself very insolently towards the subdean at that very time.

We do not learn if Mr. Ottway mended his ways. Some of the Bishop's congregation also come in for his admonitions.

> I preached in the Cathedral at Chester being the first Sunday in Lent to the greatest congregation that ever I saw a sermon of Repentance. God give a blessing to it. . . . I rebuked as they deserved Mrs. Brown, Mrs. Crutchley, Mrs Eaton and her sister for talking and laughing in the Church; and they accused Mr. Hudleston for being as guilty as themselves.

The last week of the record is taken up with a very full note of the proceedings at Magdalen College, where Dr. Hough had been installed as President by the Fellows.

The entries in the diary are very regular almost daily, and many of them are just memoranda of trivial events.

Among the many people with whom he becomes acquainted is Pepys. He notes that the Bishop of Oxford " promised to bring me acquainted with Mr. Peepes," and a few days later he had a conversation with him. But we get no comment or description.

Very little can be gathered about his family. He mentions his wife, one son who was a clergyman, and another whom he refers to as " my ungracious son Richard," who was studying medicine.

The brief diary, which in all probability is only a fragment of a larger journal, was first printed from the original MS. by the Camden Society in 1843.

JOHN MORE

ALL we know of John More is that he was born in 1654, and after going to Oxford took Deacon's orders in 1678, was ordained as Priest in 1679, and became Rector of Earls Croom.

In 1699 he went over to the Baptists and was formally baptised by Elizen Hathway. The extracts from his diary cover the period from 1694 to 1696 and 1697-8 to 1700, and tell us something of his rupture with the Church. He appears to have been a man of a somewhat *exalté* disposition, not to say eccentric. We can trace by a few entries, not always very explicit, his desertion from the Church.

> My aunt expostulated briskly with me about communion with dissenters and the rumour of my going off to them.

> I had not lain long awake when I heard one knock at the door I found Phil Battard of Aston. He told me he came to have me along to the Bishop as from the Lord he hoped. I rose and he told me he was for preaching all and giving to the poor and following Christ and going to Jerusalem. I suspected him discomposed. He said the old cap wing in my dream was the Bishop that their parson was dead and miserably rotten he was a great drinker—seemed disorderly even to phrenzy.

He records later that his " service " is laid aside.

> I rested from my ordinary labours by order of the Bishop after I had just finished a little thing on the Sabbath [this was printed].

> This day I am denied admittance at Norton Church.

> This morning it came into my thoughts to be baptised at Pirton Pool where I had misspent my time and lived not so purely as becomes a Christian and a Minister of the Gospel.

This evening I heard they had a design of putting me out of the Parsonage house for preaching in a private house.

Finally he is baptised, and while in Gloucester he sees " the heavens opened extremely."

He is of a poetic nature, as we see from the following entries :

Mem : to write a poem to Mr. Dryden to excite him to Pious Poetry instead of lewd amorous things.

A merry swallow singing after sunset when they could scarce be seen on the pool before my door, the wind being high and cold.

This evening I heard the nightingale after I had been praying at John Westbury's.

Composed above 6 score verses in all to-day on the presumed reasons of the change of season.

After some meditation of the Lords withdrawing me from all Society for a nearer union and communion with Himself I took my violin and being refreshed with the harmony . . . in singing psalms these words came into my mind.

> Lord what a harmony's in strings
> and none in living human things
> Look on the jarring world once more
> Bring all in order as before
> Man's sins untuned the whole creation
> O send another Reformation.

More was unconventional and had a sublime disregard for public opinion.

I went through Worcester with a handkerchief on my head and also through the country resolving never to wear a wig more that I might not make my brother to offend.

He takes to wearing a white cap.

A neighbour objecting against my white cap I said the mountains and hills wear white caps, I am in the mode.

On the subject of his health he says on one occasion :

I had stomach pains as usual before illuminations.

The journal is only a fragment, but it gives us a glimpse of an odd man. The manuscript transcript of the original is in the British Museum.

CELIA FIENNES

IN the preface to her diary Celia Fiennes, in expectation that it may fall into the hands of her relations, states the motive which led her to make careful notes of all that she saw on her many journeys on horseback about the country in the reigns of

William and Mary and Anne. She recommends travel in England so that people may get a better idea of their own country, which will "cure the evil itch of overvaluing foreign parts." She does not write for publication, and is very modest with regard to her literary capacity. She says:

> As most I converse with knows both the freedom and Easyness I speak and write as well as my defect in all, so they will not expect exactness or politeness in this book, tho' such Embellishments might have adorned the descriptions and suited the nicer taste.

The diary is peculiar; it is not divided up into days with dates. In fact, no date is mentioned in it except the years 1695 and 1697. But the notes she makes are quite obviously written on the day and on the spot, except perhaps the descriptions of London and the Lord Mayor's Show.

All we know of Celia Fiennes is that she was a daughter of Colonel Nathaniel Fiennes, a Parliamentarian officer, and a sister of the 3rd Viscount Saye and Sele. We can tell by the diary that she was an indefatigable traveller, a very observant woman and quite an exceptional product of her times. The diary is a sort of guide-book. She gives in minute detail descriptions of towns, palaces, country houses and gardens, as well as the industries of the places she passes through. Here and there, however, we can gather something of her opinions, more especially on the subject of religion. She makes several disparaging remarks about Papists, and Quakers do not meet with her approval.

> Where 4 men and 2 women spoke one, after another had done, but it seem'd such a Confusion and so incoherent that it very much moved my compassion and pitty to see their delusion and Ignorance and no less Excited my thankfulness for the Grace of God that upheld others from such Errors.

The sight of a lighthouse on a rock near Plymouth calls forth the following remarks:

> From this you have a Good reflection on ye great Care and provision ye wise God makes for all persons and things in his Creation, that there should be in some places where there is any difficulty rocks Even in the midst of ye deep which can be made use of for a Constant Guide and mark for the passengers on their voyages, but the Earth is full of ye goodness of ye Lord and so is this Great Sea wherein are innumerable beings created and preserved by the same almighty hand whose is the Earth and all things there in he is Lord of all.

At Truro she has a conversation with "an ordinary plain woman," and she is "edified by her conversation and ye pitch of soul resignation to ye will of God." But these interludes on religion are rare. She of course notes the weather, the distances covered and the state of the roads, which are sometimes very heavy.

From hence to Leister which they Call but 13 miles but ye longest 13 I ever went and ye most tiresome being full of sloughs y^t I was near 11 hours going but 25 mile—a footman Could have gone much faster than I could Ride.

The stones were so slippery Crossing the channels that my horse was quite down on his nose but did at length recover himself and so I was not thrown off or injured which I desire to bless God for as for the many preservations I mett with.

Before I Came to Alsford forceing my horse out of the hollow way his feete failed and he Could noe wayes recover himself and soe I was shott off his neck upon the Bank but noe harm I bless God and as soone as he Could role himself up stood stock still by me which I Looked on as a Great mercy—indeed mercy and truth all wayes have attended me.

In one summer she covers a distance of 1551 miles. She was not always alone. On one occasion she mentions " my sister, self and maid," on another her mother, and on returning to London after an expedition of 635 miles she talks of " all our Company."

But the value of Celia Fiennes' diary rests in the picture it gives of country houses, gardens, and the towns, fashionable watering-places, and villages of England at the end of the seventeenth century, for there is very little literature of this decription belonging to that period. Her language is by no means florid. Indeed, her vocabulary is somewhat limited. An expression of praise she uses over and over again in connection with cathedrals, houses, gardens, etc., is that they are " neat." But in a simple way she gives quite effectively little pictures of what she sees, and uses many quaint but happy expressions, as, for instance, when she says of the spire of Salisbury Cathedral :

it appears to us below as sharpe as a Dagger, Yet in the compass on the top as bigg as a cart wheele.

One or two of her descriptions may be quoted :

I went on the side of a high hill below which the river Trent rann and turned its silver stream forward and backward into S.S. which looked very pleasant Circling about ye fine meadows in their flourishing tyme bedecked with hay almost Ripe and flowers.

The Duke of Bedford's garden.

In the square just by the dineing roome window all sorts of pots of flowers and Curious greens, fine orange, Cittron and Lemon trees and mirtles, striped ffilleroy and ye fine aloes plant. On the side of this you pass under an arch into a Cherry garden in the midst of which stands a figure of stone resembling an old weeder woman used in the garden and my Lord would have her Effigie which is done so like and her Clothes so well that at first I took it to be a Real Living body.

Lord Chesterfield's house.

Ye house has a visto quite thro' by a glass bellcony door into ye gardens and so to ye park beyond on that side. Ye front have something surprising in it ; its all of free stone which is dipt in oyle that adds a varnish to its Lustre as well as security to its foundations. Ye Roofe is not flatt as our Modern buildings yet garrit windows Come out on ye tileing which is all flatt. None of ye windows are sashes which in my opinion is ye only thing it wants to render it a Compleate building.

When she visits watering-places she bathes or samples the waters. At Harrogate, " setting aside ye papist ffancyes of it," she finds the waters after she had bathed in them " Eased a great pain I used to have in my head," and at Buxton she drinks " part of a cupfull " of the waters, " the taste is not unpleasant but Rather like Milk, they say it is Diaretick."

Cathedrals are described at great length ; most of them are " neat," but Winchester is " to be admired for its Largeness not its neatness or Curiosity." She notes everything as she passes along—local customs, local industries, prices, architecture, antiquities. Sometimes she stays with friends or relations, but often she has to put up in " sorry inns." Here is one of her experiences :

Ye Loft as they called it which was over the other roomes was sheltered but with a hurdle ; here I was fforced to take up my abode and ye Landlady brought me out her best sheetes which served to secure my own sheetes from her dirty blankets and Indeed I had her fine sheete to spread over ye top of the Clothes ; but noe sleepe Could I get they burning twiff and their Chimneys are sort of fflews or open tunnills y^t ye smoake does annoy the roomes.

Meals are often mentioned :

We Eate very good Codfish and Salmon and at a pretty Cheape rate.

This [Derby] is a dear place for Strangers notwithstanding ye plentyfullness of all provisions. My Dinner cost me 5s and 8d only two servant men with me and I had but a shoulder of mutton and bread and beer.

[In Devonshire.] They scald their creame and milk in most parts of those Countrys and so its a sort of Clouted Creame as we Call it with a Little sugar and so put on ye top of ye apple Pye. I was much pleased with my supper though not with the Custome of the Country which is a universall smoking both men women and children have all their pipes of tobacco in their mouths and soe sit round the fire smoking which was not delightfull to me when I went down to talke with my Landlady for information of any matter and Customs amongst them.

To conclude, we will take a typical entry of a day's journey:

Thence I went to Nantwich 5 long miles. Nantwich is a pretty large town and well built ; here are ye salt springs of which they make salt and many salterns which were a boyling ye salt. This is a pretty Rich land ; you must travel on a Causey ; I went 3 miles on a Causey through much wood. Its from Nantwich to Chester town 14 long miles ye wayes being deep ; its much on Enclosures and I passed by severall large pooles of waters, but what I wondered at was y^t tho' this shire is remarkable for a greate deale of greate Cheeses and Dairys I did not see more than 20 or 30 Cowes in a troope feeding, but on Enquiry find ye Custome of ye Country to joyn their milking together of a whole village and so make their great Cheeses.

Celia Fiennes complains in her preface that members of Parliament are often " ignorant of anything but the name of the place for which they serve in Parliament," and she recommends specially her own sex to study " those things which tends to Improve the mind and makes our Lives pleasant and comfortable."

The diary, under the name of *Through England on a Side Saddle in the Time of William and Mary*, was not published till 1888.

RUGGE AND LUTTRELL

ALTHOUGH referred to as diaries, the records of Rugge and Luttrell can better be described as annals. They are collections of extracts taken largely from contemporary news sheets and concern only the public events of the day.

Thomas Rugge (son of a canon of Westminster) covers the period from 1659 to 1672, devoting the greater part of his record to the events of 1661–1662. He calls it " Mercurius Politicus Redivivus." The manuscript is in the British Museum. It has been useful to historians, but it has never been printed.

Narcissus Luttrell, who was educated at St. John's College, Cambridge, was a collector of manuscripts and books. He lived in Chelsea. His record is called :

A Brief Historicall Relation of State affairs from Sep. 1678 to April 1714.

In giving excerpts from contemporary newspapers he often confuses the date of the issue of newspaper with the date of the events related. These annals have been printed. Luttrell, however, also kept a private diary. It is neatly written in English, but in Greek characters in a small notebook. The entries are brief and very irregular. He writes for a fortnight, then there are several blank pages, then again he writes for a few days.

sometimes only two or three days, sometimes for more than a week. But there are far more blank pages than written pages in the book, which was begun in November, 1722, the last entry being made in 1724. The diary is only concerned with the very brief recital of quite ordinary events. Only one sample entry need be given:

Nov. 5. Rose this morning at 8-30 to prayers in Chamber then down and into garden dressed after and breakfasted about 10 and being gunpowder treason day I would have gone to Church but the rain hindered me so did odd things at home, and in the evening I went not out to dinner after 2 and dined after 3 so unto the garden and had a tree dug up did business all the evening in the parlor went about 9 up into Chamber after 12 so to prayers and to bed at 2.

Each entry begins "Rose this morning," and the expression "did odd things" is very frequent.

I did odd things till 6 and drunk green tea after with son I eat no butter so did odd matters all the evening.

The curious thing is that, although the pages are not divided up for days, he seems to leave just the amount of space sufficient for the long periods in which he neglected to write. Though meagre and quite without interest, it is a curious production, as one does not quite see why he wrote at all, why if he repeatedly failed to write regularly he kept on beginning again, and why Greek characters should have been used for such very trivial notes.

The following diaries in this century may also be briefly noted:

WILLIAM AYSHCOMBE

The notebook in which William Ayshcombe made a few entries between 1608 and 1633 could be regarded merely as memoranda of miscellaneous incidents connected with other people, were it not for the first two entries, which are of a peculiarly personal character. These entries may be quoted in full:

1608. I was much importuned to marry my Lady Garrarde's daughter of Dorney by Windsor Mrs. Martha Garrard, a fine gentlewomen truly. I sawe her and no more.

1609. I was importuned to see a brave spirited gentlewomen named Mrs. Kate Howarde beinge one of the two daughters and heyres of the Viscount Binden's brother. I saw her not far from Bath was earnestly sollicited to proceede; being halfe afraid of the greatness of her spirit, I did not. Shee was since more worthily bestowed and she was most worthy so to be.

The notebook, which was discovered at Brymore, where John Pym lived at one time, is included in the tenth Report of the Historical Manuscripts Commission.

The Rev. T. Dugard

This diary is only remarkable on account of its form and appearance. The book measures about 4 by 2½ inches. The writing is so small that a page contains an average of sixty-eight lines, sometimes over seventy. It is illegible without a magnifying glass, nevertheless the handwriting is exquisitely neat. The whole diary, which covers a period of eleven years from 1632 to 1643, is written in abbreviated Latin. The entries are practically daily and only amount to two or three lines, births, deaths, letters written, books read, and subjects taught are noted. "*Institui discip*" : with a Bible reference. "*Scripsi ad Patrem*" or some one else. "*Legi*" with the name of the book. The heading at the beginning is in cypher, and spare sheets are occupied by long lists of births, deaths, preachers, bailiffs, those present at Assizes and his correspondents. The minuteness and neatness is kept up to the last page. This alone, apart from the matter, suggests peculiar characteristics in the author.

The MS. is in the British Museum, Add. MS. 23146.

John Manners, Earl of Rutland

This is a brief diary kept by the Earl of Rutland while he was in attendance on Charles I in 1639 between March 30 and the pacification of Berwick. Its title, "a journall of private observacions for my-selfe," raises a hope that it may contain some indiscretions or dis-closures. Unfortunately it is a purely official account of the King's movements, councils, advances of troops and journeys to York, Durham, Newcastle, etc. Manners was a moderate Parliamentarian, and indulges in no particular expressions of admiration for the King. He gives an account of a Council at York at which Lord Say and Lord Brooke hesitated to take the new oath of allegiance and he notes one conversation with the King.

The document is only a little bit of history from a contemporary witness ; it is included in the Historical Manuscripts Commission's volumes.

Jacob Bee

The diary of Jacob Bee, who was a tradesman of Durham, extends from September 5, 1681, to February 27, 1706. With the exception of the description of a murder, no entry exceeds four or five lines. The great majority of days contain bare one-line records of deaths, marriages, accidents, weather phenomena, and election results. One or two of the rather fuller entries may be given :

1683. Sep. 18. Seven bouchers should have played at football with seven glovers, being Tuesday, this year above, and my man Christopher went without leave to play.

1684. 4. Nov. A foot race was runn betwixt Fairebearnes a butcher and a countrey man called John Upton and runn upon Eliott-moore, the hardest run that ever any did see. The countrey man were upon hard termes being runn so nerely that scarce any could judge, when they had but one hundred yards to runn whether should have it.

1684/5. Jan. 17. John Borrow departed this life and 'twas reported that he see a coach drawn by six swine, all black, and a black man satt upon the cotch box. He fell sick upon't and dyed and of his death severall apparations appeared after.

This diary is unfortunately too scrappy for any deductions to be made from it. It is included in the Surtees Society's collections.

RICHARD STAPLEY

The diary of Richard Stapley, of Hickstead Place, in Sussex, is little more than the account book kept between 1682 and 1710. He not only notes the witnesses of his money transactions, but also where they took place, whether at the horseblock or in the open fields, in the kitchen, hall or parlour, and even at which table the payment was made.

Paid Mr. Steward for Dr. Comber's paraphrase on ye Common Prayer 20s and 6d for carriage. I paid it at ye end of ye kitchen table next ye chamber stairs door and nobody in ye room but he and I. No it was ye end of ye table next ye parlour.

Paid Dec. 29 to Mr. John Whitpaine for writing a copy of an exemplification of my father's will the sum of 20s at John Ffields house, called the Royal Oak in Hurst town. There was in ye room called ye Beard's-end room alias ye Hall in ye which I paid him Thomas Ffloud etc etc.

Besides purchases, taxes, loans and presents he notes the weather and details with regard to the harvest. The only incident described is the catching and eating of an enormous trout which supplied supper for six people.

The Sussex Archæological Society published the diary in 1849.

JOHN BUFTON

In the last decade of the seventeenth century John Bufton, of Coggeshall, in Essex, made entries on two old almanacks of matters of local interest such as burials, funeral accounts, church repairs, the installation of bells, the setting up of a ducking stool in the church pond, the earthquake in 1692, and a brief mention of public events. The following entries with regard to a witch are the only ones of any special interest :

July 13. 1699. The widow Comon was put into the river to see if she would sink because she was suspected to be a witch and she did not sink but swim.

July 19. She was tryed again and then she swam again and did not sink.

July 24. The widow Comon was tryed a third time by putting her into the river and she swam and did not sink.

Dec. 27. The widow Comon that was counted a witch was buried.

Witches were condemned to death and burned at a much later date than this.

There is nothing personal in Bufton's records. They are quoted fully in the Essex Archæological Society's *Transactions*, vol. 1.

EIGHTEENTH CENTURY

JOHN WESLEY

THERE is no printed English diary which in point of view of length and regularity can surpass the diaries and journals kept by John Wesley. He lived till he was 88 (1703–1791), and he kept a diary for practically 66 years (1725–1791). The daily, sometimes hourly, memoranda are called his diaries; the enlarged, fuller and more than once transcribed versions his Journal. The diaries began when he was at Oxford; only extracts from these earlier ones are available, and many volumes, specially in the later years, are lost. The printed and published Journal began in 1735, and is complete up to 24 October, 1790; the last volume of the diaries goes on up to 24 February, 1791, with daily memoranda. He died on March 2. The standard edition of the Journal extends to eight large volumes. As the personal record of a life it is, therefore, the most voluminous that has been published. As a diary, although kept with scrupulous regularity and recording as it does all his public activities and many of his thoughts, it certainly cannot be ranked among the best. Nevertheless, Wesley did not write for publication, nor did he write because he thought his career of importance. He began long before he had any notion of the great stir he was going to make. He wrote, we are told, " for the clearing of his own mind that he might see his life in black and white and so be in a position to judge accurately as to his own motives, attainments, doings, and failures."[1] He also rewrote sections of the Journal for his mother, other members of his family and friends. It is " the most amazing record of human exertion ever penned or endured,"[2] as Mr. Birrell says, and he goes on to picture the exhausting and almost unbearable strain on a political candidate of the three weeks of a contested

---

[1] Standard Edition of *Wesley's Journal*, Vol. 1.
[2] Appreciation in Abridged Edition.

JOHN WESLEY

election, concluding : " Well, John Wesley contested the three kingdoms in the cause of Christ during a campaign which lasted forty years." And indeed that is what strikes one most in trying to read through the thousands of pages—not the moral excellence of the austere religious organizer, but the astounding physical strength and nervous energy of the man. From such an abnormal giant we must expect a certain insensitiveness. Just as one who enjoys perfect health finds it difficult to sympathise with the ailments of others who are not so fortunate, so also he whose armour of self-confident righteousness is complete is apt to be intolerant of the failures of his ill-equipped fellows. Wesley was practically always well in health, and if he was sympathetic to sinners it was because they afforded him an opportunity to save them. Wesley kept his resolutions, and one of them was never to laugh, " no, not for a moment."

The pedestal is too high, we cannot reach him, and it is extraordinarily tiring even to attempt to follow him in his interminable journeys and his unending sermons. It is not because we are disappointed at not finding the frivolous, it is because we fail to find the human, that the Journal does not appeal to us as perhaps it ought. Nevertheless, as a record of the great religious revival, a testimony of marvellously sustained enthusiasm and a chronicle of travel in the United Kingdom in the eighteenth century, the Journal is undoubtedly a most remarkable document.

The earliest diaries were not easy to decipher. The entries are generally brief, but Wesley employed either shorthand or cipher or abbreviated longhand. At the very beginning he sets down :

A general Rule in all actions of Life

Whenever you are to do an action, consider how God did or would do the like and do you immitate His example.

Then follow " General Rules of Employing Time " and " General Rules as to Intention." Regulation was the keynote of his life and of his religious system. In these early years there are a good many brief notes of self-reproach, resolutions for self-discipline and private spiritual exercises. After his ordination in 1725 he begins preaching, but we only get just the bare note of the place and date.

The published Journal begins with his voyage to Georgia in 1835, which lasted a little over two years and ended in a serious dispute. But we cannot follow Wesley chronologically through his long life, which, with the exception of a few months in 1738 in Germany visiting the Moravians and a tour in Holland in 1783, was spent within the United Kingdom. It will be best to give illustrative extracts from the vast record of certain aspects of his character and of incidents in his career.

When the earlier years have passed, the note of self-condemnation disappears and the tone becomes increasingly self-confident.

In 1738 he lays down four resolutions, and such was the unflinching determination and austerity of his character that there is every reason to believe that he carried them out so far as mortal man could:

1. To use absolute openness and unreserve with all I should converse with.
2. To labour after continual seriousness, not willingly indulging in any the least levity of behaviour, or in laughter; no, not for a moment.
3. To spare no word which does not tend to the glory of God; in particular not to talk of worldly things. Others may, nay, must. But what is that to thee? and
4. To take no pleasure which does not tend to the glory of God; thanking God every moment for all I do take and therefore rejecting every sort and degree of it which I feel I cannot so thank Him in and for.

In the same year later on he makes an important confession of faith, and describes a sort of awakening which took place while he was listening to a sermon.

I felt my heart strangely warmed. I felt I did trust in Christ, Christ alone, for salvation; and an assurance was given me that He had taken away my sins, even mine, and saved me from the law of sin and death. I began to pray with all my might for those who had in a more especial manner despitefully used me and persecuted me.

The self-confidence which perhaps finds its origin here, and which grew in Wesley as he continued his work, was not just ordinary human conceit, but a profound conviction which acted as a burning inspiration and potent incentive in all his activities.

The secret of his immense physical strength he attributes—apart from the grand cause, " the good pleasure of God who doeth whatsoever pleaseth him "—to:

(1) My constantly rising at four for about fifty years.
(2) My generally preaching at five in the morning; one of the most healthy exercises in the world.
(3) My never travelling less, by sea or land, than four thousand five hundred miles in a year.

At the age of 77 he says he had not felt lowness of spirits for one quarter of an hour since he was born. At 80 he fell down a flight of stone stairs.

My head rebounded once or twice from the edge of the stone stairs. But it felt to me exactly as if I had fallen on a cushion or pillow.

At 83 he declares he is never tired either with writing, preaching or travelling, and at 85 that he has never lost a night's sleep since he was born. There are times when he has a sore throat, a cough or a headache, but almost invariably he dismisses it and goes on with his work in spite of it, attributing its disappearance to the intervention of Providence. Even when a cloud shields him from the rays of a hot sun while he is preaching he reads in the coincidence a special sign of God's favour. Not till he is in his eighty-seventh year does he admit the waning of his physical powers. Then he writes:

I am now an old man decayed from head to foot. My eyes are dim; my right hand shakes much; my mouth is hot and dry every morning; I have a lingering fever almost every day; my motion is weak and slow. However, blessed be God, I do not slack my labour; I can preach and write still.

On one occasion only, in 1753, is he alarmed about his health. He has fever, and when he goes home after preaching he sits down and writes his own epitaph, " to prevent vile panegyric." He describes himself as " a brand plucked from the burning... not having after his debts are paid ten pounds behind him."

The Journal is mainly composed of Wesley's preaching record. Journey after journey to all parts of the United Kingdom occupy week after week, month after month: " I look upon the world as my parish," he said; and as he rode from place to place he read his book on horseback. When he was 67 he said that although he had ridden over a hundred thousand miles, covering sometimes 90 miles in one day, no horse had ever stumbled with him while he rode with a slack rein. He preached sometimes every day of the week, sometimes two or three times in the day. He preached in churches when he was allowed to; he preached in halls, in theatres, in rooms, but best of all he loved preaching in the open air in fields, in churchyards, and even in the streets. It was Whitefield who converted him to this practice. In the earlier years he sometimes encountered bitter and violent opposition, and not infrequently he ran considerable danger. But neither opposition, fatigue, nor weather ever deterred him. We will give a series of typical extracts:

1738. I preached at six at St. Lawrence's; at ten in St. Catherine Cree's church; and in the afternoon at St. John's Wapping. I believe it pleased God to bless the first sermon most because it gave most offence.

1742. *London, Long Lane.* At length they began throwing large stones upon the house which, forcing their way wherever they came, fell down together with the tiles among the people so that they were in danger of their lives.

1743. We reached Gwennap a little before six and found the plain covered from end to end. It was supposed there were ten thousand people to whom I preached Christ our wisdom, righteousness, sanctification and redemption. I could not conclude till it was so dark we could scarce see one another. And there was on all sides the deepest attention; none speaking, stirring, or scarce looking aside.

We had not gone a hundred yards when the mob of Walsal came pouring in like a flood and bore down all before them. . . . To attempt to speak was vain for the noise on every side was like the roaring of the sea. So they dragged me along till they came to the town, where seeing the door of a large house open, I attempted to go in; but a man catching me by the hair pulled me back into the middle of the mob. They made no more stop till they had carried me through the main street from one end of the town to the other. I continued speaking all the time to those within hearing feeling no pain or weariness.

1748. *Bolton.* They then began to throw stones; at the same time some got upon the cross behind me to push me down; on which I could not but observe how God overrules even the minutest circumstances. One man was bawling just at my ear when a stone struck him on the cheek and he was still. A second was forcing his way down to me till another stone hit him on the forehead . . . the third, being got close to me, stretched out his hand and in the instant a sharp stone came upon the joints of his fingers. He shook his hand and was very quiet till I concluded my discourse and went away.

1750. *Holyhead.* In the evening I was surprised to see instead of some poor plain people a room full of men daubed with gold and silver . . . several of them (I afterwards learned) being eminently wicked men. I delivered my soul but they could in no wise bear it.

1751. *London.* [After he had sprained his ankle.] I was carried to the Foundery and preached, kneeling (as I could not stand) on part of the twenty third Psalm.

1759. A vast majority of the immense congregation in Moorfields were deeply serious. . . . What building except St. Paul's church would contain such a congregation, and if it would what human voice could have reached them there ? By repeated observations I find I can command twice the number in the open air that I can under a roof.

1764. *Liverpool.* In the evening the house was fuller if possible than the night before. I preached on the "one thing needful" and the rich behaved as seriously as the poor. Only one young gentlewoman (I heard) laughed much. Poor thing! Doubtless she thought "I laugh prettily."

1769. *Freshpool.* The beasts of the people were tolerably quiet till I had nearly finished my sermon. They then lifted up their voice, especially one, called a gentleman who had filled his pocket with rotten eggs ; but a young man coming unawares, clapped his hands on each side and mashed them all at once. In an instant he was perfume all over ; though it was not so sweet as balsam.

1773. *Waterford.* As I was drawing to a conclusion some of the Papists set on their work in earnest. They knocked down John Christian with two or three more who endeavoured to quiet them and then began to roar like the waves of the sea ; but hitherto could they come and no farther.

In some thousands of sermons Wesley must have repeated himself very often. But his enthusiasm was terrific and he attracted multitudes who were affected by his excited eloquence. For so practical a man his belief in divine interpositions and wonders is rather surprising. Time after time he refers to the most ordinary occurrences as giving proof of God's intervention. One day when he was tired and his horse was lame he writes :

I thought—cannot God heal either man or beast by any means or without any ?—immediately my headache ceased and my horses lameness in the same instant.

He also writes down the most childish stories of supposed miraculous events.

In 1741 he has an estrangement from Whitefield, who, he says,

told me, he and I preached two different gospels and therefore he not only would not join with or give me the right hand of fellowship but was resolved publicly to preach against me and my brother, wheresoever he preached at all.

In later years they come together again, and it appears from the following entry that his superiority over his rival preacher lay in his physical strength.

I breakfasted with Mr. Whitefield who seemed to be an old, old man being fairly worn out in his Master's service, though he has hardly seen fifty years and yet it pleases God that I who am now in my sixty-third year, find no disorder, no weakness, no decay, no difference from what I was at five and twenty ; only that I have fewer teeth and more grey hairs.

A little later there is an entry :

Mr. Whitefield called upon me. He breathes nothing but peace and love.

And afterwards he refers to him as his " old friend and fellow labourer."

Wesley married in 1751.

For many years I remained single because I believed I could be more useful in a single than in a married state. And I praise God who enabled me to do so. I now fully believe that in my present circumstances I might be more useful in a married state ; into which upon this clear conviction and by the advice of my friends I entered a few days later.

Once or twice he mentions his wife as accompanying him on his journeys. But whatever great virtues Wesley had he can hardly have been very domestic. In 1771, January 23, he writes :

> For what cause I know not to this day —— (his wife) set out for Newcastle purposing " never to return." *Non eam reliqui ; non dimisi ; non revocabo.*

And no further mention of her occurs in the Journal. He was no^t " lover of quiet days " ; rural pursuits did not appeal to him at all.

Ceaseless activity—preaching, reading, writing—was the rule of his life, and never did he allow an opportunity to slip of trying to convert his fellow-men to a better life. Riding from Newport-Pagnell he is overtaken by " a serious man," who enters into conversation with him which ends in a warm dispute.

> He then grew warmer and warmer ; told me I was rotten at heart and supposed I was one of John Wesley's followers. I told him " No, I am John Wesley himself." Upon which he would gladly have run away out right. But being the better mounted of the two, I kept close to his side and endeavoured to show him his heart till we came into the streets of Northampton.

On another occasion near Newcastle he meets a cock-fighter.

> I met a gentleman in the streets cursing and swearing in so dreadful a manner that I could not but stop him. He soon grew calmer ; told me he must treat me with a glass of wine ; and that he would come and hear me only he was afraid I should say something against the fighting of cocks.

At Bath he tackles Beau Nash.

> " Sir, did you ever hear me preach ? " " No." " How then can you judge of what you never heard ? " " Sir, by common report." " Common report is not enough. Give me leave, Sir, to ask, Is not your name Nash ? " " My name is Nash." " Sir, I dare not judge of you by common report ; I think it is not enough to judge by." Here he paused a while and having recovered himself said : " I desire to know what this people comes here for " : on which one replied " Sir, leave him to me ; let an old woman answer him. You Mr. Nash take care of your body ; we take care of our souls ; and for the food of our souls we come here." He replied not a word but walked away.

Wesley's reading was mainly theological but there are occasional comments on other subjects. He reads Rousseau on Education and bursts out :

> But how was I disappointed ! Sure a more consummate coxcomb never saw the sun ! How amazingly full of himself.

Of the arts we hear very little. He approves a performance of the Messiah at Bristol which he says exceeded his expectation. But he disapproves in general of oratorios because :

> One is singing the same words ten times over ; the other singing different words by different persons at one and the same time.

The mothers of great men are often found to be remarkable women. Wesley's mother, of whom he writes a great deal in his Journal when she dies in 1742, bears out this theory. The mother of nineteen children, she was a woman of strong character, but a stern and forbidding disciplinarian. Her children were brought up " to fear the rod and to cry softly," " the odious noise of the crying of children was rarely heard in the house." Her main object was " to conquer the will of the children betimes." She knew Latin and Greek and was herself a preacher. Of her nineteen children only six survived. As Mr. Birrell says : " The mother of the Wesleys thought more of her children's souls than of their bodies." From her it was, however, that John Wesley inherited his marvellous powers of self-discipline and his genius for organization. His imperious ambition drove him forward, and he succeeded in establishing a great new religious movement which at the time of his death numbered a hundred thousand members and now counts its members in Great Britain and America by millions.

The Journal deals fully with the inauguration of the Holy Club and the gradual growth of the new organization. It makes frequent reference, too, to the brutality of many of the judges, the harshness of the magistrate, the awful condition of the prisons, and the drunkenness, squalor and misery that existed in towns.

To Methodists the Journal is an invaluable record of the inauguration of their great movement. To the ordinary reader it cannot appeal so much.

THE EARL OF EGMONT

THE Historical Manuscripts Commission have published the first volume of the diary of Viscount Percival, afterwards 1st Earl of Egmont. It covers the years 1730 to 1733. The whole manuscript consists of twelve folio volumes extending from 1730 to 1747. In addition to this there are some fragmentary entries for the year 1728–9 in the British Museum. We have the great advantage in the Historical Manuscripts Commission's volume of having the complete diary without the often irritating omissions which most editors seem obliged to make.

Egmont kept a diary for at least eighteen or nineteen years, probably longer, as when he was 15 he expressed his intention of keeping one. Many instances have been given of diarists who wrote for longer periods, but there is certainly no instance of anyone who kept so voluminous a diary. The four years 1730–1733 cover 477 closely printed pages, and there are single entries of three to four thousand words. His diligence and assiduity as a diarist are astonishing. It is all punctiliously and laboriously written out in longhand, and the entries are daily except for short periods when he is away on a holiday. Public affairs occupy his attention chiefly, and his records of parliamentary debates are the fullest that exist of the period during which he served as a member of the House of Commons. He himself spoke seldom, but he had great powers of concentrated attention and almost verbal memory. He gives therefore practically the whole debate more fully than it is given to-day in a good newspaper report. For this reason his diary acquires special historical importance; it takes the place of a Hansard for the period. He comments but little, he does not select the chief speeches, but every speaker is reported with an occasional descriptive word such as " a sorry speech " or " a bantering speech." Political conversations and committees are treated with the same full exactitude. He writes comparatively little of a personal character and indulges in no self-analysis, and makes few reflections apart from his opinions on public affairs. Sermons are recorded, plays mentioned, and there is a good deal about music, of which he was very fond.

Before entering the British House of Commons Percival had served in the Irish Parliament. He married in 1710, and we can see from his diary that his marriage was a happy one.

This day I have been 21 years married and I acknowledge God's blessing that I have lived so many years in full happiness with my dear wife.

This day I have been married twenty two years and I bless God that I have lived so long with the best wife, the best Christian, the best mother and the best mistress of her servants living; and that not only the world thinks so but that I am myself sensible of it.

Perusing the very lengthy and detailed entries not only of debates but of conversations, one sees the man very clearly: without marked literary talent, with no conspicuous parliamentary abilities, he was thoughtful, very conscientious, and noticeably and exceptionally high-minded for a politician of that era, although some of the political usages which he refers to may make us smile. He was independent in his views and very persistent, more especially where his son's interests were concerned. He was formally religious. No Sunday passed without observance of the duties of prayers and sermon, and often of "communicating" also, and if public worship was not possible there were invariably " prayers and sermon " at home. Percival took himself very seriously, and we should doubt if he had any sense of humour. Like so many diarists, he never fails to note down the words of Royalty, even when the conversations are of no sort of interest.

The commanding figure in the early years of George II was Sir Robert Walpole. Percival is a personal friend of his and a political supporter, and Horace Walpole, who was a sort of go-between through whom approaches to the great minister were made, also figures largely in the diary. The following passage shows that Percival could be very critical of his chief:

Sir Robert Walpole . . . found there are certain occasions where he cannot carry points; it is this meanness of his (the prostitution of the character of a first minister in assisting and strenuously supporting the defence of dunghill worms, let their cause be ever so unjust, against men of honour, birth and fortune, and that in person too) that gains him so much ill will; . . . Sir Robert like the altars of refuge in old times, is the asylum of little unworthy wretches who submitting to dirty work, endear themselves to him and get his protection first and then his favour which as he is first Minister is sure to draw after it the countenance of the Court . . . the King can seldom know the merits and character of private persons but from the first Minister who we see has no so great regard for any as for these little pickthanks and scrubs for whom he risks his character and the character of his high station.

Percival had no difficulty in getting his advance in the peerage out of Walpole. We find the very familiar excuse that he does not want it for himself, but

> the world thought there was something in quality and my own household pressed me to ask for it.

It is true that he was not ambitious for himself. He explains this to George II.

> I waited on the King and told him that though loving my ease, I never yet would be in Parliament, yet having observed in all reigns that the first that was summoned was always the most troublesome to the Prince I was resolved to stand that I might contribute my poor services to the settlement of affairs.

It is interesting, and indeed surprising, to read of the degree of excitement caused by certain proposals in Parliament which have now passed entirely into oblivion. An entry may be quoted with regard to Walpole's unpopular Excise scheme which even he failed to carry through.

> We learned that last night the City rang their bells for joy, the Bill was dropped and made more bonfires and illuminations than ever was known. They broke the windows of the Post Office and of all other houses not illuminated and would have done it of the Parliament House while we were sitting if they could have come within reach of them. They burnt Sir Robert in effigy with Sarah Malcome in several places and in others dressed up a pole and whipped it.

Among other matters which engaged the attention of Parliament was the investigation of the operations of the Charitable Corporation which resulted in the expulsion of prominent members of the House of Commons. In connection with this question he notes how ladies were first admitted into the gallery of the House.

> This day I carried my wife and daughter Kitty to the House of Commons to hear Sir Archibald Grant make his defence. So many ladies said to be undone by the managers of the Charitable Corporation, induced the Speaker to indulge ladies to be present in the gallery and witnesses of the justice the Parliament are doing on those vile persons.

When he retired from Parliament and wishes his son to take his place, long drawn-out complications ensue with regard to Harwich, his constituency, which end in serious " altercations " between him and the Walpoles. The son, afterwards 2nd Earl

THE EARL OF EGMONT

of Egmont, father of Percival, the Prime Minister, showed marked political ability at an early age. His father discovers that he is the author of two pamphlets.

<small>They are the first essays of this kind and he made me promise not to acquaint any but my wife that he wrote them. He need not be ashamed of them and few children at nineteen years old would have done so well.</small>

But later on Percival is much dismayed when he finds that his son had run through £2,000 during his stay in Ireland. How he reprimanded him we do not know, but he confides his annoyance to his diary.

There are, however, no further references to trouble between father and son, and Percival throws himself heart and soul into the business of getting his son a seat in the House of Commons.

The arrangements and intrigues with regard to Harwich, which occupy many long entries, illustrate the astonishing methods by which elections were arranged in those days. The Walpoles, however, for various reasons were not entirely sympathetic, but Percival never misses an opportunity of pressing his son's claims. "A strange return for my personal regard to Sir R. Walpole," he writes on hearing some unfavourable news.

At last the quarrel becomes serious.

<small>As I was coming out of Court Sir Robert Walpole came in, and in a familiar kind sort of way asking me how I did offered me his hand but I drew back mine and in a respectful cool way said only to him " Your humble servant, Sir."</small>

The Walpoles try to patch things up, but Percival continues to "be much heated at Sir Robert Walpole's ill usage of me," and eventually, although this comes later than the period covered by the printed volume, his son is returned for another constituency. Percival took an active part in the enterprise for the colonisation of Georgia, and the proceedings of the Georgia Committee are very fully reported. Cordial as were Egmont's relations with the Royal Family, he does not appear to have had a very high opinion of their judgment ; and their praise leaves him cold.

In 1731 he gives a character sketch of Frederick Prince of Wales :

<small>The character of the Prince is this : he has no reigning passion, if it be it is to pass the evening with six or seven others over a glass of wine and hear them talk of a variety of things ; but he does not drink. He loves play and plays to win that he may supply his pleasures and generosity which last are great but so ill placed that he often wants wherewithal to do a well-placed kindness, by giving to unworthy objects. He has had several mistresses and</small>

now keeps one an apothecary's daughter of Kingston ; but is not nice in his choice and talks more of feats this way than he acts. He can talk gravely according to his company but is sometimes more childish than becomes his age. He thinks he knows business but attends to none ; likes to be flattered. He is good natured and if he meets with a good Ministry may satisfy his people ; he is extremely dutiful to his parents who do not return it in love and seem to neglect him by letting him do as he will, but they keep him short of money.

With the Queen (Caroline of Anspach) he is on very intimate terms. He has long and interesting conversations with her, for he says " she reads and converses on a multitude of things more than our sex generally does." One example may be given in which the diarist himself seems to have expressed some very sound ideas to her majesty :

1732. April 29. Went to Court where the King and Queen talked a great deal to me, she took notice of my collection of heads and said it must be very curious and fine [these " heads " are referred to in another entry as being " in wax "] but wondered I did not work upon it in Winter. I said I had not time. " No " said she " when you rise at four o'clock ? When do you go to bed ? " I said, at ten. " That is," said she " sleeping six hours which is long enough for anybody." We then talked of the vices of the age and she said she thought the world as good as it was formerly. I said it ought to be so considering what a good example we had before us but there were fashionable vices that reigned more one age than another, as cheating and overreaching our neighbour does now more than ever occasioned by riches, trade and the great increase of the city, for populous towns have more roguery than little ones, for here men may hide it but when men lived more in the country as in former times, there was not that knowledge how to cheat neither the temptation nor opportunity given. " May be " replied the Queen " you are for reducing people to poverty to make them honest." " Not so," replied I " but great wealth occasions luxury and luxury extravagance and extravagance want and want knavery."

In contrast to this entry there are many lengthy pages devoted to the petty question of the precedence of Irish peers in some procession. Sometimes he makes very long transcriptions of sermons, and his religious inclinations can be noted by the frequent references to " prayers and sermon " at home. The only very short entries are those where he simply notes " stayed at home." These moments of leisure were probably devoted to writing up the long reports, and we must remember that he got up at four o'clock. He gives a very full and touching account of his " sister Dering's " death and his endeavours to comfort her in her last hours. Day by day the details of her illness are recorded with all the religious consolations with which he tries to soften her last moments. When she dies he writes :

She died away more gradually than a lamp going out or a lamb falling to sleep and they who were in the room, for I could not bear to be there, said they never in their lives saw nor heard of so composed and gentle and sweet an end.

His own health is occasionally referred to.

I stayed all day still at home on account of my soar throat and drew two teeth.

This day I visited Mr. John Temple who gave me for my rheumatic pains a bottle of right old verjuice and advised me to take a glass of it with a toast in it every morning fasting and going to bed and to rub my joints with it after it is well warmed, to continue this three weeks.

Still confined by the blow on my leg which I got this day sennit coming out of Court by a chair, and for which Mr. Dickens the surgeon daily attends me.

Percival's love of music is shown conspicuously throughout the diary. He goes frequently to the "Vocal Club" to "excellent Concerts of Music" and gives regular concerts in his own house. A few quotations on this subject may be given beginning with two which occur in the manuscript fragments of 1728–9.

At night I went to the Crown tavern to hear the musick (the Academy of Vocal Music) which the gentlemen of the King's Chapel have every fortnight there, being an attempt to restore ancient Church Musick.

1730. In the evening I went to my sister Percival to hear Signer Fabri who sings tenor in our Opera, perform, and I engaged him to teach my daughter at three guineas for ten times.

The Prince (Frederick, Prince of Wales) seems to have had a desire to join his orchestra :

He was learning the bass viol for he could not always be in company. I answered the pleasure of life lay in little things. He said he hoped soon to play well enough to be admitted of my concert and have my wife hear him. I answered it would be the greatest honour I could ever expect.

"Hendel from Hanover" he refers to as

a man of the vastest genius and skill in music that perhaps has lived since Orpheus. The great variety of manner in his compositions whether serious or brisk whether for the Church or the stage or the chamber and that agreeable mixture of styles that are in his works, that fire and spirit far surpassing his brother musicians soon gave him preference over Bononcini with the English.

Sympathetic as he was to musicians, his lordship seems to have been tinged with a sense of the profession's comparative social inferiority when he says that a salary of five hundred pounds a year was " a sum which no musician ever had before from any prince nor ought to have."

Once on his birthday he describes his own position with some self-satisfaction.

1731. July 12. This day being my birthday, I complete my age of forty eight years and enter upon my forty ninth. I bless God that hitherto I have had neither gout nor stone but enjoy a perfect state of health. Many others are His mercies to me. I am in possession of a good name and of a fortune greater than what my father left. . . . I have a wife after my own heart being perfect in every virtue and without alloy and three children sound in body and mind and dutiful. My son gives himself to useful things and promises to make a considerable man if he can be it without breach of his integrity and virtue which he is remarkable for : and my daughters have made great progress in their exercises. I count it my highest felicity that at the same time that I am perfectly sensible of my happiness, I am ready to part with it all and to change this life for a better when God pleases : the thought of death carries no sting with it for me. Blessed be God !

Two more volumes of Egmont's diary are to appear.

FANNY BURNEY (Madame d'Arblay)

IF ever there was a diarist, Fanny Burney was one. Yet in a close perusal of the eight volumes of her diary and letters it is not always easy to detach the journal from the letters. In fact, the clear distinction that there is between diary writing and letter writing becomes in the case of Fanny Burney obscured. Letters divided up by daily dates can be counted as journal, but towards the end we get sections of what is called " narrative," which constitute memoirs and cannot be regarded as journal. The combination of the three, the journal, the letters and the narratives, give us as full a picture of the authoress in the earlier days as it is possible to get. The private meditations, which are of a religious character, would add still further to our knowledge, but they have not been published.

There is no need to give a preliminary sketch of so well known a literary character as the author of *Evelina*. The analysis of her diary will in itself allow us to pass in rapid review the chief incidents in her long life, which divides itself more or less into five distinct periods : childhood, early life at home, court life, married life, and widowhood.

As to her motive and method we must glance through the whole diary to find the key.

The dedication of the journal, which was begun on March 27, 1768, when she was 15 years old, begins :

> To have some account of my thoughts, manners, acquaintance, and actions, when the hour arrives in which time is more nimble than memory is the reason which induces me to keep a Journal. A Journal in which I must confess my every thought must open my whole heart ! But a thing of this kind must be addressed to somebody—I must imagine myself to be talking—talking to the most intimate friends—to one whom I should take delight in confiding and remorse in concealment : but who must this friend be ?

She comes to the conclusion it must be Nobody, and accordingly to " a certain Miss Nobody " the diary is addressed. In fact, Fanny Burney faced from the outset the question which most diarists leave unsettled or rather unrevealed, namely the practical impossibility of writing without imagining some one reading. As a child, she decided on this imaginary person, later she definitely addressed her journal to one of her sisters, to Mr. Crisp, or occasionally to her father, but this in no way altered her intention at the time that it should be private and confidential. Its intense egotism in the early years, a natural characteristic of a real diary writer, is sufficient proof of this. There are several passages which show how strong in her was the itch to record passing events.

1768. I cannot express the pleasure I have in writing down my thoughts at the very moment—my opinion of people when I first see them and how I alter or how confirm myself in it . . . there is something to me very unsatisfactory in passing year after year without even a memorandum of what you did.

She had begun at a still earlier age, but unfortunately she destroyed her earliest diaries.

1774. I burnt all up to my fifteenth year—thinking I grew too old for scribbling nonsense but as I am less young, I grow, I fear, less wise, for I cannot any long resist what I find to be irresistible, the pleasure of popping down my thoughts from time to time on paper.

When she decides to address her diary to her sister she calls it "journalizing"; and the inclination for this form of writing never failed.

1780. I am not much in cue for journalizing but I am yet less inclined for anything else.

But it was for the events and incidents and not for the deeper reflections on life that her journal was reserved.

1789. But why do I forget the resolution with which I began these my chronicles of never mixing with them my religious sentiments—opinions —hopes—fears—belief—or aspirations ? . . . I never will jumble together what I deem holy with what I know to be trivial.

And later again she refers to the entries in the diary as "poor shallow memorials." In fact, she found herself very often in what she describes as "a scribbling vein," and being surrounded as she was practically all her life through by interesting and eminent people, she was afforded ample opportunity for indulging her talent. And her talent was very remarkable. Every line she wrote is by no means worth reading. Her prolixity is tiresome, her gush, though characteristic of her time, often irritating. But she had one particular faculty which can hardly have been surpassed by any other writer, and which is really the main reason of her journal having gained such a high reputation. This was her capacity for memorising and recording conversations—not just little scraps of dialogue introduced as illustrations or as examples of how she herself scored off her interlocutors—but pages of full conversations disclosing the personalities and characteristics of the participants, sometimes with considerable humour and sometimes with intense seriousness. This is her method also in her novels. In fiction there can be no doubt she was immediately successful. But in actual life, too, while no one can pretend they are anything like verbatim reports, the conversations have just that quality which makes the painting of a great artist give a more interesting impression than a far more rigidly accurate photograph. She rarely gives any full account of the outward appearance of her characters. They break into conversation immediately, and most convincing to the reader do they seem. Fanny Burney can never be suspected of deliberate invention or misrepresentation, but her imagination must have filled up the gaps. She admits her prejudices, but fairness of mind is one of the most conspicuous characteristics of every line she wrote in her diary. " All that I relate in Journalizing," she says in a letter, "is *strictly* nay *plainly* Fact : I never in all my Life have been a Sayer of the Thing that is not, and *now* I should be not only a Knave but a Fool also in so doing, as I have other purposes for Imaginery characters than filling Letters with them."

These frequently recurring and often long conversations make the illustration of the diary by means of extracts extremely difficult. We can do little more, therefore, than refer to them. This phenomenal talent was not gradually developed, she seems practically to have been born with it. In the first year of the diary, when she was 15, she begins an entry : " I have had to-day the first real conversation I have ever had in my life except with Mr. Crisp " ; then follows a dialogue which occupies five and a half closely printed pages with no sort of clumsiness in either phrase or expression.

The early diaries, covering the period from 1768 to 1778, deal with her home life and the visitors who came to her father's house. Dr. Burney was a lover of music, engaged on a History of Music, and Fanny acted as his amanuensis. She often expresses her devotion to him : " I am never half as happy as with him," and also her affection for Mr. Crisp, who goes by the name of " Daddy." We have accounts of tea parties, plays, private theatricals, fancy dress balls; and the books she was reading are duly noted. Garrick was a frequent visitor, and specially delighted her and her brothers and sisters because he was always ready for all sorts of pranks with children. She records a conversation with her father about his forthcoming book.

> "But pray, Doctor, when shall we have the History out ? Do let me know in time that I may prepare to blow the trumpet of Fame." He then put his stick to his mouth and in a Raree-show-man's voice cried, "Here is the only true History, Gentlemen, please to buy, please to buy. Sir, I shall blow it in the very ear of yon scurvy magistrate" (meaning Sir John Hawkins who is writing the same history). He then ran on with great humour upon twenty subjects; but so much of his drollery belongs to his voice, looks and manner that *writing* loses it almost all.

She also greatly admired Garrick's acting. In Richard III she says :

> Garrick was sublimely horrible. Good heavens—how he made me shudder whenever he appeared ! It is inconceivable how terribly great he is in this character.

In many of the conversations which took place round her she did not participate, though she often listened attentively enough.

> Dr. Shepherd, Mr. Twiss and my father conversed upon foreign countries and Susy and I sat very snug together amused either by ourselves or them as we chose.

We must pass from the outpourings of the young girl which occupy the best part of two volumes. They often show remarkable penetration in character reading and unexpectedly mature reflections. But the sheer facility of writing was rather a snare.

In the second period, from 1778 to 1786, we get a far more elaborate account of her pursuits and her friends and acquaintances. The two outstanding features of this section of the diary are the publication of *Evelina* and her friendship with Dr. Johnson. She begins 1778 with the following announcement in her facetious manner :

> This year was ushered in by a grand and most important event ! At the latter end of January the literary world was favoured with the first publication of the ingenious learned and most profound Fanny Burney ! I doubt not but this memorable affair will in future times mark the period whence chronologers will date the zenith of the polite arts in this island.

As the whole business of writing and publication had been done secretly without even the knowledge of her father she was naturally inclined at first to treat the whole thing as a huge joke.

But the immediate unexpected and amazing success of her first novel must have gone far to turn her head, and in her diary she records every possible reference to it, and all the multifarious accidents and incidents connected with her discovered authorship. Not only do we have every word uttered by Dr. Johnson on the subject, Burke's praise, Sheridan's appreciation, and Sir Joshua Reynolds' all night sitting over it, but the comment of every one she meets is recorded in full for some years after the event. The storing up of these pleasant and indeed very remarkable tributes to her talent is one of the surest proofs that publication was very far from Fanny Burney's mind when she began to write her diary.

Dr. Johnson seems, more than anyone who has ever lived, to have had the effect on people of making them run off and write down every word he said and describe every gesture he made, every noise that came from him. Fanny Burney, who saw him frequently in these years, concentrated her talents on recording his sayings and habits and doings in a way that would have made Boswell very envious had he been able to read her diary in his lifetime. Indeed, we gather from her interview with him that he suspected she had some valuable material stored away somewhere.

"Yes madam"—says Boswell—" you must give me some of your choice little notes of the Doctor's: we have seen him long enough upon stilts; I want to show him in a new light. Grave Sam and great Sam and Solemn Sam and learned Sam—all these he has appeared over and over. Now I want to entwine a wreath of the graces across his brow; I want to show him as gay Sam, agreeable Sam, pleasant Sam; so you must help me with some of his beautiful billets to yourself."

I evaded, declaring I had not any stores at hand. He proposed a thousand curious expedients to get at them but I was invincible.

It was a curious interview, for Boswell proceeded to take out of his pocket proofs of his Life of Johnson and read them to Miss Burney at the gates of the Queen's Lodge at Windsor, with a crowd gathering round them to her embarrassment and dismay.

Her first impression of Dr. Johnson comes in her early diary in 1777:

In the midst of this performance Dr. Johnson was announced. He is indeed very ill favoured; is tall and stout; but stoops terribly; he is almost bent double. His mouth is almost constantly opening and shutting as if he was chewing. He has a strange method of frequently twirling his fingers and twisting his hands. His body is in continual agitation see-sawing up and down; his feet are never a moment quiet; and in short his whole person is in perpetual motion. His dress too considering the times and that he had meant to put on his *best becomes* being engaged to dine in a large company was as much out of the common road as his figure ; he had a large wig, snuff colour coat and gold buttons but no ruffles to his shirt doughty fists and black worsted stockings.

Her frequent meetings with him in the following years are all carefully described. He had a very genuine affection for her and she worshipped him.

But Dr. Johnson's approbation ! It almost crazed me with agreeable surprise—it gave me such a flight of spirits that I danced a jig to Mr. Crisp without any preparation, music or explanation.

A little while ago I went into the music room where he was *tête à tête* with Mrs. Thrale, and calling me to him he took my hand and made me sit next him in a manner that seemed truly affectionate. " Sir," cried I, " I was much afraid I was going out of your favour ! " " Why so ? What should make you think so ? " " Why I don't know—my silence, I believe. I began to fear you would give me up." " No, my darling ! my dear little Burney, no, when I give you up——" " What then, Sir ? " cried Mrs. Thrale. " Why I don't know ; for whoever could give her up would deserve worse than I can say ; I know not what would be bad enough."

Mrs. Thrale says Fanny's modesty is really beyond bounds :

"That madam is another wonder " answered my dear, dear Dr. Johnson " for modesty with her is neither pretence nor decorum ; 'tis an ingredient of her nature ; for she who could part with such a work (Evelina) for twenty pounds, could know so little of its worth or of her own as to leave no possible doubt of her humility."

Dr. Johnson has been very unwell indeed. Once I was quite frightened about him, but he continues his strange discipline—starving, mercury, opium ; and though for a time half demolished by its severity, he always in the end rises superior both to the disease and the remedy—which commonly is the most alarming of the two. His kindness for me I think if possible still increased ; he actually *bores* everybody so about me that the folks even complain of it. I must, however, acknowledge I feel but little pity for their fatigue.

Apart from conversations we get little character sketches and touches of humour.

Mr. R.—whose trite, settled, tonish emptiness of discourse is a never failing source of laughter and diversion.

Mrs. Streatfield—she is very lively and an excellent mimic and is I think as much superior to the daughter in natural gifts as her daughter is to her in acquired ones ; and how infinitely preferable are parts without education to education without parts.

Burke. He is tall, his figure is noble, his air commanding, his address graceful, his voice is clear, penetrating, sonorous and powerful ; his language is copious various and eloquent, his manners are attractive, his conversation is delightful.

Mrs. Siddons. She behaved with great propriety very calm, modest quiet and unaffected. She has a very fine countenance and her eyes look both intelligent and soft. She has however a steadiness in her manner and deportment by no means engaging.

In 1786, through the instrumentality of Mrs. Delany, who lived at Windsor, Fanny was offered and accepted the post of second keeper of the robes to Queen Charlotte in succession to Mrs. Haggerdorn, at a salary of £200 a year. The section of her diary which covers the five years during which she held this appointment is the most entertaining, although it is a record of an imprisonment and menial servitude to which she never ought to have been subjected. Her duties were to answer the royal bell early in the morning and help the Queen to dress. The curling and powdering of her Majesty's hair also occupied a great deal of time. She occasionally read to the Queen, filled her snuff box, looked after the dog basket, and ran messages, but the waiting and standing and attendance at functions proved gradually a physical strain far beyond her capacity. She presided at the tea equipage of the equerries-in-waiting in the absence of her colleague and she had opportunities for intercourse with the princes and princesses. However much she may have grown to hate the life at the end, she never lost a rather pathetic worship of royalty towards whom her critical faculties are never brought into play. They are referred to as " the sweet Queen " and " the excellent King " or " the most beloved of monarchs," and on one occasion she feels inclined to " throw herself at the King's feet." They " condescend " and their messages are always " gracious." The diary which she kept regularly from daily noted memoranda brings the royal atmosphere at Windsor and Kew and occasionally at St. James's before us with wonderful realism.

The description of her first meeting with George III and the Queen at Mrs. Delany's before her appointment occupies no less than twenty-three printed pages. We can only give a short extract from the conversation :

" Pray does Miss Burney draw, too ? " asked the King. The ' too ' was pronounced very civilly.

" I believe not sir " answered Mrs. Delany " at least she does not tell."

" Oh " cried he laughing " that's nothing ! she is not apt to tell ; she never does tell, you know !—Her father told me that himself. He told me the whole history of her *Evelina*. And I shall never forget his face when he spoke of his feelings at first taking up the book ! He looked quite frightened, just as if he was doing it that moment ! I never can forget his face while I live ! "

Then coming up close to me he said,

" But what ? what ? how was it ? "

" Sir ? " cried I, not well understanding him.

" How came you—how happened it—what ? what ? "

" I—I only wrote, sir, for my own amusement—only in some odd, idle hours."

" But your publishing—your printing—how was that ?

" That was only, sir, only because——"

I hesitated most abominable not knowing how to tell him a long story and growing terribly confused at these questions ; besides, to say the truth, his own " what ? what ? " so reminded me of those vile Probationary Odes that in the midst of all my flutter I was really hardly able to keep my countenance. The *What* was then repeated with so earnest a look that forced to say something I stammeringly answered.

" I thought—sir, it would look well in print ! " I do really flatter myself this is the silliest speech I ever made ! I am quite provoked with myself for it ; but a fear of laughing made me eager to utter anything and by no means conscious till I had spoken of what I was saying.

He laughed very heartily himself—well he might—and walked away to enjoy it crying out " very fair indeed ! that's being very fair and honest."

The King was invariably kind to her, and took occasion now and again to have little talks with her. Here is his Majesty's opinion on Shakespeare :

" Was there ever " cried he " such stuff as great part of Shakespeare ? only one must not say so ! But what think you ? What ? Is there not sad stuff ? What ?—What ? "

" Yes, indeed, I think so, sir, though mixed with such excellences that——"

" Oh," cried he laughing good humouredly " I know it is not to be said ! But it's true. Only it's Shakespeare and nobody dare abuse him."

Then he enumerated many of the characters and parts of plays that he objected to ; and when he had run them over finished with again laughing and exclaiming,

" But one should be stoned for saying so ! "

The account the diarist gives of her encounter with the King in Kew Gardens, when he had not yet recovered from his first attack of insanity, is, in spite of its serio-comic character, one of the most dramatic in the journal. She running for her life, the King in hot pursuit shouting after her, the attendants and doctors bringing up the rear endeavouring to check the King. Finally she stops and then comes a flood of conversation, not by any means all of it mad.

What a conversation followed ! When he saw me fearless he grew more and more alive and made me walk close by his side. . . . Everybody that came uppermost in his mind he mentioned ; he seemed to have such remains of his flightiness as heated his imagination without deranging his reason and robbed him of all control over his speech though nearly in his perfect state of mind as to his opinions.

Of "the sweet Queen" whom she saw daily we get a more finished portrait, though it is always biased by the infatuation for royalty. Queen Charlotte was kind, domestic and punctilious and with her full share of royal inconsiderateness. But of all the characters in this part, or indeed any part, of the diary there is nothing to equal Fanny Burney's account of her colleague, the first keeper of the robes, Mrs. Schwellenberg, described by Macaulay as "a hateful old toadeater, as illiterate as a chamber-maid, as proud as a whole German Chapter, rude, peevish, unable to bear solitude, unable to conduct herself with common decency in society." A series of extracts from the diary will be the best way of describing this extraordinary person.

One of the equerries mentioned a newspaper paragraph in which the Queen's name had appeared.

"What for you tell me that!"
"Ma'am, I—I only said— It is not me ma'am but the newspapers——"
"What for you have such newspapers? I tell you the same—it is—what you call—I don't like such thing!"
"But ma'am——"
"Oh, upon my verd, I might tell you once, when you name the Queen, it is —what you call—I can't bear it! When it is nobody else with all my heart! I might not care for that—but when it is the Queen—I tell you the same, Colonel—it makes me—what you call—perspire."

A clergyman offers to read out to Mrs. Schwellenberg and asks what he shall read:

"No" cried she "I wont have nothing what you call novels, what you call romances, what you call histories—I might not read such what you call stuff—not I!" [this was a hit at Fanny].

We went to town for the drawing room and I caught a most severe cold by being obliged to have the glass down on my side to suit Mrs. Schwellenberg though the sharpest wind blew that ever attacked a poor phiz.

A terrible journey indeed Mrs. Schwellenberg finding it expedient to have the glass down on my side whence there blew a sharp wind which so painfully attacked my eyes that they were inflamed even before we arrived in town.

On a subsequent occasion Mr. de Luc is bold enough to put the glass up.

"Put down that glass," was the immediate order. "Do it Mr. de Luc when I tell you I will have it! When you been too cold you might bear it!"
"It is not for me ma'am but poor Miss Burney."

"Oh, poor Miss Burney might bear it the same; put it down Mr. de Luc without I will get out! It is my coach. I will have it selfs! I might go alone in it or with one or with what you call nobody when I please!" ...
... Oh ver well! when you don't like it (sitting with her back to the horses) don't do it! What did the poor Haggerdorn bear it when the blood was all running down from her eyes."

On yet another occasion when Fanny put up her muff as protection in the carriage she declared in a fury "she never no never would trouble any won to air with her again but go always selfs." When the equerries neglect all conversation with Mrs. Schwellenberg:

> She protested that if they did not mind she would have them no more and let them make tea for themselves. "Oh, yes, I will put an end to it! your humble servant! when they wont talk to me they may stay; comical men! they bin bears!"

She kept frogs.

> "But I can make them croak when I will when I only go so to my snuff box knock knock knock they croak all what I please."

When Fanny did not talk because she was tired:

> "You tired! What have you done? when I used to do so much more—you tired? What have you to do but to be happy? have you the laces to buy? have you the wardrobe to part? have you,—you tired? Vell, what will come next when you have every happiness—you might not be tired. No, I can't bear it."

> My coadjutrix was now grown so fretful and affronting that though we only met at dinner it was hard to support her most unprovoked harshness.

When at the time of her proposed retirement Miss Burney and her father declined the alternative offer of six months' holiday, Mrs. Schwellenberg's fury was boundless.

> A scene almost horrible ensued when I told Cerbera the offer was refused. She was too much enraged for disguise and uttered the most furious expressions of indignant contempt at our proceedings.

When the final parting came the old gorgon undoubtedly was moved:

> She would take no leave of me, but wished me better hastily and saying we should soon meet she hurried suddenly out of the room. Poor woman! If her temper were not so irascible I really believe her heart would be by no means wanting in kindness.

After her release she confesses in a retrospect:

> Poor Mrs. Schwellenberg so wore, wasted, and tortured all my little leisure that my time for repose was, in fact, my time of greatest labour.

Court life is illustrated by many other curious and interesting portraits; the extraordinary Mr. Turbulent (her name for the Rev. C. de Guiffardière), who occasionally flings himself on his knees at her feet; Mr. Fairly (Colonel Stephen Digby), with whom she has long conversations; the facetious equerry Colonel Goldsworthy, the future King William IV, of whom Schwellenberg says, " Dat Prince Villiam—oders de Duke of Clarence—bin raelly very merry—oders vat you call tipsy," and many other people eminent and humble. The unutterably tiresome court ceremonials and functions are fully described. But in the history of court ritual surely the following ceremony is unique :

> At Weymouth. The King bathes and with great success ; a machine follows the Royal one into the sea filled with fiddlers who play " God save the King " as His Majesty takes his plunge.

The Queen gave Fanny Burney tickets for the trial of Warren Hastings in Westminster Hall. Here she meets Windham, and the series of conversations she records with him as she watches the proceedings are perhaps the most striking in the journal. By means of these dialogues she brings the whole scene in detail to our eyes with unconscious and yet perfect skill. She was strongly prejudiced in favour of Hastings, and Windham was one of the Managers of the prosecution. Curiously enough Fanny Burney is not even mentioned in Windham's diary, though he generally gives the names of people he meets.

Of course it never occurred to her royal mistress that the exacting life at court was detrimental to the literary career of the already remarkable authoress. And it came as a painful surprise to her Majesty when Miss Burney and her father, urged by many friends, including Windham, Walpole, and Boswell, at last decided on her resignation. At odd intervals she did find time to write, and she tells us she is at work on her tragedies. Unfavourable as the atmosphere no doubt was, and infrequent as the moments of leisure were in a life of " hard fagging," it is far too much to say that her five years of court service permanently damaged her literary career any more than it was permanently damaging to her health, although its continuance might have been fatal. Surely she had collected enough copy for many a novel, not to say farce, in her unique experiences at Windsor and Kew.

Although this is no place to enlarge on Fanny Burney's literary accomplishments, we may note that even in her diary so long as she adopts what we may call the " Evelina " style—pure, fresh, spontaneous, slightly ironical and often witty—she is unrivalled. But time and circumstances—not only her confinement in the court, but a desire to emulate heavier metal of the Johnsonian type—produced a pomposity, a heaviness, and a pretentiousness which ruined her published work and can also be traced in her diary. The rather delicate growth of pure imagination was not only checked by circumstances, but would seem to have been choked by too excellent a memory and too keen a power of observation. These, however, were a valuable equipment for diary writing, and that is why the diary stands first among the productions from her pen.

After her release, in which she greatly rejoices, she returns once or twice to court. During a short attendance at St. James's she says :

Indeed I was half dead with only two days' and nights' exertion. 'Tis amazing how I ever went through all that is passed.

Back with her friends once again, she travels about, and her diary shows her continued interest in people. At her sister's house, which was frequented by a group of French exiles, she meets General d'Arblay.

He seems to me a true *militaire, franc et loyal*—open as the day—warmly affectionate to his friends—intelligent ready and amusing in conversation with a great share of *gaieté* de cœur and at the same time, of *naiveté* and *bonne foi*.

She marries him in 1793. From 1801 to 1812 she was in Paris and again during the Hundred Days, and she describes Brussels at the time of the Battle of Waterloo. The diary becomes intermittent in these later years, but in Paris she writes very fully, and although much of it is interesting, the light touch has gone. As Horace Walpole said, "This author knew the world and penetrated characters before she had stepped over the threshold ; and now she has seen so much of it she has little or no penetration at all."

There are no gems worth extracting. Even her description of Napoleon is commonplace and flat. Towards the end letters rather than diary tell her story. Throughout her life she was a prolific letter writer, and her journal was really a sort of overflow of this habit.

The journal is an instance of literary talent, carrying the diarist a good deal beyond what is natural in diary writing and overlaying the spontaneous sincerity of daily memoranda with quite another element.

Hogg, in his Life of Shelley, gives an amusing account of Madame d'Arblay's voluble and egotistical conversation and her powers of exaggeration. In fact, he makes her out to be an intolerable bore.

Her husband, who apparently forsook her, died in 1818, and before her own death, which occurred in 1840, she also lost her son.

In her old age Madame d'Arblay herself carefully arranged and annotated the volumes of her diary, and consigned them to her niece, Mrs. Barrett, the daughter of her sister Charlotte, with full permission to publish them. This act of the old lady looking back on her juvenile adventures was very natural, even though at the time they were written the girl and young woman had no actual thought of reaching the public eye. The later diaries were first published in 1842, edited by Mrs. Barrett. Two volumes of the early diaries, edited by Mrs. A. R. Ellis, were published in 1889. In 1904 a new edition of the later diaries and letters in six volumes was issued by Mr. Austin Dobson.

THE RIGHT HON. WILLIAM WINDHAM

WINDHAM'S diary, which he kept for many years, is disappointing from the point of view of giving a picture of his times or of providing personal notes on the host of interesting people with whom he came in contact. But, as will be seen, it has rather a peculiar interest from the way in which it throws light on his character and disposition and reveals the inner working of his mind and certain qualities of thought which could not have otherwise been discovered from his speeches and letters.

Born in 1750, William Windham was educated at Eton and University College, Oxford. After serving as Chief Secretary to Lord Northington, Lord-Lieutenant of Ireland, he was returned as member of Parliament for Norwich in 1784. He remained in alliance with the Whigs until the outbreak of the French Revolution, when he joined Pitt. In 1794 he was made Secretary-at-War and a privy councillor. He opposed all negotiations for peace with France and lost his seat in 1802. He returned to the House of Commons as member for St. Mawes, in Cornwall, but declined a place in Pitt's cabinet in 1804. When the ministry of "All the Talents" was formed in 1806 he became Secretary of State for War and the Colonies. After the two subsequent dissolutions he sat for the boroughs of New Romney and Higham Ferrers consecutively. He died in 1810 in consequence of an operation necessitated by an accident and was buried at Felbrigg, his home near Cromer, for which he had a very special affection. In 1798 he married Cecelia Forest, but he had no children.

A public estimate of his political position and character can be given in the words of Earl Grey, who in the House of Lords at the time of Windham's death said: " It was his misfortune at different times to differ from that distinguished and regretted character; yet in the heat of political disagreement he never ceased to admire his many and splendid virtues. He was a man of great original and commanding genius with a mind cultivated with the richest stores of intellectual wealth and a fancy winged to the highest flights of a most captivating imagery, of sound and spotless integrity with a warm spirit but a generous heart, and of a courage and determination so characteristic as to hold him forward as the strong example of what the old English heart could effect and endure. He had indeed his faults, but they seemed like the skilful disposition of shade in works of art to make the impression of his virtues more striking and gave additional grandeur to the outline of his character."

Making all due allowance for exaggeration in parliamentary obituaries and the hyperbole of eighteenth century periods, this testimonial shows us that Windham was a man of no small distinction. Another contemporary view of him may be given from the pages of another diary. Fanny Burney writes : " He is one of the most agreeable spirited wellbred and brilliant conversers I have ever spoken with . . . a man of family and fortune a very pleasing though not handsome face a very elegant figure and an air of fashion and vivacity."

It is as well to have this outside estimate before us, because in his diary we see him from an entirely different angle. It is a curious mixture of dull record and intimate self-analysis. He tells us very little of his political opinions and narrates no events of any special moment, and although he associates with all the most interesting people of the day he tells us, with one exception, nothing whatever about them. Lists even of the most eminent mortals are of no sort of interest in themselves. But it is tantalizing to get so near Fox, Burke, Pitt, Grey, Nelson, Talleyrand, Boswell, Sir Joshua Reynolds, Mrs. Siddons, etc., etc., and yet to get no syllable of how they looked or what they said.

The one exception is notable. He was a friend of Dr. Johnson's. For him he had a great admiration, and Dr. Johnson unquestionably exercised a considerable influence over Windham's method and manner of confronting the difficulties of life. There is a note of a conversation which took place before Windham went to Ireland, that is to say before he kept a diary, in which the following sayings of the Doctor occur :

> Never be afraid to think yourself fit for anything for which your friends think you fit.
> You will become an able negotiator ; a very pretty rascal. . . .
> No one in Ireland wears even the mask of incorruption. No one professes to do for sixpence what he can get a shilling for doing.

It was undoubtedly on Dr. Johnson's advice that he began his diary in 1784. In that year in August we get a very full memorandum of a conversation which took place between them at Ashbourne, chiefly on literary questions. On December 7 he visits him in his bedchamber,

> where after placing me next him on a chair he sitting in his usual place on the east side of the room he put into my hands two small volumes (an edition of the New Testament) saying " *Extremum hoc munus morientis habeto.*" He then proceeded to observe that I was entering upon a life which would lead me deeply into all the business of the world ; that he did not condemn civil employment but that it was a state of great danger ; and that he had therefore one piece of advice earnestly to impress upon me—that I would set apart every seventh day for the care of my soul ; that one day, the seventh, should be employed in repenting what was amiss in the six preceding and for fortifying my virtue for the six to come ; that such a portion of time was surely little enough for the meditation of eternity.

After recommending his servant to him and asking Windham to be his protector, Johnson expresses an emphatic opinion in favour of revealed religion and his reasons for accepting all the evidence in support of it. Five days later the diary records another visit in which Windham urges him to take nourishment, but Johnson dismisses the subject with " It is all very childish ; let us hear no more of it." Later in the day they have this last interview :

> I then said that I hoped he would forgive my earnestness—or something to that effect ; when he replied eagerly " that from me nothing would be necessary by way of apology " adding with great fervour, in words which I shall (I hope) never forget " God bless you, my dear Windham, through Jesus Christ " ; and concluding with a wish that we might meet in some humble portion of that happiness which God might finally vouchsafe to repentant sinners. These were the last words I ever heard him speak. I hurried out of the room with tears in my eyes and more affected than I had been on any former occasion.

Windham began diary writing in 1784 and continued it practically to the end of his life. On several occasions he deplores his failure to write regularly, and we gather quite clearly from these entries the underlying motive which made him keep a diary at all. In 1789 he says :

> I have no reason to alter the judgment given in the outset of the last volume that this practice of journal writing leads one insensibly into a habit of composition, strengthens the powers of recollection and by showing how one's time is actually disposed of suggests the means and excites the desire of disposing of it to greater advantage.

And again in 1791 :

> It is to be regretted that I have not by a more regular observance of the practice of journal writing ascertained the extent to which this habit has been

carried. It is more to be regretted that a habit known at all times to be so salutary and now found to be so easily practicable should not have been begun years and years ago. What a difference it would have made at the time! What a difference it would have made in my present condition and in all the future fortune of my life! It is not too much to say that to this single circumstance considering the way in which habits propagate each other, the whole difference may be ascribed of my being something or nothing.

In fact, he regarded keeping a diary as an intellectual and moral exercise. He records his intellectual pursuits, and notes the books he reads. The scope of his studies was immense; he wrote often in Latin, and many of the authors he refers to are very obscure. Besides Pluto, Livy, Thucydides, Horace, Erasmus, Voltaire, Rousseau, Condorcet, we find him absorbed in Lucan, Petavius, Scoppius, Thuanus, Themistius, Heliodorus, Phalereus, etc. Every moment his mind appears to have been occupied with deep intellectual exercises. We read, for instance, many entries such as these:

> Dr. Parr lent me to take in the chaise a treatise of Andronicus Rhodius as also one of Pletho.

> While I was dressing added a line or two to the Latin poem I was meditating.

> From eight till ten have been completing the conspectus of the books "De Sectione" till twenty before one: finished with great attention and great comfort the formulae extracted from Guignée for the construction of quadratic equations.

> In my pocket besides the volume of Livy I had been reading I took with me the collections of Greek epigrams with translations and begun a version with happy success.

> At breakfast or dinner I have generally made her (his niece) read some of Plutarch's Apothegms to me.

> My thoughts during the drive were employed in settling the question relative to the pressure of fluids.

> Set off by eleven; read Aristotle with little intermission all the way.

> Went to bed about one after beginning Spanish grammar.

Mathematics were his special hobby. He not only spends hours in studying them, but makes calculations in his head at odd moments.

> Tried an instance of multiplication in my head; the problem required a sum of 4 places into 1 of 3. I executed it without mistake in little less than ten minutes.

> A fall of rain and snow made my ride, both from the cold and uneasiness of the storm against my face, as unpleasant as any I recollect to have had. I continued notwithstanding to keep my mind tolerably well abstracted and

concluded a verse or two in some epigrams I was translating and settled a question about the increments of logarithms.

While sitting for his portrait to Sir Joshua Reynolds he multiplies 6824 by 2632.

He watches himself, disciplines himself, analyses his powers of concentration, the effect on him of interruptions, of company, of solitude, and he constantly blames himself for not doing enough—" I tremble lest my powers of thought are not what they ought to be." He is in fear at times of " a decline of faculties," and when he finds himself going into society more often he notes " circumstances altogether new and alarming." The very common failing of forgetting a name fills him " with the most alarming apprehensions." He fears " a decay of faculties," and at great length examines the causes of the phenomenon and notes down instances of failure in recollection whenever they occur. Sometimes he seems to fear that his intellectualism is of a too narrow and arid character.

My information goes no further than my studies and all that knowledge which is floating in the world and which to a mind properly prepared affords its chief nourishment has been wholly lost to me : kept off by negligence on the one hand and a perverse fancy on the other : and leaving me like some exotic in a greenhouse, to the precarious and imperfect supply of art.

His self-depreciation arises from an exaggerated humility, but it is quite genuine.

This habit of indecision if some means are not found to stop its progress and abate its malignity will corrupt and eat away my understanding to the very core ; it wastes my time, consumes my strength, converts comfort into vexation and distress, deprives me of various pleasures and involves me in innumerable difficulties. Some canon must be framed for proceeding in such cases.

My habits of thought are not quite what they ought to be but I tremble lest my powers of thought are not what they ought to be. I certainly have continually alarming instances to confirm the fears first conceived during the course of the preceding Summer.

Journey would have been comfortable if I had not been tormented and depressed by recollection of my own folly.

His low opinion of himself comes out more particularly in the references to his speeches in Parliament. He had a very high standard, and seems hardly ever to have been satisfied with his efforts. The testimony of his contemporaries, however, shows that he very greatly underrated his powers. Lord Lansdowne thought he had the best parliamentary address of any man he had ever seen, and Lord Chief Justice Denman declared unhesitatingly that Windham's speech on the Law of Evidence was the best speech he had heard during his life. Pitt, too, declared that his speeches were the finest productions possible of warm imagination and fancy.

Windham's constant misgivings with regard to his own powers may be best illustrated by the following extracts :

1785. The heat of the House disordered my faculties and enfeebled my powers and brought on a state of inability from which I could never recover sufficiently to venture to rise.

I thought my performance inferior and conceived others thought so too. . . . It was a mere effusion and though delivered in a forcible and perhaps graceful manner contained nothing more than anyone would have thought of in conversation.

1786. Tempted to speak on an incidental point in the debate and succeeded so ill where I think I might have succeeded so well . . . I am afraid what I said was awkwardly and cumbrously stated.

1793. Resolved to speak and succeeded fortunately in some parts beyond what I had reason to expect.

Made speech (a singularly bad one) on Fox's motion.

1798. My infatuation in not speaking exceeds all that I have ever known in myself or could conceive. . . . The loss to me is something incalculable and my regret is such as I know not what to do with myself. It breaks my slumbers and makes me incapable of doing anything.

1799. Spoke following Sheridan ; missed and mismanaged a good many things.

1800. Though rising without embarrassment and no distrust of myself somehow or other got confused and bewildered and in consequence prolix.

1805. Day of my motion. Spoke I am afraid three hours and a half ; " o'erflowing but not full."

1810. Spoke after Huskisson. Well satisfied not because everything very good in what I said but from a feel of power in myself in saying it.

His health occupies him from time to time, and he analyses elaborately his symptoms, the exact effect on him of early rising or staying in bed, the state of his digestive organs when dining alone compared with a dinner in company, the " alarming symptoms " brought about by low spirits, the effect on his stomach of tea, chocolate, and porter, and his giddiness, lumbago, and nose bleeding.

His entries with regard to his official work are rare and generally quite perfunctory and dull. As he gets more and more absorbed by his official duties the diary becomes more scrappy, a mere register of the people he met and of his movements. One might expect from all this that this rather pedantic but modest scholar never unbent and was of a uniformly serious if not melancholy disposition. It is, therefore, with surprise that we come upon entries of this description :

> After tea I grew into spirits more than ordinary so as to make me dance and sing about the room. . . .
>
> My spirits may be said in fact to be over good for instead of pressing me forward to vigorous application they have broken out in singing and dancing. [He sings " Viene o caro " but declares his voice is harsh and feeble and proceeds to a diagnosis of the causes.]
>
> It was here Mr. Barkes bedroom was adjoining to mine and that I apprehend that he must have overheard me singing. I went to bed in great spirits.

Here, too, is a sidelight on the dignified legislators of those times :

> The debate lasted till half past seven. In our way from the House we were boyish enough to amuse ourselves with throwing stones at each other during our progress through the Park and oranges when we came into St. James's street.

To trace further the lighter and more frivolous side of Windham's character we find that he was a devotee of prize fighting and gives far more vivid accounts of the " battles " he sees than of any debates in Parliament and breaks into critical descriptions of the combatants such as we never get of his political colleagues. Even on his way to Council he " took this opportunity of stealing to see a battle of which I had just had notice." He was too a constant playgoer and had a great admiration for Mrs. Siddons, with whom he exchanged several letters.

> Drove to Mrs. Siddons' in order to communicate a hint on a passage in Lady Macbeth which she was to act the next night.
>
> After the play went with Miss Kemble to Mrs. Siddons' dressing-room : met Sheridan there with whom I sat in the waiting room and who pressed me to sup at his house with Fox and North.
>
> Mrs. Siddons did Rosalind much better than the first time but not equal to her tragedy ; there is a want of hilarity in it ; it is just but not easy. The highest praise that can be given to her comedy is that it is the perfection of art ; but her tragedy is the perfection of nature.
>
> Opera for the first time. Dance of Bacchus and Ariadne. We have advanced to the point of seeing people dance naked.

Balloons were among the curious things which occupied his thoughts in the earlier days :

> Did not rise till past nine : from that time till eleven did little more than indulge in idle reveries about balloons.

> The greater part of the time till now one o'clock spent in foolish reveries about balloons.

> Went home with Horsley to whom I showed my idea about balloons.

At last he goes up in one himself and expresses his satisfaction in a very elaborate way, not at the conduct of the balloon, but at his own conduct in being quite unimpressed by any sensation of danger or apprehension. Dr. Burney mentions Windham's " Balloon Diary " in one of his letters to his daughter.

But Windham's lighter moments form only a very occasional relief to his habitual seriousness.

In 1790 he makes reflections on his loneliness :

> I felt that strong sense of the unhappiness of my own celibacy—that lively conception of pleasure I had lost—that gloomy apprehension of the conviction which I should feel of this hereafter clouding all my prospects, relaxing all my motives and in an especial manner destroying all enjoyment.

He marries in 1798. But the fact is only recorded quite baldly, and we get no intimate details with regard to his domestic relationships. Nor was the diary kept for recording the critical public events through which he lived, although they must of course have absorbed a large amount of his attention. He writes far less regularly in later years, but when he does write the entries consist of bare records of dinners, meetings, journeys, interspersed with self-disciplinary resolutions with regard to the disposition of his time. For instance, the year of the outbreak of the French Revolution, we only get three bald and uninteresting references to it.

In 1793 he goes over to France and is conducted actually into the trenches :

> It was not without anxiety that I ventured into a situation so new and untried as that in which I was about to enter. It was impossible to tell the effect of circumstances which have been found occasionally to operate so strangely on minds not distinguishable beforehand from the rest of the world. How could I be certain that the same might not happen to me as happened to certain persons that one knows of. . . . The result of the trial answered I am happy to say to my most sanguine expectations. I think with confidence that during any part of the time I could have multiplied if necessary a sum in my head. .

In June, 1810, Windham underwent the operation which caused his death. The last entry in the manuscript diary runs: "This day sentence has been passed upon me."[1]

The diary may be dull reading for anyone who expects entertainment; it is of little value to students of history, and we must go elsewhere for knowledge of Windham's career. But from the psychological point of view it has interest, for it reveals the careful endeavours at self-regulation and self-mastery of a man who might easily have been supposed to be solely engrossed in the affairs of State or in the scholastic studies for which he was noted.

Referring to Windham's diary, Lord Rosebery says: "Unhappily he was fated to be something of a suicide for he dealt an almost mortal blow to his own reputation. For we cannot doubt that it would have stood much higher but for his diary. And yet he himself set store by it as if one would think he regarded it as a sure base for his future fame ... any judicious friend would have put it without hesitation behind the fire."[2]

We are inclined to think this is altogether too severe. If only the enhancement of a reputation and the further embellishment of Windham's charms and spectacular talents are required, the diary undoubtedly is no help. But if a closer knowledge of the man is what we seek, his own self-exposure prompted by his "irritable conscience" gives us just the unexpected shadows and relief which help to make the portrait far more living than those which are generally provided in the case of public men by exterior estimates, however elaborate they may be.

Extracts from the diary were published in 1866 by Mrs. Henry Baring. Greville, who examined the manuscript, says there were twenty-eight volumes. We can judge by this that a great deal has been cut.

---

[1] Quoted in *Lady Holland's Journal*, Vol. II, p. 255.
[2] *Miscellanies—Literary and Historical*, by Lord Rosebery.

EIGHTEENTH CENTURY

MINOR DIARIES

MARY, COUNTESS COWPER

LORD COWPER was Lord Chancellor in the reign of George I. He married Mary Clavering in 1706, for some unknown reason, secretly. In 1714 she became a Lady of the Bedchamber to the Princess of Wales (Caroline of Anspach) and began to keep a diary of her court experiences. The diary, or rather what remains of it, covers four years up to 1716, and after a break there are some scattered entries of the year 1720.

There is nothing in the diary but court gossip, intrigue and scandal, but Lady Cowper writes in a very lively and unconventional style. She begins:

> The perpetual Lies that One hears have determined me, in spite of my want of Leisure to write down all the Events that are worth remembering while I am at Court.

She says, further, that she intends it only for her own use, a rough draft which " I intend hereafter to revise and digest into a better Method."

The entries are irregular, sometimes daily, sometimes at longer intervals, but always giving the fresh impression of the moment. Here is a sample of her manner of recording the day's doings:

> 1714. Nov. 21. I went to Chapel which concluded the service of my Week. I received a thousand Marks of my Mistress's Favour, as embracing me, kissing me, saying the kindest Things and telling me that she was truly sorry my Week of Waiting was so near out. I am so charmed with her good Nature and good Qualities that I shall never think I can do enough to please her. I am sure if being sincerely true and just to her will be any Means to merit her Favour I shall have it, for I am come into the Court with Resolution never to tell a Lie; and I hope I find the good Effects of it for she reposes more Confidence in what I say than in any others upon that very Account. A great Bustle was heard this Day at the Chapel. It was the Countess of

Nottingham who was going out before Church was done (like a true High Churchwoman) to take her Place behind the Princess's Chair-back in the Drawing room preferring to make her Court to an earthly rather than to a heavenly Power. I was ill from standing so long upon my Feet for which Reason I did undress me as soon as I came Home and stayed within for two Days to recover myself.

Her character sketches are not always very charitable. Here is a description of one of her colleagues:

The Duchess of Shrewsbury had some extraordinary Talents and it was impossible to hate her so much as her Lord, though she was engaged in the same ill Design. She had a wonderful Art at entertaining and diverting People, though she would sometimes exceed the Bounds of Decency. She had a great memory, had read a good deal and spoke three languages to Perfection; but then with all her Prate and Noise she was the most cunning designing woman alive.

George I, who speaks to her in French, was apparently capable of making jokes:

I never saw the King in better Humour than this night. He said a World of sprightly Things.

Her family pester her to get them soft sinecure jobs. Her brother-in-law wants to be put in " the Commission of the Salt Office," so does her uncle; her cousin pleads to get into " the Wine License " and her aunt asks for " a place about the Princess," and " high words " arise because she cannot please them all. The German and English elements in the court do not always appear to have hit it off:

Countess of Buckenburgh said that the English women did not look like Women of Quality but made themselves look as pitifully and sneakingly as they could; that they hold their Heads down and look always in a Fright whereas those that are Foreigners hold up their Heads and hold out their Breasts and make themselves look as great and stately as they can, and more nobly and more like Quality than the others. To which Lady Deloraine replied: " We show our Quality by our Births and Titles, Madam, and not by sticking out our Bosoms."

Lady Cowper becomes exasperated by the tiresome attentions of Mademoiselle Schutz, a niece of Baron Bernstorff's, the most prominent of the King's German Ministers.

Mademoiselle Schutz is a very unreasonable Body and would take no Hints I wished to be alone.

I had a letter from Mademoiselle Schutz to offer to come to stay with me all Day. I thank her for Nothing. I had too much of her Impertinence last Night.

She tries to borrow Lady Cowper's jewels, she insists on accompanying her to Court, she is "always upon the Spunge"; in fact she seems to have been difficult to shake off, and apparently was not a beauty.

> Mademoiselle Schutz is sitting for her Picture to one Constantine a French Refugee; 'tis most horridly done and so unfortunately like, that Anybody may know it and yet the ugliest Thing in the World.

Lady Cowper is sometimes entrusted with important errands to such people as the Archbishop of Canterbury and others, but for the most part all she records is court politics; and the strained relationship between the King and the Prince and the attempts at reconciliation form the chief theme of many of her entries. Judging by some of the remarks she notes down in 1720, she herself seems to have fallen out of favour.

Of herself Lady Cowper tells us practically nothing. It would almost seem as if she thought incidents connected with the court were suitable material for a diary, but domestic affairs were too intimate to write about. Nevertheless, we can detect something of her devotion to her husband, whom she refers to as "the dear fellow" when she writes in 1716.

> My Lord still ill. I am out of my Wits to see him suffer which I declare is ten times worse than Death to me, and would rather live with him all my Life on Bread and Cheese up three Pair of Stairs than be all this World can make me and at the same Time see him suffer.

She writes a little prayer once on her birthday; she mentions sermons, one of them "intolerably Dull to the Degree of an Opiate." She goes to the play frequently. Here is her account of taking the Princess to see Betterton's "The Wanton Wife":

> Went to the Play with my Mistress; and to my great Satisfaction she liked it as well as any Play she had seen; and it certainly is not more obscene than all Comedies are. It were to be wished our Stage was chaster; and I cannot but hope now it is under Mr. Steel's Direction it will mend.

George I had appointed Steele to the curious office of "Surveyor of the Royal Stables and Governor of the King's Comedians."

Lord Cowper resigned his office in 1720, and the various incidents connected with his resignation come in for notice with all the other intrigues. He died in 1723, and his wife died three months later at the age of 39.

Lady Cowper writes with such complete naturalness and so obviously without a thought of publication (as, for instance, when she starts an entry "Bit in the Night—I'm afraid by a Bug") that, although the Diary contains nothing of great importance, one gets a very good idea of the atmosphere of the early Georgian court.

THOMAS MARCHANT

THOMAS MARCHANT, of Little Park, Hurstpierpoint, Sussex, kept a diary from September 29, 1714, to June 26, 1728, with two breaks, one of five months, the other of nearly four years. The entries are irregular, occasionally only half a dozen occurring in one month. They are generally very brief. It may be included as an instance of a fairly full diary which is exclusively confined to a record of occupations, business and events. From the psychological point of view it has little interest, nevertheless it gives some picture of the life of an independent yeoman farmer of the time, and is not without value as a contemporary illustration of manners and customs.

Marchant, in addition to his agricultural pursuits, was a freshwater fish trader, and he gives many details with regard to the stocking of his ponds. He also registers his various payments and purchases. On one or two occasions he " drank too much " or " drank enough," but these occasional excesses do not trouble him. He frequently misses Sunday church, " having a bad headache." There are many single-line entries, some of which are curious as showing what he thought worth recording. For instance:

1715. Jan. 14. My son John began his accidence.

March 15. Paid my Uncle Courtness 15d for a small bottle of Daffy's Elixir.

Sep. 30. We had a dish of green peas for dinner to-day.

1716. Jan. 30. Paid Ball 2s for a bottle of Brandy.

Dec. 15. Paid J. Parsons 1s for shaving my head and tying my wig two or three times.

1717. Dec. 20. Ben Shove went to Lewes for a bottle of claret.

1718. Jan. 31. The mountebank still here.

1722. Aug. 13. Nanny sick with the measles.

26. Kitty the same.

29. Molly Balcombe the same.

1728. Jan. 19. A very wet day. Did nothing but eat and drink and sit by the fire all day and hard work I found it.

He always refers to the tinker as " my Lord Treep " and to the farrier as " my Lord Burt." His wife's doings are also recorded, but he expresses no opinion about her. Her purchases are entered :

Doomsday of Horsham brought my wife a new pair of jumps instead of stays. She paid him 36s 6 for them.

Marchant became land steward to the Duke of Somerset, who resided at Petworth, having married Elizabeth, Baroness Percy. Although business meetings with him are mentioned, we learn nothing about this nobleman except that on one occasion " he was in a cursed bad humour about the dung carts." The general impression the diary gives of its author is of a shrewd, humorous, active man, practical, rather close, easy going and entirely unreflecting.

The MS. of the diary was handed down in the family and lent in 1873 for reproduction in the Sussex Archæological Collections.

THE REV. JOHN THOMLINSON

THOMLINSON, of Blencogo, curate of Rothbury and subsequently rector of Glenfield, Leicestershire (b. 1692, d. 1762), began keeping a diary when he was at St. John's College, Cambridge, and it is probable that he kept up the habit for many years. A third part of the manuscript is taken up with extracts he wrote out from his earlier diary which he had kept " in loose papers." The remainder is complete between July 24, 1717, and January 9, 1718/9, and after a break where the diaries are missing a less consecutive record of the years 1721 and 1722. Judging by the complete section of the diary, Thomlinson was a regular writer, never missing a day. But this diary has several peculiar features. He writes fully, but refers comparatively little to local incidents or to births, deaths, marriages. Day after day often he writes down, not his doings, but some anecdote or bit of information quite irrelevant to his own pursuits. For instance, in January, 1717/8, he writes on immediately consecutive days about rattlesnakes (Jan. 19); the natives of Virginia (Jan. 20); dolphins (Jan. 21); whales (Jan. 22); sharks (Jan. 23); the rivers of the world (Jan. 24). It would seem as if he were making notes on what he was reading or collecting anecdotes, as a *raconteur*, for future use. There is a certain amount of erudition in some of his remarks, and he comments on public events; on the other hand, he never fails to recount the grossest local scandals. In addition to this, however, there is a good deal to be gathered about himself which is very far from being to his credit. He quotes incessantly his two uncles John and Robert. He was curate to Uncle John, and Uncle Robert was also a parson. The distinguishing feature of the diary is his endeavour to find a rich wife and the advice given him by his uncles with regard to his material advancement. His shameless pursuit of young ladies and calculations as to their incomes, his self-complacent materialism and his relish of unsavoury scandals, show him up in a most unfavourable light. He is quite sophisticated and there is a complete absence of *naïveté* in his comments. No note of passion, of love, or remorse, or even of disappointment, occurs anywhere. In his daily entries he must have been quite unaware that he was recording anything discreditable to himself. He probably regarded himself as an attractive Don Juan ; but the diary gives him away.

He refers to his own sermons in a very conceited way, and is always calculating how he can get a good living.

After leaving Rothbury he makes desperate efforts to become chaplain to the Duke of Wharton (the most notorious profligate of the day), but nothing comes of it. We cannot imagine that the Duke was anxious to have any sort of chaplain, even one of this type. Nevertheless, John Thomlinson was no fool. He evidently read a great deal, and he makes critical comments on his studies, as, for instance :

1718. Aug. 3. Eachard's history commended by Dr. Ellison. Uncle says he never heard it commended before—he flags in his Roman history, the two first volumes only good—Dryden corrected his first volume which made it excellent. Collier's History not good—tho' he rubs up his witt and lards his book with sententious and quaint expressions in most pages.

" Uncle says," " Uncle told me," " Uncle thinks," etc., occur very often. In fact, Uncle John seems to have interfered in matters both great and small. From marriage down to " Uncle found fault with my wig for being so light said I should have a darker one."

The pursuit of the young ladies is so ludicrous that it is worth quoting, although the frequent changes make it difficult to follow.

We begin with Miss Nicolson, daughter of the Bishop of Carlisle.

1717. July 31. " Uncle John has spoke to the Bishop of Carlisle about his daughter." But immediately after comes : " if I do not like her Aunt thinks he will be for her of Alnwick." This was Miss Potts, who was kept going for some time. But in August Uncle John says : " Mr. Collingwood is an honest man and he has got a daughter for you if you'll have her—he will give her perhaps £7 or 800—but what's that to twelve thousand which your father and I have." Uncle John goes further in September, and in conversation with Mr. Collingwood says : " Come, you'll not advance £500 with your daughter not £50 either." In October young John is taken to see " yon damsel of Mr. Collingwood's." His only comment is " she's like a Flanders mare . . . had a very mean dinner but a bottle of wine " ; and later in the month : " Uncle . . . would have Dolly but I am resolved against it. Our dinner was well drest but I cannot approve her person." Uncle Robert was against this match ; he " had rather I should have Mr. Douglas' daughter than Dolly Collingwood but he has one in view with £3000 whose father is the most likely man too to gett me a living of any man he knows."

Meanwhile Miss Ord was in the running because her father had the gift of a good living. She was " religious and good natured," " not a woman of parts or extraordinary sense but enough to manage a house."

In April, 1718, he writes : ". . . tryed one woman and did not like her I was to try another shortly and if I found her answer the description I intended to attack her very briskly and reduce her by storm." (It is impossible to say to which of them he refers.) In June, 1718, Jesse Hall appears on the scene, but only for a moment, and in the following January he makes an entry showing he is afraid of an entanglement, but the lady's name is left blank.

After the break in the diary when he had left Rothbury his affections turn to Mrs. Lawson, and a few months later to Nancy Repington, with whom he goes very far ; " no bait shall catch me but my dearest lady," he writes to her, " I'm all hers heart, estate, etc." At the same time Cousin Polly is spoken of. We feel Mary Repington, referred to as " the lady of Amington," will be the favoured one when " the Bishop of London's lady " turns up with a living of £300 a year and " she has £1,200 and other sisters may die." He is in great perplexity as to " whether my words may not have engaged me I cannot well recollect." And then the diary ends. As a matter of fact he eventually marries quite another lady, the daughter of his patron at Glenfield, in Leicestershire, James Winstanley. We know nothing of his subsequent history except the date of his death, and after reading the diary that exists we feel very little inclination to learn more.

Nevertheless, this is an instance of a diary which, however unpleasing it may be, is quite spontaneous and honest and therefore portrays the character of the writer more vividly than letters or second-hand observations of others could do and gives a truer picture of him than if he had attempted to explain himself by means of self-analysis.

The manuscript is in the British Museum (Add. MS. 22560), and was printed by the Surtees Society.

JOHN BYROM

FROM 1722 to 1744 John Byrom kept a very full and detailed diary. But it must be confessed that, although Byrom was an extremely learned man and came in contact with many interesting people, there is very little that is either arresting or entertaining in his long daily records. Born in 1692 at Kersal Cell, near Manchester, Byrom was educated at Merchant Taylors School and Trinity College, Cambridge. He studied medicine, he was a theologian, a mathematician, and a poet and hymn writer, but his attention was chiefly occupied with the system of shorthand which he invented. From the artistic, philosophic, and human point of view shorthand is not an inspiring subject, and his absorption in it, which appears by his constant references to it in the diary, does not make him specially attractive. He shows himself, however, to be very domestic, and while we have the record of conversations and discussions on religious and scientific subjects he is not above telling us when he plays chess or backgammon, when he goes to the play, exactly what he eats and drinks, and particulars with regard to his wife and children. In April, 1726, he confesses something about his motive in keeping a journal:

> I find that though what I set down in this kind of journal is nonsense for the most part yet that these nonsenses help to recollect times and persons and things upon occasion and serve at least to some purpose as to writing shorthand; therefore I must not, I think, discontinue it any longer, but only if I have a mind omit some trifling articles; though when I consider that it is the most trifling things sometimes that help us to recover more material things I do not know that I should omit trifles; they may be of use to me though to others they would appear ridiculous; but as nobody is to see them but myself, I will let myself take any notes, never so trifling, for my own use.

It is clear, therefore, that it was a private record, never intended for publication, and it often shows an astonishing power of memory. He seems to have had a misgiving about going on with it, for we find at the end of an entry in June, 1736, " Qy. to abolish this journal when I came home."

He was engaged in a book on shorthand (which was not published till after his death), he teaches shorthand to a large number of pupils, he discusses his system with his friends, he founds a shorthand society, he takes down sermons in shorthand, and he criticises other systems of shorthand.

Byrom generally writes from Abington's coffee-house, which seems to have been his headquarters. He habitually begins the record of the day by giving the time of his rising, which is often very late, as he stays up late at night.

> Rose at ten very hearty but not so alert as yesterday.

> Rose at twelve my hand trembled very much but I was very hearty ; had milk porridge to breakfast, had a mackerel to dinner.

> The coffee tasted very good after my fasting since morning, that is, since twelve or one o'clock—fine morning indeed, you idle rogue !

> Rose at twelve—why no sooner ?—God be merciful to me a sinner.

For the most part the entries, though full, are dull. When he travels there is rather more colour in his descriptions. But the longer entries are taken up with his discussions generally on theological subjects. Though an adherent of the Church of England, he is something of a mystic, and he is interested in various Nonconformist sects. He tries to win back a young lady referred to as F. H. from Quakerism to the Church. This leads to certain misunderstandings.

> Mr. Walker said that Abel Strethall had spoke to him to know if he had heard anything of her and wondered at my going there and thought it very odd that I should converse with a young woman of twenty one, which I thought a little carnal of friend Abel.

Many eminent people of the day become interested in his system of shorthand. He has discussions with Butler (author of the *Analogy*), William Law (the Nonjuror), the Wesleys, Warburton, Bentley, and many others, amongst whom was a gentleman who rejoiced in the name of Dr. Anodyne Necklace. Byrom was a member of the Royal Society and describes meetings and controversies there under the presidency of Sir Hans Sloane. His discussions with his friends, related at considerable length, range over a large variety of topics—the Creation, religion, fluxions, the signs of the Zodiac, poetry, mathematics, Hebrew, etc., etc., but they are generally long-winded and rather obscure.

Brimful of information on every conceivable subject, we can imagine Byrom must have been rather a bore. It would indeed be difficult to have any light intercourse with a man who in his spare moments was engaged in reading Capellus against Buxtorf, Clenardi, Meursius, Carpzovius, Jamblicus *de Mysteriis*' Gohorius, Avenerius, Daubuz on the Revelations, Gutherius' *Offices*, Ebu Yokdam, Rusbrochius, Dachsel on Hebrew accents, Lactantius and Passeratius.

He has lighter moods, no doubt, but we get no sense of enjoyment or fun from his recital of his less serious occupations. For instance, when he goes to a masquerade there is only the following perfunctory reference :

> They talked of going to the masquerade. Ord gave me a ticket, he lent me a black coat and waistcoat and bag gown and sent for a wig from the barber's ; Mr. Folks had another gown and Heyrick's hat without his rose: the man could not get us a coach so we walked to Common Garden and took two chairs. My chair 1s.

We don't believe he enjoyed himself, and we cannot help feeling that in his black coat and waistcoat he was longing to be back with Gohorius and Rusbrochius. On another occasion, when his friends talk of masquerades and plays, he says, " I was grieved in spirit for myself and them."

The whole diary of course is written in shorthand, and in 1728, on a visit to Cambridge, he comes across another shorthand diary, —the greatest of all diaries—" five large volumes quarto being a journal of Mr. Pepys ; I did not know the method but they were writ very plain." The shorthand expert, however, passes them by, and is only interested in the various books on systems of shorthand in the Pepysian Library. His own work was published in 1767, four years after his death.

At the time of the rebellion Byrom showed Jacobite sympathies, but the last entry in the diary is dated January 27, 1744, and the rest of his career is illustrated by a number of his letters. In the early part of the nineteenth century a large collection of his papers was discovered in the two family residences of Kersall Cell and Quay Street. The diary was deciphered and eventually published by the Cheetham Society between 1854 and 1857, together with letters and other memoranda. There is an attractive portrait of the author at the beginning of the volumes showing a youthful, pleasant and refined face with a very high forehead.

ELIZABETH BYROM

ALTHOUGH only a fragment, this diary is the earliest woman's diary in this collection. Elizabeth, known as " Beppy," was John Byrom's eldest daughter. She was born in 1722, and died unmarried in 1801. She inherited the diary writing instinct of her father, or perhaps was taught by him to keep one, and it is not improbable that this is only a part of a fuller journal. The entries, which become regular and daily after November 25, begin on August 14, 1745, and end on January 23, 1746, covering the period of the Pretender's entry into Manchester. Byrom himself refers to these events in letters, but not in his diary. While there is nothing remarkable about this record, Beppy's style is simpler and more graphic than her father's, and we get quite a good idea of the invasion of the Jacobites, with whom she, like her father, was in obvious sympathy. There are only a few references to domestic details and the movements of her family. One or two entries begin with the word " smoothing," which means that she was occupied in ironing clothes, and she buys " a blue and white gown " for 12s., after things have quieted down she goes " a hunting " and has good sport.

The following extracts may be given, though without the consecutive entries no impression of the full story can be given:

1745. Aug. 14. Great talk of the Pretender coming.

Sep. 26. The Presbyterians are sending everything that's valuable away, wives, children and all for fear of the rebels.

Nov. 16. An express is come that Carlisle is surrendered to the rebels and the next day the castle. General Wade is gone to the relief of it, but went two days march and turned again ; they were two days without any provisions. Capt. Barlow has writ a most dismal account of them, that they are so numbed with cold and their limbs mortify and they die very fast.

Nov. 27. The Prince lay at Lawyer Starkey's Preston last night : he has marched from Carlisle on foot at the head of his army ; he was dressed in a Scotch plaid, a blue silk waistcoat with silver lace and a Scotch bonnet with J.R. on it.

Nov. 28. About 3 o'clock to-day came into town two men in Highland dress and a woman behind one of them with a drum on her knee and for all the loyal work that our Presbyterians have made, they took possession of the town as one may say for immediately after they were light they beat up for volunteers for P.C.

Nov. 30. I dressed me up in my white gown and went up to my aunt Brearcliffe's and an officer called on us to go see the Prince, we went to Mr. Fletcher's and saw him get a horseback and a noble sight it is, I would not have missed it for a great deal of money ; his horse had stood an hour in the court without stirring and as soon as he got on he began a-dancing and capering as he was proud of his burden and when he rid out of the court he was received with as much joy and shouting almost as if he had been king without any dispute, indeed I think scarce anybody that saw him could dispute it.

Dec. 12. Smoothing ; my brother came and fetched me to see the Duke [of Cumberland] we all went up to Aunt Brearcliffe's, stayed there all day, saw nothing but the light horse and hussars which went straight through the town.

Dec. 19. Yesterday was the fast ; to-day at my Uncle's at dinner, it is the first time of my uncle's going out, my aunt keeps her bed ; where the Highlanders did not care to pay they drew bills upon the Duke of Kingston or some other great man ; we have abundance of lies about them, they are killed, taken, surrounded, and got clean away all two or three times of a day.

Dec. 29. He [The Rev. A. Ward] preached in the afternoon a most furious sermon against popery. Mr. Lewthwaite and Mr. Johnson drank tea at my uncle's. Mr. L. and my mama had a great scolding bout about these Highlanders, he abuses them most strangely ; we stayed the evening.

1746. Jan. 3. The Presbyterians have made two effigies of the Prince, one in his Scot dress and one in his English dress, and carried them up and down the town and raised a great mob which was headed by some of the great Presbyterian gentlemen and went to all the houses in town where any were gone from and broke their windows . . . they were very rude and they carried their bunch of rags down to Mr. Dakenfield's and the Justice out of his great courage got a gun and shot at it, and then it was brought into the house, and he wrung it by the nose, then his wife and daughter were introduced and had the honour to slap it in the face, and so on till they all were tired and drunk for all the heads of the Presbyterians were at the Angel and gave the mob drink ; then they hung it upon the signpost then quartered it, then threw it into the fire ; somebody threw a piece of it into the drink which put them into a violent passion.

Another account of an eye-witness of the events in Manchester in these exciting days is given in the Lancashire and Cheshire Antiquarian Society's *Transactions*, Vol. VII, in the form of daily memoranda written down by Thomas Walley, one of the constables. His account is more official, but not so full or picturesque as Beppy Byrom's. Her diary is printed with her father's in the Cheetham Society's volume XLIV.

JOHN HOBSON

THE diary of John Hobson, of Dodworth Green, Yorkshire, begins on January 1, 1725, and ends on January 27, 1734–5. The entries are irregular, an interval of several days often occurring between them. He writes of local incidents and accidents, visits, and gossip, the purchase of cattle, and the visits of friends for the most part in quite a perfunctory way. But the distinguishing feature of the diary is the astonishing number of deaths he records, so that the journal reads like a page from the church register except that marriages and births occur very rarely. Never can any man have attended so many funerals. The cause of this excessive mortality among his friends and acquaintances is not mentioned except on one or two occasions from accidents or "died of pleuritick fever," "died of the small pox." The latter disease, which was the scourge of the time, may account for many of the deaths. If he has no local deaths to record he mentions the decease of prominent people, "The King of Denmark dead," "The Duke of Leeds dead." Indeed, John Hobson seems to have had a morbid interest in Death and goes out of his way to discover its ravages.

May 8. 1730. Observ'd a great many fresh graves at Bradfield churchyard. There has been above 60 buried there in a short time.

It is not surprising, therefore, that his own death should have been a subject of interest to him. There is absolutely no personal note in the diary till April, 1729, when on the 15th he spends the morning "in meditating on the ill posture of my affairs." The infirmity of his parents, the carelessness of his servants and his debts

depressed my spirits so much and made me so weak that at nine o'clock when I got up I supposed myself dying for several hours. I thank God I had no fearfull thoughts nor was not at all discouraged at the apprehensions of death which I thought every minute approaching but took what care I could to spend that small portion of time I thought I had left to my best spirituall advantage.

The Sacrament is administered to him and he says :

When I think how suddenly death may overtake one it will make me lead a more circumspect life for the future and always have regard to my latter end.

The doctor who blisters him

found quickly that it was mentall as well as corporeall distemper and told me I had the hypochondriack passion upon me, which then I could not believe, as being a meer stranger to that distemper but found his words very true for I was afterwards very often so much disordered in my thoughts that I could not rest nor govern them.

But he recovers and is well enough to record the death of two other people on the two succeeding days.

He falls ill again in 1732, " there was but small hope of my recovery." He has the Sacrament again, and again recovers, and is able to announce the death of a friend and his father's death, which he does without any expressions of regret.

The large number of names mentioned makes the journal valuable from the point of view of local history. Otherwise it is only just possible to catch a glimpse of the personality of the writer. By a curious irony the date of the diarist's own death is not recorded anywhere.

The diary was communicated by Mr. Joseph Wilkinson to the Surtees Society.

WALTER GALE

ONLY extracts exist of the diary of Walter Gale, schoolmaster, of Mayfield. It was discovered at Hastings spread out in a garden to be dried for the purpose of lighting fires. The portion rescued from the flames covers intermittently the period from 1749 to 1759. It begins on the appointment of Gale as schoolmaster at Mayfield at a salary of £16 a year. He was a versatile man, however, and made money in other ways besides teaching. He paints inn signs, designs quilts, waistcoats, neckerchiefs, and there is also an entry " finished diamending two heelbands and three-quarter pieces of a pair of shoes for Squire Baker's lady."

The diary, which is not kept with daily regularity, is an astonishing mixture of a record of drinks and sermons. The entries of the former are more frequent than of the latter. Incessantly we have " he treated me with a quartern of gin " ; " he treated me with a mugg of fivepenny " ; " he treated me with a quartern of brandy and a mugg of ale " ; " we sat down with the aldermen and drank raisin wine—very good ! " The text of the Sunday sermon is always given, and sometimes his conviviality and his piety are combined in one entry.

Sunday April 6. (1749) I went to Church at Hothley. Text from St. Matthew " Take no thought saying What shall we eat and what shall we drink and wherewithal shall we be clothed," and I went to Jones's where I spent 2d and here came Thomas Cornwall and treated me with a pint of twopenny.

On one occasion he falls from a high bank in the dark. This was after partaking of a quartern of brandy, a pint of fivepenny and a mug of mild beer. An accident on horseback described in detail takes place after visiting " Mr. Bridge's who entertained me well." Drink also appears to have been his remedy in illness : " Having taken three pills I went to Peerless for a 1d worth of warm ale." A Mr. Rogers presents him with a book entitled *A Caution to Swearers.* But the schoolmaster never indulges in self-depreciation or remorse over his failings.

It is not surprising that Gale should have come to cross purposes with the trustees of the school. John Kent, who appears to have been a very irascible old gentleman, led the attack.

1750. May 26. Old Kent came and I went with him to Mr. Baker ; they said they should have a ragged congregation of scholars who should sit together in the new gallery and that they should insist on my sitting with them ; to this I did not assent.

1758. Tuesday April 25. I met the old man, who, without any provocation on my part or saying a word to him, loaded me with opprobrious language and told me the report of the town was that I was a drunken, saucey, covetious fellow and concluded with his opinion that I had neither good breeding nor honesty. In answer I disallowed the report of the old man charged upon the town ; I allowed there might be a little truth in my being covetuous but as to drunkenness and sauciness, it was utterly false.

The incident of his fall off " the high bank " got about :

Old Kent came to the knowledge of the above journey and told it to the Rev. Mr. Downall in a false manner, much to my disadvantage ; he said I got drunk and that that was the occasion of my falling and that not being contented with what I had had, I went into the town that night for more.

Foreseeing trouble, Gale got up a testimonial to himself from his neighbours, certifying to his good qualities, " his attachment to church and state, his sober life, and conversation." But old Kent continued to visit the school and make trouble.

The old man entered the school with George Wilmhurst and Eliz. Hook and said they should be taught free. I asked him how many I was to teach free ; without any further ado he flew into a violent passion. Among other abusive and scurrilous language he said I was an upstart, runnagate, beggarly dog ; that I picked his pocket and that I never knew how to teach a school in my life . . . he clinched his fist in my face—made a motion to strike me and declared he would break my head. He did not strike me but withdrew in a wonderful heat and ended all with his general maxim "The greater scholler the greater rogue."

One more outburst of Kent's is recorded:

> I was told by Mr. Downer that the day before James had been so indiscreet as to suffer Richardson's boy George to bring beer into the school, and, old Kent coming in before the mug was out, the boy asked him to drink; thereupon he fell into a great heat and drove the boy out of the school.

Except for the account of these disputes very little mention is made of the school or the scholars. The schoolmaster's interests were evidently in other directions.

One of his references to smuggling may be quoted:

> I set out for Laughton after drinking a quatern of gin and came to Whitesmiths where was a hurley bolloo about Mr. Plummer's (now a custom house officer) having seized a horse loaded with 3 anchors of brandy which was carried off by him and two soldiers.

The end part of the diary is unfortunately lost. But Gale held his place till 1771, long after his formidable adversary old Kent was laid in his grave. However, in spite of the invariable self-complacency of this diarist, his manner of living eventually brought him into trouble. On October 18, 1771, it was resolved by the trustees, *nem. con.*,

> That the schoolmaster, Mr. Walter Gale, be removed from the school for neglecting the duties thereof and that he have notice to leave the same the next quarter day.

The diary was published by the Sussex Archæological Society.

GEORGE BUBB DODINGTON (Lord Melcombe)

IF only Bubb Dodington had written a diary about the more domestic side of his life,—if only he had displayed himself as a wit, a friend of wits, scholars, and authors, and given some of his literary and social experiences,—we should no doubt have been greatly entertained. As it is, his diary, covering the years from 1749 to the beginning of 1761 (the year before his death), is just a long rather involved register of political intrigue. In many diaries there is an abundance of self-reproach. Here we get a complete contrast. The keynote of Bubb Dodington's diary is self-justification. He seems anxious to throw the most favourable light he can on the sordid intrigues in which he was continually engaged as an unashamed political place-hunter.

The diary was published by Mr. Henry Penruddocke Wyndham in 1785. It had been bequeathed to him with other papers by Mr. Thomas Wyndham, Dodington's cousin, with an injunction that only those should be published which may " in some degree do honour " to Lord Melcombe's memory. Mr. Henry Wyndham hesitated on the propriety of publishing the diary, as " it shows his political conduct (however palliated by the ingenuity of his own pen) to have been wholly directed by the base motives of avarice, vanity, and selfishness." But the very careful way in which Dodington had written out the whole diary afresh forces the editor to the conclusion that he " wrote for the publick and that he intended his diary should in a future season be produced to light." Accordingly he had no compunction in having it printed.

Bubb Dodington, born in 1691, was returned for Parliament as member for Winchelsea in 1715. Subsequently he sat for Bridgwater. For sixteen years he was a Lord of the Treasury. In 1744 he was Treasurer of the Navy under Henry Pelham and again in 1755 under Newcastle and Fox. He succeeded the year before he died in getting a peerage.

Political backstairs intrigue is not a very inspiring, nor indeed a very interesting, theme at any time. In the days of George II there was so much of it and its ramifications were so involved that it is difficult now to follow, and one has some reluctance, or rather disinclination, to make any attempt to disentangle the threads. Dodington's venality and tergiversations were so marked that he became a target for political satires, caricatures and pamphlets, and it is not surprising when we find him complaining of the publication of " the vilest and most rancorous pamphlet against me."

It is quite impossible to follow him through the political maze. Extracts must be picked out here and there to illustrate his endeavours to be on the winning side and to get the best he can for himself.

In 1749 he resigns his post as Treasurer of the Navy in order to throw his lot in with Frederick, Prince of Wales, who, as we know, lived in bitter rivalry with his father. We get a full account of the bargain. The Prince offers him £2,000 a year, Bubb Dodington goes through the form of saying he would prefer to take the post of Treasurer of the Chambers " without any salary." The Prince of course refuses.

He then immediately added that we must settle what was to happen in reversion and said he thought a Peerage with the management of the House of Lords and the seals of Secretary of State for the southern province would be a proper station for me if I approved of it. Perceiving me to be under much confusion at this unexpected offer and at a loss how to express myself, he stopped me and then said, I now promise you on the word and honour of a Prince that as soon as I come to the Crown I will give you a peerage and the Seals of the Southern province. Upon my endeavouring to thank him he repeated the same words and added (putting back his chair) and I give you leave to kiss my hand upon it now by way of acceptance ; which I did accordingly.

But they were both of them counting their chicks before they were hatched, and when the Prince most provokingly died less than two years later all Bubb Dodington's schemes were overturned. While he was with the Prince, however, there were dissensions in the camp, and he was accused of having forced himself on the Prince, which accusation in many pages of the diary he elaborately repudiates. The royal animosity against Frederick was kept up after his death. We are told in the diary that in the funeral procession " there was not an English Lord, nor one Bishop, and only one Irish Lord."

No refreshment was provided for those who did attend, and they " were forced to bespeak a great cold dinner from a common tavern in the neighbourhood."

For a moment after Frederick's death Dodington is depressed. He writes :

I have done enough and henceforth shall live to myself the years which God in his mercy grant me unless I am called upon to assist.

Nevertheless he soon begins making advances to Pelham and offers him " all the services in his power." The difficulty is to get round the King, so he keeps on protesting, " it was never my intention to offend His Majesty." At the same time he keeps up intimate relations with the widowed Princess, who is much exercised about the upbringing and education of her children, specially Prince George. One one of these visits he writes :

I waited on the Princess and staid with her two hours. Much freedom and condescension—rather too much of the first on my side.

He was quite a friend of the family, as we see by this domestic scene.

I went to Leicester House expecting a small company and a little musick but found nobody but her Royal Highness. She made me draw a stool and sit by the fire side. Soon after came in the Prince of Wales [George III] and Prince Edward and then the Lady Augusta all in undress and took their stools and sat round the fire with us. We continued talking of familiar occurrences till between ten and eleven with the ease and unreservedness and unconstraint as if one had dropped into a sister's house that had a family to pass the evening.

His plots with Pelham cease because Pelham dies in 1754, so then he starts with the Duke of Newcastle. With him he reaches a degree of cordiality which raises his highest hopes; he says to the Duke :

> I would not even be in the right against him and I was very sure I would never again be in the wrong against him for which I hoped his Grace would be my caution. He said he would with all his heart. He took me in his arms and kissed me twice with strong assurances of affection and service.

This on March 21. But on March 27 he notes :

> Notwithstanding the fine conversation of last Thursday all the employments were given away.

So when in the following month he has another long interview with the Duke he concludes his account of it :

> He made great professions of good wishes, good will, best endeavours etc. etc. which weigh with me as much as the breath they were composed of.

But his struggle for place and recognition continues, "for," he openly confesses, "I was determined to make some sort of figure in life." But the immensely long interviews and conversations, in which there is very little about policy and nothing whatever about principle, are fatiguing, and sufficient quotations have been given to show what Bubb Dodington was after. As already related, he eventually succeeded in getting his reappointment as Treasurer of the Navy, after which it is not surprising to read that "Her Royal Highness received me very coolly." A year before he died he was given a peerage, so perhaps his ambitions were more or less satisfied.

A good many sidelights on elections and electoral methods occur in the diary. He expresses indignation at the methods of his opponents, as if his own were above reproach. We may find fault with our electoral system to-day, but we can congratulate ourselves that there is some improvement on those days when an election at which under 350 votes were polled cost the candidate £5,000, as was the case with Dodington at Bridgwater.

A most unfavourable criticism of Bubb Dodington occurs in Egmont's diary. Horace Walpole in the course of a conversation with Egmont in 1733, after describing how Dodington " does perfectly govern " the Prince of Wales, adds that he is " the vilest man, vain, ambitious, loose and never to be satisfied. He wants now to be a Lord and when he is that he will want to be a Duke."

Several poems were dedicated to Bubb Dodington and he himself was the writer of occasional verse. We learn through Cumberland, Lord Halifax's secretary, something about the showy and tasteless splendour in which he lived; with his vast figure arrayed in gorgeous brocades he would loll after dinner in his chair in lethargic slumbers and wake up to produce an occasional flash of wit or to read selections, often of the coarsest kind, even to the ladies. It is a pity that his diary does not reflect any of his wit or his apparently eccentric humours.

JOHN BAKER

BAKER, who was a solicitor and barrister of the Inner Temple, kept a regular diary from 1750 to 1779. He carried on his business in London and was a wealthy man, having married an heiress, Miss Ryan, whose sister married Cardinal Manning's grandfather. In 1771 he came to reside at Horsham, in Sussex, when he was 59, and it is only the diary from that date that is available for examination. The entries are very regular, describing his daily occupations and giving the names of a multitude of friends with whom he came in contact. The style is peculiar and individual; words in Latin, French, and other languages are inserted here and there with amusing effect. He always refers to his wife as *Uxor*. For instance :

Uxor and 2 Pattys and I to Col. Leland's in coach and 4. Home to dinner. *Soir* home.

Mrs. Drury came and went with y[em] in *carosse à quatre*. Mrs. Blunt *seule*. Mr. Tridcroft and sisters *là*. Mr. Blunt had been *à cheval* to within 5 miles of Guildford.

J.P.B. out shooting, *ne tua rien*.

Uxor went *hier* in chaise *con* little Patty to see Mrs. Blunt.

Brother brought a letter from each of his daughters to me with a waistcoat made by *l'ainée*, also a letter from Mr. William Johnson which shall read *cras*.

Dined *seul*. *Après midi* walked old walk to mill.

Colonel Leland we saw not, he out shooting. Rest of day *à l'ordinaire*.
Soir picquet. Drank two pint bottles of cowslip wine.

Mr. Blunt called and asked me to dine at his house to-day. I went *portant* first time *ma belle culotte noire*. Found Mr. Thomas White and Mr. B.'s two *fils cadets*.

His occupations are not particularly interesting. In addition to dinners and entertainments and dances at *l'assemblée*, his chief form of amusement seems to have been looking on at cricket matches, which he describes.

And here is an example of a dance :

We all went to Mr. George Waller's, the " Anchor " *où* a dance [Here follows a list of names] N B All marked X danced continually changing partners. Began soon after 7 danced till 9, then drank tea, then danced till 12, then supped in another room . . . then the ladies to dancing room and went to singing and the gentlemen who sat down to supper after ladies gone went backward and forward to rooms where they were singing. At near 2 began three or four more dances and broke up at 3.

We have records of his occasional reading :

Read Boccacio's Novel of " Tedaldo and Emmelina." *Après midi* took " Ninon de l'Enclos."

Mr. Waller sent for " Drake's Voyage " same I gave Jack Manning at Barbadoes and I lent him Pennant's " First Tour."

Read " Emma " said to be Lady Ferguson's and several other books.

Edward came home with me and took back " Lord Herbert of Cherbury."

All day reading " Abbé Rayner."

He gives his daughters curious reading in the shape of trials.

Girls read Mary Modders trial for bigamy.

Girls read at night Colonel James Turner's Trial but *si mal elle sortit pleurant*.

He plays bowls and cards and draughts, and although hot punch and other drinks are mentioned on only one occasion does he seem to have gone too far.

Afternoon *ni cartes ni* bowls. Drank a little hard and walked in garden. A little dance, *sans violon*, only one dance.

He takes no interest in public affairs, and the only incident recorded which does not immediately concern him and his neighbours, except trials in the district which he several times describes, is the quarrel and duel between John Scawen and Fitzgerald, of which he gives an account in some detail.

Although there is no personal note or attempt at self-revelation, there is a certain intimacy in the homely details which seems to bring one into close proximity to the diarist so that when *Uxor* falls ill one can feel his bitter grief behind the reticent notes on her illness.

> *Uxor* exceeding ill at night. . . . *Uxor* much better *ce soir*. [The use of French shows a rise of spirits]. . . . *Uxor* exceeding low to-night.

And then *Uxor* dies and there is a most affecting scene. For once he breaks his bare record of events by exclaiming, " Good God, how terrible and racking it was." He spends a fortnight in retirement in his own grounds without any communication with his friends. Then he resumes his ordinary life.

But there is a special feature in the diary which throws a good deal of light on John Baker's disposition. Many diarists make occasional references to their ailments. But Baker gives the closest attention to his physical infirmities, and makes a very detailed analysis of his illness, the remedies used, and the effects obtained, sometimes in French, sometimes in plain English. These notes, however, would only be suitable for a medical journal, and a few typical extracts alone can be given here :

> Was taken with a violent ague—drank hot punch and Madeira negus—found myself heavy with that—slept well rest of night ; drank much milk and water, wonderfully refreshing—which sat pleasingly on my stomach.

> Took castor oil a very large dose at ½ past 4, lay till ¼ before 7 *quand une belle opération mais c'était la seule*.

> Awoke *ce matin* with a violent pain . . . took warm water, honey, rum, turlington, then a mug of warm water and souring then wood strawberry brandy. However eat nothing but a little broth to dinner and at picquet broad glass of gin punch and turlington. Afterwards mug small beer and sugar—to bed soon after ten.

> Went to Church. Thought to stay to Sacrament but sermon began just before twelve and very cold and pain in bowels, so did not.

His health, in fact, undoubtedly caused him anxiety. He may have been a hypochondriac, but judging by the remedies he took he must certainly have aggravated any trouble he may have had.

The year before he died (1777) he makes the following entry, which shows a sad depression from his usual cheerfulness :

> Sep. 28. My father died wanting 22 days of completing his 66th year I want more than four months of completing my 66 year which I think it utterly impossible I shall ever do, for I grow daily weaker. The sea baths nor sea air has any effect to make me better but all are flat and useless, and I have

neither pleasure nor amendment from them. 'Tis a vain struggle to attempt to lengthen this poor remnant of life. Even if it could be prolonged it is not worth holding. I have no business above ground. I consume hourly and both my feelings and my countenance make me look upon myself as a dead man.

Sept. 29. I believe the glass of milk and gin and the five or six glasses of arrack Punch I drank at Mrs. Bell's heated me too much, pains in hips, left thigh, and knee exceeding stiff. In night both knee bones ached. Left thigh aches and knee burns.

John Baker also made an elaborate daily weather chart.

The diary, bound in vellum, was left by Cardinal Manning to his niece, Mrs. Gasquet, who gave it to Mr. Wilfred Scawen Blunt. It forms part of the papers at Newbuildings, and the portion of it from which the above extracts are taken was communicated by Mr. Blunt to the Sussex Archæological Collections in 1909.

DR. RUTTY

THERE are many instances of diaries which have been kept chiefly for the purpose of spiritual correction, though other matters may also find a place in them. The long prayers, the pages of self-depreciation, the exaggerated humility, make rather tedious reading. Dr. John Rutty's "spiritual diary," although it is exclusively concerned with his inner life and contains hardly any mention at all of events or domestic matters, differs both in form and style from any of the others and must be regarded as a unique production. Dr. Johnson was much diverted and laughed heartily when parts of the diary were read to him. And indeed, as will be seen by the following extracts, there is something peculiarly funny in Dr. Rutty's entries. Unfortunately, too, we find ourselves laughing at the doctor and not with him, for his humour is quite unconscious. But we are disposed to take a more serious view when we have the whole diary before us and can see the patient and ceaseless endeavour of a really spiritually-minded man to combat his failings. He did not begin diary writing till he was 56, and he continued till within four months of his death at the age of 77 (1753 to 1774). He can have had no thought of publication when he began his diary, but after continuing for twelve years or so he decided that its publication might be helpful to others.

It is his laconic, ejaculatory, epigrammatic style that makes the diary notable. It reminds one in its short paragraphs sometimes of the Psalms and sometimes of the book of Jeremiah. There is no doubt Rutty modelled his style on the Bible. He says:

> There is a beautiful laconism in the holy scriptures; but many preachers and authors seem to think to be heard for their much speaking and writing: but they bring their jewels in a deal of chaff.

John Rutty was born in Wiltshire, of Quaker parents, in 1698. He was educated at Leyden, took his medical degree in 1723, and settled down to a practice in Dublin in 1724. He wrote several learned medical books as well as a history of the Quakers in Ireland. He was a much esteemed and successful physician, and to his friends he appeared a humble, self-sacrificing, temperate man of pleasing temper and charitable disposition. But inwardly he was consumed with the notion that he was a prey to drink, gluttony and bad temper, and his diary records his unceasing struggle with these failings, and the entries recording his failures and resolutions continue ceaselessly throughout the diary, which in the earlier years is kept with almost daily regularity.

Before singling out special extracts for quotation with regard to his lapses, it will be as well to give a sample page as an illustration of his biblical style.

Third Month 1758.
9. Went into the country and took the spiritual book with me lest the natural should encroach.
10. Struggled and got to meeting: Satan avant! for God is bringing forward in a degree suitable to conviction.
I have sucked at the breasts of this world and am not satisfied.
Exercised with retention of fees.
A rarity—a spiritual conference in a visit.
O for more of the chaste tender preserving fear in drinking!
Feasted beyond bounds.
12. Rose too late: O the dull body!
13. This day an acquaintance broke deeply in my debt; the deception great and the loss considerable: Lord thou has smitten: sanctify the event.
15. Thus doth the Lord embitter my sweets and bring a partial blast on my labours and why? To wean from the world. Amen. My friendships moulder.
18. O what a favour this to be planted in the true church out of Babylon and its corruptions and where every motive draws to a holy life agreeable to the doctrine and precepts of our Lord.
Seven patients without a penny even as usual.

The references to drink and gluttony are very numerous; we can only give the most striking:

Feasted again a little beyond the sacred medium.

Feasting beyond the holy bounds.

O that I may not abuse riches ! Certain it is I often have, in guzzling.

Feasted, not innocently, in not refusing the bumper.

I feasted pretty moderately; but with this notable difference in solitary and social eating, that in the last I eat more like a swine.

An hypochondriac obnubilation from wind and indigestion.

A little incubus last night on too much spinage.

A little of the beast in drinking.

Although I dined with the saints I drank rather beyond bounds.

A little swinish at dinner.

Piggish at meals.

A little piggish in stuffing with vegetables.

Ate and drank swinishly: nature wants less.

I rather exceed in solids at dinner.

Take care, take care of the fumes of cyder and whiskey, tremble at the mixture.

Gripes from excess.

A little of the beast in drinking.

Ate as a swine to-day.

The dose of drink precious to the publick meeting was somewhat too large.

Time after time he feasts on "bread and water" to correct himself, and the occasions of overeating become gradually less frequent, till in later years we get the following entry :

A sensible advancement in victory over the sin that used so easily to beset me.

The reports on temper may be treated in the same way :

Twice, unbridled choler.

Weak, and fretful. Licked spittle in two places insolent in two others.

Brittle again.

A sudden eruption of ferocity.

A black evening : a fit of downright anger on a supposed injury and for want of timely resisting, it proceeded : Lord pardon.

In-appetent and morbidly peevish with lassitude and coldness.

A frappish cholerick day.

Snappish on fasting.

Cursed snappishness to those under me on a bodily indisposition.

Learn to repine less at small evils and flea bites, thou pitiful Jack Straw!

Flatulent and cross on a slight occasion.

Some doggedness on provocation.

Snappish. Lord shall this sin which so easily besets be never never overcome.

At my return home upon provocation I struck my servant.

Miserably and sinfully peevish : double the guard.

A little crabbed with two incurables.

And the year before he died :

A sweet whisper that God will hear my petition for freedom from quickness to anger.

Early rising troubled him too :

Too idle in bed to-day : O flesh, thou clog!

Lay a little too late for this day ; rouse soul, death is at the door.

Some of his more general aphorisms may also be given :

I have been putting the cart (i.e. the body) before the horse (i.e. the soul) all my life : but God is turning me about since my last signal visitation.

The medical profession exhibits strongly the vanity and wickedness of the world where the more work the less pay.

O, what a trial is prosperity! The reins must be held tighter in time of plenty.

Saw myself in the clear vision to be top heavy and the necessity there is for my growing less in the branch and more in the root.

Spent my mattin in spiritual fox hunting.

He always makes a note about " meeting," sometimes it is " sweet," " luminous," and " profitable," at other times " dull " and " barren," and once " my fire was almost extinguished by my drowsiness." He hates loquacity and prolixity :

I also saw the vulgar error of long preaching and text spinning.

The afternoon meeting was partly silent, partly loquacious ; the silent part was more edifying than the preaching ; what a pity it is that some persons know not when to leave off !

Disapproval is shown of play-going and he rejoices when a play house is converted into a house of prayer.

God opened a way to deal with play haunters in a social capacity : but O the deadness of our spiritual socios.

Drew up a paper against play haunting.

He more than once expresses his admiration for women. On one occasion he writes :

The natural volubility of that sex beyond all comparison superior in effect to what is delivered by some of us dull reasoners renders them far better speakers and fitter instruments for a superior power to animate and direct.

His devoted attention to his poorer patients is shown in many entries :

Eight patients of which six paupers.

Eight patients but all pennyless.

Eleven visits and no fee, blessed be the Lord.

Attended nine patients six of which were the glorious poor.

There is less about his own health than one would expect in the diary of a doctor. It may be noted, perhaps not irrelevantly, that a treatise *De Diarrhœa* was his thesis when he took his doctor's degree. In addition to " heaviness of the body," " vapourish from indigestion," " flatulence," etc., we have references, as time goes on, to " optical tremours," and in 1766 he writes :

An embittering dispensation of sore eyes and dull ears the first taking me off from my darling delights of reading and writing and the second from conversation : Lord I kiss thy rod.

The old man keeps up his vigilant guard over himself to the end, continually asking, " What lack I yet ? " A few months before his death he is still concerned at his " unsubdued ferocity," and in the last two entries he is still watchful but hopeful :

12th Month 3. 1774. Conscious that of late no fleshly indulgence hath taken place : beware that it creep not on now in the days of infirmity and sitting by the fire ; ·I dare not trust my own heart.

8. The voice of God now sounds louder in my great infirmity of being scarcely able to bear the cold.

In addition to the ordinary entries in the diary there are paragraphs headed " Soliloquies " and sometimes " Question " and

"Answer." In 1768 he inserts "a short spiritual Chronology" in which he gives an account of the spiritual side of his early life before he began to keep a diary.

Dr. Rutty may have been spiritually eccentric, but he never bores us with diffuse sanctimonious outpourings. In spite of his violent self-reproach he was probably only a very convivial and sociable companion. It would perhaps be cynical to suggest that the passage of time and increasing old age brought in the natural course a mitigation of the impulses to anger and excess. Let us rather take his word for it that "God gained ground," for, as he says in his preface, "Sanctification is not the work of a day nor a week nor a year; the Christian warfare ceaseth not but with our lives."

The diary was printed and published in 1776.

MRS. BROWNE

ALL our women diarists were either themselves people of reputation or were connected with more or less eminent personages. Mrs. Browne is the one exception. We know nothing of her except what she tells us in a very entertaining little diary she kept from November 17, 1754, to August 4, 1757, which is contained in a small paper book of not more than thirty pages.[1]

Mrs. Browne accompanied Braddock's expedition to Virginia and sailed from Gravesend on board the *London*, on which her brother was one of the officers. We gather from her entries, which are not daily but occasional, that she had been a widow for about two years and had left her children behind her in England. Her daughter Charlotte dies while she is away, which causes her great grief. Of her personal appearance we catch just a glimpse from the remark made to her by a Quaker whom she comes across on her travels. "Thou seems full Bulky to travel," he says, "but thou art young and that will enable thee." Bulky or not, she evidently had great energy, rode and marched hundreds of miles and put up with extreme discomforts as the expedition passed from Bellham to Fort Cumberland, to Frederick's Town, Philadelphia, and New York.

---

[1] The MS. of this diary is in the possession of Mr. S. A. Courtauld of the Howe, Halstead, Essex, by whose kind permission extracts are given.

The ship's passage occupied from November 17 till March 23. The *London* " was laden with stores for the hospital."

Mrs. Browne is interested in humanity and has a gossipy style. We learn a good deal about some of her fellow-passengers, their behaviour, their quarrels, which she calls " squalls," and other incidents of the voyage. Her troubles begin early :

Dec. 5. At 4 in the morning made Mizen Head and we all expected to have been lost. I being Mr. Cherrington's Banker he came to my state room and said ; Mrs. Browne get up and if you please put my Purse in your Pockett. But remember Lady you are not dressing for court. I dressed myself immediately and came on Deck and found my brother tying two Planks together for us to set upon but at last we happily got clear.

Mr. Cherrington, of whom we shall hear a good deal more, seems generally to have been mixed up in the rows. Here are some of the " squalls " :

Being Sunday Mr. Cherrington and Mr. Bass had a Squall on Deck. Mr. Bass had severall times given hints of Miss Davis, a friendly fair of Mr. Cherrington's. He insisted on his explaining himself which Mr. Bass did but not in the lady's favour. Many ill-natured Truths were said. Mr. Bass was forbid coming into the Cabin ; but he told him he had as much right as himself, so he kept his footing, but Mr. Cherrington not being able to bear the insolence of the little fellow mov'd off to Cork.

Being Sunday a great Squall on Deck between Mr Cherrington and Capt. Browne it began about the loss of some water gruel and ended with the great favour I had rec'd to have my Cabbin in the Steerage.

A great squall on Deck with Mr. Lash the Mate and Mr. Black the Clerk of the Hospitall about the tapping of some Beer, Mr. Lash ordered it to be tap'd Mr. Black forbid it. At which Mr. Lash in a great rage told him that it was as thick as Hell and he should never taste it, that it was but the other day he carried a knot on his Back but now he was so much on his Hizy Prizy there was no speaking to him. The day ended with a Dispute in the Cabbin with Mr. Cherrington and Mr. Couch.

In another dispute Mr. Cherrington said : " It was not clear to him why so many of his sheep should die and not one of ours." Later, however, one of his sheep " brought forth a fine lamb."

Mr. Couch is a gentleman who suffers terribly from sea sickness and remains in his cabin,

deep in the Horrors and will neither eat, drink or speak and is at a loss to tell whether he is alive or dead.

Mrs. Browne has to discharge her maid Betty when she arrives in Bellhaven, having found of mine in her box a pair of Ruffles, a pair of stockings and an apron.

To Mr. and Mrs. Barbut she makes rather sarcastic references. They were evidently late risers.

Mr. Barbut up and a mending of stockings his wife fast asleep.

And when there is bad weather,

the reason of it was, as the Men say because Mr. Barbut heav'd out so soon being up before 11.

Mrs. Barbut up by 8 this morning but the sailors desired her to tumble in again or else they should have a bad wind.

But Mrs. Barbut's intellectual powers must have been surprising, judging by the following entry :

Mr. Cherrington learnt Mrs. Barbut to read and construe Greek in an Hour.

Or perhaps it was Mr. Cherrington's remarkable skill as a teacher.

Some months after their arrival Mrs. Browne comes across Mrs. Barbut again in Philadelphia.

Nov. 28. My old shipmate Mrs. Barbut came to see me but she was so full of engagements she could not afford me an Hour of her Company. She was dressed like a Butterfly which put me in mind of June instead of November.

At Frederick's Town in Maryland she goes to a Ball,

which was compos'd of Romans, Jews and Hereticks who in this town flock together. The Ladys danced without Stays or Hoops and it ended with a Jig from each Lady.

Drink specially on board ship figures very prominently. There is great lamentation when it is discovered that thirty gallons of brandy had run out :

Pompey the Negroe all most turn'd white on the thoughts of it but Mr. Lash the Mate said it was all run to Hell but they should have good Grog the next time that they pump'd the Ship.

Mr. Black " drank so much grog he was at a loss how to go to bed." And there are two references to the Parson which show he was not an abstainer :

Sunday but had no Prayers till afternoon our Parson being indispos'd by drinking too much grog the night before.

And later ashore :

The officer and the Parson replenished their Bowl so often that they began to be very joyous untill their Servant told them that their Horses were lost at which the Parson much inrag'd and pop'd out an oath.

Mr. Cherrington, however, was able to withstand the allurements of drink. When they cast anchor in Hampton Roads,

4 officers came on Board; drank out 15 Bottles of Port: all in the Cabbin drunk (but Mr. Cherrington).

We lose sight of Mr. Cherrington for awhile after the landing. But Mrs. Browne is joined by her old friend again on the journey to Philadelphia.

We supt and desired to have 2 Beds but the Mistress of the house said she presumed we were Man and Wife and that one would do. Mr. Cherrington said it was true I was his Wife but it was very seldom he was favoured with part of my Bed. She said she was sorry of it and at last complied. I was favoured with a Bed of Down and Mr. Cherrington with a Bed of Straw.

At another inn :

Mr. Cherrington and I not being of the same opinion as to my Sex in general we had many Disputes. Several Ill-natured Truths were said on both Sides. It ended with my telling him he did nothing but say and unsay and that he was so unaccountable a riddle I knew not what to make of him. He made a low Bow and said he was much obliged to me and retired.

In spite of Mr. Cherrington's apparently quarrelsome disposition Mrs. Browne was devoted to him, and when he returns home she writes :

Dec. 1. 1756. Mr. Cherrington left Albany for England in whom I have lost all my friends in one.

After the death of her brother in July, 1755, she sometimes finds her position misunderstood. At New York, for instance :

The Dutch had a very bad opinion of me saying I could not be good to come so far without a husband.

The Dutch said I was General Braddock's Miss but she [Miss Miller an old friend] has convinced them that I was not for that her Father had known me Maid, Wife and Widow and that nobody could say anything bad of me.

Mrs. Browne makes brief notes with regard to the military events and the fighting, and in the latter part of the diary her personal remarks are less frequent. Her health suffers a good deal from the hardship of riding and marching and many entries are taken up with comments on her " disorder." She ends her diary abruptly on August 4, 1757, with the words : " There ends my Journal having so much Business on my Hands that I cannot spare the Time to write it." What her "business" was is not clear, but we very much regret that it should have prevented her from continuing her very human and amusing little record. Mrs. Browne's diary is far better worth printing than many of the diaries that have been published.

HENRY FIELDING

THE author of *Tom Jones* was not a regular diarist, but we have from his pen published after his death a brief journal of his voyage to Lisbon. This voyage was undertaken at the end of his life in 1754, when he was suffering acutely from dropsy and the doctors had recommended him to seek a milder climate. So ill was he that he had completely lost the use of his limbs and had to be hoisted like a dead weight or carried about helplessly in a chair. He had to undergo the operation of being tapped frequently, and to all intents and purposes he was a dying man, and what is more he knew it. Added to this the discomforts on the ship were unusual even for those days, and owing to the vagaries of the wind the voyage occupied no less than fifty days. It is astonishing in the circumstances that he should have written at all. "Yet," as Mr. Austin Dobson says, "so indomitable is his gallantry of spirit, so irrepressible his joy of life, so insatiable still his 'curious' eye for humanity that a fresh face or a new sensation makes the old fire flame up once more and he writes as if he had not a care in the world." His own description of himself, however, on his departure is sufficiently harrowing:

> Upon my entrance into the boat I presented a spectacle of the highest horror. The total loss of limbs was apparent to all who saw me and my face contained marks of a most diseased state if not of death itself. Indeed so ghastly was my countenance that timorous women with child had abstained from my house for fear of the ill consequences of looking at me.

He describes the captain:

> He wore a sword of no ordinary length by his side with which he swaggered in his cabin among the wretches his passengers whom he had stowed in cupboards on each side. He was a person of very singular character. He had taken it into his head that he was a gentleman from those very reasons that proved he was not one; and to shew himself a fine gentleman by a behaviour which seemed to insinuate he had never seen one.

The wind being unfavourable they hung about the English coast off the Isle of Wight and off Devonshire till late in July. Every incident is described, the captain's moods and tempers, the food and the storms; and one is often made to forget the state of health of the writer himself. A series of extracts touching on some of the incidents will give an idea of this singular journal:

> My poor wife after passing a night in the utmost torments of the toothache resolved to have it drawn. I dispatched, therefore, a servant to Wapping to bring in haste, the best toothdrawer he could find. He soon found out a female of great eminence in the art; but when he brought her to the boat at the waterside they were informed that the ship was gone.
>
> My wife continued the whole day in a state of dozing; and my other females whose sickness did not abate by the rolling of the ship at anchor seemed more inclined to empty their stomachs than to fill them. Thus I passed the whole day by myself and the evening concluded with the captain.

" A most tragical incident " takes place. A kitten falls overboard. The sails are slackened and all hands are employed to recover the poor animal. Fielding expresses his surprise at the captain's " extreme tenderness," and remarks: " If puss had had nine thousand instead of nine lives I concluded they had all been lost." A sailor jumps overboard and returns with the cat in his mouth. At first the cat shows no signs of life, and the captain

> having felt his loss like a man he resolved to show he could bear it like one, and having declared he had rather have lost a cask of rum or brandy, betook himself to threshing at backgammon with the Portuguese friar.

Subsequently the cat recovers, " to the great joy of the good captain."

After a dinner off beans and bacon in a barn near Ryde he writes:

> We completed the best, the pleasantest and the merriest meal with more appetite, more real solid luxury and more festivity than was ever seen in an entertainment at White's.

The description of Mrs. Humphrys, the farmer's wife, with whom they lodged at Ryde, is in the novelist's best style. Part of it must be given:

> She was a short squat woman; her head was closely joined to her shoulders where it was fixed somewhat awry; every feature of her countenance was sharp and pointed; her face was furrowed with the smallpox; and her complexion which seemed to be able to turn milk to curds not a little resembled

in colour such milk as had already undergone that operation. She appeared indeed to have many symptoms of a deep jaundice in her look; but the strength and firmness of her voice overbalanced them all. . . . She differed as I have said in every particular from her husband; but very remarkably in this, that as it was impossible to displease him, so it was impossible to please her; and as no art could remove a smile from his countenance, so could no art carry it into hers.

The continued delays exasperate the captain:

The Captain now grew outrageous and declaring open war with the wind took a resolution more bold than wise of sailing in defiance of it and in its teeth. . . . The wind began in the captain's own language to freshen: and indeed it freshened so much that before ten it blew a perfect hurricane . . . and continued to blow with such violence that the ship ran above eight knots an hour during this whole day and tempestuous night till bed time. I was obliged to betake myself once more to my solitude; for my women were again all down in their sea sickness and the captain was busy on deck.

He realises that there is danger, and says

this would have given no small alarm to a man who had either not learnt what it is to die or known what it is to be miserable. And my dear wife and child must pardon me if what I did not conceive to be any great evil to myself I was not much terrified with the thoughts of happening to them.

He adds the following remark which shows that he was writing for publication:

Can I say that I had no fear; indeed I cannot, reader, I was afraid for thee lest thou shouldst have been deprived of that pleasure thou art now enjoying.

But after all this storm they were still off the coast of Devonshire. Fielding buys cider and the captain " drest himself in scarlet " and went off to pay a visit to a Devonshire squire. However, although the captain declares the ship is bewitched, they do eventually get away. They encounter more foul weather in which the unfortunate invalid suffers and the captain appears to be quite unsympathetic.

We went only at the rate of four miles an hour but with so uneasy a motion continually rolling from side to side that I suffered more than I had done in our whole voyage; my bowels being almost twisted out of my belly. However the day was very serene and bright and the captain who was in high spirits affirmed he had never passed a pleasanter at sea.

At last they arrive, but Lisbon does not appeal to him:

About seven in the evening I got into a chaise on shore and was driven through the nastiest city in the world.

Fielding died within two months of his arrival.

The diary is not exclusively taken up with a recital of incidents of the voyage, there are long digressions, some of them entirely irrelevant; they are partly political and controversial and partly philosophic. There is a disquisition on cider, on the morals of sailors, on the career of a ship's captain and on liberty.

Two versions of the diary were published. The first one in which passages were suppressed was issued in 1755, and a longer version in 1762.

Considering the circumstances, the Journal may not be classed among Fielding's best works, but it discloses his character, his fortitude, and his patience, and gives us more knowledge of him than can be derived from his other books.

THOMAS TURNER

TURNER kept a general store at East Hoathly, Sussex. He was born at Groombridge, in Kent, in 1728. His diary, which was originally contained in one hundred and sixteen memorandum books, of which only a few have been lost, extends over a period of eleven years from February 2, 1754, to July 3, 1765. It is an amazing production, containing as it does the most outspoken confessions combined with almost ridiculous penitence and pretentious moralising. While he treats his diary as a sort of confessional, at the same time he records many ordinary events. His sincerity, of which his style might at first make one suspicious, is unquestionable. At the same time Turner was writing deliberately for posterity ("those who may happen to peruse my memoirs") and hoped no doubt that the elaboration of his remorse might outweigh the gravity of his frequent lapses. Drink was his failing, and it may well be doubted if he ever conquered it. His stilted and sententious style can be explained by the fact that he was a great reader, without in all probability being highly educated. He reads poetry, theology, history and novels and with obvious enjoyment.

" Clarissa Harlow," he says, " I look upon as a very well wrote thing tho' it must be allowed it is too prolix."

He gives long extracts from Pope's translation of the *Odyssey*, he quotes advice given by *Madame de Maintenon*, he reads out *Tillotson's Sermons* to his friends, he reads the last book of *Para-*

dise Lost twice and says, " it exceeds anything I ever read for sublimity of language and beauty of similies." *As You Like It, Othello,* and the *Taming of the Shrew* are commended by him, and many other books are mentioned. In fact, he confesses to " a too great delight in reading."

He draws up rules of proper regimen, which include early rising, an abstemious diet, moderation in drinking, and " always to go to bed at or before ten o'clock." The spirit, in fact, seems constantly to have been willing, but the flesh was extraordinarily weak even for the eighteenth century. His lapses are always recorded with the immediate renewal of resolution.

Came home drunk ; but I think never to exceed the bounds of moderation more.

We drank one bowl of punch and two muggs of bumboo and I came home in liquor. Oh with what horrors does it fill my heart to think I should be guilty of doing so and on a Sunday too ! Let me once more endeavour never, no never, to be guilty of the same again.

Not quite so sober at home all day and I know I behaved like an ass . . . not like one that calls himself a Christian. Oh, how unworthy I am of that name.

What can I say in my own behalf for getting drunk ? Sure I am a direct fool.

I cannot say I came home sober though I was far from being bad company.

I came home but to my shame do I say it very much in liquor [and next day]. Pretty bad all day with the stings of a guilty and tormenting conscience.

I came home after eleven after staying in Mr. Porter's wood near an hour and a half the liquer opperating so much in the head that it made my legs useless.

But it would be unfair not to give instances in which he did control himself, though in the first quotation the word sober seems to be used in a relative sense.

We came home—I may say quite sober considering the house we was at, though undoubtedly the worst for drinking and having I believe contracted a slight inpediment in my speech, occasioned by the fumes of the liquor operating too furiously on my brain.

Thank God very sober as was all the company (except Dame Durrant).

Came home about three minutes past twelve—sober. Oh, how comfortable does that word sound in my ears !

The orgies he describes in great detail show that his friends and acquaintances were no better than he was himself.

After supper our behaviour was far from that of serious, harmless mirth; it was downright obstreperious mixed with a great deal of folly and stupidity. Our diversion was dancing or jumping about without a violin or any musick singing of foolish healths and drinking all the time as fast as it could be poured down and the parson of the parish (Mr. Porter) was among the mixed multitude [Then follow the usual qualms of conscience.]

But three days later Mr. Porter, his wife and a party turned up at Turner's house, burst into his bedroom, and

drew me out of bed, as the common phrase is topsy turvey; but however at the intercession of Mr. Porter they permitted me to put on my . . . and instead of my upper cloaths they gave me time to put on my wife's petticoats and in this manner they made me dance without shoes and stockings untill they had emptied the bottle of wine and also a bottle of my beer [he goes on to express horror and indignation ending à propos of Mr. Porter] 'the precepts delivered from the pulpit on Sunday tho' delivered with the greatest ardour must lose a great deal of their efficacy by such examples.'

We continued drinking like horses, as the vulgar phrase is, and singing till many of us were very drunk, and then we went to dancing and pulling of wigs, caps, and hats; and thus we continued in this frantic manner behaving more like mad people than they that profess the name of Christians.

Other orgies at Mr. Porter's house and at his own house are recorded, and he sums up:

Now I hope all revelling for this season is over; and may I never more be discomposed with so much drink or by the noise of an obstreperous multitude but that I may calm my troubled mind and sooth my disturbed conscience.

The celebrations of victories were also occasions for intemperate rejoicing. Mr. Coates, the Duke of Newcastle's agent at Halland, invited them all to several feasts. Turner always goes, though he knows beforehand what the result will be:

If I goe, I must drink just as they please or otherwise, I shall be called a poor singular fellow. If I stay at home I shall be stigmatised with the name of being a poor, proud, ill-natured wretch and perhaps disoblige Mr. Coates.

The Duke himself gives a banquet. Turner was not one of the guests, but no doubt he was helping Mr. Coates.

1759. Sunday Aug. 5. I spent most part of the day in going to and fro from Halland there being a public day where there was to dine with his Grace the Duke of Newcastle, the Earls of Ashburnham and Northampton, Lord Viscount Gage, the Lord Abergavenny and two judges of assize, and a great number of gentlemen there being, I think upward of forty coaches chariots etc. I came home about seven not thoroughly sober. I think it is a scene that loudly calls for the detestation of the serious and considerating people to see the sabbath prophaned and turned into a day of luxury and debauchery; there being no less than ten cooks, four of which were French, and perhaps fifty more, as busy as if it had been a rejoicing day. There was such hazzaing that made the very foundations almost of the house to shake and all this by the order and the approbation of almost the next man to the King. Oh! What countenance does such behaviour in a person of his Grace's rank give to levity drunkenness and all sorts of immorality.

Turner's married life was not harmonious, and his mother-in-law, Mrs. Slater, made matters worse by "having a very great volubility of tongue for invective and especially if I am the subject." Having had "words" with his wife (Peggy) he writes:

> Oh what happiness must there be in the married state when there is a sincere regard on both sides and each partie truly satisfied with each other's merits! But it is impossible for tongue or pen to express the uneasiness that attends the contrary.

However, he confesses that in spite of "anemosityes and disentions" were he single he would do the same again—"I mean, make her my wife who is so now."

> I think I have tried all experiments to make our life's happy but they have all failed. The opposition seems to be naturally in our tempers—not arising from spitefulness but an opposition that seems indicated by our very make and constitution.

Peggy after a period in which she is "prodigiously" ill dies, and her husband with characteristic remorse displays the warmest affection for her memory.

> How do I lament my present irregular and very unpleasant life for what I used to lead in my dear Peggy's time.
> Oh! How pleasant was the even spent after a busy day in my dear Peggy's time.

He finds that in solitude "a certain roughness and boisterousness of disposition has seized my mind," and that he is reduced to a "great degree of moroseness that is neither agreeable to myself nor can my company be so to others." In fact he cannot get on without "the company of the more softer sex," so he begins courting Molly Hicks, "my charmer." But he has doubts:

> This courting does not well agree with my constitution and perhaps it may be only taking pains to create more pains.

However, he marries Molly on June 19, 1765, and on July 3 he writes:

> I have, it's true, not married a learned lady nor is she a gay one, but I trust she is good natured and one that will use her utmost endeavour to make me

happy. As to her fortune, I shall one day have something considerable and there seems to be rather a flowing stream. Well, here let us drop the subject and begin a new one.

But here, unfortunately, the diary ends, so we do not know whether he was as happy with Molly Hicks as he imagined himself to have been with Peggy, after her death ; nor do we learn whether he ever conquered the sad habit which caused him so many stings of conscience.

We have only space for the above quotations on reading, drink, and marriage, but Turner writes much else about his business and its ups and downs, about race meetings, journeys, and local customs and incidents. And he moralises in his entertaining way about all his pursuits as well as about public events.

The manuscript of the diary is in the possession of his descendants and was communicated in 1859 to the Sussex Archæological Society.

JOHN DAWSON

JOHN DAWSON, of Brunton, only kept a diary from March 8 to December 31, 1761. When the Northumberland Militia was first embodied in 1759 under an Act of Parliament passed 30 George II, John Dawson was appointed to be captain of a Tynedale Company. The diary is almost exclusively concerned with the doings of the militia during the year 1761. The entries are recorded daily throughout the whole period, but they are very brief, giving notes of mob risings, riots, trials, punishments, courts martial, etc., and the names of the people with whom he came in contact. Judging by the first half-dozen entries, however, Dawson seems at first to have intended to keep a very much fuller journal containing his views and opinions. For instance, on March 6 he writes :

> Surely the best scholars are the best citizens for here I find those whose minds are least cultivated are absolutely very indifferent company ; I should say dangerous company—half an hour is badly spent amongst many of them. Surely it may be called, without impropriety, premeditated murder of time.

And again the next day :

> Awakened this morning about 4 o'clock and arose at 6. Without a good knowledge of the Scriptures a man never can make a tolerable figure in Society ; the best and wisest men have been in all ages and in all nations the

strongest advocates for the sacred writings but with the abandoned and ignorant we find the reverse. A man starving of hunger would be deem'd a madman to refuse victuals offered to him but how must we term a man who refuses to eat of the bread of life to whom immortality is offered and yet rejected. What fools men are !

Then comes on the same day " this morning I attended a court martial," and unfortunately never again up to the close of the diary does Dawson give any of his illuminating philosophic reflections, even though on several days the only entry is " at home all day " and two or three times " peace and quietness." The bald daily record hardly contains even any descriptive epithets. On one occasion he makes a fuller note ; it discloses the sort of atmosphere he lived in, which cannot have been conducive to philosophic reflection.

June 6. N.B. Mr. Soulsbye came to town last Thursday ; he had not been 10 minutes in the room till he saw :—
1. The Mayor of Berwick and Captain Romer ready for a boxing match.
2. Noise, Drunkenness and confusion.
3. The Major down with his breeches and up with his shirt and shew'd his belly above the navel.
4. The major mob'd at night and N.B. Major damn your soul, what do you want. Major steady, Major steady Saturday evening for ever.

Apart from his official duties he seems to have been superintending his son Jack's education.

Oct. 2. Still reading the English grammar with Jack.

Oct. 7. Jack began to write and construe his *Propria quae maribus* this morning.

Nov. 23. I find from Mr. Rumney's conversation that my son Jack follows the very method of Mr. Romney's scholars as to the preter perfect tense and supines of which he was master some time ago.

Dec. 25. Jack began Cordery on Wednesday sen' night.

The diary ends : " Here I finish this journal begun the 8th of March last past. My fingers still very weak."

The Rev. Thomas Stephens, vicar of Horsley in Ridesdale, communicated extracts of the diary to the Proceedings of the Newcastle Antiquarian Society and it also appears in the Surtees Society's collection.

It is one of those diaries in which the little glimpses of the writer's personality make one regret there is not more.

LADY MARY COKE

THE voluminous journal kept by Lady Mary Coke extends from 1766 to 1791. It is written for the most part in the form of letters to her sister, Lady Strafford, and was actually despatched to her from time to time. On Lady Strafford's death the journal was addressed to Lord Strafford. When he died Lady Mary Coke discontinued writing her journal. As there is consciousness throughout of an almost immediate recipient, the diary has none of the features of the usual private diary, and as it is written practically daily, it has none of the merits of a general survey which a letter can give. In fact, it falls between two stools and has very little to recommend it. Lady Mary Coke was the daughter of John, Duke of Argyll; she was born in 1726. When she was 21 she married Viscount Coke, and after two years of constant disagreement they separated. During the remainder of her long life, for she lived till she was 84, she went about in society, travelled abroad and associated with many notable people. Lady Louisa Stuart, in a memoir of the family, describes her thus: "She had the reputation of cleverness when young and in spite of all her absurdity could not be called a silly woman: but she was so eminently wrong headed, her understanding lay smothered under so much pride, self conceit, prejudice, obstinacy and violence of temper, that you knew not where to look for it, and seldom indeed did you catch such a distinct view of it as certified its existence."

Horace Walpole, who dedicated the *Castle of Otranto* to her, referred to her as "violent, absurd and mad." From such an eccentric character as this one might expect something peculiarly entertaining, but the journal, though often very silly, is generally very dull. It contains health notes, a few domestic details, references to the people she meets, her movements and travels, her gains and losses at cards, and an immense quantity of gossip, especially about the Royal Family for whose favour and smiles she was always seeking. In fact, Horace Walpole said: "if all the sovereigns of Europe combined to slight her she still would put her trust in the next generation of Princes."

She kept her journal private and had no intention of publishing it. In 1767 she writes:

> Lady Spencer came to see me and found me writing my journal. She desired I wou'd let her read it. She wou'd be content with a single page; but as much as I love her I cou'd not consent. I felt ashamed thou' I told

her some years hence I thought it might be an amusement, at least it would have one thing to recommend it—that everything that was found in it might be depended upon for truth.

How far it was true that the Duke of York wanted to marry her is not known. She anyhow cherished the romance. After his death there are entries beginning :

I drempt of the Duke.

I drempt again last night of the Duke.

I drempt a great deal about Colonel Bradenel relating to the advice he had given the poor Duke not to marry me.

When she quarrels with Walpole, she writes :

I have not the same pleasure in meatting him as I used to have since I know him to be so false to me. Thank God I could not be so to anybody !

She does not deal exclusively with the great world, and although there are no reflections, no thoughts, opinions, or meditations, there are several entries of a more domestic character, such as :

I had a bad pain in my head when I got up, but was in hopes going to my house in the country would take it off, but I had so many vexations when I came there 'twas no wonder it grew worse. My gardener had run away and a Butcher at Kensington had drove away five and twenty of my sheep.

The journal is only of family interest. The part from 1766 to 1774 was privately printed in 1889 in four large volumes in order to preserve it; only the headings of the journal of the last seventeen years are given.

JAMES HARRIS, EARL OF MALMESBURY

THE diary extracts given in the four-volume biography of Lord Malmesbury amount to nothing more than links between the long despatches and letters which tell the story of his distinguished career. Nevertheless, he kept a pretty regular diary from 1767, when he was 22, up to 1809. He was entrusted with many important diplomatic missions, notably in Berlin and Paris. The diary is a typical diplomatic diary, filled with visits, travel, functions, dinners, political and diplomatic conversations, etc., entirely objective, without a word about himself or his family. There are anecdotes of Frederick the Great and his flutes and of many other royal personages and statesmen. Anyone making a close study of the foreign policy of the period might find some interesting sidelights in his memoranda, but as a human document the diary is quite colourless.

Among the delicate duties entrusted to Lord Malmesbury was that of marrying Caroline of Brunswick by proxy for the Prince of Wales (afterwards George IV). He sees it through and gives the whole scene at the Grand Ducal Court. Even at the time he has some misgivings about the Princess's manners and disposition, but he brings her to London, and the account of her husband's first meeting with her is worth quoting :

> I according to the established etiquette introduced the Princess Caroline to him. She very properly in consequence of my saying to her it was the right mode of proceeding, attempted to kneel to him. He raised her (gracefully enough) and embraced her, said barely one word, turned round, retired to a distant part of the apartment and calling to me said : " Harris, I am not well ; pray get me a glass of brandy." I said " Sir, had you not better have a glass of water ? "—upon which he, much out of humour, said with an oath " *No* : I will go directly to the Queen " and away he went.

From the first the whole thing was a miserable failure, and the Princess's behaviour, which was " flippant, rattling, affecting raillery and wit and throwing out coarse vulgar hints," did not improve matters. So that Lord Malmesbury finally says about the transaction, " I lament very much having taken any share, purely passive as it was."

His important diplomatic work in Madrid, The Hague, Berlin, and more especially in France, where he was engaged in the fruitless negotiations in Paris and Lille during 1796 and 1797, are better related by his despatches than by his diary.

From 1809 until the close of his life in 1820, however, Lord Malmesbury gave up his ordinary diary and kept a " Self controlling Journal." This was of a very different character and has not been published. It appears to have been much more in the style of an eighteenth-century divine. The final entry, written a fortnight before his death in 1820, can be quoted :

> Thou hast completed thy seventy fourth year having been permitted to live longer than any of thy ancestors as far back as 1606. Thy existence has been without any great misfortune and without any acute disease and has been one for which thou ought'st to be extremely grateful. Be so, in praise and thanksgiving towards the Supreme Being and by preparing thyself to employ the remnant of it wisely and discreetly. The next step will probably be the last. Strive not to delay the period of its arrival nor lament at its near

approach. Thou are too exhausted, both in mind and body, to be of service to thy country, thy friends or family. Thou art fortunate in leaving thy children well and happy; be content to join thy parent Earth calmly and with becoming resignation. Such is thy imperious duty—Vale.

THOMAS GRAY

THERE are two fragments of diary written by the poet Gray. The first is some notes on his journey in France in 1739, when he was 23, which are so brief that there is only a bare mention of the places he visits and hardly any description except of his ascent to the Grande Chartreuse. He expresses no personal feelings whatever, and does not even refer to his travelling companion, Horace Walpole.

The second is his Journal in the Lakes, begun on September 30, 1769, and concluded on December 22 of the same year. Gray was not a diary writer, and the Journal was only composed for his friend Dr. Wharton's amusement. The scenery inspired him, but when he returns " to the smoky, ugly, busy town of Leeds I dropped all further thoughts of my journal."

Though it consists of little more than descriptions of scenery written practically daily as he travels about, a reader can soon detect, as he peruses the few pages, that it is not the usual banal effusion that is met with so often in diaries. It wants to be read all through to get the atmosphere; quotations cannot convey it. The restraint and simplicity of the language, the absence of exuberant purple patches, can only be appreciated by consecutive reading. As, however, the whole diary cannot be transcribed, extracts must be given.

In the evening walked alone down to the Lake by the side of Crow Park after sunset and saw the solemn colouring of night draw on, the last gleam of sunshine fading away on the hill tops, the deep serene of the waters and the long shadows of the mountains thrown across them till they nearly touched the hithermost shore. At distance heard the murmur of many waterfalls not audible in the daytime. Wished for the moon but she was *dark to me and silent hidden in her vacant interlunar cave.*

From the shore a low promontory pushes itself far into the water and on it stands a white village with the parish church rising in the midst of it, hanging enclosures, cornfields and meadows green as an emerald, with their trees and hedges and cattle fill up the whole space from the edge of the water. Just opposite to you is a large farm house at the bottom of a steep smooth lawn embosomed in old woods which climb half way up the mountain side and discover above them a broken line of crags that crown the scene. Not a single red tile, no flaming gentleman's house or garden walls break in upon the repose of this little unsuspected paradise but all is peace, rusticity and happy poverty in its neatest most becoming attire.

On the cliffs above hung a few goats; one of them danced and scratched an ear with its hind foot in a place where I could not have stood still for all beneath the moon.

He mentions his food:

For me I went no further than the farmer's at Grange; his mother and he brought us butter that Siserah would have jumped at though not in a lordly dish, bowls of milk, thin oaten cakes and ale; and we carried a cold tongue thither with us.

And he gives a "receipt to dress Perch," which he declares is excellent. He relates romantic stories he hears, he mentions a few people in connection with the houses he sees, but he indulges in no meditations and expresses no opinions.

The diary is contained in the first volume of the works of Thomas Gray, edited by Mr. Edmund Gosse.

STROTHER

ALTHOUGH only the record of a single year, devoid of historical interest and of little note from a local and archæological point of view, the diary of Strother, the draper's assistant, deserves special notice as a production of psychological value owing to the light it throws on the personality of its obscure young author, whose Christian name even we do not know.

We gather that he came to Hull from York at the age of 15, and remained in the shop for six years. He begins his diary during the last of these years on August 8, 1784, when he was 21. The first entry runs thus:

I have often thought of keeping a journal of all my thoughts and proceedings and by referring to it may sometimes aid my memory and please myself with reading in some future period past occurrences.

And he says later: "These writings are for my own private perusal."

He then proceeds with careful daily entries in which, in addition to notes on the weather, burials, intercourse with friends, records of prices, reports of sermons and details with regard to his health, he indulges in philosophic reflections, confesses his aspirations and describes his depressions. The writing throughout is neat and clear, the language rather stilted, and while he takes himself very seriously, he has a sense of humour and gives very sound moral judgments.

With a good knowledge of French, with a smattering of Hebrew, and being able to write shorthand, he naturally aspires to a better position. But his various attempts to get commercial employment abroad do not succeed, anyhow during the period in which he writes.

He and his friends form a society " with a design to improve ourselves in the art of speaking and reasoning for the better enabling us to hold a conversation with propriety," and he expresses great contempt for people " who read books and cannot tell about what they have read."

One of the debates is on the following subject :

> Whether may a man derive more solid instruction from Prosperity or Adversity . . . which I shall consider more fully at Leisure and have for my present amusement translated the 31st Fable from la Fontaine (the Lion and the Gnat).

He is very fond of argument, which he carries on with his friends on every conceivable subject :

> I told Burton in an argument that the head is clearer in the morning than at night because the fumes of provisions rise from the Belly and as a support for what I said a vapour arises from Meat when stewed on the fire, and if so why may not the same be in the Belly which is both warm and moist.

He fears, however, after a while that the Debating Society " teaches us more to prate than to speak," and he notices that one member " loves oysters, buttered buns, and all better than any of the Company." The Society, which is known as " The Sentimental Society," finally breaks up owing to the high cost of their room and the resignation of other members.

He gives amusing accounts of some of his friends :

> Mr. Ellerington a man of high imagination . . . he is one of those characters who are fond of holding chit chat and love to hear tongues wag and never is more happy and contented than when he can hold gossip over a pot of ale ; but I do not think he is a drunkard although his nose is red and of a tolerable size so that when he lifts a gill pot to his mouth nosy goes half way in.

His ambition is to get some position abroad, and he copies out the letters, some in French, which he writes on the subject. He finds himself, he says, at the age of 21, with no other prospect than that of struggling thro' the world with few advantages. So despair is wrong. I'll therefore make the best of a bad market and endeavour in 3 or 4 years' time to settle myself in as advantageous a manner as possible and hazard my little all in foreign commerce.

He enlists his mother's assistance, and in one of his letters to her he writes :

> I beg you will write your letter to them plainer and spell better than you do to me that you may give y^m no occasion to laugh and satirize on your style of writing.

When she does not reply he fears she is offended :

> If she is she will show a spirit more like rich pye crust that cannot bear touching.

But his endeavours to get a better situation are in vain, and when he goes to York in July it is either to another shop or a shop of his own.

His moral tone is always high. He expresses at some length and particularly well his indignation with a friend whose advice on moral questions is contrary to his practices. On the subject of gaming he says :

> It ought to hurt the pride of a gentleman to make an equal of one that is so much his inferior both in morals and everything else. If he loves cards or Dice rather let him amuse himself with his known equals ; but a true bred gentleman heartily despises such amusements which are only fit for grovelling spirits.

Here is another of his aphorisms :

> There is as much virtue in Private Life as in Public ; the first is rather in obscurity amongst men, therefore we seldom hear of it. The latter seldom wants a Trumpeter to sound forth its praise.

Health details occur from time to time :

> The little liquor that I drank got into my head and quite metamorphosed me to be dull and strangely stupid.

Eating too much bread and quenching his thirst with a lot of water produces disturbing symptoms :

> I will eat less of my favourite bread and drink something more substantial than flip flap water.

And there is a long and elaborate account of the removal of a corn on his left little toe, which he does by means of " Lapis

Infernalis," with the result that he burns his finger and is prevented from writing for some weeks. However, he keeps memoranda and the very conscientious diary record does not suffer.

His depressions are frequent.

> In looking over my Journal—I find in several places only observations of the weather to fill up the day which is a sad, but too true sign of want of occurrences to fill the page and scenes as if I had shut myself from the world or had not thought sufficient to make up the deficiency whereas I have been confined behind the counter and prevented from committing my sentiments to paper.
>
> I have been here 6 years having visited my mother 3 times and she has visited me once. I have kept myself from many unlucky mischances which several of my comrades have run into.

Then follows a great deal of philosophising, naïve perhaps but not in the least self-righteous. He tells some amusing anecdotes, describes at length Sir Roger de Coverley, his favourite dance, draws pictures of some coins he finds, and after saying, " I am fond of genealogies and particularly of virtuous men," he proceeds to fill several pages with a very careful account of his own family.

In York he makes a new resolution :

> I have often thought of keeping a Journal for a week of every thought, word and deed that might occur to memory for as we must give an account of our actions and how every hour is spent so this week's Journal may inform me in what manner I generally spend my time. I never fixt any resolution of the kind before.

He then begins very conscientiously to attempt the impossible. From July 5 to July 12 he tries to put down everything—how every hour of the day is spent, what he eats and to whom he talks. His handwriting becomes more untidy and the short sentences more scrappy. We can only quote a part :

> Sold very little this morning—only taken 6/- . . .—came in with haughty spirit and pedantic manners. . . . Hum'd a tune or two all the while my corn pain'd me greatly . . . read the Spectator . . . [measuring cloth]. For the future I shall measure by the selvage tho' not agreeable to the strictest rules of honesty. . . . Walked out of Bootham bar and my thoughts turn'd upon myself that I have not an address sufficiently polite for a good shopkeeper and I know but little how to proceed in improving according to the common rules so that I must learn by observing other Tradesmen and endeavouring to imitate them or strike out some other method of my own :

After a description of a service in the Cathedral at which the Archbishop and Judges were present, and of an accident and adventure with a riotous companion, there are a few lines on the last day, July 12, and then comes the end of the note-book of

260 pages and the end of the diary with the following pathetic statement on the last page :

And now I have filled this book but perhaps shall not fill another. I have learnt by keeping this Journal that I have been discontent more than was profitable and that it is not proper for a Tradesman to keep a Journal without he has enough of Time and plentifull fortune.
I began Sunday 8 of Aug. 1784 and now conclude Sunday 17 July 1785 at 7 o'clock in the evening.

We are left with the hope that Strother eventually found a position better suited to his capacities and with a regret that his eminently successful attempt at diary writing should have been curtailed by his modesty.

The original MS. is in the British Museum. In 1912 the Rev. Cæsar Caine produced a printed edition of it.

THE LADIES OF LLANGOLLEN

THE romantic story of the Ladies of Llangollen is so unique, and one may almost say fantastic, that it might easily be supposed that tradition, local gossip and hearsay had woven the highly-coloured strands of fiction over the bare threads of whatever there may have been of fact. There are, however, in existence diaries kept by the Ladies themselves which fully testify to the authenticity of the accounts given of them.

We must resist the temptation of entering at length into the history of the two ladies who lived together for over fifty years in Plas Newydd, a curious Gothic cottage in the Valley of Llangollen. But in order to explain and give a frame to the diary extracts which will be quoted a brief outline of their story must be related.

Lady Eleanor Butler, a sister of the 17th Earl of Ormonde, was a high-spirited and independent young woman who conceived a loathing for the idea of marriage. Exasperated by the matrimonial plans her relations tried to make for her and impatient with the restrictions imposed on her in her aunt's house in Ireland, she decided to " elope " with her friend Sarah Ponsonby, a daughter of Chambre Brabazon Ponsonby and cousin of the Earl of Bessborough. Her first attempt, which was unsuccessful, was some time in the early seventeen-seventies, when she was 33, and Sarah Ponsonby about 17. The second attempt, whether it was again a flight or whether she waited till her friend was of age, anyhow ended in the two friends settling as tenants of Plas Newydd without any further protest from their relations. There they remained together for over fifty years, never sleeping away from home for a single night.

There they passed their time, carrying on an extensive correspondence, reading, drawing, gardening and making little excursions in the neighbourhood. There, in spite of their love of retirement, they received many guests, among whom may be named Miss Seward, Madame de Genlis, the Duke of Wellington, Lord Edward Fitzgerald, the Duke of York, Prince Puckler Muskau, de Quincey, Walter Scott, Wordsworth and Charles Mathews, the actor. Some special fascination in the ladies must have attracted such visitors. They were cultivated and well read, they spoke French with ease, and their charm and originality is dwelt upon in several of the accounts of them which have been handed down by those whom they entertained. Their costume and appearance was very singular. With short powdered hair, tall hats, waistcoats, cravats, and riding habits they looked when seated more like two old gentlemen. Lady Eleanor wore orders and decorations which had been presented to her by the Bourbon family. There they sat surrounded by strange curios in their well-filled library, into which the sun pierced through stained-glass windows and which was lighted at night by a prismatic lantern of coloured glass.

But the most remarkable thing about these so-called recluses was their devotion to one another, which not only stood the test of time, but was kept up all through at an almost ecstatic pitch, as we shall see by the diary extracts. Lady Eleanor died in 1829, when she was nearly 90; Miss Ponsonby died three years later.

As to diaries, only fragments remain, but they are of so regular and minute a character that we may well suppose that one of the two ladies may have kept one throughout the whole period. It would be in keeping with their methodical and punctual habits.

Lady Eleanor's diary,[1] from which our quotations come, covers three months from September 15 to December 14, 1785; that is to say, after they had been resident in Llangollen for about ten years. It is contained in a little book measuring about 4 inches square, bound by herself in buff coloured paper. Every day is

[1] These quotations are published for the first time by kind permission of the Marquis of Ormonde, to whom the diary belongs.

accounted for. The handwriting is a marvel of neatness, but can only be read easily by the aid of a magnifying glass. The lines and margins are as straight as those of a printed book and there is not a single erasure throughout. The occupations of almost every hour are set down. Every day begins with the hour of rising and a weather report. Scenery is described in detail and often with enthusiasm. The gardener's doings, the visits of guests, books read, and all the little trivial incidents of their daily life are carefully entered. Sarah Ponsonby is referred to as " my Sally," " my beloved," " the darling of my heart," " the joy of my life." At the end of each entry the day is summed up in a phrase of which the following are examples :

a silent happy day.

an undisturbed peaceful day.

a day of sentiment and delight.

[after visitors] a tumultuous day.

a day of delight and uninterrupted retirement.

sweet converse with the delight of my heart.

We will first give two full specimen entries :

Sep. 18. Rose at seven. soft morning inclined to rain. went the rounds after Breakfast. Our shoes from Chirk. vile. scolded Thomas for growing fat. from ten till one writing and reading (La Rivalité) to my beloved. She drawing. spent half an hour in the shrubery. mild grey day. from half past one till three reading. from four till seven read to my Sally finished la Rivalité began Warton on Milton. in the Shrubery till eight. Powell returned from Wrexham. no letters. eight till nine read l'Esprit des croisades. papered our Hair. an uninterrupted delightful day.

Dec. 12. Rose at nine. all the mountains covered with snow. a loaded gloomy sky. the most piercing Bitter cold sharp Wind. Letter by the Oswestry Post from the Burnetts. from Mr. Chambre the contents of which will be ever gratefully remembered by us. from my friend Boissiere enclosing a pattern of paper a Vignette avec envelope done by a Protegée of His. some poor tawdry french creature who (like a cameleon) lives upon air in some garret in London. mem. to write to Mrs. Simpson and recommend her to her protection and oblige my friend Boissiere. wrote to the Burnetts. from eleven till two each writing. at two went the Home circuit. most penetrating cold and the sharpest wind. gloomy sky. Sent Powell to Tower. the poor Whalleys very ill. from half past two till Three read Rousseau to my beloved. She at her Plan. After dinner went round the gardens cold beyond imagination. the Library is exquisitely warm and comfortable. From five till eight read (Rousseau finished the 14th tome) to my beloved. She drawing her plan. from eight till ten I read Madame Sévigné. A day of the most perfect and sweet retirement.

During this period of three months they read fourteen volumes of Rousseau, who is referred to as "beloved," while Voltaire is noted as "that detested Voltaire." A subsequent diary shows the enormous amount of literature they consumed, history, memoirs and classics in French, Italian and English. Miss Ponsonby's drawing consisted often of maps of Wales or of the world or sometimes plans. Lady Eleanor says:

> My beloved finished her map (of the world) with a neatness and accuracy peculiar to herself. The writing and ornament particularly beautiful.

Lady Eleanor superintended the gardening operations; she goes the round every morning and notes what Powell the gardener is about, whether he is mowing, raking, planting or "scuffling in the shrubery," and sometimes scolds him. The entry "Margaret extremely indelicate" might at first be taken to refer to a domestic servant, but a later entry shows who Margaret was. There were guests, and "she came and showed herself and was milked before them."

They brewed their own beer. This year she notes:

> Brewed again. all our Beer proving sour owing to the dishonesty and negligence of the vestal whom for her malpractices we discarded last August.

Guests dropped in frequently, specially the Whalley family, who lived in the neighbourhood.

> Mr. Whalley came staid till two. melancholy, languid and interesting· gave him a melon and a pencil.

But visits from the outside were not always appreciated. The Whalleys called one day when the ladies were occupied with a friend drawing up their wills, and Lady Eleanor writes:

> Wished them at the deuce for interrupting us.

We also find:

> Colonel Mydelton smoked and we ran off sick to death.

> John Jones stayed till three. provincial politics how I hate them.

Nothing they disliked more than a pretentious or patronising air on the part of their visitors. General Yorke, who succeeded them at Plas Newydd, relates how on one occasion Lady Eleanor was describing a visit of this sort, but as her memory was failing at the time she appealed to her companion, "Did we like him,

Sarah Ponsonby ? " " We hated him, Eleanor," was the reply ; and she continued her tale by repeating " *We hated him.*"

Curious as their costume was, we see by the following entry that they were very particular :

> The habits we have so long expected arrived by the stage coach—that detestable Donnes—instead of the dark violet colour we so expressly ordered he sent a vulgar ordinary snuff colour like a Farmer's coat and in place of the plain simple Buttons which we chose has sent a paltry dullish Taudry three coloured thing like a Fairing. Just looked at them, observed with fury the total mistake of our order, packed them up and returned them to him by the same coach in which they came.

In illness the mutual devotion of the two ladies becomes very apparent.

> I awoke with a violent headache. kept my bed all day. How can I acknowledge the kindness and tenderness of my Beloved Sally who never for a moment left me but sat reading and drawing till ten o'clock at night.

> My Sally my tender, my sweet love lay beside me holding and supporting my head till one o'clock. When I by much entreaty prevailed with her to rise and get her breakfast.

Their financial circumstances remained rather a mystery. They talked over their " poverty " and occasionally " presents " helped them. There was evidently one from Mr. Chambre in the entry of December 12 above quoted. Lady Eleanor talks over their affairs with the Talbots.

> Mr. Talbot has a perfect recollection of the provision which was made for me in my brother's marriage settlement. They agree in thinking I have been barbarously cheated. I also acquainted them with my having signed, sealed and delivered my last Will and Testament. That I might secure all I am possessed of or entitled to to the Beloved of my Heart. They will see justice done her when I am no more.

In the last entry, December 14, she notes : " looking over correcting and binding this Journal."

One quotation alone from Miss Ponsonby's diary in the year 1788 is available.[1] It is in precisely the same style, Lady Eleanor is referred to as " my beloved," and the entry ends, " a day of sweet and silent retirement." But this diary and the others, if they existed, cannot be traced. Miss Ponsonby kept the accounts, and a few quotations from her account book [1] may be given as an instance of how much may be learned from a recital of items of expenditure. The accounts are filled with small generosities.

[1] Quoted in *A Swan and Her Friends*, by E. V. Lucas.

	£	s	d.
A travelling boy for the kindness with which he gave us some pinks.		1	
Lodowick's unfortunate daughter		1	
Poor woman 4d. Irish woman 1s 6d.		1.	10.
John Rogers, for bad work		2.	6.
Tinker for spoiling tea kettle		1.	3.
Ale from " Hand " not fit to be drunk			6.
Powdered Hair Tax	3.	3.	0.
Four little boys at chimney fire			6.
Halston gardener with horrid melon		2.	6.
Mr. Salmon for cleaning our teeth	1.	1.	0.
Muffins for kitchen quality			6.
Old, dirty, ungrateful Lloyd			6.
Carline's man with cart full of disappointment		2.	6.
Brandy for our landlord's cough			3.

Among other extracts are " Eels and trout for Mrs. Piozzi " and " Pair of Turkies, expectation of Miss Seward."

It is unfortunate that we have no diary comment on some of the eminent guests who visited Llangollen valley.

ELIZABETH, LADY HOLLAND

ELIZABETH VASSALL was born in 1771. At the age of 15 she was married to Sir Godfrey Webster, of Battle Abbey. She had three children, but the marriage was an unhappy one. She met Lord Holland in 1794 and separated from her husband. After obtaining a divorce she married Lord Holland in 1797. The celebrated hostess of Holland House is described thus by Greville when she died in 1845 : " Lady Holland contrived to assemble round her to the last a great society comprising almost everybody that was conspicuous, remarkable and agreeable. . . . She was often capricious, tyrannical and troublesome, liking to provoke and disappoint and thwart her acquaintances and she was often obliging, good-natured, and considerate to the same people. . . . She could not live alone for a single minute ; she never was alone and even in her moments of greatest grief it was not in solitude but in society that she sought her consolation."

From a woman of so marked a character, who had been through bitter private experiences and became the centre of the most remarkable political salon ever known in London, one might expect a diary of peculiar interest. The published extracts from her diary between 1791 and 1811, filling two volumes, are, however, a great disappointment. Neither the social, political, nor the personal entries in her diary are in any way noteworthy. The personal notes are unnaturally stilted and cold, and the political and social comments fall very far behind Greville or even some of the minor social diarists of the time. She thought it worth while to make a pretty full record of her travels and social entertainments and even to reflect on personal experiences. She did not lack literary talent, but she seems to have been entirely devoid of the spontaneity and reckless, careless ease which make some diaries entertaining. Her gossip is not as amusing even as Lady Charlotte Bury's, her political notes are never very illuminating, and what we get of the personal side is colourless and conventional. It would almost seem as if she were writing for eventual publication when she makes this sort of entry on the tragedy of her first marriage.

1793. Jan. 27. This fatal day seven years gave me in the bloom and innocence of fifteen to the power of a being who has made me execrate my life since it has belonged to him. Despair often prompts me to a remedy within my reach. . . . My mind is worked up to a state of savage exaltation and impels me to act with fury that proceeds more from passion and deep despair than I can in calmer moments justify. Often times in the gloom of midnight I feel a desire to curtail my grief and but for an unaccountable shudder than creeps over me, ere this the deed of rashness would be executed.

If she thought she was near committing suicide when she sat down and wrote this, she was very much mistaken. We get occasional glimpses of the advances made to her by various men, but she does not always give the name. For instance, in 1794 she writes :

Surprise and embarassment have completely overset me. Oh ! what vile animals men are with headstrong passions. Now ! I have heard from the lips of one who affects morality and domestic virtues maxims that would revolt all but the most depraved. . . . One night coming from the Pergola I was compelled to get out of the carriage to avoid his pressing importunities.

She is annoyed by Tierney's attentions :

I had a long walk upon the terrace with Tierney. I was in an eloquent *veine* and happily conveyed all I intended to express without the rigorous exterior of forbidding prudery. I think I convinced him his attentions offended and his hope insulted me, that I was firmly attached at home, and tho' I felt at present no resentment towards him yet I should if his pretensions continued.

When she hears of the suicide of her first husband, she writes:

> I could not hear of his death without emotion and was for some time considerably agitated. But my God! how was I overcome when Drew showed me a hasty note written to him by Hodges to apprise me of the manner of his death. He shot himself, he added, in consequence of heavy losses at play. With him dies all resentment and great as my injuries have been willingly would I renounce all that may accrue to me from this dreadful event to restore him again to existence with the certainty of his paying the natural debt of nature. Unhappy man! What must have been the agony of his mind to rouse him to commit a deed of such horror. Peace to his soul and may he find the mercy I would bestow.

In 1797 there is an interval of a year in the Journal, and when she resumes it she merely records the fact of her marriage to Lord Holland. But three years previously, when she first meets him in Italy, she makes some notes about him:

> Ld Holland is quite delightful. He is eager without rashness, well bred without ceremony . . . he is totally without any party rancour; in short he is exactly what all must like, esteem and admire. His spirits are sometimes too boisterous as may occasionally overpower me, but he is good humoured enough to endure reproof.

> Ld Holland's delightful spirits cheered us so much that we called him *sal volatile* and used to spare him to one another for half an hour to enliven when either [she and Lady Bessborough] were melancholy.

She prevented her daughter by her first marriage from being given into the custody of Sir G. Webster by stating that she was dead. Of this rather dramatic episode, however, we only find brief references, such as the following:

> 1799. June 19. On this day my mother left me. During her stay I disclosed an event which has incessantly occupied my mind now 3 years. I restored to her father my little daughter Harriet who I had concealed pretending her dead.

When she loses a son in 1801 she breaks out into a long and elaborate outpouring of grief:

> Alas! to lose my pretty infant just beginning to prattle his little innocent wishes, and imagination so busily aids my grief by tracing what he might have been. . . . Ah! my child perhaps if I had not left you in the summer but stayed and watched with maternal care all your ailments I might have had you still. . . .

After a page or so of this she goes on to describe an " interesting play " at Drury Lane.

She writes a good deal about her travels in Italy, Germany and the East, and she often enters the books she is reading, which are of the most various description, comprising classics, histories, chemistry, travel, drama, and philosophy in English, French and Italian. Of the parties at Holland House there is often little more than a list of names, although she sometimes records conversations or mentions the particular people with whom she spoke. There is a long and careful account of the death of Charles James Fox, who was Lord Holland's uncle.

Not only politicians assembled at Holland House. The literary and the learned as well as society notables were among the guests. There is this entry in 1807 about Wordsworth, " one of the Lake poets," when he came to dine :

> He is much superior to his writings and his conversation is even beyond his abilities. I should almost fear he is disposed to apply his talents more towards making himself a vigorous conversationalist in the style of our friend Sharp than to improve his style of composition.

While Lady Holland's descriptions of people are often critical, they somehow do not seem quite to hit the mark. There is much political and parliamentary gossip, but it is generally involved and difficult to follow.

After all, there is no particular reason why a great hostess and conversationalist with notable social gifts should also be able to record in writing the striking incidents of an eventful life. Even the greatest have their limitations.

The diary, edited by Lord Ilchester, was published in 1909.

THOMAS GREEN

THERE are two sections of Green's diary ; the first, 1796 to 1800, which was published ; the second, 1800 to 1811, extracts from which appeared in the *Gentleman's Magazine*. The diary differs from any other diary examined in these pages. It is concerned almost exclusively with records and criticisms of books. The first part when published was entitled *The Diary of a Lover of Literature*.

Thomas Green was born at Ipswich. He entered the Inner Temple, but having a competence of his own he relinquished his profession and settled down and read and travelled. There is in the diary, therefore, no professional ambition, no study for a special object, no endeavour to write up reminiscences for publication, no quest after celebrities, and actually no mention of royalty. He read because he loved reading, and while he mentions little else than books there is in his entries an air of quiet leisure, of peaceful absorption in literature for literature's sake, and a shrewdness and balance of judgment which shows the appreciation of a real scholar in the best sense. " Accomplishment," " career," " success," must have been words unknown to him. His was not an initiating, but an appraising mind. We could wish we had a little more colour in the setting, and could see more of the surroundings of this contemplative devourer of books. There is one mention of his " transplanting roses and watering." He writes of music a good deal and occasionally of politics. But for the most part the entries, which are made six or eight times in each month, are devoted solely to the books he is reading. They are not the hurried memoranda of the daily diarist recording events, but the carefully written reviews of a critic. The writing gave him pleasure. He says in 1803 :

> This closes the 7th year of my Diary a work from which both in the performance and in the retrospect I have derived still more delight than I expected.

He has a very wide range of reading, and it is impossible to enumerate all the books he digests. Cicero he admires and Livy " a sound and satisfactory historian." Johnson is a favourite, Gibbon's memoir he praises, and Burke's " plenitude of thought fertility of fancy and viguour of argumentution." He reads *Gil Blas* for the tenth time and re-reads the *Arabian Nights*, " to whose facinating influence I am quite ductile." A very long disquisition on Rousseau begins :

> Rousseau is a character who has by turns transported me with the most violent and opposite emotions of delight and disgust, admiration and contempt, indignation and pity : but my ultimate opinion of him drawn as it is from a pretty attentive consideration of his writings and actions will not I think easily be changed.

Sometimes his comments can be very severe :

> Read Maurice's Richmond Hill. However he may struggle to assume the poet I will venture to pronounce him not to be one. There are no traces of fine sensibility and his specious images are whipped round and round again in endless and tiresome succession. His vanity, for he boasts of writing Richmond in immortal verse, is more than equalled by his servile fawning contemptible adulation of the great.

There are philosophic and religious speculations. He writes at some length in defence of annihilation as against a future life, and later he notes :

Had a long and late discussion with Miss Barchard after supper on the doctrine of annihilation—congenial theme to my afflicted spirit.

After hearing a sermon in which the preacher deliberately avoided the question of the authenticity of the passage on which he was enlarging, Green writes:

Was this ignorance, a pious fraud or merely a total want of candour?

He enjoys music, and insists more than once in his notes that mere proficiency is not enough both in singing and playing, "a cultivated understanding and refined sensibility" are essential.

He describes his travels and the sights he sees in a few of the entries, but there is nothing remarkable in this part of the diary.

When he published the first section in 1803 he is very modest in his preface and calls it "the idlest work probably that was ever composed."

A fresh edition of this diary might well be published, with the second portion from the *Gentleman's Magazine* added.

The following Diaries in this century may also be briefly noted:—

ADMIRAL SIR GEORGE ROOKE

The two diaries kept by Sir George Rooke are typical sailor's diaries of a purely professional character. The first records events from April to October, 1700, when he was in command of the expedition in the Sound which was one of the episodes in the War of the Spanish Succession.

The entries, which are daily, give the usual nautical information about wind and weather as well as instructions and results of councils. The diary is written partly in the third person.

The second diary is concerned with an attack on Cadiz and Vigo in 1702, and extends from June, 1701, to January, 1703, ending up with the thanks he received from Parliament on his return. The entries are all brief and technical.

He wastes no unnecessary words about the King's death.

March 8. At 8 this morning his Majesty died and at nine we went towards Portsmouth and came this evening to Godalming.

And his religious exercises are related with the same brevity as his movements or the changes of the wind.

Received the sacrament at Queenborough.

Despatches, orders and resolutions in council are written out in full. The diary was published by the Navy Record Society in 1897.

PETER OLIVER

This diary shows the intention of the author to write a record of his life, but when it came to keeping it up in diary form he does not go beyond making brief business entries or one-line references to public events. From 1741 to 1781 he writes up a pretty full account of his career. He was born at Boston, U.S.A., and came over to England, where he practised as a doctor. In 1778 he writes a eulogy of his wife, who died in that year, but this was not written at the time. The actual diary does not begin till 1781, and then the entries are very brief and concern only his goings and comings, the weather, the movements of his family and references to the great public events at the end of the eighteenth and beginning of the nineteenth centuries. It concludes in 1821. Medical details occur from time to time. He describes a *post mortem* ; he notes that " Mr. Whitewood made me a set of artificial teeth for the upper jaw, very nice and elegant," and the entry " Peggy's nose gains fast " may or may not be medical.

The manuscript of the diary, which is contained in a small note-book of seventy pages, is in the British Museum (Eg. MS. 2674).

THOMAS GYLL

Solicitor-General of the County Palatine of Durham, Recorder of the City of Durham and historian and antiquary, Thomas Gyll kept a diary from 1748 to 1778, two years before he died at the age of 80. It is nothing more than a recital of deaths, births, and marriages of people in the district and eminent people in other parts. There are references to architectural changes in the Cathedral and the appointment and reception of a new Bishop. Sometimes he makes a very short comment after registering the date of a death, such as : " very good sense and cheerful temper," " very rich," " had insured a great deal," " a hopeful young man," " she was a woman of no consequence. *Ebria, garrula,*" " was reckoned to sing a base in perfection," etc. He records a picturesque funeral where five women preceded the coffin in hoods of white Irish linen and the bearers were eight widows in hoods and scarfs of the same linen.

Once only does he forget his official manner and express his feelings :

1763. Dec. 30. Mr. Hartley did not invite me to his dinner as he usually had done for many years on a groundless and shameful pretense. The Lord forgive him. I do, but he is *inexorabilis acer.*

The diary was obviously kept as a useful record for local antiquaries. It has very little human interest.

A transcript of the diary was made for the Surtees Society by Canon Raine.

MRS. POWYS

Caroline Girle was taught by her father to keep a diary. Born in 1739, she began at 17 to write diary letters to her father and then to keep a regular journal of her own. Her various productions cover the period from 1756 to 1808. She married Philip Powys and lived at Hardwick House, Oxfordshire.

Mrs. Powys' diary is a typical social diary recording movements, descriptions of scenery, family births and deaths, notes on the weather, comments on plays and as many references as possible to the Royal Family. She makes lists of people at dances and parties and she even includes *menus*. After a ball at Bath she writes :

> I will now put down the names of the nobility I remember to have been there tho' I've no doubt I shall omit many.

Then follows a list which occupies more than a page ending " besides Baronets and their wives inumerable." There is nothing of the smallest interest in any part of the long diary, which can only have value as a family record. She never indulges in personal opinions and there is very little character or colour in her memoranda. It serves as a good instance of the hopeless dullness of these social registers.

NINETEENTH CENTURY

B. R. HAYDON

HAYDON'S diary can certainly be ranked as one of the most remarkable ever written. It covers practically his whole life, and is contained in twenty-seven folio volumes interspersed with sketches. With few breaks it is written daily. But the diary is much more than merely full and regular, it gives a vivid, highly-coloured, even blatant picture of the extraordinary career of this extraordinary man. Everything about him was excessive; never has lack of reserve and restraint been carried to such a pitch. He painted the most gigantic pictures, his conceit was immeasurable, his ambition was limitless, in moments of exaltation he soared to the giddiest heights, his self-reproach was frantic, his depressions literally suicidal, the depth of his despair unfathomable, his friendships rapturous, his enmities violent, he worked far too hard, he idled for days and weeks together, and all these exaggerations are reflected with mirror-like accuracy in the pages of his diary. Egotism can never have reached such a height. He was an egomaniac. But when he can leave himself for a moment and describe others, recount incidents, and repeat conversation, we find so skilful and brilliant a pen that the character sketches and pen portraits which we try to commend in many other diaries seem lifeless and flat compared to his. He fancied himself, of course, as an artist, and it must be admitted, in spite of a few qualified successes which he always greatly exaggerated, he was an absolute failure; he fancied himself as a letter writer and as a lecturer, and he was fairly good in both capacities, although in his letters he could not be depended upon to steer clear of rant and fustian. But he never says, as we might well expect, " this diary of mine is going to be one of the most extraordinary and interesting human documents ever penned," and yet it is. As Sir Sidney Colvin says in his Life of Keats, speaking of Haydon : " In truth Haydon's chief intellectual power was as an observer and his best instrument the pen. Readers of his journal and correspondence know how vividly and tellingly he can relate an experience or touch off a character. In this gift of striking out a human portrait in words he stood second in his age, if second to Hazlitt alone and in our later literature there has been no one to beat him except Carlyle." But outside the diary, where in his writing he aims higher, " trying to become imaginative and impressive we find only the same self-satisfied void turgidity and proof of spiritual hollowness disguised by temperamental fervour, as in his paintings."

It is clear that he wrote for publication a sort of apologia, or vindication of his life. His motive is more or less disclosed in the following entry :

> I acquired in early life a great love of the journals of others and Johnson's recommendation to keep them honestly I always bore in mind. I have kept one for thirty four years. It is the history in fact of my mind and in all my lectures I had only to refer to them for such and such opinions to look when such and such thoughts had occurred and I found my journals an absolute capital to draw upon. I hope that my journals, if ever they are thought worthy of publication may give as much pleasure to others as other journals have given a delight to me.

And again we find at a later date :

> I write this without a single shilling in the world, with a large picture before me not half done, yet with a soul aspiring, ardent, confident—trusting on God for protection and support. . . . I shall read this again with delight and others will read it with wonder.

Needless to say Haydon began an autobiography covering his life from his birth in 1786 up to 1820, but the autobiography is largely composed of extracts copied out from his journals. From 1820 to 1846 the journals alone exist.

We cannot follow the ups and downs of his career nor touch on all the multitude of incidents in his life. He paints a large number of pictures, he is generally engaged in controversy, whether it is the defence of the Elgin marbles, furious attacks on the Academy or attempts to make the Government patronise art. He is nearly always in debt ; he sponges shamefully on his friends ; he reads a great deal ; he is close friends with a number of interesting people, including Wilkie, Keats, Wordsworth, Scott, Leigh Hunt, Lamb, Hazlitt, etc. ; he comes into close contact with many statesmen ; he marries, has children, and shows an unfailing devotion to his wife ; he travels, he lectures and he writes. But it is naturally impossible out of this voluminous record to give anything more than a few illustrative extracts, and even that is difficult, as there are throughout comparatively few short entries.

One habit of Haydon's not yet referred to was his outpourings and supplications to the Almighty. The diary is literally deluged in them. Like everything else, it is overdone. Pages of imprecation, of penitence, of importunate solicitation, of demands for triumph, in fact " begging letters dispatched to the Almighty," as they have been well described. Nevertheless they are absolutely sincere. As these prayers are the accompaniment or peroration of so many entries, some examples of them may be given.

> God in heaven, on my knees, I pray it may be my lot to realise my idea of art before I die, and I will yield my soul into Thy hands with rapture. Amen with all my soul.
>
> O God, on my knees I humbly, humbly, humbly pray Thee to enable me to go through it. Let no difficulties obstruct me, no ill health impede me, and let no sin displease Thee from its commencement to its conclusion. Oh save me from prison on the confines of which I am now hovering. I have no employment, no resources, a large family and no hope. In thee alone I always trust. Oh let me not now trust in vain. Grant, O God, that the education of my children, my duties to my love and to Society, may not be sacrificed in proceeding with this great work (it will be my greatest). Bless its commencement, its progression, its conclusion and its effect for the sake of the intellectual elevation of my great and glorious country.
>
> Oh Almighty God ! It is now thirty years since I commenced my picture of Solomon ; though deserted by the world, my family, father, friends, Thou knowest well that I trusted in Thee ; that Thou didst inspire my spirit with a fiery confidence ; that Thou didst whisper me to endure as seeing One who is invisible : Thou knowest I never doubted though without money, though in debt, though oppressed. I prayed for thy blessing on my commencing labours. Thou carriedst me through to victory and triumph and exultation.
>
> I ask from my heart Thou good Being to be saved with my family from the fatal ruin which must overwhelm me and them without Thy interference promising repentance sincere and intense.

Occasionally the inclination for prayer is not so acute :

> Sent my children to church but did not read prayers to myself which is wicked and ungrateful. The reason is I am in no danger pecuniarily—felt no want of God's protection and forget his past mercies. This shows what human gratitude is.

And once he has a misgiving that his importunity towards the Almighty has been overdone :

Perhaps I have presumed too much on the goodness of my Creator—appealed to Him too much and too freely.

The best way to give some idea of Haydon's alternating moods of wild elation or of utter despair will be to give a series of extracts which concern his painting and his debts. His excitement over the conception, composition and the performance of his painting, and even over the varnishing of his pictures, is so well described in some entries which cover days or weeks that a reader cannot help catching some of the frenzy of enthusiasm that consumed him. But here the briefer references must suffice.

1815. Never have I had such irresistible and perpetual urgings of future greatness. I have been like a man with air balloons under his arm pits and ether in his soul. While I was painting walking or thinking beaming flashes of energy followed and impressed me.

1823. Well I am in prison. So were Bacon, Raleigh, Cervantes. Vanity! Vanity! Here's a consolation! I started from sleep repeatedly during the night from the songs and roarings of the other prisoners.

1824. Completed my yesterday's work and obliged to sally forth to get money in consequence of the bullying insolence of a short, wicked-eyed, wrinkled, waddling, gin-drinking, dirty, ruffled landlady—poor old bit of asthmatic humanity! As I was finishing the faun's foot in she bounced and demanded the four pounds with the air of an old demirep duchess. I irritated her by my smile and turned her out. I sat down quietly and finished my foot. Fielding should have seen the old devil.

Passed in desponding on the future. Not a shilling in the world. Sold nothing and not likely to. Baker called and was insolent. If he were to stop the supplies God knows what would become of my children. Landlord called—kind and sorry. Butcher called, respectful but disappointed. Tailor good-humoured and willing to wait.

I saw the head of Lazarus as the hand of Christ after a year's absence, and if God in his mercy spare that picture my posthumous reputation is secured. O God! Grant it may reach the National Gallery in a few years and be placed in fair competition with Sebastian del Piombo. I ask no more to obtain fair justice from the world.

I leave off wearied and commence in disgust. I candidly confess I find my glorious art a bore.

1825. My fits continue. I am all fits—fits of work, fits of idleness, fits of reading, fits of walking, fits of Italian, fits of Greek, fits of Latin, fits of French, fits of Napoleon, fits of the navy, fits of the army, fits of religion. My dear Mary's lovely face is the only thing that has escaped—a fit that never varies.

1826. Reinagle said he thought me infamously used and wondered I had not gone mad or died. 'Where is your Solomon, Mr. Haydon?' 'Hung up in a grocer's shop.' 'Where your Jerusalem?' 'In a ware room in

Holborn.' 'Where your Lazarus?' 'In an upholsterer's shop in Mount Street.' 'And your Macbeth?' 'In Chancery.' 'Your Pharaoh?' 'In an attic pledged.' 'My God and your Crucifixion?' 'In a hayloft.' 'And Silenus?' 'Sold for half price.'

1827. I do not despair; and something whispers me that I shall yet do greater things than I have ever yet done and that my knowledge will not be suffered to leave the world without a period arriving of full development.

To relieve the pressure of necessity he took to portrait painting, which he loathed :

1830. Finished a rascally portrait, the last I have got—a poor, pale faced, skinny creature who was biting his lips to make them look red, rubbing his hair, and asking me if I did not think he had a good eye.

1831. A quarter to nine. This moment I have conceived my background stronger than ever. I strode about the room imitating the blast of a trumpet —my cheeks full of blood and my heart beating with a glorious heat. Oh who would change these moments for a throne ?

Another last day of another year. What have I to say ? Nothing but that after forty five years I have been more irresolute, more idle, more doting, more unworthy of my name than any preceding year of my life.

1835. The agony of my necessities is really dreadful. For this year I have principally supported myself by the help of my landlord and by pawning everything of any value I have left until at last it is come to my clothes a thing in all my wants I never did before. I literally to-day sent out my dinner suit which cost £10 and got £2.15 on it for to-night's necessities. Oh it is dreadful beyond expression ! I could not go to dearest Mary and ask her for her little jewelries ; but I am now if invited to dinner without a dress to dine in.

1836. Set my palette to-day, the first time these eleven weeks and three days. I relished the oil ; could have tasted the colour ; rubbed my cheeks with the brushes and kissed the palette.

1840. It is extraordinary that with a large canvas in the house I always feel as if Satan crossing Chaos was no match for me. My heart beats ; my breast broadens ; my height rises ; my cheek warms. How I would swell in a Vatican or a dome of St. Paul's ! O God bless me before I die. Why such talents—why such desires—such longings if to pine in hopeless ambition and endless agonies ? In Thee I trust O God.

I want to get that broad style of imitating nature I see in the great masters— not in Vandyke, but in Titian, Correggio, Angelo, Tintoretto, Rembrandt and Reynolds. Founded as I am I know I could improve on it ; I'll try.

1842. Thank God with all my soul and all my nature my children have witnessed the harassing agonies under which I have ever painted ; and the very name of painting—the very name of high art—the very thought of a picture gives them a hideous and disgusting taste in their mouths. Thank God, not one of my boys, nor my girl can draw a straight line even with a ruler much less without one. And I pray God on my knees with my forehead bent to the earth and my lips to the dust that he will in his mercy afflict them with every other passion appetite or misery, with wretchedness, disease, insanity, or gabbling idiotism rather than a longing for painting—that scorned miserable art—that greater imposture than the human species it imitates.

Three days later:

Huzza—huzza—huzza and one cheer more! My cartoon is up and makes my heart beat as all large bare spaces do and ever have done. Difficulties to conquer. Victories to win. Enemies to beat. The nation to please. The honour of England to be kept up. Huzza—huzza—huzza and one cheer more!

Though Haydon was the moving spirit in pressing for the decoration of the House of Lords, when the opportunity for executing the great decorative work came, his cartoons were rejected and he was passed over. He never recovered from the bitterness of the disappointment.

1834. Went and removed my cartoons. Thus ends the cartoon contest, and as the first inventor and beginner of this mode of rousing the people when they were pronounced incapable of relishing refined works of art without colour I am deeply wounded at the insult inflicted. These journals witness under what trials I began them—how I called on my Creator for His blessing—how I trusted in Him and how I have been degraded, insulted, harassed. O Lord thou knowest best. I submit. Amen.

Still his fits of optimism return:

Alexander the Great was before me—a mutton chop on the coals. I had just written to Wordsworth. . . . My chop was cooked to a tee; I ate like a Red Indian; and drank the cool translucent with a gusto a wine connoisseur knows not. I then thought the distant cloud was too much advanced so toning it down with black I hit the mark and pronounced the work done—*Io Pœ-an!* and I fell on my knees and thanked God and bowed my forehead and touched the ground and sprung up my heart beating at the anticipation of greater work and a more terrific struggle. This is B. R. Haydon—the *real* man—may he live a thousand years! and here he sneezed—lucky!

Haydon's enthusiasm was infectious; it blinded his friends to the mediocre character of his performances as an artist. But it is a great tribute to his personality that he should have attracted so many of the best minds of the day to his studio. When he has to change his quarters owing to debt, he writes:

What pleasure have I enjoyed in this study! In it have talked to Walter Scott, Wordsworth, Keats, Proctor, Belzoni, Campbell, Canova, Cuvier, Lamb, Knowles, Hazlitt, Wilkie and other spirits of the time. And above all thy sweet and sacred face, my Mary, was its chief grace, its ornament, its sunbeam.

It is after one of the evenings of discussion in his studio that he catches with a single happy phrase the exact reflection of the passing mood and scene:

> Spent a delightful evening with old friends. . . . When they were gone I felt the solitude of the scattered chairs.

Of course his friendships were, like everything else, rapturous to danger point, and many were ended by quarrels.

> Keats is a man after my own heart. He sympathises with me and comprehends me. We saw through each other and 1 hope are friends for ever. I only know that if I sell my picture Keats shall never want till another is done that he may have leisure for his effusions; in short he shall never want all his life.

This did not prevent him from borrowing from Keats at a time when the unfortunate poet was least able to afford it.

He describes Keats reading out his poems " in a low tremulous undertone." Keats writes a sonnet to him. Wordsworth several. Shelley's conversational opening " as to that detestable religion, the Christian," makes Haydon " like a stag at bay and resolved to gore without mercy." With Leigh Hunt, with Reynolds and others he quarrelled. His capricious humours are all depicted in the pages of the diary. The best of all the scenes perhaps is the description of the dinner when Lamb was drunk and chaffed most unmercifully a pompous official, Kingston, the Comptroller of Stamps. It is far too long to quote, but, as Sir Sidney Colvin says, it is " thrust before us in the insistent colour and illumination of a magic lantern picture."

A comparison of Moore and Wordsworth may be quoted showing that Haydon could appreciate a character very different from his own.

> Moore is a delightful, nay, voluptuous, refined natural creature; infinitely more unaffected than Wordsworth; not blunt and uncultivated like Chantrey or bilious and shivering like Campbell. No affectation, but a true, refined, delicate frank poet with sufficient honesty of manner to show fashion has not corrupted his native taste; making allowance for prejudices instead of condemning them, by which he seemed to have none himself; never talking of his own works from intense consciousness that everybody else did; while Wordsworth is always talking of his own productions from apprehension that they are not enough matter of conversation.

This amusing little miniature of Chantrey is also worthy of notice.

> I called on Chantrey at Brighton. I had not seen him for eight years and was astonished and interested. He took snuff in abundance. His nose at the top was bottled large and brown, his cheeks full, his person corpulent, his

air indolent, his tone a little pompous. Such were the effects of eight years' success. He sat and talked easily, lazily gazing at the sun with his legs crossed.

Haydon, too, was brought or rather forced himself with his innate effrontery into the company of statesmen. He exasperated them with his petitions and begging letters, he bored them, he pestered them, he never took a snub, he persisted and at last he succeeded in interviewing them, in painting them, and even staying with them, and we can see that, in spite of their exasperation, they were intensely amused and entertained by him. They, like everyone else, come in for praise or blame according to his mood and circumstances. As Macaulay says : " Whether you struck him or stroked him, starved him or fed him, he snapped at your hand in just the same way."

Lord Grey is in high favour at one time :

> Lord Grey was enough yesterday to make any man begin with champagne the moment he was gone. He looked like the first glass after the bursting pop.

> Lord Grey was looking the essence of mildness. He seemed disposed for a chat. In my eagerness to tell him all I wanted to know I sprang off my chair and began to explain bending my fist to enforce my argument. Lord Grey looked at me with a mild peacefulness of expression as if regarding a bit of gunpowder he had admitted to disturb his thoughts.

Lord Melbourne's interviews are described at some length. He was evidently amused by Haydon, always broke into a laugh, rubbed his hands, or " went to the glass and began to comb his hair." " God help the Minister that meddles with Art," he says to his impetuous interviewer on one occasion.

Sir Robert Peel was a very good friend to Haydon and helped him on more than one occasion. But Haydon shows little gratitude and is generally unreasonable.

Lord Egremont was one of his patrons, and while lying in bed in a magnificent chamber in Petworth, the painter muses :

> What a destiny is mine ! One year in the Bench, the companion of gamblers and scoundrels—sleeping in wretchedness and dirt on a flock bed, low and filthy with black worms crawling over my hands—another in a splendid house, the guest of rank and fashion and beauty.

But the most finished picture—needless to say not of his brush, but of his pen—is the Duke of Wellington. In a correspondence extending over some considerable period the Duke positively snubs his head off. Undismayed, Haydon persists, and he not only obtains the Duke's consent to sit, but he is invited to Walmer for a visit of several days. The Duke treats him with the most gentlemanlike courtesy, and Haydon on his side falls into adoration of " the greatest man on earth and the noblest—the conqueror of Napoleon." All the little touches about each day of the visit bring the scene before one with microscopic clearness. The Duke seated reading the newspaper with a lighted candle " on each side of his venerable head," asking him if he will have black tea or green, giving a tremendous yawn before bed time, showing him up to his room, sitting for the portrait always patiently but never looking at it (" D'ye want another sitting ? Very well, after hunting I'll come ") : telling anecdotes, putting on " a fine dashing waistcoat for the Russian Ambassador " and then in church—

Arthur Wellesley in the village church of Walmer this day was more interesting to me than at the last charge of the Guards at Waterloo.

The Duke was no doubt tickled by the whole proceeding ; we can hear him chuckling in the passage when Haydon writes :

He said : ' I hope you are satisfied. Goodbye.' I heard him go to bed after me, laughing, and he roared out to Arbuthnot ' Good-night.' I then heard him slam the door of his room No. 11 next to mine No. 10 but on the opposite side a little further along.

Amongst humbler people there is no worse instance of Haydon's ingratitude than his references to his landlord Newton, who not only allowed him to stay on without paying rent, but often helped him with money. But here again he refers at one time to his insults and then expresses later his devotion to him.

His political were no less intense than his artistic, literary and religious interests, and contained exactly the same elements of shrewdness and perception, marred by blatant over-emphasis and commonness of mind. He plunges into foreign politics, the reform movement and other questions with great zeal, and peppers his diary with scathing and enthusiastic comments. Haydon could never do things like other people, or rather the most ordinary things in his mind became transformed and distorted. A visit to Brighton would be a fairly commonplace event for most people and they would enter in their diary " went to Brighton ; bathed " ; but Haydon rushes to Brighton, where he " rolled in the sea, shouted like a savage, laved his sides like a bull in a green meadow, dived, swam, floated, and came out refreshed."

As may well be imagined, he gradually wore himself out in mind and body. Debt and disappointment got the upper hand, and his buoyant vitality was at last vanquished. In June, 1846, the entries show constant anxiety, though there are attempts at work. The last four entries may be given :

18th. O God bless me through evils of this day. Great anxiety. My landlord Newton called. I said " I see a quarter's rent in thy face but none from me." I appointed to-morrow night to see him and lay before him every iota of my position. Good hearted Newton ! I said: " Don't put in an execution." " Nothing of the sort " he replied half hurt. I sent the Duke, Wordsworth, dear Fred and Mary's heads to Miss Barrett to protect. I have the Duke's boots and hat and Lord Grey's coat and some more heads.

20th. O God bless us all through the evils of this day. Amen.
21st. Slept horribly. Prayed in sorrow and got up in agitation.
22nd. God forgive me. Amen.

Finis
of
B. R. Haydon.

Stretch me no longer on this rough world (Lear).

He made this last entry at half-past ten, and about an hour later his body was found with a frightful gash in his throat and a bullet wound in his skull. On his easel was his unfinished picture of King Alfred. On a table near was his diary open at the page of the last entry, a prayer book and a paper headed " last Thoughts of B. R. Haydon, half past ten."

In this paper, which is a sort of will divided into a number of clauses, he wrote :

In the name of my God I hope for forgiveness for the step I am about to take—a crime no doubt but if I am judged immediately hereafter I have done nothing all my life that will render me fearful of appearing before the awful consciousness of my invisible God or hesitate to explain my actions.

In earlier years he had more than once discussed the ethics of suicide in his diary ; one conclusion he came to was : " I am not so convinced of the wickedness of suicide as I am of its folly." But the continued crises, the passionate longings and repeated disappointments no doubt ended by unhinging a mind the balance of which had always been uncertain. In his last paper he asks the pardon of his wife and children, " for the additional pang —but it will be the last and released from the burthen of my ambition they will be happier and suffer less."

Haydon's pictures are forgotten ; but in his diary, by the very want of reticence, which was perhaps his chief defect, he has left a wonderful portrait of himself.

The twenty-seven manuscript volumes are in the British Museum. They were edited and used by Tom Taylor in a biography published in 1853.

BYRON

MOORE in his Life of Byron gives extracts from the poet's diary, with "the omission of some portion of its contents and unluckily too of that very portion which from its reference to the secret pursuits and feelings of the writer would most likely pique and gratify the curiosity of the reader." Byron literature is now so voluminous, and every aspect of his genius and character has been so carefully examined, that his fragmentary diary, even when complete, covers only a very small part of the ground. Nevertheless in a collection of diaries the fragments certainly deserve a prominent place, because Byron, though not a diarist in the sense that he kept a regular journal for any long period, shows in the entries he does make just the recklessness, humour and egotism which go to make a lively human document.

The three diary periods are very short, and Moore's winnowing takes place within these periods. Byron only kept a journal from November 14, 1813, to April 19, 1814, during his expedition in the Alps in 1816, and in January and February, 1821. Each time he writes daily, sometimes more than once in the day and generally at considerable length.

Some idea is given of his motive in keeping a diary in the following entry:

> This journal is a relief. When I am tired—as I generally am—out comes this and down goes everything. But I can't read it over: and God knows what contradictions it may contain. If I am sincere with myself (but I fear one lies more to one's self than to anyone else) every page should confute, refute and utterly abjure its predecessor.

He begins writing at the age of 25.

> 1813. Nov. 14. If this had been begun ten years ago and faithfully kept!!! Heigho! There are too many things I wish never to have remembered as it is. . . . At five and twenty when the better part of life is over one should be *something*; and what am I? Nothing but five and twenty—and the odd months.

When he misses writing for two days he begins:

> Two days missed in my log book: *hiatus haud deflendus*. They were as little worth recollection as the rest; and luckily laziness or society prevented me from noticing them.

Everything is noted—his reading, his writing, criticisms of the people he meets, opinions on public affairs, dinners, parties, solitude all wrapt up in general reflections on life and interspersed with details about his food, his health, and his moods. Whether he lies or tells the truth does not much signify. He writes with a natural formless spontaneity and brilliance that makes every line readable. We can but make arbitrary selections—little slices from the rather rich cake, and as the diaries are so short we will go along, lifting in chronological order bits as we pass.

The first entry contains this on speaking in the House of Lords:

> I have spoken thrice but I doubt my ever becoming an orator. My first was liked; the second and third—I don't know whether they succeeded or not. I have never yet set to it *con amore*: one must have some excuse to one's self for laziness, or inability or both and this is mine 'Company, villainous company hath been the spoil of me';—and then I have ' drunk medicines ' not to make me love others but certainly enough to hate myself.

He visits a menagerie:

> Such a conversazione! There was a hippopotamus like Lord Liverpool in the face and the Ursine Sloth hath the very voice and manner of my valet— but the tiger talked too much. The elephant took and gave me my money again—took off my hat—opened a door—trunked a whip—and behaved so well that I wish he was my butler.

A visit to the dentist:

> Went to Waite's. Teeth all right and white; but he says that I grind them in my sleep and clip the edges.

He had just finished writing "The Bride of Abydos." On November 17 we hear something of this, and also about his extraordinary diet regulations.

> Mr. Murray has offered me one thousand guineas for " The Giaour " and the " Bride of Abydos." I won't—it is too much, though I am strongly tempted merely for the *say* of it. No bad price for a fortnight's (a week each) what ?—the Gods know—it was intended to be called poetry.
> I have dined regularly to-day for the first time since Sunday last—this being Sabbath too.
> All the rest tea and dry biscuits—six *per diem*. I wish to God I had not dined now! It kills me with heaviness stupor and horrible dreams and yet it was but a pint of bucellas and fish. Meat I never touch nor much vegetable diet.

I would not so much mind a little accession of flesh—my bones can well bear it. But the worst is, the devil always came with it—till I starved him out—and I will *not* be the slave of *any* appetite. If I do err it shall be my heart at least that heralds the way. Oh my head—how it aches ? the horrors of digestion ! I wonder how Buonaparte's dinner agrees with him.

On November 22 we get this reflection when he is talking about the affairs of the world abroad :

A little *tumult* now and then is an agreeable quickener of sensation ; such as a revolution a battle or an *aventure* of any lively description.

He begins on November 23 about Ward, afterwards Lord Dudley :

Ward—I like Ward. By Mahomet I begin to think I like everybody ;—a disposition not to be encouraged—a sort of social gluttony that swallows everything set before it. But I like Ward. He is *piquant*; and in my opinion will stand very high in the House and everywhere else if he applies regularly. By the by I dine with him to-morrow which may have some influence on my opinion. It is as well not to trust one's gratitude *after* dinner. I have heard many a host libelled by his guests with his burgundy yet reeking on their rascally lips.

Philosophising on public affairs later on the same day (for there are three separate entries on this day), he says :

My hopes are limited to the arrangement of my affairs and settling either in Italy or the East (rather the last) and drinking deep of the languages and literature of both. Past events have unnerved me and all I can do is to make life an amusement and look on while others play. After all even the highest game of crowns and sceptres what is it ?

On this day, too, we get his opinion of his future wife :

Yesterday a very pretty letter from Annabella which I answered. What an odd situation and friendship is ours ! Without one spark of love on either side and produced by circumstances which in general lead to coldness on one side and aversion on the other. She is a very superior woman and very little spoiled which is strange in an heiress. . . . She is a poetess, a mathematician, a metaphysician and yet withal very kind, generous, and gentle with very little pretension. Any other head would be turned with half her acquisitions and a tenth of her advantages.

The entry on the next day ends with the following reflection :

I shall soon be six and twenty.
Is there anything in the future that can possibly console us for not being always twenty five.

Oh *Gioventù !*
Oh *Primavera !* gioventù dell' anno.
Oh *Gioventù !* primavera della vita.

The careless ease with which he scribbled down just what came into his head can be shown in the end of his entry on December 6 and the beginning of his entry on the following day:

> I shall now smoke two cigars and get me to bed. The cigars don't keep well here. They get as old as a *donna di quarant anni* in the sun of Africa. The Havannah are the best—but neither are so pleasant as a hooker or chibogue. The Turkish tobacco is mild and their horses entire—two things as they should be. I am so far obliged to this Journal that it preserves me from verse—at least from keeping it. I have just thrown a poem into the fire (which it has relighted to my great comfort) and have smoked out of my head the plan of another. I wish I could as easily get rid of thinking or at least the confusion of thought.
>
> Dec. 7. Went to bed and slept dreamlessly but not refreshingly. Awoke and up an hour before being called : but dawdled three hours in dressing. When one subtracts from life infancy (which is vegetation)—sleeping, eating and swilling—buttoning and unbuttoning—how much remains of downright existence ? The summer of a dormouse.
>
> Redde [he generally spells " read " like this] the papers and tea-ed and soda watered and found that the fire was badly lighted. Lord Glenbervie wants me to go to Brighton—um !

On December 16 there is a very short entry :

> Much done but nothing to record. It is quite enough to set down my thoughts—my actions will rarely bear retrospection.

On January 16 we have Byron on marriage :

> A wife would be my salvation. . . . That she won't love me is very probable nor shall I love her. But on my system and the modern system in general that don't signify. The business (if it came to business) would probably be arranged between papa and me. She would have her own way. I am good humoured to women and docile : and if I did not fall in love with her which I should try to prevent we should be a very comfortable couple. As to conduct *that* she must look to. But *if* I love I shall be jealous—and for that reason I will not be in love. . . . I do fear my temper would lead me into some of our oriental tricks of vengeance or at any rate into a summary appeal to the court of twelve paces. So ' I'll none on't ' but e'en remain single and solitary ;—though I should like to have somebody now and then to yawn with one.

His experiment, when it came to the point, was, as we know, peculiarly unsuccessful. His wife left him after a year.

After a month's break he returns to his journal, making three entries on February 18, 1814 : one in the morning, the second at nine o'clock, the third at midnight. We will extract the following bits :

> Redde a little—wrote notes and letters and am alone which Locke says is bad company. ' Be not solitary, be not idle.' Um ! the idleness is trouble-

some but I can't see so much to regret in the solitude. The more I see of men the less I like them. If I could but say so of women too all would be well. Why can't I ? I am now six and twenty : my passions have had enough to cool them : my affections more than enough to wither them—and yet—and yet—always *yet* and *but*—' Excellent well, you are a fishmonger—get thee to a nunnery.' ' They fool me to the top of my bent.'

Napoleon ! this week will decide his fate. All seems against him but I believe and hope he will win—at least beat back the invaders. What right have we to prescribe sovereigns to France ? Oh for a republic ! [there is much more about his admiration for Napoleon] I wonder how the deuce anybody could make such a world : for what purpose dandies, for instance, were ordained—and kings—and fellows of colleges—and women of ' a certain age '—and many men of any age—and myself, most of all.

On February 27 we get a reference to a woman friend of Byron's who is perhaps not so famous as many of the others :

I always feel in better humour with myself and everything else if there is a woman within ken. Even Mrs. Mule my fire lighter—the most ancient and withered of her kind—always makes me laugh—no difficult task when I am i' the vein.

Mrs. Mule, with her gaunt and witch-like appearance, acted as a sort of scarecrow to Byron's visitors. She followed him from Bennett Street to the Albany and was actually found in his establishment in Piccadilly after he married. Byron's only reply to inquiries about her was " The poor old devil was so kind to me."

On March 17 and other dates we get a note of one of the forms of exercise he took :

I have been sparring with Jackson for exercise this morning ; and mean to continue and renew my acquaintance with the muffles.

The following on the career of any son he may have reminds one of Haydon :

If I have a wife and that wife has a son—by anybody—I will bring up mine heir in a most anti-poetical way—make him a lawyer or a pirate—or anything. But if he writes too I shall be sure he is none of mine and cut him off with a Bank token.

Towards the end we get ejaculations such as " Tired, jaded, selfish and supine—must go to bed," " my heart begins to eat itself again." Napoleon's abdication upsets him. On April 10 :

To-day I have boxed one hour—written an ode to Napoleon Boanaparte—copied it—eaten six biscuits—drunk four bottles of soda water—redde away the rest of my time.

And April 19 is the last entry :

> There is ice at both poles, north and south—all extremes are the same—misery belongs to the highest and the beggar when unsixpenced and unthroned. There is to be sure a damned insipid medium—an equinoctial line—no one knows where except upon maps and measurements.
>
> And all our *yesterdays* have lighted
> The way to dusty death.
>
> I will keep no further journal of that same hesternal torchlight and to prevent me from returning like a dog to the vomit of memory, I tear out the remaining leaves of this volume and write, in Ipecacuanha—' that the Bourbons are restored ! ! ! '   ' Hang up philosophy.'   To be sure I have long despised myself and man but I never spat in the face of my species before—' O fool !   I shall go mad ! '

Byron's second attempt at keeping a diary was during a tour in the Bernese Alps in September, 1816. Needless to say it is not a dull guide-book account of what he saw and did.

He sent it to his sister. The first he had given to Thomas Moore. His third attempt only lasted six weeks in 1820 when he was in Ravenna. " A sudden thought strikes me," he begins. " Let me begin a Journal once more." He keeps it very regularly and while it is just as spontaneous as his first attempt, it has not quite the same reckless tone. He notes his reading and writing and his depressions, but he is chiefly occupied with the intrigues of the revolutionary movement and politics. His enthusiasm is unbounded, though the leaders of the movement are a disappointing lot.

> It is not one man, nor a million but the spirit of liberty which must be spread. The waves which dash upon the shore are, one by one, broken but yet the ocean conquers nevertheless.

He is at work on " Sardanapalus " and reports about the progress of it.

> Wrote the opening lines of the intended tragedy of Sardanapalus. Rode out some miles into the forest. Misty and rainy—returned—dined—wrote some more of my tragedy. Read Diodorus Siculus—turned over Seneca and some other books. Wrote some more of the tragedy. Took a glass of grog. After having ridden hard in rainy weather and scribbled and scribbled again, the spirits (at least mine) need a little exhilaration and I don't like laudanum now as I used to do. So I have mixed a glass of strong waters and single waters which I shall now proceed to empty. Therefore and thereunto I conclude this day's diary.

He makes notes about the books he reads and expresses

more than once his great admiration for Sir Walter Scott : " wonderful man—I long to get drunk with him." Most of the entries are long, but here is a complete short one :

> Jan. 16. Read—wrote—fired pistols—returned—wrote—visited—heard music—talked nonsense—and went home. Wrote part of a Tragedy—advanced in Act I with " all deliberate speed." Bought a blanket. The weather is still muggy as a London May—mist, mizzle, the air replete with Scotticisms which though fine in the descriptions of Ossian, are somewhat tiresome in real, prosaic perspective. Politics still mysterious.

On the eve of his birthday he writes :

> To-morrow is my birthday—that is to say at twelve o'clock midnight i.e. in twelve minutes I shall have completed thirty and three years of age ! !—and I go to my bed with a heaviness of heart at having lived so long and to so little purpose.
> It is three minutes past twelve. ' 'Tis the middle of the night by the castle clock ' and I am now thirty three !
> *Eheu fugaces, Posthume, Posthume,*
> *Labuntur anni ;—*
> but I don't regret them so much for what I have done as for what I might have done.

Then follows a sort of comic epitaph on the year that has passed.

Of course he becomes deeply involved in the revolutionary activities. He writes on February 18 :

> To-day I have had no communication with my Carbonari cronies ; but in the meantime my lower apartments are full of their bayonets, fusils, cartridges and what not. I suppose they consider me as a depôt, to be sacrificed, in case of accidents. It is no great matter, supposing that Italy could be liberated, who or what is sacrificed. It is a grand object—the very *poetry* of politics. Only think—a free Italy ! ! !

In addition to arms and ammunition in his villa he apparently had birds, for we find the remark : " Beat the crow for stealing the falcon's victuals." He becomes more disinclined to write in the diary. On February 25 he says :

> Came home—my head aches—plenty of news but too tiresome to set down. I have neither read nor written nor thought but led a purely animal life all day. I mean to try a page or two before I go to bed.

On February 27 he writes one more entry in another book. He is at work on " Don Juan," he quotes a stanza from Gray's " Elegy," and ends up with a very elaborate description of his indigestion.

As a last quotation we will give the melancholy passage with which the poet ends his second diary:

> I am a lover of nature and an admirer of beauty. I can bear fatigue and welcome privation and have seen some of the noblest scenes in the world. But in all this the recollection of bitterness and more especially of recent and more home desolation which must accompany me through life preyed upon me here; and neither the music of the shepherds, the crashing of the avalanche nor the torrent, the mountain, the glacier, the forest nor the cloud have for one moment lightened the weight upon my heart nor enabled me to lose my own wretched identity in the majesty and the power and the glory around and above and beneath me.

If Byron had really kept a diary, it would certainly have ranked among the best ever written. It was not lack of egotism but lack of regular method, an essential for diary keeping, which prevented him.

CHARLES GREVILLE

ONE has only to notice the number of footnote references to Greville's Journal in any history of the period during which he wrote in order to realise the importance of his record. Greville as a commentator on contemporary events holds a unique position. He wrote history as it was in the making; and other political and social diaries of the nineteenth century fade into insignificance when compared with his very full and detailed chronicle. As clerk of the council under four monarchs, and a man of fashion, he had specially favourable opportunities for collecting the materials he wanted, but he also had the gift of being able to relate the intrigues and inner workings of the machine of government and of society in such a way as to make a reader live in his times. It is an objective diary, of course, and has not the personal and psychological interest of a diary such as Pepys', but it is not dryly impersonal, for he often expresses his own opinions and moralises when he feels inclined.

Greville wrote for publication. He entrusted the ninety-three quarto note-books to Henry Reeve, with an injunction that he should " print such portions of them as might be thought of public interest whenever that could be done without inconvenience to living persons."

In 1865 Mr. Reeve published a few extracts from the diaries from 1814 to 1827. But in 1875 the publication of the full series began with the Journals of the reigns of George IV and William IV. Five large editions were sold in the first year, but some passages caused extreme offence and had to be suppressed. In 1885 and 1887 the second and third series of the volumes were published.

Greville's method was not merely to register public events, but to relate the inner causes which led up to them. It is all very personal. His character sketches are well drawn and spontaneously written at the moment. They are racy but often rather superficial, and his political survey does not contain any profound analysis of motives and principles. At times there is great elaboration of circumstances which seemed important when written but which have ceased to have any sort of interest to-day. Greville, however, gives the most graphic contemporary account of the relationships and intercourse between the members of the governing class in the country that has ever been produced. His work differs from other contemporary histories like Clarendon's or Wraxall's memoirs because he adopted the regular diary form and gave the fresh impression of the day. In communicating the manuscript to a friend he remarks : " You will find public characters freely, flippantly perhaps and frequently very severely dealt with ; in some cases you will be surprised to see my opinions of certain men, some of whom, in many respects, I may perhaps think differently of now." A passing judgment may not have the same value as a considered survey after the lapse of years, but it has value of its own, as an opinion of the moment and the ease and felicity of expression in the case of Greville bring the events and persons described very close to one.

It will be unnecessary to quote very much from the well-known passages in the eight printed volumes. Although the diary consists mainly of a narrative of political and public events, the subjective personal element is present and the man himself can be discovered by something more than his style as a diarist historian.

Greville was a handsome and accomplished man of fashion who served as clerk of the council for nearly forty years. He was friends with many public men and was consulted by them, and he was an active member of the Turf. His contemporaries would no doubt have been very much surprised had they known with what fullness and freedom, and we may add with what literary talent, he was describing them and their doings. He had no great pretensions with regard to the record he was making. In one entry he says :

> As I don't write history I omit to note such facts as are recorded in the newspapers and merely mention the odd things I pick up which are not generally known and which may hereafter throw some light on those which are.

He is overcome, too, occasionally by the diarist's misgiving as to whether it is worth while going on with his record, and he analyses the whole principle of diary keeping more fully perhaps than any other diarist.

In 1843 he writes :

> I have serious thoughts of giving up this journal altogether and yet I am reluctant to do so for it has been for many years an occasional and sometimes a constant and brisk amusement to me but I feel that it is neither one thing nor another and not worth the trouble of continuing. I have no inclination like some diarists to put down day by day all the trifles they see, hear or do. . . . I am reluctant to spoil a quantity of paper with mere trash which whatever accident may make it or what value it may possibly acquire by age is too trivial now to set down without a feeling of mixed shame and disgust.

His gossip—and there is a good deal of it—is political. He says :

> I hardly ever record the scandalous stories of the day unless they relate to characters or events but what relates to public men is different from the loves and friendships of the idiots of society.

It is interesting to read his opinion on other diaries and diarists. He sees the manuscript of Windham's diary, and notes how it abounds with expressions of self-reproach. He adopts Windham's practice of only writing on one side of the page. In 1838 for a moment he considers making his diary more personal, but he says :

> I always contemplate the possibility that hereafter my journal will be read by the public always greedy of such things and I regard with alarm and dislike the notion of its containing a heap of twaddle and trash concerning matters appertaining to myself which nobody else will care three straws about.

But he acknowledges that a strong stimulus to keep such a diary proceeds from having read Scott's and Byron's. He is mercilessly critical of Fanny Burney's diary. While he pays a tribute to her talent for recording conversations, and acknowledges that there are interesting passages, he says :

> They are overlaid by an enormous quantity of trash and twaddle and there is a continuous stream of mawkish sentimentality, loyalty, devotion, sensibility and a display of feelings and virtues which are very provoking.

Occasionally he moralises, and unexpectedly he actually indulges like a true diarist in self-disparagement. This is interesting because he was definitely writing an historical narrative for publication, and it shows how sooner or later a regular diary writer must notice himself. After an evening in 1834 at Holland House, where "a vast depression came over my spirits," he reflects at length on his ignorance :

> He who wastes his early years in horse racing and all sorts of idleness figuring away among the dissolute and the foolish must be content to play an inferior part among the learned and the wise. . . . Reflections of this sort

make me very uncomfortable and I am ready to cry with vexation when I think of my mispent life. If I was insensible to a higher order of merit and indifferent to a nobler kind of praise, I should be happier far ; but to be tormented with the sentiment of an honourable ambition and with the aspirations after better things and at the same time so sunk in sloth and bad habits as to be incapable of exertions without which their objects are unattainable is of all conditions the worst.

There is a sincerity in this which makes us prefer it to Thoresby's groanings of the soul. This is not an isolated instance ; he returns to it several times :

When I see what other men have done, how they have read and thought, a sort of despair comes over me, a deep and bitter sensation of regret ' for time mispent and talents misapplied ' not the less bitter from being coupled with a hopelessness of remedial industry and of doing better things.

Read Macintosh's Life in the carriage which made me dreadfully disgusted with my racing *métier*. What a life as compared with mine !

Yet such are the caprices of fortune that for one person who has heard of or read a line of Macintosh to-day there are hundreds who have heard of and read extracts from Greville.

His devotion to the Turf does not prevent him from inveighing against betting and gambling and racing with great violence, and, like so many diarists, the discharge of passionate self-condemnation does not prevent him from continuing in exactly the same way :

1830. A month nearly since I have written a line ; always racing and always idleness.

1834. The degrading nature of the occupation mixing with the lowest of mankind and absorbed in the business for the sole purpose of getting money, the consciousness of a sort of degradation of intellect, the conviction of the deteriorating effects upon both the feelings and the understanding which are produced, the sort of dram drinking excitement of it—all these things and these thoughts torment me and often turn my pleasure into pain.

1837. One day I resolve to extricate myself entirely from the whole concern to sell all my horses and pursue other occupations and objects of interest and then these resolutions wax faint and I again find myself buying fresh animals entering into fresh speculations and just as deeply engaged as ever.

Not till 1854 does he make up his mind to give up racing, and by that time he seems to be tired of politics too.

I am every day more confirmed in my resolution to get rid of my race horses. . . . The two objects I now have in view are this and to get out of my office. I want to be independent and be able to go where and do what I like for the short remainder of my life. . . . Of politics I am heartily sick and can take but little interest in either governments or the individuals who compose them.

Finally, in 1855, we have the following entry :

All last week at Newmarket and probably very nearly for the last time as an owner of race horses for I have now got rid of them all and am almost off the turf after being on it more or less for about forty years.

On his birthday he sometimes breaks into moralising :

1838. How we wince at our reflections and still go on in the same courses ! how we resolve and break our resolutions ! It is a common error to wish we could recall the past and be young again and swear what things we would do if another opportunity was offered us. All vanity, folly and falsehood.

1847. My birthday, a day of no joy to me which I always gladly hasten over. There is no pleasure in reaching one's fifty third year and in a retrospect full of shame and a prospect without hope ; for shameful it is to have wasted one's faculties and to have consumed in idleness and frivolous if not mischievous, pleasures that time which if well employed might have produced good fruit full of honour and of real solid permanent satisfaction. And what is there to look forward to at my time of life ? Nothing but increasing infirmities and the privations and distresses which they will occasion.

This side of Greville's Journal is little known because so much material is found by historians in his descriptions and comments on public affairs, but it is interesting if we are taking into account the diarist as well as his diary; and the opportunity allowed us of discovering something of the personality of the author makes us enjoy all the more his views and impressions of public affairs. The note of depression and self-blame coming from a man who writes comparatively little of his own private life has a perfectly genuine ring about it, but it only occurs in the earlier years. He often mentions his health, specially his gout when it prevents him from getting about, and he notes his gains or losses in racing from time to time. The entries are quite irregular, as he writes nothing unless he has gathered material with regard to parliamentary or foreign affairs. He was personally acquainted with most of the prominent men and women of the day, and he is therefore able to get his information from the fountain head.

We will make a few selections from his character sketches as examples of his writing :

(*William IV*) The King has been to Woolwich, inspecting the artillery, to whom he gave a dinner, with toasts and hip, hip, hurrahing, and three times three, himself giving the time. I tremble for him ; at present he is only a mountebank but he bids fair to be a maniac.

After dinner he made a number of speeches, so ridiculous and nonsensical, beyond all belief but to those who heard them, rambling from one subject to another repeating the same thing over and over again and altogether such a mass of confusion, trash, and imbecility as made one blush and laugh at the same time.

The other day he gave a dinner to one of the regiments at Windsor and as usual he made a parcel of foolish speeches in one of which after descanting upon their exploits in Spain against the French, he went on : " Talking of France, I must say that whether at peace or at war with that country I shall always consider her as our natural enemy and whoever may be her King or ruler I shall keep a watchful eye for the purpose of repressing her ambitious encroachments." If he was not such an ass that nobody does anything but laugh at what he says, this would be very important. Such as he is, it is nothing. ' What can you expect ' (as I forget who said) ' from a man with a head like a pine apple.' His head is just of that shape.

It is difficult to imagine anything more irksome for a Government beset with difficulties like this than to have to discuss the various details of their measures with a silly bustling old fellow who cannot possibly comprehend the scope and bearing of anything.

With regard to the Duke of Wellington, his estimates vary from time to time, but from the political point of view he is very critical :

I am by no means easy as to the Duke of Wellington's sufficiency to meet such difficulties ; the habits of his mind are not those of patient investigation, profound knowledge of human nature and cool discriminating sagacity. He is exceedingly quick of apprehension but deceived by his own quickness into thinking he knows more than he does. He has amazing confidence in himself which is fostered by the deference of those around him and the long experience of his military successes. He is upon ordinary occasions right-headed and sensible but he is beset by weaknesses and passions which must and continually do, blind his judgment.

This was written in 1831. Seven years later he appends a note retracting having said he was ever a little man, but otherwise confirming his opinion. On Wellington's death he sums up his character at some length.

About Macaulay he writes a great deal, critically and unfavourably at first, and afterwards, when he gets to know him, much more sympathetically. He gives a very amusing description of his first meeting him at Holland House in 1832 without knowing who he was. He sits next to " a common looking man in black," whom he sets down " for a dull fellow." He is so overcome when he discovers who it is that " perspiration burst from every pore of my face." He is unfavourably impressed :

Not a ray of intellect beams from his countenance ; a lump of more ordinary clay never enclosed a powerful mind and lively imagination.

Later again he writes:

His figure, face, voice, manner are all bad; he astonishes and instructs, he sometimes entertains, seldom amuses, and still seldomer pleases. He wants variety, elasticity, gracefulness; his is a roaring torrent, and not a meandering stream of talk.

Macaulay indeed is a great talker and pours forth floods of knowledge on all subjects; but the gracefulness, lightness, and variety are wanting in his talk which are so conspicuous in his writings; there is not enough of alloy in the metal of his conversation; it is too didactic, it is all too good and not sufficiently flexible, plastic, and diversified for general society.

But in later years he refers to him as "an unrivalled and delightful talker." In 1841 he describes a dinner at Holland House in which he gives the most entertaining account of Macaulay's overpowering knowledge. Whatever subject of conversation arose, from the "Fathers of the Church" to "dolls," Macaulay capped everyone else and exhibited special technical knowledge. At a country house party where Macaulay, Rogers and many others are present, Greville remarks: "Rogers will revive to-morrow when Macaulay goes." On Macaulay's death Greville writes a rather exagger ed eulogy of his history.

It is the colour and personal opinion which Greville puts into his entries that make his record so readable. The parliamentary crises are developed with great skill because of his close contact with the chief actors. His account of the passing of the Reform Bill is a specially valuable contribution to history. He follows the foreign situation and the developments of international policy with particular attention. The revolutions of 1848 fill him with horror; he attributes it all to "democracy and philanthropy" which, he writes, "leave behind them—and all Europe exhibits the result—a mass of ruin, terror and despair." We find him in 1853 making a very shrewd diagnosis of future events when he says, "if ever France finds it her interest to go to war Italy will be her mark."

His parliamentary record is the fullest part of his chronicle. People are rather apt to believe that in the good old days there was a dignity and decorum about our parliamentarians the absence of which they deplore to-day. When, however, we read the following, we need not be greatly concerned about the deterioration in parliamentary manners:

1846. The debate in the House of Commons came to a close at last wound up by a speech of Disraeli's, very clever, in which he hacked and mangled Peel with the most unsparing severity and positively tortured his victim. It was a miserable and degrading spectacle. The whole mass of the protectionists cheered him with vociferous delight making the roof ring again; and when Peel spoke they screamed and hooted at him in the most brutal manner. When he vindicated himself and talked of honour and conscience they assailed him with shouts of derision and gestures of contempt.

There are, of course, many references to Queen Victoria too well known to be quoted here. The Queen was very indignant when the first instalment of the journal was published. The light thrown on her uncles was a little too bright.

Greville only makes very occasional references to anything but public affairs. He gives an account of an early railway journey and has a very appreciative word to say about the introduction of chloroform. There are, however, portions of his journal which are devoted to his travels in Italy and Germany. His descriptions, written with spirit and with a seeing eye, are a good deal above the average diarist's travel notes.

As time goes on he becomes more occupied with literary pursuits and less interested in politics. He resigns his office in 1859 at the age of 65, but notes the fact with hardly any comment.

On November 13, 1860, after having neglected to write for three months, he deliberately concludes his journal :

> I take my pen in hand to record my determination to bring this journal (which is no journal at all) to an end.

The reason he assigns is that he is out of touch with public affairs and only hears what is known to all the world.

The complete accuracy of Greville's diary was by no means universally accepted. This is shown by the famous comment made on it :

> For fifty years he listened at the door,
> He heard some secrets and invented more.

WILLIAM COBBETT

To include a book like Cobbett's *Rural Rides* among diaries may at first be thought to be stretching the meaning of the word "diary" beyond its legitimate limits. But on closer consideration it will be found that the *Rural Rides* fulfills very exactly the necessary conditions which constitute diary writing. The book is essentially a journal the entries of which are freshly written on the actual day, and the fact that it contains much else than a bare record of the events of each day in no way invalidates its character as a diary.

As we are only indirectly concerned with the careers of our diarists, no more than a brief reminder of Cobbett's eventful life need be given. Grandson of a farm labourer and son of a small farmer, he was born at Farnham in 1766. He was employed as a boy in the fields, and received little education except what he gave himself. "Born in a farm-house bred up at the plough tail with a smock frock on my back," as he describes himself. Being of an adventurous disposition he soon left home and became successively an attorney's clerk, a soldier in a regiment quartered at St. John's, New Brunswick, a student in France, a teacher of English in Wilmington, Delaware, and a bookseller in Philadelphia. He then began writing pamphlets and books and editing newspapers. His manner and method constantly brought him into trouble, and on his return to England he was, as editor of the *Weekly Political Register*, more than once brought to trial and fined. In 1809 his bitter comments on the flogging of some militiamen at Ely, which had been carried out with the aid of a body of German troops, brought down on him the monstrous sentence of two years' imprisonment with a fine of £1,000. In 1830 he entered Parliament as member for Oldham. His speeches were very unconventional and he was an effective debater, though Greville in his diary speaks disparagingly of his efforts. He commenced his first speech with the remark: " It appears to me that since I have been sitting here, I have heard a great deal of vain and unprofitable conversation." A fellow-member describes him thus : " An elderly, respectable-looking, red-faced gentleman, in a dust-coloured coat and drab breeches with gaiters, tall and strongly built with sharp eyes, a round and ruddy countenance, smallish features and a peculiarly cynical mouth."

The prevailing idea which seemed to pervade all Cobbett's views was a hatred of tyranny and a sympathy with the minority. The agricultural labourer was the class of the community in which he was the most interested and whose cause he specially espoused. A master of invective and sarcasm, his pen served him best in showing up scandals and attacking his opponents. In his private life he was charmingly domestic and displayed great kindliness. He died in 1835. As well as pamphlets and newspaper articles, he turned out a large number of books. His rural rides took place between 1821 and 1832. The object in view was the investigation on the spot of the state of agriculture, and his journal was specifically written for publication. The freshly-gathered experiences, the lucidity and vigour of the style and the interesting reflection of his personality which appears in the entries, make the *Rural Rides* stand out as the masterpiece of Cobbett's writing and a book unique of its kind in English literature.

In 1821 he left London and rode through Bucks, Hants, Wilts, Gloucester and Hereford, returning by way of Oxford, and later in the year he went into Kent and through Norfolk and Suffolk.

In 1822 he had three trips which included Hertford, Buckingham and Huntingdon, as well as the south-eastern counties. Both in 1823 and 1825 Sussex, Surrey and Hants were again visited ; Wiltshire, Somerset and Gloucester in the following year. 1829 saw him in Hertfordshire and later in Norfolk and Suffolk, and during the last tour in 1832, which was more purely political in its character, he was in Northumberland and Durham.

He seldom writes his experiences of the day, which are given minutely in diary form, without going off into a diatribe against certain statesmen and fulminating against political scandals.

It is impossible, of course, to follow him on his journeys and to note the daily incidents, nor can anything like an adequate review of his conclusions be given by extracts. Indeed, to break into one of Cobbett's paragraphs spoils very considerably the swing and zest of his writing. The country as he describes it daily stretches out before his readers with intense reality, not only because Cobbett as a son of the soil knows how to bring its sights and sounds and breath before us, but because he sat down then and there and wrote away after his ride, however many miles he had covered. After a rainy day one almost expects to see the page stained with drops.

I set off from Fifield this morning and got here about one o'clock with my clothes wet. While they are drying and while a mutton chop is getting ready I sit down to make some notes of what I have seen since I left Enford; but here comes my dinner and I must put off my notes till I have dined.

Ever since the middle of March I have been trying remedies for the whooping cough and have I believe tried everything except riding wet to the skin two or three hours amongst the clouds on the South Downs. . . . This is really a soaking day thus far. I got here at nine o'clock. I stripped off my coat and put it by the kitchen fire. In a parlour just eight feet square I have another fire and have dried my shirt on my back. We shall see what this does for the whooping cough.

I staid at Reigate yesterday and came to the Wen [this is the way he always describes London] to-day every step of the way in rain; as good a soaking as any devotee of St Swithin ever underwent for his sake. I promised that I would give an account of the effect which the soaking on the South Downs had upon the whooping cough. I do not recommend the remedy to others but this I will say that I had a spell of the whooping cough the day before I got that soaking and that I have not had a single spell since.

This is practically the only mention of his health in the Journal. But we get some insight into the Spartan habits which kept him so fit, and it comes as a pleasant relief after the many examples we have had of guzzling and toping:

Many days I have no breakfast and no dinner. I went from Devizes to Highwater without breaking my fast a distance of more than thirty miles. I sometimes take from a friend's house a little bit of meat between two bits of bread which I eat as I ride along; but whatever I save from this fasting work, I think I have a clear right to give away; and, accordingly, I generally put the amount in copper into my waistcoat pocket and dispose of it during the day. I know well that I am the better for not stuffing and blowing myself out and with my savings I make many and many a happy boy; and now and then I give a whole family a good meal with the cost of a breakfast or a dinner that would have done me mischief.

And in another place he tells us how he never has more than two meals a day when he is at home with a little tea or milk and water to drink, and with characteristic conceit asks if any man can do more bodily and mental work than he does.

As he passes along he comments on the soil, the state of the crops, the harvest, and especially the trees; there are constant references to his favourite acacia and to splendid oak trees and disparaging remarks about fir trees " and other rubbish "; the potato he describes as " a soul degrading and man enslaving root "; he pictures country houses and cottages; he has much to say on the wages of the labourers and their condition; and he tilts with vigorous and eloquent invective against his pet aversions—the debt resulting from the war, paper money, parliament (which he calls The Thing), large towns, parsons, Jews and Quakers. Seeing so many depopulated villages, and churches far too large for their parishes, he pours his sarcasm on those who declared the population was rising, though as a matter of fact they were quite right. If he enters a cathedral, it is not to admire the architecture, but to reflect with bitterness over the Reformation:

(*Winchester.*) The " service " was now begun. There is a dean and God knows how many prebends belonging to this immensely rich bishopric and chapter; and there were at this " service " two or three men and five or six boys in white surplices with a congregation of fifteen women and four men. Gracious God! If William of Wykham could at that moment have been raised from his tomb. If Saint Swithin whose name the Cathedral bears or Alfred the Great to whom St Swithin was tutor; if either of these could have come and had been told that that was now carried on by men who talked of the " damnable errors " of those who founded that very Church!

(*Salisbury.*) I at last turned in at a doorway to my left where I found a priest and his congregation assembled. It was a parson of some sort with a white covering on him and five women and four men; when I arrived there were five couple of us. I joined the congregation until they came to the litany and then being monstrously hungry I did not think myself bound to stay any longer. I wonder what the founders would say if they could rise from the grave and see such a congregation as this in this most magnificent and beautiful Cathedral? I wonder what they would say if they could know to what purpose the endowments of this Cathedral are now applied; and above all things, I wonder what they would say if they could see the half starved labourers that now minister to the luxuries of those who wallow in the wealth of those endowments.

Out of the many appreciations he gives in the daily records of his rides of country scenery let us select a few descriptions of special beauty.

(*Sussex.*) Woodland countries are interesting on many accounts. Not so much on account of their masses of green leaves as on account of their variety of sights and sounds and incidents that they afford. Even in Winter the coppices are beautiful to the eye while they comfort the mind with the idea of shelter and warmth. In spring they change their hue from day to day during two whole months which is about the time from the appearance of the delicate leaves of the birch to the full expansion of those of the ash; and even before the leaves come at all to intercept the view, what in the vegetable creation is so delightful to behold as the bed of a coppice bespringled with primroses and bluebells? The opening of the birch leaves is the signal for the pheasant to begin to crow, for the blackbird to whistle and the thrush to sing; and just when the oak buds begin to look reddish and not a day before, the whole tribe of finches burst forth in songs from every bough while the lark imitating them all, carries the joyous sounds to the sky.

(*Hampshire.*) On we trotted up this pretty green lane; and indeed we had been coming gently and generally up hill for a good while. The lane was between highish banks and pretty high stuff growing on the banks so that we could see no distance from us and could receive not the smallest hint of what was so near at hand. The lane had a little turn towards the end; so that, out we came, all in a moment at the very edge of the hanger! And never in all my life was I so surprised and so delighted! I pulled up my horse and sat and looked; and it was like looking from the top of a castle into the sea except that the valley was land and not water. I looked at my servant to see what effect this unexpected sight had upon him. His surprise was as great as mine. Those who had so strenuously dwelt on the dirt and dangers of this rout had said not a word about the beauties, the matchless beauties of the scenery.

(*Near Ipswich.*) A lark very near to me in a ploughed field rose from the ground and was saluting the sun with his delightful song. He was got about as high as the dome of St. Paul's having me for a motionless and admiring auditor when the hen started up from nearly the same spot whence the cock had risen, flew up and passed close by him. I could not hear what she said; but supposed that she must have given him a pretty smart reprimand; for down she came upon the ground and he ceasing to sing took a twirl in the air and came down after her.

Oh! the thousands of linnets all singing together on one tree in the sand hills of Surrey! Oh! the carolling in the coppices and the dingles of Hampshire and Sussex and Kent! At this moment (5 o'clock in the morning) the groves at Barm-Elm are echoing with the warblings of thousands upon thousands of birds. The thrush begins a little before it is light; next the blackbird; next the lark begins to rise; all the rest begin the moment the sun gives the signal; and from the hedges, the bushes, from the middle and the topmost twigs of the trees comes the singing of endless variety; from the long dead grass comes the sound of the sweet and soft voice of the white throat or nettle tom while the loud and merry song of the lark, the songster himself out of sight, seems to descend from the sky.

As a contrast to these, let us hear Cobbett on towns.

Brighton is naturally a place of resort for expectants and a shifty ugly-looking swarm is of course assembled there. . . . You may always know them by their lank jaws, the stiffener round their necks, their false sholders, hips, and haunches, their half whiskers and by their skin colour of veal kidney suet warmed a little and then powdered with dirty dust.

Westbury, a nasty odious rotten borough, a really rotten place. It has cloth factories in it and they seem to be ready to tumble down as well as many of the houses. God's curse seems to be upon most of these rotten boroughs.

Deal is a villainous place. It is full of filthy looking people. . . . Rottenness and putridity is excellent for land but bad for Boroughs.

Cheltenham which is what they call a " watering place " that is to say a place to which East India plunderers, West India floggers, English tax-gorgers, together with gluttons drunkards and debauchees of all descriptions female as well as male, resort at the suggestion of silently laughing quacks in the hope of getting rid of the bodily consequences of their manifold sins and iniquities, when I enter a place like this I always feel disposed to squeeze my nose with my fingers. It is nonsense, to be sure, but I conceive that every two legged creature that I see coming near me is about to cover me with the poisonous proceeds of its impurities.

Cobbett is never on stronger ground than when he is condemning the growth of large towns. We can hardly imagine what his language would be were he to see the dimensions to which they have grown to-day.

Have I not for twenty long years been regretting the existence of these unnatural embossments ; these white swellings, these odious wens, produced by Corruption and engendering crime and misery and slavery ? . . . But what is to be the fate of the great wen of all ? The monster called by the silly coxcombs of the press " the metropolis of the Empire " ?

He constantly returns to this theme. Reflecting on the decreasing population and the poverty of the country side, he exclaims : " and yet you hear the jolter heads congratulating one another upon the increase of Manchester and such places." And at the end of one of his rides he says : " For the present, however, farewell to the country and now for the Wen and its villainous corruptions."

It was the condition of the people whom he saw with his own eyes that infuriated Cobbett, caused his outbursts of anger and his determination to continue the political struggle—the pretty girls " ragged as colts and as pale as ashes " with their " blue arms and lips," the miserable poverty, the dwellings " little better than pig beds," the human wretchedness and want of decent food—these sights make him cry—and we can almost hear him shouting it out, " And this is *prosperity* is it ? These Oh ! Pitt ! are the fruits of thy hellish system " ; and then we get pages of invective.

Tired after his day and on one occasion putting in a parenthesis (" for I want to go to bed ") nevertheless he writes three or four pages of attack on Canning. Indeed, nearly half the journal is political, and we often have complete reports of the speeches he makes to farmers and others. But however effective Cobbett may have been as a political controversialist, however amusing his sallies against ministers and Parliaments, that side of him can be fully examined by a study of his speeches, articles and pamphlets. In his journal we are, therefore, more inclined to pick out the episodes and opinions which give us a more intimate view of the man. For instance, what could be more human and charming than the little incident with his son Richard, who was his companion on one of his rides ?

One of the loops that held the strap of Richard's little portmanteau broke, and it became necessary for me to fasten the portmanteau on before me, upon my saddle. This, which was not the work of more than five minutes, would, had I had a breakfast, have been nothing at all, and indeed, matter of laughter. But now it was something. It was his "fault" for capering and jerking about "so." I jumped off saying "Here! I will carry it myself." And then I began to take off the remaining strap, pulling with great violence and in great haste. Just at this time, my eyes met his in which I saw great surprise; and feeling the just rebuke feeling heartily ashamed of myself, I instantly changed my tone and manner cast the blame upon the sadler and talked of the effectual means which we would take to prevent the like in the future.

Of course he draws a moral from the incident :

If such was the effect produced upon me by the want of food for only two or three hours me who had dined well the day before and eaten toast and butter the over-night . . . if this mere absence of a breakfast could thus put me out of temper, how great are the allowances that we ought to make for the poor creatures who in this once happy and now miserable country are doomed to lead a life of constant labour and of half starvation.

After ministers of state, ministers of religion are the most frequent target for Cobbett's wrath. We will give his account of a sermon.

When I came to the place the parson was got into prayer. His hand clenched together and held up his face turned up and back so as to be nearly parallel with the ceiling and he was bawling away with his "do thou" and "mayst thou" and "may we" enough to stun one. . . . After a deal of this rigmarole called prayer came the preaching . . . such a mixture of whining cant and of foppish affectation I scarcely ever heard in my life. (He gives the text.) . . . after as neat a dish of nonsense and impertinences as one could wish to have served up came the distinction between the *ungodly* and the *sinner*. . . . Both he positively told us were to be damned.

As he travels about the landowners are naturally the class which stirs him to exasperation, though now and again he praises the efforts of certain individuals. At Salisbury he fairly lets himself go, and breaks out in one of the longest entries in his journal, thus :

The baseness, the foul, the stinking, the carrion baseness of the fellows that call themselves "country gentlemen" is, that the wretches while railing against the poor and the poor rates ; while affecting to believe that the poor are wicked and lazy ; while complaining that the poor, the working people, are too numerous and that the country villages are too populous ; the carrion baseness of these wretches is that while they are thus bold with regard to the working people, they never whisper a word against pensioners, placemen, soldiers, parsons, fund holders, tax gatherers or taxeaters ! They say not a word against the prolific dead-weight, to whom they give a premium for breeding while they want to check the population of labourers ! They never say a word about the too great populousness of the Wen ; nor about that of

Liverpool, Manchester, Cheltenham and the like! Oh! they are the most cowardly the very basest, the most scandalously base reptiles that ever were warmed into life by the rays of the sun!

Outside this class and the politicians Cobbett does not express any opinion on individuals in other walks of life. But we get in one passage his opinion of Dr. Johnson, to whom he refers as "a teacher of moping and melancholy."

If the writings of this time serving, mean, dastardly old pensioner had got a firm hold of the minds of the people at large, the people would have been bereft of their very souls. These writings, aided by the charm of pompous sound were fast making their way, till light, reason and the French revolution came to drive them into oblivion.

His son Richard, aged 11, has a passion for fox-hunting. His father sees danger here, but says nothing discouraging about fox-hunting. He craftily ends his discourse by declaring:

"but all gentlemen that go a foxhunting (I hope God will forgive me for the lie) are scholars, Richard. It is not the riding nor the scarlet coats that make them gentlemen; it is their scholarship." What he thought I do not know; for he sat as mute as a fish and I could not see his countenance. "So," said I "you must now begin to learn something; and you must begin to learn arithmetic."

After a long discourse on how to teach arithmetic to children, he ends up:

Nothing is so dangerous as supposing that you have eight wonders of the world. I have no pretensions to any such possession. I look upon my boy like other boys in general. Their fathers can teach arithmetic as well as I; and if they have not a mind to pursue my method they must pursue their own. Let them apply to the outside of the head and to the back if they like; let them bargain for thumps and the birch rod; it is their affair not mine. I never saw in my house a child that was afraid; that was in any fear whatsoever; that was ever for a moment under any sort of apprehension on account of the learning of anything; and I never in my life gave a command, an order, a request or even advice to look into any book; and I am satisfied that the way to make children dunces, to make them detest books and justify that detestation is to tease them and bother them upon the subject.

We must be satisfied with these brief extracts from a very voluminous journal. They suffice perhaps to show us the man. We see Cobbett in the pages of his country diary a mass of prejudices, boiling over with rage at injustice, vain, egotistical and raging with uncontrolled fury against all, specially those highly placed, who disagreed with him. We see too a man saturated with the love of nature, kindly, domestic, witty and infinitely shrewd, readily moved to anger by a political challenge, but as readily moved to love by the song of a lark.

QUEEN VICTORIA

1832, Wednesday August 1. We left K.P. (Kensington Palace) at 6 min. past 7 and went through the Lowerfield gate to the right. We went on and turned to the left by the new road to Regent's Park. The road and scenery is beautiful. 20 min. to 9. We have just changed horses at Barnet a very pretty little town. 5 min. past ½ past 9. We have just changed horses at St. Albans. The situation is very pretty and there is a beautiful old Abbey there. 5 min. past 10. The country is beautiful here ; they have begun to cut the corn ; it is so golden and fine that I think they will have a very good harvest at least here. There are also pretty hills and trees. 20 minutes past 10. We have just passed a most beautiful old house in a fine park with splendid trees. A ¼ to 11. We have just changed horses at Dunstable there was a fair there the booths filled with fruit, ribbons etc. looked very pretty. The town seems old and there is a fine abbey before it. The country is very bleak and chalky. 12 minutes to 12. We have just changed horses at Brick hill. The country is very beautiful about here. 19 min. to 1. We have just changed horses at Stony Stratford. The country is very pretty. About ½ past one o'clock we arrived at Towcester and landed there. At 14 minutes past 2 we left it. At ¼ past 3. We have just changed horses at Daventry. The road continues to be very dusty. 1 minute past ½ past 3. We have just passed through Braunston where there is a curious spire. The Oxford Canal is close to the town. 1 min. to 4. We have just changed horses at Dunchurch and it is raining.

This is the first paragraph of the first entry in Queen Victoria's diary which she began writing at the age of 13. There is nothing in the least remarkable in a child eagerly writing in great detail the first entry in a new diary book. But there is something very remarkable in the fact that the child continued to write and that the child, who lived to the age of 82, filled over a hundred volumes with practically daily entries, kept up to the very end of her life. In later years the lady-in-waiting wrote the details of the functions while she herself noted her personal impressions. Of these hundred volumes only extracts have been published covering the period before her marriage 1832–1840 (published in 1912) and extracts taken from the diaries between 1848–1862 and published under the title of *Leaves from the Journal of our Life in the High-*

lands and *More Leaves* (1862–1882), both of them published during the Queen's lifetime, the first in 1868, the second in 1883.

Future generations may read Queen Victoria's diary, we have only got these scrupulously edited extracts. Editing, as we have already had occasion to notice, does not improve the quality of a diary, and often deprives us of much that might be of real human interest. In the case of a sovereign who died so recently editing becomes not only a personal but an official matter. In the earlier diaries the dots and spaces are tantalizing; in the latter *Leaves* the passages were selected by the Queen herself, the editor knowing that anything from her pen would be likely to reach a very large public. As a diary they are of little value. The early diaries, in spite of omissions, do disclose to a considerable extent the personality of the writer.

The Queen, Sir Arthur Helps tells us in the preface to the *Leaves*, declared " that she had no skill whatever in authorship," and indeed it is apparent enough throughout that her literary skill was very limited. It was not Fanny Burney's facility for expression which induced her to keep a diary, nor was there any desire for introspection, or self-analysis which a Windham might show; nor like Wesley, another lifelong diarist, did she wish to impart a lesson to her fellows by precept and example. She simply acquired the habit which she regarded as a duty and diligently noted events as a help, no doubt, to her memory, which, as time proved, became wonderfully reliable.

But Queen Victoria, except perhaps in the first year or so of her diaries, must have been aware that the diary of a sovereign was certain one day to see the light. She might therefore have posed for the picture, she might have written with her eye fixed on posterity, she might have painted her own portrait with the consciousness of her position in history. She did nothing of the kind. And this brings us to the leading feature in the diary which the published extracts illustrate quite sufficiently. It is the most natural, unsophisticated and ingenuous document that can be imagined. There is no pose, no pretence, and more especially no pretension, about it. The Queen did not have the advantage of being brought up like Edward VI by an Ascham. The precincts of an early nineteenth-century court did not constitute a favourable atmosphere for intellectual development. She was taught to be punctilious, and in spite of the awkward and uncomfortable position of her mother, the Duchess of Kent, her inclinations were intensely domestic. Punctilious domesticity is essentially the characteristic of that period, and the reaction from it which has been pushed to the opposite extreme in the twentieth century will make many feel that her manner, her habit of mind, her taste, and her method belong to an age they have grown to regard with something like contempt. Nothing would be easier than to make fun in the modern spirit of the period and of the person whose name it takes and who is the incarnation of it. The Queen's demonstrative raptures, her superlatives, her limited vocabulary, do not contribute to literary finish or thoughtful penetration. Moreover, as Lord Melbourne said, " the life of Kings and Queens is not very amusing," and " Uncle Leopold " (the King of the Belgians) went so far as to say it was " very tiresome." In fact, the *métier* of a monarch is not at all conducive to interest or entertainment in diary writing. Ceremonies, functions, banquets, and parties are dull to read about, however many great people may have been present at them. Besides this, her indiscretions and probably too some of her criticisms have all been carefully cut out. Nobody can suppose that Queen Victoria throughout her life used superlatives only in praise. Nevertheless, while we find no brilliant phrases, no epigrams, no profound thought and no artistry whatever, and while the official blue pencil has no doubt deprived us of much that might be interesting and amusing, the faithful and wonderfully simple sincerity of the writer marks every page we have and probably every page in the hundred volumes. In fact it would not be too much to say that the young Queen infects one with her enthusiasm for simple things. This ingenuousness is the feature that will claim attention more in centuries to come than in the immediately succeeding period when a revulsion against the domestic virtues is the fashion of the time.

Whatever faults the Queen may have had, she was never indifferent to what was passing round her. She was intensely interested in life and full of vitality and energy. " I *love* to be *employed*; I *hate* to be *idle*," she writes when she is 16, and would have written the same when she was 60. Her sorrows and joys were acute and she never restrained herself in recording them. So far as we are allowed to see, the sorrows are all for losses by death. Hers was not a temperament given to morbid dejection, but like all royal personages she was inclined to revel in woe. She cannot find new words to express her feelings, so she underlines the old ones. But she is quite incapable of affectation. She enters so conscientiously into the duties and obligations of her isolated and artificial position as to make one understand how she accepted it quite naturally. She revealed herself far more than she knew in her daily jottings. The early diaries give the clue to her manner and method of diary writing, the later volumes show that she did not change her style in middle age, and had we the hundredth volume before us we should certainly find the same *naïveté*, the same emphasis, the same absolutely unaffected and childlike sincerity. The exterior visions we have first of the girl in sweeping habit and feathered hat galloping along surrounded by ministers and courtiers, then of the tiara'd, crinolined, radiant, Crystal Palace Queen, then of the rarely seen, rather cross-looking widow in a carriage, and finally of the softened and smiling old lady of the Jubilees, correspond to no similar interior or mental changes. In spite of the great sorrow which robbed her of the one person whom she could treat as an equal and who saved her from her complete isolation, she really remained the same. She stored up her experiences carefully and found that their extent and the accurate recollection of them served her well and proved a rather formidable weapon in her old age.

The entries of the early diaries contain little more than records of events and ceremonies given very fully with a punctilious regard for accuracy in titles and relationships. The smaller as well as the greater pursuits are faithfully recorded. For instance, an afternoon in 1832 is entered thus :

At one we lunched. I then played on the piano and at a little before 3 played billiards downstairs with Victoire and then went out walking. When I came home I first worked and then we blew soap-bubbles.

And a visit to Plymouth in 1833 :

At about ½ past 9 we went on board the *dear little Emerald*. We were to be towed up to Plymouth. Mama and Lehzen were very sick and I was sick for about ½ an hour. At 1 I had a hot mutton chop on deck.

In 1837 she gives quite an amusing account of a game of chess :

The rest of the evening I sat on the sofa with dearest Aunt Louise who played at chess with me to *teach* me and Lord Melbourne sat near me. Lord Tavistock, Lord Palmerston, Mrs. Cavendish, Sir J. Hobhouse and Mme de Mérode sat round the table. Lord Melbourne, Lord Palmerston, Sir J. Hobhouse, and later too Lord Conyngham all gave me advice and all *different* advice about my playing at chess and *all* got so *eager* that it was very amusing ; in particular Lord Palmerston and Sir J. Hobhouse who differed totally and got quite excited and serious about it. Between them all I got quite beat and Aunt Louise triumphed over my Council of Ministers !

She loved playgoing, and many entries are occupied with descriptions of plays and criticisms of actors. Her appreciation acting remained throughout her life, and was as strong when she was 80 as when she was 18.

On her sixteenth birthday she gives a long and elaborate description of all the presents she receives, but she thinks she must preface it by a few reflections in the copy-book morality strain:

> To-day my 16th birthday ! How very old that sounds ; but I feel that the two years to come till I attain my 18th are the most important of any almost. I now only begin to appreciate my lessons and hope from this time on to make great progress.

Throughout the diaries it will be found that the Queen's sorrows were produced almost exclusively by the death of her friends and relations. Mourning was a duty, and mourning was a function. We see it at the age of 16 when a nurse who " was not a pleasant person " dies and she writes : " it would be very wrong if I did not feel her death," and she breaks out constantly into " awful " and " dreadful " when recording the death of anyone she knew. This attitude towards death was what she was taught by the deans and bishops, and it must be remembered that black hearses, plumes, mourning bands, crape, heavy horse cloths, drawn blinds, and all the rest of the hideous paraphernalia of mourning had been introduced by the Hanoverians and reached their highest pitch in the nineteenth century as the privilege of the rich and the ambition of the poor. It was this way of regarding demonstrations of mourning as a duty and as a sign of affection that induced the Queen to exceed all limits when her husband died. To her all the years it lasted it was a sacred duty. No one dared tell her that it was the most excessive self-indulgence.

Religion occurs in the diary occasionally in the form of thanksgiving to God, accounts of sermons and Church ceremonies. But she is determined not to be troubled by the confusions of religious speculation. She writes at the age of 19 when the tenets of various sects are explained to her:

> I said one could get oneself quite puzzled by thinking too much about these matters and that I thought it was wrong to do so.

And a year later:

> I said that the use of the church was that it made one think of what one would otherwise not think of.

She finds time on the very day of her accession to write a full account of the momentous scene—and even to insert a brief reflection :

Since it has pleased Providence to place me in this station I shall do my utmost to fulfil my duty towards my country. I am very young and perhaps in many though not in all things inexperienced but I am sure that very few have more real good will and more real desire to do what is fit and right than I have.

After her accession a large part of her diary is taken up with records of her conversations with Lord Melbourne. He was her first Prime Minister, her confidential adviser and her political coach, and before her accession she had not come into close contact with any intelligent people. She is therefore very naturally impressed by him. As Mr. Strachey[1] says : " Upon every page Lord M is present, Lord M is speaking, Lord M is being amusing, instructive, delightful and affectionate at once, while Victoria drinks in the honeyed words, laughs till she shows her gums, tries hard to remember and runs off as soon as she is left alone to put it all down." In addition to politics, they discuss books, plays, education, food, clothes, gardens, and in fact every conceivable topic that comes up. This is the sort of thing :

1837. Lord Melbourne rode near me the whole time. The more I see of him and the more I know of him, the more I like and appreciate his fine and honest character. I have seen a great deal of him every day these last 5 weeks and I have always found him in good humour, kind, good and most agreeable : I have seen him in my Closet for Political affairs, I have ridden out with him (every day) I have sat near him constantly at and after dinner and talked about all sorts of things and have always found him a kind and most excellent and very agreeable man. I am very fond of him.

1838. I asked Lord Melbourne how he liked my dress. He said he thought it " very pretty " and that " it did very well." He is so natural and funny and nice about *toilette* and has very good taste, I think.

1839. Said to Lord M I was never satisfied with my own reading and thought I put the wrong emphasis upon words ; he said " no you read very well ; I thought you read it very well this morning " ; and I said I often felt so conscious of saying stupid things in conversation and that I thought I was often very childish " You've no reason to think that " said Lord M and that I feared I often asked him tiresome and indiscreet questions and bored him " Never the least " he replied " You ought to ask."

Talked of my being so silent which I thought wrong and uncivil as I hated it in others. " Silence is a good thing " said Lord M " if you have nothing to say." I said I hated it in others and that it annoyed me when he was silent. " I'm afraid I am so sometimes " he said " won't say a word." Yes I said that nothing could be got out of him sometimes. " And that you dislike ? " he said. Yes, I said, it made me unhappy, which made him laugh.

---

[1] *Queen Victoria*, by Lytton Strachey.

Talked to Lord M of his being tired and I said he mustn't go to sleep before so many people for that he generally snored ! *" That proclaims it too much,"* he said, in which I *quite* agreed.

In her historical conversations with Lord Melbourne we get her opinions on some of her predecessors. She is very much shocked at the way Henry VIII treated his wives. " Spoke of Charles I whom I thought much to blame." " I observed that Richard III was a very bad man : Lord Melbourne also thinks he was a horrid man," and she makes him tell her many anecdotes about George III and George IV.

Dancing was a great joy to her, and she describes balls with great enthusiasm. " I never enjoyed myself more. We were all so merry." " It was a lovely ball, so gay, so nice, and I felt so happy and so merry."

When Prince Albert appears on the scene the intensity of rapture reaches a superlative degree.

First of all with his brother Ernest,

those *dearest* beloved Cousins whom I *do* love so *very very* dearly ; *much more dearly* than any other cousins in the world.

" It was with some emotion that I beheld Albert who is *beautiful* . . . he is so handsome and pleasing . . . he dances so beautifully," etc., and she describes " his exquisite nose," and " delicate mustachios and slight but very slight whiskers." Her reluctance to marry disappears and the intimacy advances : " I played 2 games of Tactics with dear Albert and 2 at Fox and Geese. Stayed up till 20 m. past 11. A delightful evening." Two days later she describes her proposal.

At about ½ p. 12 I sent for Albert : he came to the Closet where I was alone and after a few minutes I said to him that I thought he must be aware *why* I wished him to come here—and that it would make me *too happy* if he would consent to what I wished (to marry me). We embraced each other and he was *so* kind and *so* affectionate. I told him I was quite unworthy of him— he said he would be very happy " das Leben mit dir zu zubringen " and was so kind and seemed so happy that I really felt it was the happiest moment in my life.

In the afternoon she sees Lord Melbourne, and after some preliminary remarks about the weather and Lord Huntingdon's rank,

I then began and said I got well through this with Albert " Oh ! you have " said Lord M.

Under the ingenuous innocence and simplicity and among the

sincere confessions of her own shortcomings, one looks for traces of the development of the Queen's determination which Greville described as her peremptory disposition and which some may have characterised as obstinacy, and one finds them.

On the subject of vaccination Lord Melbourne has some difficulty in persuading her:

> Said to Lord M. I should resist about this vaccination; "Oh! no you'll do it," he said kindly: I said No and that no one could force me to it; he agreed in that but strongly urged it and said earnestly "*Do.*"

After she had been two years on the throne Lord Melbourne tells her:

> I said to Stanley it's far better that the Queen should be thought high and decided than that she should be thought weak. 'By God!' he said 'they don't think that of her; you needn't be afraid of that.' Lord M. seemed to say this with pleasure.

Politically her first exhibition of determination was with Sir Robert Peel over the question of her retaining the Ladies of the Bedchamber on the change of government. Here is part of the account she gives to Lord Melbourne of the proceedings:

> Soon after this, Sir Robert said "Now about the Ladies" upon which I said I could *not* give up *any* of my Ladies and never had imagined such a thing; he asked if I meant to retain *all*; *all* I said; the Mistress of the Robes and the Ladies of the Bedchamber? he asked. I replied *all* . . . *they* were of more consequence than the others and I could *not* consent and that it had never been done before; he said I was a Queen Regnant and that made the difference; not here, I said—and I maintained my right.

Whether the Queen was right or wrong is not the question. At the age of 20 she stood up to Sir Robert Peel, so that he refused to form a government.

Over the question of the rank to be given to Prince Albert she expresses herself very forcibly to Lord Melbourne and she ends her record of the conversation:

> I feared I vexed him, kind, good man as he looked, I think, grieved at my pertinacity.

And we notice the order of the last words in the last published entry describing her marriage:

> We took leave of Mama and drove off at near 4; I and Albert alone.

It will not be difficult to find other examples of "pertinacity" when the many other volumes of the diary appear.

She mentions the books she reads, and of course the books Lord Melbourne recommends her to read, but she was not a great reader, although she conscientiously ploughed through some rather stiff volumes.

Although in one entry she says she dislikes " to hear nothing else but Politics and always Politics," she took a sufficiently close interest in affairs to have a strong political bias, and it was some little time before she overcame her prejudice against Sir Robert Peel. Parallels to this also would be found later in her reign.

Leaves from the Journal of our Life in the Highlands are simply descriptive extracts of expeditions in Scotland lifted out of the Queen's diaries. The Queen was at first reluctant to publish them, but her scruples were overcome by editor and publisher. They knew, no doubt, that an author counts more than a book with the public, and that anything written by the Sovereign, no matter what it was, would be safe to have an immense success. Moreover, at the time of publication the Queen in her retirement had become a very distant unknown figure. A book showing she was an ordinary human being with simple domestic tastes was likely to be appreciated, so descriptions of her expeditions and pursuits at Balmoral were collected and printed.

The style is very much the same as the style of the early diaries, but the entries are so much cut and trimmed and edited for public consumption that the charm of personality is almost entirely eliminated, and there remains only bald records of the days which gave her great happiness, or in the second volume recollections of and regrets over past happiness. The domestic scenes presented and rather sentimentally described appealed to a majority of those who read them, and the picture of the fond wife and in the second volume of the sorrowing widow came to constitute the sole conception of the Queen in the eyes of her people. They had not seen the earlier diaries, they were not allowed to see anything else. Ordinary people revelled in being able to read something written by a Queen; superior people laughed at the childish narratives, which were entirely devoid of literary merit or political interest. Neither of them wondered whether they were not being presented with a very incomplete picture, nor did they pause to speculate what that part of the diary recorded which they were not allowed to see. In fact, they were all rather taken in.

For instance, they read that in October, 1868, the Queen, accompanied by her gillies and attendants, went to a housewarming at a little house at Glassalt Shiel, where reels were danced and whisky toddy drunk, Ross played the pipes, and the cook, the housemaids, the stablemen, and the policeman joined the party. But they were not told that a week or two earlier the Queen was writing to Disraeli practically dictating to him with regard to certain ecclesiastical appointments and getting her own way.[1]

Again in September, 1874, they read a description of the homecoming of the Duke and Duchess of Edinburgh with " Brown in full dress on the rumble " ; Marie " in a brown travelling dress with a hat," the playing of the pipes, the dancing of reels, and the drinking of healths. But they did not hear that in the same month the Queen was having important consultations with Disraeli, who wrote from Balmoral to Lady Bradford saying, " She opened all her heart and mind to me and rose immensely in my intellectual estimation. Free from all shyness she spoke with great animation and happy expressions, showed not only perception but discrimination of character and was most interesting and amusing."[2]

There is little that is worth quoting from the *Leaves*. The rapture over life in the Highlands occurs again and again.

> There is a great peculiarity about the Highlands and the Highlanders; and they are such a chivalrous, fine active people. Our stay among them was so delightful. Independently of the beautiful scenery there was a quiet, a retirement, a wildness, a liberty, and a solitude that had such a charm for us.

> The pure mountain air was most refreshing. All seemed to breathe freedom and peace and to make one forget the world and its sad turmoils.

She goes for long expeditions of several days to remote parts of the Highlands *incognito*, and the amusement and entertainment of being able to behave and be regarded as an ordinary mortal entranced her. They were the only little ventures she ever made in the Haroun al-Raschid style. We get accounts of her visits to cottages and her conversations with the old women. She shows the same interest and accurate knowledge of the relationships and careers of her gillies, pipers, attendants, dressers and wardrobe women as for those of the Royal Family and the aristocracy. And of course in the first volume Albert's sporting exploits and doings figure very largely. There are accounts, too, of the rejoicings over the fall of Sebastopol and the reception of the news of the death of the Duke of Wellington.

An instance of how one diarist can be checked by another

---
[1] *Life of Benjamin Disraeli*, Vol. V, 64–67.
[2] Ibid., Vol. V, p. 344.

occurs in her entry of September 13, 1850. Lord Carlisle, as we shall see, notes that the Queen, in her anxiety at seeing the Prince Consort rush to the rescue of two men who were in danger in the river, "pinched me very much." And the Queen writes:

> There was a cry for help and a general rush including Albert towards the spot which frightened me so much that I grasped Lord Carlisle's arm in great agony.

The Queen made £2,500 by the publication of the *Leaves*, and with the money she founded university and school bursaries for the people at Balmoral.

As already noted, so far as diary is concerned between 1840 and 1900, these little scraps of what may be called holiday notes tell us very little, although at the time of their publication they were eagerly read as giving a complete picture of the Queen. Since then we have had two volumes of her letters, two volumes of her early diaries and her correspondence with Disraeli. There in a great deal more to come. The portrait is still incomplete.

So far as she was at all conscious of any reader as she wrote, it seems clear that the Queen wrote for herself in her old age, and marginal notes in the diaries show that she re-read them. Their eventual fate, she, like many other diarists, probably never considered.

The full disclosure of the life and activities of Queen Victoria is not going to reveal that the childishness, ingenuousness and simplicity were a pose, and that hidden behind this there was a Machiavellian figure of masterly intellectual powers. Nothing as crude as that. If we may venture to prophesy, when the whole story is known—and the hundred volumes of the diary will reveal more than all the histories and memoirs—it will be found that what we see of her already in the material published is a true picture. She *was* ingenuous, she was simple, she was entirely without affectation, she was not highly educated, she was punctilious and domestic, she had strong prejudices and she was obstinate. But it will be found also that there was a very pronounced personality, formed partly by the immense range of her experience which was carefully stored in a very retentive memory, partly too by an individual charm, which struck as much those who came in contact with her in the last years of her life as the ministers who were assembled round the table at Kensington Palace on June 20, 1837; and that this personality, enhanced by a very rare distinction of manner and bearing, by no means habitual with sovereigns, gave her a curiously indefinable but very strong influence over all who were brought into relation with her, were they monarchs, ministers of State or gillies. Moreover, she was well aware of her own limitations, and would never attempt to assert herself unless she was quite sure of her ground. In fact, Queen Victoria will be found to be a notable instance of the triumph of character where knowledge and talents might have failed. The image of the devoted wife and sorrowing widow did very well for public consumption while she lived ; she was quite content to leave it at that, and every one accepted it as authentic.

Whether she interfered where she ought not to have, whether she showed unfair bias, whether she was constitutional or unconstitutional, are matters open to dispute. The conclusion that will eventually emerge will be that she impressed her personality to an unsuspected degree on her surroundings, and that the authority which came from such simple sources was more baffling and irresistible than the decrees of an autocrat.

CAROLINE FOX

IN the Introduction the opinion has been ventured that Caroline Fox stands first among English women diarists. This opinion should be qualified by adding, " judging by what we see of her journal"; because her editor gives only extracts which, numerous as they are, are confined for the most part to objective memoranda ; and he remarks in the preliminary memoir, " It is hoped that nothing will be found in these pages which should seem like drawing aside the curtains that ought to be left covering the inner life of all." We are always coming across these curtains, and we must frankly confess that from the point of view of a reader they are a nuisance. The inner life is the very life we want to hear about, and without any question in the case of Caroline Fox a closer view of herself would be in the very highest sense of the word edifying. While a Quaker and devoted to religion in the narrower meaning of the word, she displays such breadth of view, such wise philosophic penetration, such balanced and well-proportioned opinions and such an apparent absence of vain outbursts of self-reproach, that her account of her inner conflicts and of life's struggles about which she must have written would have been specially interesting. The curtains, we are glad to say, have not been effectively closed on all her subjective reflections, and when we light on such reflections or on references to religion they are never oppressively serious, never dry and never accompanied by painful puffs of strained earnestness.

It may be said that the journal comes under the category of social diaries against which disparaging criticism has been levelled. It does to some extent. But the society is her own, and although she was acquainted with people of note, she is not hunting celebrities, there is no breathless strain to collect snippets of gossip or to introduce lists of great names. There is no pursuit of notoriety. It is the calm atmosphere of easy and interesting intercourse, reproduced not only faithfully but with the skill that makes the arguments and opinions expressed attractive to a reader. Not the verbatim method of Fanny

Burney, which must entail a great deal of invention, but the epitome produced by a mind which is absolutely up to the level of the talkers or disputants.

The diary is difficult to describe. It is one of the minority which should be read from cover to cover. It includes the years 1835 to 1871. She was 16 when she began it. Her home was at Penjerick, in Cornwall. Her father, one of the well-known Quaker family, was a distinguished scientific man; and it was the conversation of his friends that the young girl began to note with wonderfully precocious powers of understanding and appreciation.

The always vexed question of motive in journal writing seems in the case of Caroline Fox to be more or less explained by an entry she makes in 1855 soon after the death of her brother, to whom she was specially devoted. She writes:

> I could fill volumes with remembrances and personal historiettes of interesting people but for whom should I record them now?

In the early years one is struck by the maturity and restraint of the style as well as by the alertness of her powers of observation. She was an exact contemporary of Queen Victoria, and there is as little similarity in the style and mental vision of the two girls as there was in their circumstances and surroundings.

It is true that in Caroline Fox's diary as given to us there is hardly enough childishness to be quite natural, and had it not been that she was evidently endowed with a sense of humour her intellectuality might at times have become rather excessive.

When she is 17 she gives an amusing description of the Begum of Oude, whom she meets in London, whose face was one "of quick sagacity but extreme ugliness."

> She and Papa talked a little theology, she of course began it. "I believe but one God very bad not to think so; you believe Jesus Christ was prophet?" Papa said "Not a prophet but the son of God." "How you think so, God Almighty never marry."

Caroline Fox became close friends with **John Sterling, John Stuart Mill** and **the Carlyles**, and it is her record of conversations with them that has made her diary of special interest. Mill she describes as

> a man of extraordinary power and genius, the founder of a new school in metaphysics and a most charming companion.

The conversations invariably fall into a more or less philosophic strain, and she gives Mill's opinions with a clearness and precision which he himself could not have surpassed.

Mill unburdens himself to her, tells her of his childhood, and expresses doubt about the intellectual discipline to which he was subjected.

> This method of early intense application he would not recommend to others; in most cases it would not answer, and where it does the buoyancy of youth is entirely superseded by the maturity of manhood and action is very likely to be merged in reflection.

He takes the most lively interest in the Quakers and asks her all about them. He concocts for her " an almanack of the odours that scent the air " arranged chronologically according to months, beginning with the laurel and ending with the lime.

With Sterling her conversations range over a large field, but she manages so to arrange the arguments and opinions as to make every entry attract a reader's rapt attention.

We may give an example of a full entry which incidentally shows the diarist's inclination for introspection.

> At one o'clock J. Sterling entered and announced he had bought Dr. Donelly's house! How little did we think of such a climax a month since and even now I cannot realise it. They intend moving early in the summer. We talked about motives ; he does not like too much self scrutiny and would rather advise " Take the best and wisest course, do what you know is right, and then don't puzzle yourself in weighing your motives ; forget yourself in the object of your striving as much as possible ; any examination which brings Self under any colours into the foreground is bad." I don't altogether agree with him here for a hearty sincere inlook tends I think in no manner to self glorification. He talked of the strange breaking up of Sects and bodies, everywhere remarkable, with a half melancholy sagacity mixed with wondering uncertainty. There is so much of the destructive spirit abroad that the creative or at least the constructive must be cherished. After a very interesting hour or two we separated.

The first time she sees Carlyle is in 1840 at one of his lectures on " Hero Worship."

> Carlyle soon appeared and looked as if he felt a well dressed London crowd scarcely the arena for him to figure in as a popular lecturer. He is a tall, robust looking man ; rugged simplicity and indomitable strength are in his face and such a glow of genius in it—not always smouldering there but flashing from his beautiful grey eyes, from the remoteness of their deep setting under that massive brow. His manner is very quiet but he speaks like one tremendously convinced of what he utters and who had much—very much—in him that was quite unutterable, quite unfit to be uttered to the uninitiated ear ; and when the Englishman's sense of beauty or truth exhibited itself in vociferous cheers, he would impatiently almost contemptuously wave his hand as if that were not the sort of homage which Truth demanded. He began in a

rather low nervous voice with a broad Scotch accent but it soon grew firm and shrank not abashed from its great task.

Then follows a clear epitome of the whole lecture. Of Carlyle's forlorn view of his physical health she speaks, telling how one day he said to Dr. Calvert:

Well, I can't wish Satan anything worse than to try to digest for all eternity with my stomach; we shouldn't want fire and brimstone then.

Here is Carlyle on Mill:

He is still too fond of demonstrating everything. If John Mill were to get up to heaven he would hardly be content till he had made out how it all was.

She goes frequently to see the Carlyles, has long talks with Mrs. Carlyle, and then the great man comes in.

Carlyle wandered down to tea looking dusky and aggrieved at having to live in such a generation; but he was very cordial to us notwithstanding.

Sterling knows she keeps a diary, and asks her why she does not describe the appearance of people as well as their conversation. She immediately starts on him, and not only do we get his appearance but a wonderfully penetrating sketch of his character, which ends:

In argument he commonly listens to his antagonists sentiments with a smile less of conscious superiority than of affectionate contempt—I mean what would express " Poor dear! she knows no better." In argument on deep or serious subjects however he looks earnest enough and throws his ponderous strength into reasoning and feeling; small chance then for the antagonist who ventures to come to blows! He can make him and his arguments look so small; for truth to tell, he dearly loves this indomitable strength of his; and I doubt any human power bringing him to an acknowledgment of a mistake with the consequent conviction tht the other party was right. Sterling possesses a quickness and delicacy of perception quite feminine and with it a power of originating deep and striking thoughts and making them the foundation of a regular and compact series of consequences and deductions such as only a man, and a man of extraordinary power of close thinking and clearness of vision, can attain unto. He is singularly uninfluenced by the opinions of others, preferring on the whole to run counter to them than make any approach to a compromise.

Here is her description of Wordsworth:

He is a man of middle height and not very striking appearance, the low part of the face retreating a little; his eye of a somewhat French diplomatic character with heavy eye lids and none of the flashing one connects with poetic genius. When speaking earnestly his manner and voice become extremely energetic; and the peculiar emphasis and even accent he throws into some words add considerably to their force. He evidently loves the monologue style of conversation but shows great candour in giving due consideration to any remarks which others may make. His manner is simple, his general appearance that of the abstract thinker whom his subject gradually warms into poetry.

Caroline Fox's own opinions and reflections do not occur at all frequently. She was no egotist, she was interested in studying others. But occasionally we have glimpses of her calm philosophic disposition. A few of these entries may be quoted :

How I like things to be done quietly and without fuss. It is the fuss and bustle principle which must proclaim itself until it is hoarse that wars against Truth and Heroism. Let Truth be done in silence " till it is forced to speak " and then should it only whisper, all those whom it may concern will hear.

But—I ventured to say—rather than this harassing search amongst the multitude of conflicting rays which show but an infinite number of tiny light beams would it not be wiser in simplicity and faith to direct the earnest gaze upward where all rays of light converge in one glorious focus and inward if one ray is permitted to shine there to guide the teachable spirit through this misty half-developed chaos of a world.

I have assumed a name to-day for my religious principles—Quaker Catholicism—having direct spiritual teaching for its distinctive dogma yet recognising the high worth of all other forms of Faith ; a system in the sense of inclusion, not exclusion ; an appreciation of the universal and various teachings of the spirit, through the faculties given us or independent of them.

My birthday ; it seems as if my future life might well be spent in giving thanks for all the mercies of the past.

The full year is coming to an end. How much of anxiety and pain and grief it has contained, but how much too of support and strength and comfort granted through all, difficulties conquered, paths made clear, duties made pleasant, very much to strengthen our faith and to animate our love. Our home life now looks clear and bright and we all go on cheerily together ; the sense of change is everywhere but the presence of the Changeless one is nearer still.

But, as we have said, the serious note is never overstressed. The ridiculous is always able to amuse her.

At meeting a Friend spoke very sweetly but from circumstances over which she had little control her sermon forcibly reminded me of " going to Bexico to zee the Bunkies."

A damsel belonging to Barclay's establishment being here I thought it right " to try and do her good " so I asked her after many unsuccessful questions if she had not heard of the Lord's coming into the World. " Why " she said, " I may have done so but I have forgot it." " But surely you must have heard your master read about it and heard of it at school and church and chapel." " Very likely I have " said she placidly " but it has quite slipped my memory ! " and this uttered with a lamb-like face and a mild blue eye.

She introduces, too, a number of good stories which are far above the average anecdotes often collected in diaries. We may quote one :

> Talked of Taylor, Irving, Coleridge, and Charles Lamb being together; and the conversation turning on Mahomet, Irving reprobated him in his strongest manner as a prince of imposters without earnestness and without faith. Taylor thinking him not fairly used defended him with much spirit. On going away Taylor could not find his hat and was looking about for it when Charles Lamb volunteered his assistance with the query "Taylor, did you come in a h-h-hat or a t-t-t-turban ?"

She refers to her health occasionally, but probably the editor has cut out many of these passages. Her weather remarks differ from the usual perfunctory note :

> Such a beautiful day, that one felt quite confused how to make the most of it and accordingly frittered it away.
>
> A wet day and all its luxuries.
>
> A fine day and all its liabilities.

There is a good account of her miraculous escape from a bull which pursued her. She lay insensible on the ground, the fierce animal pawing and snorting but never touching her. She describes the curious thoughts that coursed through her dazed brain as she lay on the ground.

Caroline Fox travelled abroad several times, and in 1863 went with her father to Spain. In spite of her failing health in the last years, she always remained cheerful, and she was going the round of the cottages with New Year gifts a fortnight before she died in 1871, at the age of 52.

Her journals, together with some of her letters, were published with her sister's consent in 1882.

GENERAL GORDON

DURING the Taiping revolt in China, when Gordon conducted the successful operations which eventually culminated in the complete suppression of the revolutionary movement, for a few weeks in 1863 he kept a diary. It is written in the third person, very brief and exclusively concerned with military matters. It was subsequently published with notes and explanation by S. Mossman, but it does not call for any comment.

Gordon's reputation was made in China, but public interest in him centres round the great tragedy which closed his career twenty years later. We have from his pen a complete daily diary kept by him at Khartoum in 1884 from September 10 up to December 14, six weeks before he was killed.

No sketch of Gordon's adventurous career is needed, he is far too well-known a national figure. As we are only concerned here with the period covered by his diary, it will be sufficient to say that in January, 1884, he was ordered to Khartoum to report on the best method of carrying out the evacuation of the Soudan, and was appointed Governor-General by the Khedive.

This is a diary dealing with a very special set of circumstances and events, and we might easily be led into a discussion of the ins and outs and the rights and wrongs of the policy pursued, and be drawn into the heated controversy which raged at the time and continued a long time after the fall of Khartoum. We must take special care, therefore, to observe the practice which has been followed throughout in the examination of diaries, namely, to concentrate our attention on the diary itself from the point of view of the diarist and not from the point of view of the events he records. We shall see the events, therefore, through Gordon's spectacles, and however much there may be to be said for or against his actions and opinions, that must be left to the historical student; it does not concern us here.

The journal consists of six volumes, each one of which was

sent down at intervals from Khartoum wrapped up in a handkerchief or a glasscloth. It gives a complete and detailed narrative of events and the most outspoken expressions of opinion. While the soldier and administrator deals with the daily occurrences of the memorable siege, it is not by any means a dry military record. The style is unconventional and relieved with touches of satirical humour, and the story told of those days of tragic apprehension is intensely human and eminently readable. Gordon had the reputation of being eccentric in matters of religion, but there is in the diary far less than one might expect of definitely religious character apart from quotations from the Bible. In every page of it we can see his character, masterful, determined, obstinate, human, sometimes apprehensive, but never despairing, turning his impatience and indignation at the follies to which he was being sacrificed into jest and firmly resolved not to betray those around him who were sharing with him the ever-growing danger. Like the man in Edgar Allan Poe's story, he saw the walls closing in on him. Now and again the inevitable disaster strikes him, but he never dwells on it long.

Gordon wrote for publication. He wanted the Government and the country to know what he thought and to learn the true story of events. Each section of the journal was marked, " This journal will want pruning out if thought necessary to publish." Very few pages were omitted when the whole journal appeared in print.

The military details are all carefully set out and often accompanied by maps and diagrams : raids, rumours with regard to the Mahdi's position, reports from spies, the despatch of messengers, calculations of the quantity of stores and ammunition, and the daily events in the garrison and town. Trifles, too, are not omitted, as when he is stung by a scorpion in his sponge and when a mouse comes on to the table and eats out of his plate. He draws little pictures and caricatures now and then. There is a sketch of an Egyptian official with large collars under which he writes : " Mr. Gladstone has a rival up here in shirt collars." The funny side of things struck him as he wrote and he cannot help bringing it in. He has a peculiar way of breaking away from a subject which he thinks is getting tiresome and suddenly writing an imaginary dialogue or making some apparently irrelevant but humorous reflections.

Various forms and instances of treachery were the chief cause of harassment to Gordon. Apostasy even on the part of Europeans was not uncommon. On this he writes :

It is not a small thing for a European for fear of death to deny our faith; it was not so in old times and it should not be regarded as if it was taking off one coat and putting on another. If the Christian faith is a myth then let men throw it off but it is mean and dishonourable to do so merely to save one's life if one believes it is the true faith. . . . Treachery never succeeds and however matters may end, it is better to fall with clean hands than to be mixed up with dubious acts and dubious men. I am using this argument with them, in saying : " You ask me to become a Mussulman to save my life and you yourself acknowledge Mahomet Achmet as the Mahdi to save your lives; why, if we go on this principle we will be adopting every religion whose adherents threaten our existence, for you know and own when you are safe that Mahomet Achmet is *not* the Mahdi."

Deplorable as much of the material was which he had on his side (for it must be remembered he had not a single British soldier), the idea of throwing them over or letting them down never entered his head. In addition to his garrison the civil population numbered about 40,000. But let us hear Gordon on diplomatists. They are the chief object of his irony, not always perhaps quite fairly, but, considering his position, very naturally :

We are an honest nation but our diplomatists are conies and not *officially* honest.

I must say I do not love diplomatists as a rule (and I can fancy the turning up of noses at my venturing to express an opinion on them) I mean in their official attire, for, personally, the few I know are most agreeable . . . but taking them on their rostrum with their satellites, from their chiefs down to the smaller fry no one can imagine a more unsatisfactory lot of men to have to do anything with.

I am sure I should like that fellow Egerton (acting agent and consul-general at Cairo). There is a light hearted jocularity about his communications and I should think the cares of life sat easily on him. Notice the slip in the margin. He wishes to know *exactly* " day, hour and minute " that he (Gordon) expects to be in " difficulties as to provisions and ammunition." Now I really think if Egerton was to turn over the " archives " (a delicious word) of his office he would see we had been in difficulties for provisions for some months. It is as if a man on the bank having seen his friend in a river already bobbed down two or three times hails " I say, old fellow, let us know when we are to throw you the life buoy, I know you have bobbed down two or three times, but it is a pity to throw you the life buoy until you really are *in extremis*, and I want to know *exactly* for I am a man brought up in a school of exactitude though I did *forget* (?) to date my June telegram about that Beduin escort contract."

" I must say I hate our diplomatists." Under this remark there is a very funny caricature of Egerton and Evelyn Baring. Egerton says " I can't believe it, it is too dreadful," and Baring : " Most serious ! Is it not ? He calls us humbugs ! *arrant humbugs !* "

Evelyn Baring (afterwards Lord Cromer), who, it will be remembered, never approved of Gordon's mission, comes in also for his share of the diarist's irony. Gordon writes a dozen lines and then crosses them out, and goes on :

> All the scratched out portion is abuse of Baring. Some one said "If you feel angry, then write your angry letter and then tear it up." It certainly does relieve the mind to write one's bile and it is good also to scratch it out for I daresay Baring is doing his duty better than I am; he is certainly more patriotic if patriotism consists in obedience to the existing Government of one's country.

There was a rumour that Baring himself was coming up.

> If Baring does bump his way up here (on a camel) as British Commissioner I shall consider he has expiated his faults and shall forgive him.

And later we have an amusing imaginary speech by Baring arriving, " every bone in my body dislocated with those beastly camels," and expressing horror at the deplorable tone of Gordon's journal.

Lord Granville, of course, is a special target for his bitterest sarcasm. He depicts him at Walmer reading his *Times* and enlarging with impatience and indignation on the fact that Khartoum was still holding out. Some of these passages, however, are suppressed by the editor.

In the following extract he includes himself in his laugh :

> We seldom realise our position. In ten or twelve years time Baring, Lord Wolseley, myself, Evelyn Wood etc. will have no teeth, and will be deaf; some of us will be quite *passé* ; no one will come and court us ; new Barings, new Lord Wolseleys will have arisen who will call us " bloaks " and " twaddlers." " Oh ! for goodness' sake come away, then ! Is that dreadful bore coming ? If once he gets along side of you, you are in for half an hour " will be the remark of some young captain of the present time on seeing you enter the Club.

In the middle of his entry on October 22 he suddenly breaks off into a skit on a debate in the House of Lords :

> House of Lords . . . in answer to questions put by the . . . of . . . replied that the noble marquis seemed to take a special delight in asking questions which he knew he (. . .) could not answer. He could say he had given a deal of time and attention to the affairs of the Soudan, but he frankly acknowledged that the names of places and people were so mixed up that it was impossible to get a true view of the case (a laugh). The noble Marquis asked what the policy of His Majesty's Government was ? It was as if he asked the policy of a log floating down stream ; it was going to the sea, as any one who had an ounce of brains could see. Well, that was the policy of it, only it was a decided policy and a straightforward one to drift along and take advantage of every circumstance. His Lordship deprecated the frequent

questioning on subjects which, as His Lordship had said, he knew nothing about and further did not care to know anything about.

His indignation with the Government is more serious : " I should be an angel (which I am not needless to say) if I was not rabid with Her Majesty's Government," he writes ; and this brings us to his constant survey of the position and his reiteration time after time that the *rescue of the garrison* is the real object.

As for " evacuation " it is one thing ; as for " ratting out " it is another. I am quite of advice as to No. 1 but I will be no party to No. 2.

I altogether decline the imputation that the projected expedition has come out to relieve me. It has come out to *Save our national honour* in extricating the garrisons from a position our action in Egypt has placed these garrisons.

My idea is to induce Her Majesty's Government to undertake the extrication of all people or garrisons now hemmed in or captive and that if this is not their programme then to resign my commission and do what I can to attain it (the object).

I hope I am not going down to History as being the cause of this expedition for I decline the imputation. *The expedition comes up to deliver the garrisons.*

Oh ! our Government, our Government ! What has it not to answer for ? Not to *me* but to these poor people. I declare if I thought the town wished the Mahdi, I would give up ; so much do I respect free will.

And here is a remarkable prophetic utterance.

We are a wonderful people ; it was never our Government which made us a great nation ; our Government has been ever the drag on our wheels. It is of course on the cards that Kartoum is taken under the nose of the expeditionary force which will be *just too late.*

Although they occur again and again with frequency we will only give one more of these emphatic statements.

It may be urged I was named Governor-General " in order to carry out the evacuation of the Soudan " and that I am bound to carry that out, which is quite correct, but I was named for *Evacuation of Soudan*, not to run away from Kartoum and leave the garrisons elsewhere to their fate.

Of course, as he explains more than once, if it were a question of saving his skin he could easily have escaped.

As for the Mahdi, Gordon's opinion of him is lowered when he hears that he puts pepper under his nails and then when he receives visitors touches his eyes and weeps copiously.

I must confess that the pepper business has sickened me ; I had hitherto hoped I had to do with a regular fanatic, who believed in his mission, but when one comes to pepper in the finger nails, it is rather humiliating to have to succumb to him and somehow I have the belief that I shall not have to do so. One cannot help being amused at this pepper business. Those who come in for pardon come in on their knees with a halter round their neck. The Mahdi rises having scratched his eyes and obtained a copious flow of tears and takes off his halter ! As the production of tears is generally considered the proof of sincerity I would recommend the Mahdi's recipe to Cabinet Ministers justifying some job.

But speaking as a soldier, he says :

From a professional military point of view and speaking materially I wish I was the Mahdi and I would laugh at all Europe.

Spies and stragglers were constantly coming over from the Mahdi with information, often not very reliable.

From what the sergeant major says, it appears that I am not more liked by the Mahdi than I am elsewhere—a nuisance ! and a bore !

A horse escaped from the Arabs, formerly belonging to the Government. It gave *no* information, but from its action may be supposed *not to believe the Mahdi.*

He makes the best of his Egyptian garrison, although they are often exasperating.

I declare my people do in a feeble way what is wanted, and do not deserve the character of cowards ; they bear defeat far better than other peoples and they are good tempered over it. We English are the cream, all acknowledge that, but we will not exist on two dates a day as these men do, without a murmur.

I boxed the telegraph clerk's ear for not giving me the telegram last night (after repeated orders that no consideration was to prevent his coming to me) ; and then as my conscience pricked me I gave him 5 dollars. He said he did not mind if I killed him—I was his father (a chocolate-coloured youth of twenty). I know all this is brutal—*abrutissant* as Hansall calls it—but what is one to do ? If you cut their pay you hurt their families. I am an advocate for summary and quick punishment which hurts only the defaulter.

It is really amusing to find (when one can scarcely call one's life one's own) one's servant already with one wife (which most men find is enough) coming and asking leave for three days to take another wife.

The question of trusting people was of course always coming up. He generalises on it in the following way :

There is one great question, and if you know a person, say K, is faithless and is seeking his own, ought one to be down on him ? We have an example in our Lord. He knew Judas was going to betray Him ; from which I infer, if we know even that K is going to rat or be faithless unless he K gives positive proof of such intention, we ought to treat K as J of whom we have no suspicion of treachery. I am inclined (satanically I own) to distrust everyone i.e. I trust every one. I believe that circumstances may arise when self interest will almost compel your nearest relative to betray you to some extent. Man is an essentially treacherous animal ; and although the psalmist said *in his haste* " all men are liars " I think he might have said the same *at his leisure.*

On the subject of fear he gives an opinion very different from the popular clap-trap generally expressed on the subject.

During our blockade we have often discussed the question of being frightened which, in the world's view a man should never be. For my part I am always frightened and very much so. I fear the future of all engagements. It is not the fear of death ; that is past, thank God ; but I fear defeat and its consequences. I do not believe a bit in the calm unmoved man. I think it is only he does not show it outwardly. Thence I conclude no commander of forces ought to live closely in relation with his subordinates who watch him like lynxes, for there is no contagion equal to that of fear.

By the following entry he does not appear to suffer from homesickness :

I dwell on the joy of never seeing Great Britain again with its horrid wearisome dinner parties and miseries. How we can put up with those things passes my imagination. It is a perfect bondage. At those dinner parties we are all in masks saying what we do not believe, eating and drinking things we do not want and then abusing one another. I would sooner live like a Dervish with the Mahdi than go out to dinner every night in London.

The Arab attacks become more frequent ; more often as November passes does Gordon realise the closing in of the walls. The steamer *Abbas* is lost, with Colonel Stewart on board—a catastrophe which haunts him.

Nov. 15. If not relieved for a month our food supply fails.

Nov. 16. If we do get out of this mess it is a miracle.

Almost the worst side of his terrible position was that he had no one whom he could trust. He talks of " volleys of lies," " tissues of lies," and an adjutant-major who " told me two cold lies in two days so I bundled him out." He says :

What has been the painful position for me is that there is not one person on whom I can rely. . . . My patience is almost exhausted with this continuous apparently never ending trial ; there is not one department which I have not to superintend as closely as if I was its direct head.

Dec. 11. The Arabs fired three shells at the Palace from Goba ; two went into the water, one passed over the palace. This always irritates me, for it is so personal and from one's own soldiers too ! It is not very pleasant also to feel at any moment you may have a shell in your room, for the creatures fire at all hours.

Dec. 13. *If some effort is not made before ten days' time the town will fall.* It is inexplicable this delay.

The last entry must be given in full.

Dec. 14. Arabs fired two shells at the Palace this morning: 566 ardebs dhoora (forage) in store; also 83,525 okes of biscuit! 10.30 a.m. The steamers are down at Omdurman engaging the Arabs consequently I am on tenterhooks! 11.30 steamers returned; *the Bordeen* was struck by a shell in her battery; we had only one man wounded. We are going to send down *the Bordeen* to-morrow with this journal. If I was in command of the two hundred men of the Expeditionary Force which are all that are necessary for the movement I should stop just below Halfeyeh and attack the Arabs at that place before I came on here to Kartoum. I should then communicate with the North Fort and act according to circumstances. Now *mark this* if the Expeditionary Force, and I ask for no more than two hundred men, does not come in ten days, *the town may fall*; and I have done my best for the honour of my country. Good bye,

C. G. GORDON

Khartoum fell on January 26, and Gordon was killed. The relief force under Sir Charles Wilson arrived on January 28, as the diary had foretold " just too late." Gordon must have continued keeping a journal, but his record of the last act of the tragedy is lost.

He wrote for others to read. But how differently from the conventional soldier! The diary is filled with shrewd and excellent general reflections quite apart from his opinions on his particular position. From its perusal one certainly does not get the impression of a gloomy unpractical and rather fanatical idealist; but no doubt additional and perhaps more personal knowledge can be gained of his character from the many letters he wrote.

The journals were published in 1885 with an introduction by A. Egmont Hake and notes by Sir Henry Gordon.

NINETEENTH CENTURY

MINOR DIARIES

GENERAL DYOTT

UNLIKE many soldiers who have kept diaries just to record the incidents of a particular campaign, Dyott kept a diary from the age of 20 till a year before he died. He was born in 1761 and died in 1846, so the diary (1781–1845) covers a period of sixty-four years. It fills sixteen volumes, and in its original form consists of about 500,000 words. It is a good instance of a regular and very full recital of events conscientiously noted by an honest, unreflecting, and unobservant man. He calls his life " strange and eventful," but it is neither ; it is just the ordinary routine of an active soldier sent about on various duties and of a country gentleman in retirement. The bare recital of events, what he does, where he goes, whom he meets, is practically unrelieved by any criticisms, thoughts or reflections which might make it readable. However, in so long a record we cannot fail to get some personal impression of the General himself. Conventional reticence curiously combined with a desire to keep a full account of his life in itself gives us a clue to his character. In writing he was thinking of his family. He says :

> If in threescore years I am able to entertain myself and family with perusing the transactions of my juvenile days (the sole purpose of this my journal) I shall be perfectly satisfied.

And very much later he writes, in beginning a new volume, that when he is no more, the journal may " afford my children some amusement and not improbably a feeling thought of their old father."

William Dyott began service as a soldier in Ireland; he was for some years in the garrison in Nova Scotia, he saw active service in the West Indies, he was sent to Egypt, he travelled on the Continent, he took part in the ill-fated Walcheren Expedition, and in 1826 he settled down in the home of his ancestors at Freeford, in Staffordshire. In his youth he enjoys himself, and we get frequent accounts of "vastly elegant dinners," "devilish good suppers," "joyous nights," "bumper toasts," etc. In Nova Scotia he makes friends with Prince William (afterwards William IV), and throughout his life he comes in contact with royalties who are always "uncommonly gracious" and he is "highly honoured" on each occasion by his intercourse with them. His account of Prince William in 1787 is not impressive. It consists almost entirely of drinking episodes:

> After supper he gave five or six bumper toasts.
>
> He was in great spirits and we all got a little inebriated.
>
> There were just twenty dined and we drank sixty three bottles of wine.
>
> His Royal Highness whenever a person did not fill a bumper always called out 'I see some of God Almighty's daylight in that glass, Sir: banish it.'

Dyott explains in recording instances of the Prince's graciousness:

> I cannot avoid mentioning these little circumstances : it is so very flattering to be taken such particular notice of by so great a person.

However, in later years, when William becomes King, he is more critical:

> I have little hesitation in auguring that William's will not be a reign to which any great benefits are likely to accrue to the nation from kingly exertion.

For George III, to whom he was A.D.C., he has unbounded admiration. But of George IV he says:

> A more accomplished Prince could not be as to address and manner, but as King of a great empire future historians will not have material to supply many princely traits of a great man.

At Queen Victoria's accession he has grave misgivings:

> A very young Queen coming to the throne of this mighty Empire, brought up and subject to the control of a weak, capricious mother, surrounded by the parent's chosen advisers from distinguished democratick councillors, gives token of unpropitious times to come.

Dyott expresses strong Tory views with uncompromising

vigour. Catholic Emancipation and the Reform movement are regarded by him with horror and the prospect of a Repeal of the Corn Laws rouses him to indignation. He even refuses to take part in the celebrations at Lichfield on the Queen's accession because the Mayor was "a rank radical." He notices with regret "a sad evil spirit among the *lower* orders," and declares "there is nothing to be more dreaded than popular power." He strongly disapproves of Elizabeth Fry's attempts at prison reform, and personally objects at the Stafford quarter sessions to the formation of a society to visit prisons. His counter proposal which he carries is to erect eight cells for solitary confinement. He writes: "It is my intention to make them as irksome and lonely to the individual as possible in order to obtain the desired effect."

Dyott was very domestic. He loves being with his wife and children. It is startling and tragic, therefore, suddenly to come on an entry in 1814 stating that his wife, who was an invalid, wished to separate from him. She had fallen in love with another man, with whom she eloped, and the General never saw her again. But it must have cost him a good deal to note down this incident, considering he never indulges in any indiscreet expression with regard to his inner feelings. He says, "she had long shown symptoms of unkindness and inattention"; but he never noted it in his diary. And except in connection with the business of the Divorce Bill and the news of her death he does not allude to her again. His children are a great blessing to him, and the careers of his two boys are often referred to. We hear a good deal about all his adventures, about his country life and attendance on the bench, and it may seem curious that we cannot quote more. But the General's style does not attract or excite. There is an immense quantity of this sort of thing:

> My hope of experiencing that felicity [going home] appears to me in a very glimmering light; nor can I determine what limits to fix for my duration in this most unhospitable clime. All I can conclude definitely is to remain with my regiment till I acquire the first step an officer can consider as real promotion in the profession I am embarked in. Towards the end of the month the season began to be milder and for the first four days of April the snow and frost etc. etc.

We need not even conclude the quotation, for there is really no end to it, nor can we cull any gems from his foreign travel; the General's artistic side was not his strongest. Here is his description of one of the greatest art galleries in the world at Florence :

> The collection of paintings, statues, and busts extremely numerous and of the first masters, in a high state of preservation and open to the public every day.

But flitting in a very odd way through the pages of this tedious and voluminous journal, or rather peeping now and again through the heavy curtain of the General's correct and conventional discourse, is a strange figure never fully described—a cousin, Miss Bakewell. She is upsetting, annoying, irritating, but she is a cousin and has to be tolerated. We can feel the General with his pen trying in vain to keep her out of the important chronicle of his life. For a little more of Miss Bakewell we would have gladly dispensed with negro risings, election contests, and even royal levees.

A series of some of the short references to this incongruous person will show why our curiosity is excited.

> 1827. Miss Bakewell is one of the most singular characters I know. With much good sense, much meanness of disposition and inability of mind that leads her to acts bordering on insanity, added to great vanity and open at all points of flattery and with but few good qualities to rebut her failings.

> 1830. We dined with cousin Bakewell who lives in a strange uncomfortable and shabby way.

> 1832. I left Miss Bakewell at Freeford and found her on my return. I was not sorry to be absent during her visit.

> 1833. She was altered in her appearance and manner, having shown no symptoms of violence or ill behaviour to anyone.

> 1835. Miss Bakewell arrived. I sent horses to meet her at Burton ; a dreadful torment she is and worse than the plague.

> 1836. We arrived about three and found my wild cousin in one of her hateful fits of ill humour and insanity. I never saw her more detestable.

> 1836. Miss Bakewell left us. I and Eleanor did not lament the loss of our guest. She is the most accomplished tiresome being that nature ever manufactured. My poor Eleanor had more of her plague and torment than I had. Indeed I would not have supported ten hours a day of such a repetition of plague and pestilence.

What did Miss Bakewell look like, what did she say or do that was so exasperating ? We are never told. She was evidently something more than an ordinary bore. However, we welcome her as forming some comic relief in the otherwise ponderous memoir, although the General certainly did not regard her as a joke.

Selections from the diary were published in two volumes in 1907, edited by Reginald W. Jefferey.

FRANCES, LADY SHELLEY

THE book entitled *The Diary of Frances, Lady Shelley* contains " a private memento of scenes and events that deeply impressed her." It really only just comes under the category of a diary at all. The entries are very occasionally dated and very seldom recorded on the day itself, and they are only concerned with gossip on public events, mixed with social and society experiences. She gives a full account of her life from her birth in 1787, and begins the more or less contemporary record in December, 1813. The so-called diary consists of memoirs written up from time to time, and from the subjective point of view entirely devoid of any personal note, although the gossip is practically all of a personal character. Lady Shelley's method is shown by these remarks, which occur at the beginning of dated entries.

1815. Aug. 25. What an age since I last wrote in my journal. I must make a sort of *pot pourri* up to to-day.

1816. Sep. 16. I must fill up this interval of my diary at leisure and write while it is fresh in my memory.

The few attempts she makes at daily entries are so bald that she evidently preferred the method of writing up periods of her experiences at long intervals. She relates a great number of anecdotes. But many of the anecdotes and indeed incidents and descriptions she gives are second-hand. " Lord S. told me many anecdotes about ——," " Miss S. told me the following anecdote," " I am told that," " It is said that," " I have seen a letter from Lady ——," " I have only feebly reproduced Lady S——'s eloquent and dramatic description of," are introductory phrases of frequent occurrence.

A large part of the memoir is taken up with enthusiastic descriptions of foreign travel in Switzerland, Italy, and Vienna. Lady Shelley had a good memory and a flowing pen, but no critical faculty, and absolutely no bite or grip in her style. She undoubtedly came across a large number of celebrities. That, no doubt, was what induced her to write, and it is the account of her intimate friendship with the Duke of Wellington that made her diary worth publishing. But the ecstatic worship of the hero of Waterloo is so excessive that we do not get any real character sketch. However, this is practically the only part of the diary that is worth noting, although many of the anecdotes about him are really quite pointless.

While she longs to record his sayings, she is obliged to confess :

> Except on subjects which interest the Duke such as war and politics he prefers to listen rather than to talk consequently he seldom says anything worth noting.

> I dined at 3 o'clock to-day in order to ride with the Duke who offered to mount me on Copenhagen. A charming ride of two hours. But I found Copenhagen the most difficult horse to sit of any I had ever ridden. If the Duke had not been there I should have been frightened. He said " I believe you think the glory greater than the pleasure in riding him."

> Mounted as I was on the dear chestnut mare by the Duke's side I felt supremely happy . . . the Duke took great care of me and I never lost him for a moment. We were of course always in front ; and on descending the hill we set off to gallop round the square which we did without once pulling up, a distance of eleven miles. As usual I received endless compliments on my horsemanship.

> And now comes the moment when we parted from the Duke of Wellington a short distance on the road to Paris whither the Duke returns. So deeply did I feel the parting that I could not help crying but I do not think he saw me. After we had shaken hands for the last time Shelley and I rode back to Vertus.

Shelley is rather a shadowy figure in the diary ; he seems generally to be sent off on shooting parties. She married Sir John Shelley in 1807, and a note in the early record of her life runs :

> There is one rule from which I have never deviated during the whole course of my married life. I made it a point never to interfere in any way with my husband's mode of life ; and I never kept him from the society even of persons whose conduct I could not admire.

In addition to accounts of reviews, battle-fields, dances, plays, operas, dinner parties, museums and scenery there are anecdotes about the Prince Regent, Princess Charlotte, the Emperor of Russia, the Emperor of Austria, Talleyrand, Metternich, the Pope, Nelson, Byron, Sir Walter Scott, the Duchess of Devonshire, and Lady Caroline Lamb, to mention only a few of the great people she came across. But the pen portraits do not quite come off, although some of the anecdotes are amusing. Her few lines on Talleyrand and Sir Walter Scott will suffice as examples.

> Talleyrand seemed pleased with his *mot* and repeated it to Madame Perigord herself. This evidently delighted her for she kissed him on both cheeks repeatedly. Talleyrand then proceeded to feed her with coffee out of his own cup and used his own spoon for that purpose. He is a frightful object to look at; and rolls his tongue about in a disgusting manner; in spite of all that the French ladies find him irresistible.

Sir Walter Scott's first appearance is not prepossessing:

> A club foot white eyelashes and a clumsy figure. He has not any expression when his face is in repose; but upon an instant some remark will lighten up his whole countenance and you discover the man of genius.

The diary, edited by Mr. Richard Edgcumbe, was published in 1912.

CHARLES ABBOT (Lord Colchester)

THE editor of Lord Colchester's diaries states that "those portions which related to strictly private or family affairs have been excluded as uninteresting to the public." Of course he is quite wrong. We are therefore left with a purely official record conscientiously kept from the time Abbot entered Parliament in 1795, during his Speakership (1802–1817) until shortly before his death in 1829.

A daily record of this character is useful to historians and students, but as a diary it is difficult to digest. The very fact, however, that he thought it worth while to keep this careful register shows how attentive and exact he was in the discharge of his parliamentary duties. No rash judgments, hardly any criticisms, no note of enthusiasm or displeasure, is allowed to creep into these almost judicial pages.

The differences in parliamentary manners and customs only a hundred years ago are striking, when we find Abbot being told soon after his entry into the House that he was "disorderly" in "wearing his spurs" as "none but county members were entitled to that privilege"; or when we get the following account of a debate:

> 1796. May 10. In the House Fox moved an Address upon the state of the nation with regard to the war. He spoke from half past five till a quarter before ten. Mr. Pitt spoke till a quarter past twelve. Fox replied for three

quarters of an hour. The division at one was :—For the address 42 ; against it 216.

In the midst of debates, divisions, reports, commissions, procedure, etc., he gives very little description of the members themselves. This seems a pity when as an exception we find this very striking picture of Grattan :

1805. Grattan was as in all his printed speeches, able and various in his topics : delivered in language quaint and epigrammatic with occasional flashes of striking metaphors ; and in a manner disgustingly vain, conceited and affected. His elocution fluent ; sometimes rapid with strained pauses and strange cadences ; his action violent, throwing his body, head and arms into all sorts of absurd attitudes. He was heard with much attention but not always with admiration even by his own friends.

There is a good account of a conversation with Fox and an estimate of Pitt when he dies.

Abbot is evidently greatly impressed by royalty; remarks and conversations of the most commonplace description are carefully entered ; and the health symptoms of George III and George IV are given continually in the most elaborate detail.

There is a very long account of the dinner given by the Prince Regent to the exiled King of France in 1811, at which a table two hundred feet long was decorated with a river of water with little gudgeon in it, which widened towards the Prince's end, the water falling by cascades into a lake surrounded by vases burning perfumes under the arches of a colonnade round the lake.

The diary contains weather notes ; storms, temperature and floods are recorded.

When he goes to Italy after his retirement from the Speakership he continues to keep a diary. But the tone is the same. The politics of Italy and Europe occupy his attention, the eminent people he meets are never described or criticised, and his interview with the Pope is noted in the usual ceremonial manner.

The diary, in fact, as we have it in the three volumes published in 1861, is not human but official.

ELIZABETH FRY

FROM before the age of 16 up to the end of her life Elizabeth Fry kept a journal. She wrote in it intermittently and confined her entries very largely to religious reflections and prayers. It is described as " the outpourings of her heart, the communings between God and her own soul," and she herself describes it in the first year as "a little friend to my heart," and says, "it is next to communicating my feelings to another person . . . it is most comfortable to read it over and see the different workings of my heart and soul," and again : "writing my journal is to me expressing the feelings of my heart during the day." It was kept in fact for self-disciplinary purposes, and from time to time she does read it over. Elizabeth Fry's abnormally active and successful career as a prison reformer is well known. In addition to a vast public correspondence Elizabeth Fry found time to write often at considerable length in her diary.

Superficially such a journal as this resembles many other journals of Quakers and divines. But in the midst of the ejaculatory appeals there is a great deal of very searching self-examination and some thoughtful meditations on life. Apart from the extreme seriousness of the tone, the high-minded tenacity of purpose makes the reader conscious of a masterful personality lifted perhaps rather above the reach of the ordinary mortal, yet very human. In addition to prayer, descriptions of "meeting" and references to her work, there is frequent mention of the numberless members of her family. Besides having eleven children of her own, she herself was one of twelve. Her health also occupies her attention.

She began diary writing at a very early age, but destroyed the earliest attempts. She was not brought up as a strict Quaker, although the Gurneys were members of the Society of Friends. In the earliest entries, which are the most human, we find the young girl bent on self-discipline and questioning all her thoughts and actions.

When she is 16, in 1797, she writes :

I feel by experience how much entering into the world hurts me ; worldly company I think materially injures, it excites a false stimulus, such a love of pomp, pride, vanity, jealousy and ambition ; it leads to think about dress and such trifles and when out of it we fly to nov els and scandal or something of that kind for entertainment.

And the following year :

I have known my faults and not corrected them and now I am determined I will once more try with redoubled ardour to overcome my wicked inclinations ; I must not flirt ; I must not ever be out of temper with the children ; I must not contradict without a cause ; I must not mump when my sisters are liked and I am not ; I must not allow myself to be angry ; I must not exaggerate which I am inclined to do. I must not give way to luxury ; I must not be idle in mind, I must try to give way to every good feeling and overcome every bad.

My mind has by degrees flown from religion. I rode to Norwich and had a very serious ride there ; but meeting, and being looked at with apparent admiration by some officers brought on vanity ; and I came home full of the world as I went to town full of heaven.

Trifles occupy me far too much such as dress etc. etc. I find it easier to acknowledge my vices than my follies.

I went to the Oratorio, I enjoyed it but spoke sadly at random, what a bad habit !

I feel I am a contemptible fine lady. May I be preserved from continuing so. . . .

I am more cross, more proud, more vain, more extravagant. I lay it to my great love of gaiety and the world. I feel, I know I am falling. I do believe if I had a little true religion I should have a greater support than I have now.

I am a bubble without reason without beauty of mind or person. I am a fool. I daily fall lower in my own estimation.

The preaching of William Savery in 1798 makes a deep impression on her :

He seemed to me to overflow with true religion and to be humble and yet a man of great abilities. If I see William Savery I shall not I doubt be over fond of gaieties.

This was regarded as her conversion, and in time she became a strict Friend. Music and dancing had not been prohibited in her education, but gradually she begins to express doubt about them :

We went to hear the band which I am sorry for as I cannot get courage to tell my father, I wish I had not gone.

The danger of dancing I find is throwing me off my centre ; at times when dancing I know that I have not reason left but that I do things which in calm moments I must repent of.

I do not approve of singing in company as it leads to vanity and dissipation of mind. . . . I should be sorry quite to give up singing.

She found difficulty in adopting the correct language and saying " thee " and " thou " and she writes : " I do not feel little scruples of that importance that some other persons do." Although no one throughout her life could have been a more devoted Quaker, she is not blind to their faults, and in 1830 she writes : " Bitter experience has proved to me that Friends do rest too much on externals."

When she was 20 she married Joseph Fry. In her journal she weighs the pros and cons of marriage from the point of view of spiritual duty, and decides in favour of it.

There is much more about her domestic life in the diary than about her public life, and we are brought right into the atmosphere of a large Quaker household. After the birth of her eldest child she writes :

> I much wish to avoid my mother in law's very " cotting " plan, for a degree of hardiness I think most desirable—I think being too careful and tender really make them more subject to indisposition.

A few other references to her children may be given :

> I am at home alone with my nine children, a great and very precious charge; at times they appear too much for me at others I greatly enjoy them.
>
> All our beloved children dined with us. It really was to me a beautiful sight. Sixteen round our table happy in each other, a strong tie of love amidst the brothers and sisters and much united to us their father and mother. . . . When the cloth was removed after dinner I believed it my duty to kneel down and very fervently to pray and to return thanks to my God for all these most tenderly beloved ones. . . . After this solemn time thirteen of the sweet dear grandchildren came in.

Mrs. Fry has servant worries and mentions them more than once.

> Tried by my servants appearing dissatisfied with what I believe to be liberal things . . . I know no family who allows exactly the same indulgences and few who give the same high wages and yet I do not know of anyone so often grieved by the discontents of servants as myself.

There are many descriptions of " meeting " and of her praying and of death-bed scenes. We may pick out of the paragraphs of prayer, resolutions and self-examination one or two phrases which will show that Elizabeth Fry did not, like some others, find relief in just the repetition of conventional religious formulæ :

> I want order ; I believe it difficult to obtain but yet with perseverance attainable. The first way to obtain it appears to me to try to prevent my thoughts from rambling and to keep as steadily as possible to the object in view.
>
> I am fearful of self confidence; I feel it so different to the confidence placed in an All wise Director.
>
> From a great fear of hurting others I feel, though I believe it is not very apparent, a bowing to their opinions and not openly professing my own which tries me.

Her public work with regard to prison reform and prison schools involved a great deal of correspondence from all parts of the world, and it does not figure so prominently therefore in her private diary. But a few extracts may be given, some of which show how much she disliked the publicity and prominence into which her work brought her.

1817. I have lately been much occupied in forming a school in Newgate for the children of the poor prisoners as well as the young criminals which has brought much peace and satisfaction with it.

Our Newgate visiting could no longer be kept secret, which I endeavoured that it should be and therefore I am exposed to praise that I do not the least deserve; also to some unpleasant humiliations—for in trying to obtain helpers I must be subject to their various opinions; and also being obliged to confer at times with strangers and men in authority is to me a very unpleasant necessity.

My having been brought publicly forward in the newspapers, respecting what I have been instrumental in doing at Newgate has brought some anxiety with it; in the first place as far as I am concerned, that it may neither raise me too high nor cast me too low, that having what may appear my good works, thus published, may never lead me or others to give either the praise or glory where it is not due.

The prison and myself are become quite a show which is a very serious thing in many points.

1818. When the Queen came to speak to me which she did very kindly there was I am told a general clap. I think I may say this hardly raised me at all. . . .

1824. The burden and perplexity of the opposition to improvement in prisons is almost too much for me; it is so much against my nature to take my own defence or even that of the cause in which I am interested into my own hands.

1831. My interest in the cause of prisons remains strong and my zeal unabated; though it is curious to observe how much less is felt about it by the public generally. How little it would answer in these important duties to be much affected by the good or bad opinion of man.

She has to submit to having her portrait painted, but she yields very reluctantly :

It is not altogether what I like or approve; it is making too much of this poor tabernacle and rather exalting that part in us which should be laid low and kept low.

She expresses on several occasions grave doubts about trying to see royalty and attending dinners and functions, " how far it was safe for me thus to be cast among the great of this world " ; and again, " how far the expensive dinner is right to give," and she prevents the Lord Mayor on one occasion from proposing toasts. The stir she caused brought her inevitably very much to the front, and the way she accepted the situation shows that she never had her head turned by fame and success. She gives an account of conversations she had at dinner with Sir Robert Peel and Prince Albert, when she made the most of her opportunities, and also of the visit of the King of Prussia to Newgate, with whom she proceeded arm in arm through the prison. And in the midst of the royal courtiers and city functionaries she prays :

> I believed it my duty to kneel down before this most curious interesting and mixed company for I felt my God must be served the same everywhere and amongst all people, whatever reproach it brought me into.

And afterwards the King has dinner with her and her family at Upton Lane, and " appeared to enjoy his dinner perfectly at his ease and very happy with us."

Her great vitality and energy (for hers was far more an active than reflective temperament) is shown in all she writes. " I have got many things stirring " is an entry in 1843, that is to say when she was 63, when although ill and resting at Sandgate, she says that a place " so remarkably void of objects does not suit my active mind ... this place is unusually dull to me."

Though imbued to a great extent with characteristic Quaker optimism, she has her moments of depression, especially during periods of illness and family bereavements. On New Year's Day, 1843, she writes :

> Another year is closed and passed never to return. It appears to me that mine is rather a rapid descent into the valley of old age.

There are accounts of her journeys abroad, specially in Paris and in the Channel Islands, but they are never very descriptive or critical. She is not writing a narrative, she is communing with herself and only refers to events in so far as they affect her at the moment. Strict as she was in the religious sense, many instances might be quoted of her tolerance and broad-mindedness.

She does not often make any comment on public events, but the following is her description of the state of affairs in 1840 :

> Political commotion about the country—riots in Wales—much religious stir in the Church of England, numbers of persons becoming much the same as Roman Catholics—Popish doctrines preached openly in many of our churches—infidel principles, in the form of Socialism, gaining ground.

The last entry in her journal was written on September 16, 1845 ; she died on October 12 in the same year.

The journal is copiously quoted in the biography brought out by her daughters in 1847.

THE RIGHT HON. GEORGE ROSE

GEORGE ROSE'S diary is exclusively and somewhat dryly concerned with public affairs. He was a Member of Parliament who held several minor appointments, and his diaries and correspondence are of historical importance owing to his very close intimacy with Pitt, who figures, so to speak, as the hero of his diary, which covers the years 1800 to 1811, with the exception of 1805, which is a blank. When Pitt dies in 1806 he writes:

> Intending these notes merely as memoranda of occurrences it is not my intention to attempt to express the agony of my mind on the incalculable loss I have sustained; severe and irreparable as it is and deeply as it will be felt by me to the latest hour of my life I bow with resignation to the Power that has inflicted it.

And after the funeral:

> On my return to my own house I indulged myself with what has been very frequently the occupation of my mind during the last five weeks and will not unfrequently employ it during the remainder of my life; the reflection on the character and talents of my deceased friend and the loss I have sustained in his death, banishing entirely every consideration of an interested nature.

These extracts are quoted as the only instance in which any note of personal emotion or sentiment is allowed to creep into his record. But we can detect very unusual disinterestedness, conscientiousness and modesty in Rose when Perceval asks him to be Chancellor of the Exchequer and he refuses, feeling he can discharge his duty better by remaining at the Board of Trade. He fears he might be called upon in Perceval's absence to lead the House of Commons, and he writes: " To this most important duty I feel myself from want of eloquence quite unequal."

His conversations with George III are fully reported. He rides with him, and the little touches with regard to their horses, the scenery and the weather give his descriptions a good deal of life. One of his Majesty's observations towards the end of a ride near Lyndhurst may be quoted:

> I thank God there is but one of my children who wants courage; and I will not name *him* because he is to succeed me.

Rose is " deeply pained by this remark."

The editor of the diaries and correspondence, published in 1860, says Rose was not " at any time addicted to pleasantries, anecdotes or gossip," nor did he " take much notice of what was passing round him." He had not the qualities, in fact, to make a good diarist. His memoranda were written for his son.

LADY NUGENT

*J*AMAICA *One Hundred Years Ago* is not an alluring title for a book. One would not immediately snatch a volume with that name from the shelf of a library. And yet Lady Nugent's journal, of which this is the sub-title, is most entertaining. We have here a very good instance of how little the subject matters if the diarist is able to impart to diary entries the natural spontaneity which comes from sympathetic powers of observation. Lady Nugent had little pretensions from the literary point of view, although she wrote a few verses ; she is rather sentimental and intensely domestic, but she is able in quite a skilful though perfectly natural way to make each day tell its story.

Sir George Nugent, her husband, was appointed Lieutenant-Governor and Commander-in-Chief in Jamaica in 1801, where he remained till the beginning of 1806. Lady Nugent accompanied him and remained there till June, 1805. She kept a regular diary during this period, and there are some irregular entries (up to 1814) after she returned to England, and also in India where Sir George was Commander-in-Chief. She was the daughter of Brigadier-General Skinner of New Jersey, and was born about 1771, when New Jersey was still under the British Crown. Irish, Scotch, as well as Dutch blood flowed in her veins.

She wrote for her children and for her own amusement, and the idea of publishing her diary never entered her head. It was first privately printed after her death, and published in 1907. The appointment to Jamaica does not smile on her ; she says :

I would greatly have preferred remaining (at Hampstead) instead of playing the Governor's lady to the *blackies* : but *we* are soldiers and must have no will of our own.

The voyage out is graphically described with all its incidents and discomforts. She refers throughout to her husband, whom she calls " General N," or " my dear N," with the greatest affection, and often gets into a state about his health. She finds it very hot on their arrival :

All the gentlemen, civil and military were introduced to me before we sat down; I scarce recollect the name or visage of any of them only they all looked very bilious and very warm. One gentleman seemed to suffer exceedingly; for in spite of his constant mopping the perspiration stood like drops of crystal on his face the whole time we were at dinner.

I sat between Lord B and Colonel MacMurdo, the latter actually dripping with perspiration. He saw me looking at the drops as they fell from his forehead, poor man! and this increased them almost to a cascade.

She is not very complimentary about her husband's predecessor, who is still on the island.

I wish Lord B would wash his hands and use a nail brush for the black edges of his nails really make me sick. He has, besides, an extraordinary propensity to dip his fingers into every dish. Yesterday he absolutely helped himself to some fricassée with his dirty finger and thumb.

I behaved very ill, having placed an Aide-de-camp between me and his lordship; for really his hands were so dirty I could not have eaten anything had he been nearer.

The feasts and banquets were sometimes a high trial to her. One or two of her comments on the food may be given.

I don't wonder now at the fever the people suffer from here—such eating and drinking I never saw! Such loads of all sorts of high, rich, seasoned things, and really gallons of wine and mixed liquors as they drink! I observed some of the party to-day eat of late breakfasts as if they had never eaten before—a dish of tea, another of coffee, a bumper of claret, another large one of hock negus; then Madeira, sangaree, hot and cold meat, stews and fries, hot and cold fish, pickled and plain, peppers, ginger sweetmeats, acid fruit, sweet jellies—in short it was all as astonishing as it was disgusting.

I am not astonished at the general ill health of the men in this country, for they really eat like cormorants and drink like porpoises.

Dances are very frequent, and all officials join in them. After a formal ball, at which she had to dance with members of the Council, etc., she ends up:

But after supper I forgot all my dignity and with all my heart joined in a Scotch reel—Many followed my example and the ball concluded merrily.

A very large party in the evening and the candidates for the Chief Justices situation particularly smiling and attentive. Some of them danced merrily on the occasion and particularly when they were my partners.

The round of entertainments and her other official duties she often finds very tiring, and she notes when she is exhausted and says on one occasion:

I would give anything for a little rest and quiet but must exert myself at dinner to make the agreeable to the big wigs.

The heat, the mosquitoes, the roars of laughter from the gentlemen till a late hour and the dancing and jollity of the servants all night, all combined together to spoil our repose so that we got very little sleep, and I feel this now very much.

She notes her health and her symptoms before her first confinement. The birth of two children is recorded with great rapture : the struggles with the black nurses, the protection of the babies from scorpions, mosquitoes, and poison spiders, and all their minor ailments are fully noted. She is very religious, and there are many little phrases of prayer and thanksgiving throughout the diary. She sets to work and converts numbers of her black servants, teaches them the catechism, and has them baptised.

The blackies perfect in their prayers. Read to them this evening and intend to do so in future.

In fact, she is always kind and attentive to the coloured population, and indeed goes beyond what is considered proper.

I began the ball with an old Negro man. The gentlemen each selected a partner according to rank by age or service and we all danced. However I was not aware how much I shocked the Misses Murphy by doing this. They told me afterwards they were nearly fainting and could hardly forbear shedding a flood of tears at such an unusual and extraordinary sight.

Saw a number of black and brown ladies in the evening to please the old housekeeper ; but I don't know whether the white ladies whom I left in the drawing room when I gave audience quite approved of my conduct.

She accompanies Sir George on his journeys of inspection in the island, and is entertained by various people.

She has a visit from royalty in the shape of the king of the Mosquito Indians and his uncle, who called himself Count Stamford or the Duke of York. The king, who is eight years old, is dressed in scarlet and wears a crown, and

he cried roared and yelled horribly and began to pull off all his clothes in the most violent manner and was nearly naked before we could have him carried out of the room.

Meanwhile the uncle got drunk and had to be put to bed. The whole description is extremely funny.

Lady Nugent is often distressed at the connections formed by white men with the black population. She exclaims :

This is indeed a sad immoral country, but it is no use worrying myself.

She shows throughout a most optimistic and cheerful disposition, and we have no difficulty in believing that she and Sir George were very popular. Every day she relates her doings, the official and political transactions, the weather phenomena, more especially the storms, and the progress of her children, with the most natural and engaging frankness.

Her diary when in England is very much less good. She goes about visiting her friends, goes to a drawing-room, giving a full description of her dress and remarks on Mr. Fox's "slovenly appearance." The extracts from the Indian diary show that she no longer wrote regularly and her youthful fun has disappeared. The little baby George, who is guarded and watched with such care in Jamaica, succeeded his father as second baronet and lived to be 90.

SIR GEORGE JACKSON

THERE are four volumes of Sir George Jackson's diaries and letters covering the period from 1801 to 1816. Sir George was a diplomatist of some distinction. The most interesting period of his career was when he accompanied Sir Charles Stewart to Germany and entered Paris with the Allies in 1815. Jackson's diary reads very much like extracts from letters which he forgot to post—letters in which the almost official tone of despatches is preserved and in which hardly any personal matter is introduced. Diplomatists by their profession are brought into close touch with rulers and people of importance, and many of them keep diaries to record their official and social intercourse which must appear at the moment to be highly important. But it is not the fact of meeting a King or Minister that matters in a diary, but what you say about him; and Jackson's notes contribute very little beyond occasional anecdotes to our general knowledge of those times. That the Czar was "gracious and affable" does not tell us much, and Jackson's indignation at his not wearing the Garter when he appears in knee breeches tells us more about Jackson than about the Czar. However, he has a very strenuous time of it, sitting up all night writing with the pen sometimes dropping from his hand in his exhaustion, travelling from one place to another and sometimes finding himself very near the scene of action. He always has faith in the cause of the Allies, scoffs at the idea of invasion in 1810, and in 1813 notes that "there is a probability of their overcoming the great Boney at no very far off date."

In the same year he records " an event to make a figure in my journal," which is the fact that he is lodged at Goethe's house in Weimar, and the sketch he gives of the poet philosopher is worth quoting :

> There was a great deal of entertaining conversation for the presence of M. de Goethe put us all on our mettle. . . . The charm of his conversation, in my humble opinion, is somewhat marred by an air of pedantry which is probably due to the adulation he is accustomed to receive from his many worshippers. People here seem to hang, as it were, upon his lips and listen for his words as if an oracle were about to hold forth. It is not therefore surprising that they should flow from them in a less easy current than if he were allowed to speak with as little restraint as those from whom no unusual beauty of language, lessons of wisdom, or poetic fancies are expected each time they open their mouths. For my part I like Goethe for his good humour and pleasant manners ; for I think that a man inferior in genius and of less genial nature would have become insufferable in society if constantly dosed with flattery as he is and that much credit is due even to *him* for being so little spoiled by it.

We get accounts of visits to Holland House, dinners, balls, and plays when he is in London. More than half the volumes consists of letters, many from his brother Francis, who was also a diplomatist.

Lady Jackson, in editing the volumes, only wanted no doubt to present the picture of the official activities of the diplomatic brothers, and probably more intimate sections of the diary were omitted.

Sir George distinguished himself by his services in connection with the abolition of the Slave Trade, and died in 1861.

HENRY MARTYN

SIR JAMES STEPHEN says that Henry Martyn's " is the one heroic name that adorns the Church of England from the days of Elizabeth to our own." Son of a Cornish miner's agent, he was educated at Truro and St. John's College, Cambridge, and was senior wrangler in 1801. He was ordained at Ely, and in 1805 he went to India, where he devoted his life to missionary work. He translated the New Testament and the Prayer Book into Hindustani and the New Testament and Psalms into Persian. Owing to ill health, he obtained leave to go to Persia, where after travelling about in the greatest discomfort he died at the age of 30. From 1803 to 1812 he kept a more or less regular diary.

HENRY MARTYN

For nine months in 1809 he made his entries in Latin or Greek "for secrecy."

His intention in keeping a diary is disclosed in the following passages:

> In making this journal, I pretend not to record all that I remember; and that not on account of its minuteness for nothing is strictly so—but because in some cases it would be improper to commit it to paper. I desire to collect the *habit* of my mind, to discover my besetting sins, the occasion of calling them forth and the considerations by which I have at any time been stirred up to duty.

And a year later:

> On the review of my journal of the last year I perceived it has been of late becoming a diary of my life instead of being a register of my state of mind.

He never wholly succeeds in making it only a register of his state of mind. So far as it assumed this character, it resembles very much the journals of self-examination which have already been noticed. Martyn was a saint, a man of rigidly strict and uncompromising religion, a man for whom the world, human intercourse and even the vision of nature were filled with snares and pitfalls of evil. Self-discipline of the most rigorous description was the rule of his life, but, like many others, his self-condemnation and self-abasement when committed to writing appear altogether exaggerated. And while his wonderful record of ascetic self-discipline places him on a pedestal far beyond the reach of the ordinary mortal, the incessantly repeated expressions of penitence and remorse must fail to attract others to follow his example.

Such expressions as the following occur on every page: "I groaned under the corruption of my heart"; "my sins really deserve hell"; "my spirit groans at my unprofitableness"; "daily do I deserve the pit of destruction"; "the sense of my guilt still almost overwhelming"; "my soul groans at recording the wickedness of every day."

When the expressions are less extreme they are far more convincing. Such as, "I began to see for the first time that I must be contented to take my place among men of second rate abilities"; "recollected that I had said something sarcastic at table"; "at supper was grieved at the conversation and longed to say something effectually"; "felt chagrined in the evening at not hearing my sermon praised."

His style in preaching was evidently characteristically severe. A friend tells him so:

He then told me of my preaching that it was not calculated to win people to religion : for I set the duties of religion in so terrific a light that people were revolted.

And another friend comes up and says :

" Upon my word, Mr. Martyn, you gave us a good trimming yesterday."

Everything against himself, whether it comes from others or from his own habitual self-disparagement, goes down in the diary, and occasions outpourings of his soul to God. Had he lived an inactive life of contemplation, Martyn would probably have gone out of his mind. Instead of that, however, his life was one of most strenuous and almost inconceivable activity. Yet in the midst of prayers and imprecations his daily doings are recorded. His whole life on board ship going out on his long voyage to India is almost realistically described, his torture from sea-sickness, the storms, the indifference and open hostility of some of the crew, his failure in preaching, his attempts to convert, to pray with or to move the spirit in some of the people, all become pegs on which to hang reflections either about his own desperate sinfulness or the hopeless condition of those around him. Even the glories of the setting sun he declares have no power to charm him, so absorbed is he in the work of salvation. He revelled in opposition, adversity, struggle, discomfort and pain. It was as if he enjoyed being buffeted, and anything that softened, beautified or mitigated the trials of life seemed almost to exasperate him. He appears to resent having any human feelings at all. But he has them even to the extent of falling in love. Again here we find him regarding the young lady from the point of view of how she will help his soul or be of assistance to him in his work. One is inclined to feel that the failure of his love affair, which would have been a tragedy to a normal man, was looked upon by him as an additional cross which his Spartan nature was ready to bear. He had met her in England and had made advances to her. After he has been in India a while he decides in favour of marriage, and writes to her to come out to him. Her mother refuses her consent, and there the matter ends :

Grief and disappointment threw my soul into confusion at first but gradually, as my disorder subsided, my eyes were opened and reason resumed its office.

He continues, however, to have an affectionate correspondence with her to the end of his short life.

Martyn refers, of course, in many entries to his constant study of languages, which began before he went out and on board ship. He gained such proficiency that he could preach in Hindustani as well as do his laborious and monumental work of translation.

So far as conversions are concerned, he has no success. He admits this himself in an entry on his thirtieth birthday:

> I once used to flatter myself that when entering my thirtieth year I might have the happiness of seeing an Indian congregation of saints won to the gospel through my preaching. Alas! how far is this from being the case; scarcely even an European can I fix upon as having been awakened under my ministry since coming here.

Even allowing for his usual exaggeration with regard to his own demerits, it is clear that Martyn's success was as a scholar, not as a preacher. It may be imagined that a man of his type was entirely out of his element so far as social festivities were concerned. Although he says:

> I groan at the misery and vanity of the world and humbly adore the mercy of God which hath separated me from them,—

nevertheless he is obliged occasionally to go to dinners and other entertainments. Here is one:

> I found such a party of Dragoon officers that I could not open my mouth but was obliged to sit listening to nonsense, while the happy people of God were worshipping in his courts; but I lifted up my heart in prayer and ejaculation frequently; and was therefore so far from being inclined to conform to them that I never felt more averse to the ways and miserable merriment of the worldly.

His journey in Persia becomes more and more distressing as his fever and wretchedness increase. Even for this tough and valiant spirit the load of suffering becomes too great. But to the very end he thinks " with sweet comfort and peace of my God, in solitude my company, my friend and comforter." The last entry is written ten days before he died.

The journal, edited by Samuel Wilberforce, was published in 1839.

THOMAS CREEVEY

ALTHOUGH Greville speaks of Creevey's "copious diary," Sir Herbert Maxwell, the editor of the *Creevey Papers*, states that it never came into his hands, and expresses some doubt as to whether it ever existed. If it did, it is conceivable that his political opponents got hold of it after his death and destroyed the greater part of it. Anyhow, the *Creevey Papers* consist almost exclusively of letters and memoranda of reminiscences, and there are only a few diary extracts. These show that intermittently the great collector of gossip must have kept some sort of a diary. He certainly was well qualified to do so, because he was in a favourable position to hear all that was going on and in his writing he shows a special talent for recording the intrigues and scandals of the day with the ease and indiscretion which is very suitable for diary writing. We may regret, therefore, that there is not more of it.

Thomas Creevey, born in 1768, was for several years a Member of Parliament. The few passages in his journal from which we can quote occur between 1809—1818. There is nothing whatever in them about himself or his domestic affairs.

He relates in some detail a visit to Howick, where he has several conversations with Lord Grey, but he remarks:

> Conversation after dinner and after supper always as artificial as the devil, Lord Grey showing his spite at my conduct the last session.

He sometimes writes in the present tense:

> Mrs. Creevey receives a letter from Lady Petre begging her and me to write letters of introduction in Edinburgh for her son young Lord Petre who is going there. Mrs. Creevey asks Lord Grey to let her send a note to Alnwick to bring him and his tutor over here. Lord and Lady Grey make such difficulty about beds and in short fling such cold water upon the proposal that we drop the subject. Take notice. There was room in the house—plenty.

We cannot help sympathising with Lord Grey.

The entries in 1809 are chiefly political gossip and scandal about Mrs. Clarke, the Duke of York's mistress. In 1811 at Brighton he is highly delighted at being asked several times to the Pavilion with his wife and step-daughter, so we get some amusing references to the Prince Regent.

> We were at the Pavilion last night—Mrs. Creevey's three daughters and myself—and had a very pleasant evening. . . . About half past nine which might be a quarter of an hour after we arrived the Prince came out of the dining room. He was in the best humour, bowed and spoke to all of us and looked uncommonly well tho' very fat.
>
> The Regent sat in the musick Room almost all the time between Viotti, the famous violin player and Lady Jane Houston and he went on for hours beating his thighs the proper time for the band and singing out aloud and looking about for accompaniment from Viotti and Lady Jane. It was curious to see a Regent thus employed but he seemed in high good humour.

LADY CHARLOTTE BURY

The Regent was again all night in the Musick room and not content with presiding over the Band but actually singing and very loud too.

The Prince was very merry and seemed very well. He began to me with saying very loud that he had sent for Mrs. Creevey's physic to London.

The passages quoted in 1817 and 1818 are mostly accounts of conversations with the Duke of Wellington. He seems anxious to show on what familiar terms the Duke was with him.

We talked over English politics and upon my saying that never Government cut so contemptible a figure as ours did the last session—particularly in the defeats they sustained on the proposals to augment the establishments of the Dukes of Clarence, Kent and Cumberland upon their marriages he said " By God ! there is a great deal to be said about that. They (the Princes) are the damnedest millstone about the necks of any Government that can be imagined. They have insulted—*personally* insulted—two thirds of the gentlemen of England and how can it be wondered at that they take their revenge upon them when they get them in the House of Commons ? It is their only opportunity and I think, by God ! they are quite right to use it.

All the " Well, Creevey," " Come in here, Creevey," " Come on and dine with me, Creevey," are most carefully noted. Summing up the Duke, he writes :

It is a curious thing to have seen so much of this said Duke as I have done at different times considering the imposters that most men in power are—the insufferable pretensions one meets with in every Jack in office—the uniform frankness and simplicity of Wellington in all conversations I have heard him engaged in coupled with the unparalleled situation he holds in the world for an English subject make him to me the most interesting object I have ever seen in my life.

It is not in the diary extracts but in the letters and memoranda that the full spice of Creevey's tittle-tattle comes out.

LADY CHARLOTTE BURY

IN 1838 was published anonymously *A Diary Illustrative of the Times of George the Fourth*. It created a considerable stir and was fiercely attacked. Thackeray tore it to pieces in *Skimmings from the Diary of George IV*, by C. Yellowplush, Esq. ; but this did not prevent him using passages from it in his *Four Georges*. Tom Hood wrote :

> When I resign the world so briery
> To have across the Styx my ferrying
> O may I die without a DIARY
> And be interr'd without a BURYing !

This shows that the authorship was already suspected.

Lady Charlotte Bury, who was the author of this diary, was born in 1775. She was a daughter of John, Duke of Argyll, and became a famous beauty. She married first in 1796 John Campbell, her cousin, and in 1818 the Rev. Edward J. Bury. The latter got hold of the diary, which was originally never intended for publication, edited it and added notes, but he died before its actual publication. Lady Charlotte was a prolific novelist. She turned out novel after novel for the sake of making a little money when she found herself in reduced circumstances in later years, but no one has ever heard of any of them.

The diary is certainly a most astonishing production. Parts of it read almost like a parody or skit. Her husband evidently tampered with it, anyhow to the extent of mentioning the author herself by name and in the third person, with a view no doubt of putting people off the right scent. It covers about ten years (1810-1820) with breaks, and many of the entries occupy several pages. Scandal gossip and anecdotage served in rich profusion are heavy reading at the best of times, and we do not get much relief in the sentimental effusions of the novelist on her foreign travels. What she sees may be " sublime," " radiant," " dazzling," " transcendental," " effulgent," " enchanting," " replete with sweetness," but our attention flags. A comparison of Lady Charlotte's Journal with Fanny Burney's will strike anyone who reads the two because they both describe the Court, they are both novelists, and they both write a great deal. But in Fanny Burney there is a shrewdness, a humour, an inimitable descriptive power which we may look for in vain in Lady Charlotte's observations; in the former diary there is a reticence with regard to scandal, a rather charming propriety and even in her raptures a *naïveté* which is absent in the more worldly and sophisticated lady's writing. In another respect, however, Lady Charlotte differs again from the author of *Evelina*. In her more mature experience of the world and society she has no awe or obsequious reverence for her royal acquaintances. Fanny's " sweet Queen " becomes " the old Queen whose death would not be much regretted "; " the excellent King " becomes " the unfortunate King " whose " mind is quite gone," and Princess Charlotte who is " quite beautiful " becomes Princess Charlotte who is " neither graceful nor elegant, and extremely spread for her age." With all her faults Lady Charlotte kept her head when she was in the presence of royalty, and indeed exercised her critical faculties in this connection far more skilfully than when she was surrounded by her society friends, who all appear rather colourless, or than when she was admiring the pictures of Carlo Dolci in Italian galleries or gazing at the beauties of Italian scenery. After a ruthless pruning of the heavy and elaborate accessories in the diary, one can detach a very bold and peculiarly realistic portrait of the Regent's unfortunate wife, to whom Lady Charlotte was a lady-in-waiting. The curious thing is that whenever she is describing or criticizing or pitying her royal mistress Lady Charlotte's style seems entirely to alter ; the soaring enthusiasm vanishes, the cloying verbiage ceases, and we get trenchant phrases, acute observations and sound judgments. Though a critical she was a loyal and helpful friend to the Princess of Wales, and she certainly provides the most intimate information with regard to the extraordinary treatment of George IV's wife that has been furnished from any source.

We may therefore pass over a great deal of the diary in order to collect some of the passages which gives us this close view of Caroline of Brunswick, not because she is either an interesting or important historical personage, but because it shows off the diarist at her best. Only a small selection can be made from the many pages of conversations, confidences and revelations which the diary contains.

Sometimes there is a series of exalted sentiments in what she (the Princess) says and does that quite astonishes me and makes me rub my eyes and open my ears to know if it is the same person who condescends to talk low nonsense and sometimes even gross ribaldry. One day I think her all perfection—another I know not what to think. The tissue of her character is certainly more uneven than that of any other person. One day there is tinsel and tawdry—another worsted—another silk and satin, another gold and jewels—another *de la boue, de la crasse—que dirai-je ?*

No appetite for converse, no strength of nerves, no love for any individual who might be present could possibly enable any person who was not royal (they certainly are gifted with supernatural strength) to sit for five or six hours at table and keep vigil till morning light. Some one I remember present that night ventured to hint that morning was at hand. " Ah " said the Princess " God, He knows when we may all meet again—to tell you God's truth, when I am happy and comfortable I could sit on for ever."

The Princess gave a long and detailed account of her marriage . . . " a protestant Princess must be found—they fixed upon the Prince's cousin. To tell you God's truth I always hated it but to oblige my father, anything. But the first moment I saw my *futur* and Lady Jersey together I knew how it all was and I said to myself ' Oh, very well.' "

The old ourang outang came to dinner—more free and easy and detestable than ever. Then Her Royal Highness sang—squall—squall ! Why invite me ? After supper she continued the complaints. I cannot describe how wearisome how unavailing and injudicious the subjects of her conversation now are in general.

In regard to myself I have laid down a rule of conduct towards Her Royal Highness from which I am determined not to depart. This determination is never to give advice ; because I am quite aware that it might do me much harm and would do her no good.

The Princess is always seeking amusement and unfortunately often at the expense of prudence and propriety. She cannot endure a dull person ; she has often said to me " I can forgive any fault but that " ; and the anathema she frequently pronounces on such persons is " Mine Gott ! dat is the dullest person Gott Almighty ever did born ! "

All the time I staid and walked with her Royal Highness she cried and spoke with a desolation of heart that really made me sorry for her ; and yet at the end of our conversation, poor soul, she smiled and an expression of resignation even of content irradiated her countenance as she said " I will go on hoping for happier days. Do you think I may ? " . . . This Princess is a most peculiar person—she alternately makes me dislike and like her.

I dined at Kensington. There was no one besides the Princess except Lady ——. We dined off mutton and onions and I thought Lady —— would have *dégobbiléd* with the coarseness of the food and the horror of seeing the Princess eat to satiety.

When we arrived at the Opera to the Princess's and all her attendants' infinite surprise we saw the Regent placed between the Emperor and the King of Prussia and all the minor Princes in a box to the right. " God save the King " was performing when the Princess entered and consequently she did not sit down. . . . As soon as the air was over the whole pit turned round and applauded *her*. We who were in attendance on H.R.H. intreated her to rise and make a curtsey but she sat immoveable and at last turning round said " My dear, Punch's wife is nobody when Punch is present." We all laughed but still thought her wrong not to acknowledge the compliment paid her ; but she was right as the sequel will prove. " We shall be hissed " said Sir W. Gell. " No, no " again replied the Princess with infinite good humour " I know my business better than to take the morsel out of my husband's mouth ; I am not to seem to know that the applause is meant for me till they call my name." The Prince seemed to verify her words for he got up and bowed to the audience. . . . The fact was the Prince took the applause to himself . . . when the Opera was finished, the Prince and his supporters were applauded but not enthusiastically ; and scarcely had he left the box when the people called for the Princess and gave her a very warm applause. She then went forward and made three curtseys and hastily withdrew. I believe she acted perfectly right throughout the evening ; but everybody tells a different story and thinks differently.

After dinner her Royal Highness made a wax figure as usual and gave it an admirable addition of large horns ; then took three pins out of her garment and stuck them through and through and put the figure to roast and melt at the fire. If it was not too melancholy to have to do with this I could have died of laughing. Lady —— says the Princess indulges in this amusement whenever there are no strangers at table and she thinks H.R.H. really has a superstitious belief that destroying this effigy of her husband will bring to pass the destruction of his royal person.

And later when she meets her in Genoa :

> She (the Princess) had no rouge on, wore tidy shoes, was grown rather thinner and looked altogether uncommonly well. The first person who opened the door to me was the one whom it was impossible to mistake hearing what is reported ; six feet high, a magnificent head of black hair, pale complexion, mustachios which reach from here to London. Such is the *stork* (Pergami). But of course I only appeared to take him for an upper servant. The Princess immediately took me aside and told me all that was true and a great deal that was not.

> The same decoction of mingled falsehood and truth is in use as heretofore.

> I cannot conceive why H.R.H. invites the latter little sneaking fellow who is a decided enemy to her and a spy set over her by the Prince. I was very glad that her dress, conversation and manners happened by some lucky chance to be all perfectly proper so that unless Monsieur D told lies he could not say anything was improper.

Of course we get all the details about the Princess's houses and exploits, the political significance of the position and her visits from Brougham and Whitbread and finally the trial; though the account of the latter is in a separate memorandum. But whether with the Princess of Wales or her daughter Princess Charlotte, Lady Charlotte is always on her guard. " There is no believing," she says, " what these royal people say ; and I verily believe they do not know what they believe themselves."

Passing now to other parts of the diary, when Lady Charlotte sentimentalizes about herself, we get passages like this :

> The heart which acknowledges within it a hopeless vacuum, which has been disappointed in all its expectations has burnt out its affections to the very ashes and from nourishing every feeling to excess is forced to subside in the fixed calmness of indifference and be content with common life, such a heart must surely perish from inanition if it aspire not to the life to come.

When she misses seeing Thomas à Becket's tomb at Canterbury she says :

> I regretted not being able yesterday to visit the shrine of Thomas à Becket at Canterbury where hypocrisy paid the price of its vice by blood, and superstition trembled in its turn for having dared to usurp the power of Heaven to punish.

We get many " melancholy reflexions " on her " unhappy existence," although the richness of the style on these occasions prevents us from fully understanding what the precise causes were.

In the diary she relates a number of anecdotes, generally second-hand, and there are constant little insinuations of scandal. One or two sketches are given of people, amongst others one of Lady Caroline Lamb, with whom she makes friends.

Many letters from various correspondents besides the Princess of Wales are interspersed throughout the pages of the diary. Sir Walter Scott was among the friends who wrote to her.

In 1814 Lady Charlotte was abroad. In France, Switzerland and Italy her life seems to be occupied with sight-seeing, a certain amount of reading and collecting from acquaintances, news and gossip. " Early this morning I went about to gather up the news." There is a great deal about Madame de This, La Marquise de That and the Duchess of The Other, but it is almost impossible to read about them. Our eye only wanders across the page to catch references to the unfortunate Caroline. She keeps up a correspondence with the Princess and she meets her again in Italy.

The diary, though very full when she writes in it, has breaks. She accounts for one of them thus :

> This last week one of my overcoming periods of returning sadness stopped my pen. Suspense, astonishment, dismay have all combined to make me feel that common daily notes were trivial and insufficient to express my state of mind.

But as usual we cannot gather the precise reason of this desperate state of mind.

Lady Charlotte does not blossom out as a novelist till after the date on which the diary is concluded. But in 1818 she says :

> I am glad that people of *ton* have taken to writing novels ; it is an excellent amusement for them and also for the public.

Lady Charlotte died at the age of 86, but not " lone and neglected " as some of the biographical notices of her pretend. Her daughters were with her.

Her diary and letters were re-edited by A. Francis Steuart in 1908 without Mr. Bury's original notes and with many of the blanks, left for names, filled in.

LIEUTENANT SWABEY

THE diary kept by Lieutenant Swabey in the Peninsular War (from 1811 to the battle of Vittoria in 1813, when he was wounded) is a good example of a soldier's diary, which in addition to technical military details contains descriptions of scenery and places and some rather humorous comments. The cheerful disposition of the young diarist of 22 is quite apparent in the full entries.

We are reminded of Teonge when he says on the journey out:

> The first ceremony was that the whole dinner with the two servants and myself went bodily to leeward on the floor. I kept fast hold of a chicken by the leg and we fell to without knives and forks. I think I have not laughed so much since I left Christchurch.

He enters the books he reads, which include Dryden, Otway, a French book on Tacitus, and *Gil Blas*. He comments on the weather and tells of his riding and coursing and other amusements. But as with all soldiers on active service it is the periods of waiting and inaction that are the most trying.

> Rather troubled with a headache which was not deserved by idleness.

> I am apt to be desponding when too quiet and unemployed.

> There is such a complete vacancy and want of employment in our time that I cannot congratulate myself of a night on having done anything either useful or entertaining.

> I feel myself so constantly engaged in the daily pursuits of infantry officers in England viz : watching fishes swim under the bridge, throwing stones at pigs, etc. I am ashamed of it but have nothing else to do.

He goes out to try and find books at the priest's house, but only discovers " lives of saints, alias a compendium of ecclesiastical impositions." His descriptions of discomforts are amusing, but he always makes the best of them :

> The beds had counterpanes of satin with lace borders and fringe ornaments but oh comfort where are you gone ?

We get characteristic expressions of impatience at his superior officers :

> Confound all dilatory and spiritless generals !

The military engagements are fully described, and in many places there are additional notes inserted by him at a later date. He is much more concerned in giving a full account of the victory at Vittoria than in relating the incident of his being wounded in the knee. Afterwards, however, he chafes a good deal at being incapacitated, and finally he is invalided home.

We find on one occasion the usual diarist's misgiving at going on with his record :

I found this day as well as many of late so little worthy of being remembered that I begin to think of curtailing my plan of journal altogether and am the more tempted to do so from the habits that necessity imposes on us.

There is an account very modestly told of his trying to help a wounded French soldier: "I could not get the Frenchman out of my head." The whole incident shows a kindly and humanitarian disposition. His comments on the Portuguese are not complimentary; he very much prefers the Spaniards.

Swabey returned afterwards to active service, fought in the battle of Toulouse and also at Waterloo. But there is no further diary from his pen. In 1840 he settled in Prince Edward Island and died in 1872.

HENRY CRABB ROBINSON

IN Dr. Williams' Library in Gordon Square there are thirty-five volumes of Crabb Robinson's diaries, extending from the end of the eighteenth century to his death in 1867. He was a diarist with a big D and gave up a great part of his time to recording conversations and noting incidents in his intercourse with the many celebrated people with whom he was on friendly terms. In 1869 Thomas Sadler published three volumes giving extracts from the diary, reminiscences, and part of the correspondence. This selection has been condemned as meagre and inadequate. But a careful perusal of these volumes makes one doubt whether a further selection from the diaries would produce anything of great importance or interest except a few actual facts and dates. Crabb Robinson is described in his epitaph: "Friend and associate of Goethe and Wordsworth, Wieland and Coleridge, Flaxman and Blake, Clarkson and Charles Lamb; he honoured and loved the Great and noble in their thoughts and characters." He was undoubtedly a very sympathetic friend and had a great social gift; he was a famous conversationalist, and his breakfast parties rivalled those of Samuel Rogers.

After early experiences as a journalist he practised as a barrister long enough to acquire a modest competence, and he then appears to have devoted his life to social intercourse with men of note and became a satellite of men of genius. He was therefore in a very favourable position to observe and record; and with painstaking industry he produced not only a voluminous diary but reminiscences written subsequently amplifying and explaining

HENRY CRABB ROBINSON

many of the diary entries. The probably very unfair misgiving seems to force itself on a reader from time to time—was Crabb Robinson an awful bore ? With all his gifts and opportunities we are anyhow inclined to think that Crabb Robinson lacked the finer perceptions and the talent of pen portraiture. There is hardly a passage in which he brings the personality of the interesting characters such as Flaxman, Lamb and Wordsworth before the reader with any striking vividness. There is a mass of quite commonplace detail, but no flash of light, no telling or discriminating character sketch. His notes are immeasurably inferior to those of Caroline Fox. The letters and reminiscences would carry us further no doubt than the actual diary. But it is with the diary that we are here concerned. In it there are a good many literary judgments of his own and of his friends. But the immense collection of celebrities—for to those above mentioned must be added many others such as Hazlitt, de Quincey, Carlyle, Landor, Madame de Staël, etc., etc.—remains a list of names, not one of them really lives even though many of their opinions are related, and he cannot help noting characteristic features such as Lamb's puns. Daily contact even with the great cannot of course constantly produce illuminating observations. Character estimates of any value must be the result of collected impressions and summaries. Conscientious daily diary notes are not the best medium for giving the living impression of others unless there is special skill and perception behind them. This sort of entry, for instance, does not arrest a reader:

> In the evening I stepped over to Lamb and sat with him from ten to eleven. He was very chatty and pleasant. Pictures and poetry were the subjects of our talk.

> A delightful breakfast with Milnes—a party of eight among whom were Rogers, Carlyle, who made himself very pleasant indeed, Moore and Landor. The talk very good, equally divided. Talleyrand's recent death and the poet Blake were the subjects.

> Venice impresses me more agreeably than it did seven years ago. The monuments of its faded glory are deeply affecting. We called on the Tickners and Wordsworth accompanied them to hear Tasso chanted by gondoliers.

But although there is a great deal of this sort of style, it would be unfair not to recognize merit in many parts of the diary. He is not invariably in sympathetic agreement, drinking in words of wisdom. With Godwin in 1815 he has a hot political discussion.

> I spent the evening by appointment with Godwin. The Taylors were there. We talked politics not very comfortably. Godwin and I all but quarrelled ; both were a little angry and equally offensive to each other. Godwin was quite impassioned in asserting his hope that Buonaparte may be successful in the war. He declares his wish that all the allies that enter France now may perish and affirmed that no man who did not abandon all moral principles and love of liberty could wish otherwise. I admitted that in general foreigners have no right to interfere in the government of a country but in this case I consider foreign armies as coming to the relief of the people against the oppressions of domestic soldiers ; and in this lies the justice of the war.

With Wordsworth he walks and talks and travels. He discusses his poetry and reports his opinions. In 1816 we find him on foot and Wordsworth on horseback having a long walk in the rain.

> In the close and interesting conversation we kept up Mr. Wordsworth was not quite attentive to the road and we lost our way. . . . He is an eloquent speaker and he talked upon his own art and his own works very feelingly and very profoundly but I cannot state more than a few intelligible results for I own that much of that he said was above my comprehension [then follow notes with regard to his poems].

They travelled together in Switzerland in 1820 and in Italy in 1837. Wordsworth dedicated *Memorials of a Tour in Italy* to him. Here is a description of Shelley :

> 1817. I went to Godwin's. Mr. Shelley was there. I had never seen him before. His youth and a resemblance to Southey particularly in his voice raised a pleasing impression which was not altogether destroyed by his conversation though it is vehement, and arrogant and intolerant.

Crabb Robinson was one of the few who recognized the genius of Keats. He notes :

> There is a force wildness and originality in the works of this young poet which, if his perilous journey to Italy does not destroy him, promise to place him at the head of our next generation of poets.

Out of his gallery of portraits we should choose the picture of Blake as being the best. It begins :

> Shall I call Blake artist, genius, mystic or madman ? Probably he is all.
>
> I found him in a small room which seems to be both a working room and a bedroom. Nothing could exceed the squalid air both of the apartment and his dress ; yet there is diffused over him an air of natural gentility.

And he gives the substance of several conversations. Of Goethe there is a great deal when he revisits Weimar in 1829. He writes about the lectures of Hazlitt and Coleridge which he attends, but as Sir Sidney Colvin says " he lacked the touch which should have made his record live." It is impossible to go on picking out passages about the host of celebrities. The diary and reminiscences may be a more or less fruitful hunting ground for their biographers. Our object here is to find Crabb Robinson himself, and this fortunately we can do.

We can pass over his legal experiences, his careful recording of fees he receives ; we can pass over his travels, his adventures with a tipsy man and with a thief in the Strand, and his first journey in a train.

His meeting in the coach with Incledon, the singer, who " sang in a sort of song whisper some melodies " to him, is entertaining, as also his description of the wholesale christening of a large number of babies in a Manchester church, when he " could not repress the irreverent thought that being in the metropolis of manufactures the aid of steam and machinery might be brought in." We need only mention his love of playgoing and his admiration for Mrs. Siddons. Like a true diarist he notes little details such as a visit to the dentist, " who put in a natural tooth in the place of one I swallowed yesterday." In the thirty-five volumes there is probably much more of the private particulars which editors think it right to omit.

But there are two passages of self-analysis and introspection which reveal the man, and probably many more of these would be found in the full manuscript.

Surveying the year at the end of 1815 he says :

> I do not now fear poverty. I am not nor ever was desirous of riches but my wants do not perhaps increase in proportion to my means. My brother Thomas makes it a reproach to me that I do not indulge myself more. This I do not think a duty and shall probably not make a practice. I hope I shall not contract habits of parsimony.

In 1816 he analyses his own disposition.

> Sometimes I regret a want of sensibility in my nature but when such cases of perverted intensity of feeling are brought to my observation, I rejoice at my neutral apathetic character. . . . The older I grow the more I am satisfied on prudential grounds with the constitution of my sensitive nature. I am persuaded that there are very few persons who suffer so little pain of all kinds as I do ; and if the absence of vice be the beginning of virtue so the absence of suffering is the beginning of enjoyment. I must confess, however, that I think my own nature an object of felicitation rather than applause.

This passage, which is probably quite just, gives a clue to his apparent failure to detect the finer shades of feeling and the somewhat superficial character of his criticism of others.

But he has his moments of depression. In 1820 he writes:

> It quite affects me to remark the early decay of my faculties. I am so lethargic that I shall soon be unable to discharge the ordinary business of life; and as to all pretentions to literary taste this I must lay aside entirely. How wretched is that state, at least how low is it when a man is content to renounce all claim to respect and endeavours only to enjoy himself! Yet I am reduced to this. When my vivacity is checked by age and I have lost my companionable qualities I shall then have nothing left but a little good nature to make me tolerable even to my old acquaintances.

After writing this he lived, however, for forty-six years with his faculties unimpaired. At the end of this year he notes

> a deeper conviction than I ever had of the insignificance of my own character.

His last words at the end of 1823 are:

> As to myself I have become more and more desirous to be religious but seem to be further off than ever. Whenever I draw near, the negative side of the magnet works and I am pushed back by an invisible power.

On New Year's Eve, 1836, he sits up late, and

> when the year expired I was reading Dibdin's "Life"—a significant occupation for in idle amusement and faint pleasure was the greater part of the now closing year spent. Such are my frivolous habits that I can hardly expect to live for any profitable purpose either as respects myself or others.

But under this he notes in 1854 with some self-complacency:

> I wrote this sincerely in my sixty first year. My life has been more actively and usefully spent since I have been an elderly man.

On religion he writes in 1839:

> Oh how earnestly do I hope that I may one day be able to believe! But I feel the faith must be *given* me; I cannot gain it for myself. I will try, but I doubt my power energetically to will anything so pure and elevated.

Crabb Robinson's old age must certainly have been the most remarkable part of his life. He kept his diary fully and regularly up to January 31, 1867, five days before his death at the age of 92, so he is the oldest diarist of whom we have a record. At 86 we find him climbing to the top of an omnibus (not by the spacious staircase of the modern omnibus but by the narrow vertical ladder of sixty years ago). At 90 he goes to the play and enjoys *Twelfth Night*, and only at 91 when he goes for the last time does he confess he had little pleasure owing to "half deafness and dimness of sight."

At a dinner when he was 87 he notes:

I felt at my ease and from habit can repeat my old stories still with some effect. And I now perceive why old men repeat their stories in company. It is absolutely necessary to their retaining their station in society. When they originate nothing they can profit their juniors by recollections of the past.

He is able to take quite a detached point of view, and notes the little lapses and failures of age, so to speak, from outside. On his ninetieth birthday he writes:

My birthday. To-day I complete my ninetieth year. When people hear of my age they affect to doubt my veracity and call me a wonder. It is unusual I believe for persons of this age to retain possession of their faculties. The Germans have an uncomplimentary saying " Weeds don't spoil."

Undismayed at 91 he begins " a new clean volume " of his diary, although he adds:

The probability is that I shall never finish this volume. If alive, I shall not be able to do so.

Nearing the end he has his occasional depressions, as when he says:

I awoke early as is now usual with me; and I was in a musing mood, ruminating in an old-fashioned way. All my musings turned to self-reproach. Were I a man of sensibility or acuteness I know not what would become of me, I could not endure myself.

And later:

To-day I have felt really well and I hope that when *the* hour—the last hour—comes I shall not disgrace it.

In the very last entry he begins writing about an essay " on the qualifications of the present age for criticism," but he leaves off in the middle of a sentence with the words : " But I feel incapable to go on."

Crabb Robinson's diary has been quoted times without number by biographers and essayist writers on the early nineteenth century poets. Nevertheless our contention would still appear to hold good that the diarist rather than the subjects on which he writes is the study which attracts the most.

MARY SHELLEY

HOGG in his Life of Shelley tells us that Shelley " kept a regular journal of his daily life recording day by day all that he did read and wrote." Perhaps this diary was little more than brief memoranda, anyhow it does not seem to be in existence. Mary kept a journal of their travels, beginning in 1814, in which Shelley made several entries at first, but the latter part is entirely hers. This was published under the title of *Journal of a Six Weeks' Tour*. But after this Mary continued to keep a diary practically to the end of her life, and a large number of extracts from it are published in her biography by Mrs. Julian Marshall.

Had Mary been the wife of an obscure man it is improbable that any extracts from her diary would have ever found their way into print. There is nothing at all remarkable about it. Nevertheless, from the brief record of their wanderings and occupations, side light is cast on the poet's curious and uncomfortable domestic circumstances.

Mary was a child of 17 when she started off on her adventures. It is impossible to enter into the involved relationships of the various women who figure in Shelley's life's story. Harriet is in the background, Jane Clairmont accompanies them, and Mary's parents the Godwins obtrude into the picture incessantly. One or two of Shelley's entries at the beginning put a little life and spirit into the record, which disappear when Mary alone is responsible for the diary.

(Shelley.) In the evening Capt. Davidson came and told us that a fat lady had arrived who said I had run away with her daughter ; it was Mrs. Godwin. Jane spent the night with her mother.

It may be explained for those who are not closely conversant with the story, that Jane was Mrs. Godwin's daughter and Mrs. Godwin was Mary's step-mother.

(Shelley.) Mary is not well and all are tired of wheeled machines. Shelley is in a jocosely horrible mood.

Jane's strange vagaries are noted ; Shelley calls on Harriet, " who is certainly an odd creature " ; wanderings in Switzerland and Italy, discomforts, money troubles, and in almost every entry the literature they consumed. The diary is written in the present tense and when Mary takes up the pen we get all the details about Shelley's day, such as :

Shelley very unwell—Shelley's odd dream—Shelley and Jane go out as usual—Shelley goes out and sits in another room till 5—Shelley goes to sleep ; at 8 Shelley rises and goes out—Shelley reads Livy—In the evening Shelley, Clara and Hogg sleep—[and so on].

And then casually, as if of no more importance than what

Shelley was reading or doing, comes the birth of Mary's child, and a week or so later the following entries concealing a tragedy which she evidently has not time to enlarge on :

March 4. Read, talk, nurse. Shelley reads the Life of Chaucer. Hogg comes in the evening and sleeps.

March 5. Shelley and Clara go to town. Hogg here all day. Read Corinne and nurse my baby. In the evening talk. Shelley finishes the Life of Chaucer.

March 6. Find my baby dead. Send for Hogg. Talk. A miserable day. In the evening read Fall of the Jesuits. Hogg sleeps here.

March 9. Read and talk. Still think about my little baby. 'Tis hard indeed for a mother to lose a child . . . Hogg stays all night. Read Fontenelle Plurality of Worlds.

March 13. Shelley and Clara go to town, stay at home and think of my little dead baby.

March 19. Dream that my little baby came to life again.

This thread of tragedy under the high intellectual effort of keeping up to the level of her adored but evidently callous idol, by learning Greek and reading every book under the sun, is brought out more vividly in these curt, bald entries than the later tragedy of Shelley's death on which she writes pages and pages.

From the point of view of diary writing it is interesting to note that Mary, while Shelley lived, absorbed herself in him and only jotted down the day's events to remind her of every one of his movements and doings. After he died she left off noting daily events, and poured herself into her diary in immensely long rapturous ejaculatory self-communings. In her melancholy solitude she made her diary her companion. But it is almost impossible to read much of this sort of thing :

Mine own Shelley ! the sun knows of none to be likened to you—brave wise noble-hearted, full of learning tolerance and love.

My heart shakes with its suppressed emotions and I flag beneath the thoughts that oppress me.

Oh Shelley dear lamented beloved ! help me, raise me support me, let me not feel ever thus fallen and degraded ! my imagination is dead, my genius lost my energies sleep. Why am I not beneath that weed grown tower ?

My brow is sadly trenched, the blossom of youth faded. My mind gathers wrinkles. What will become of me ?

These are only short sentences from the long pages, and the long pages that are printed are only extracts up to 1840 from the whole diary. It is fair to say it was never intended for publication. It no doubt gave Mary great consolation, and it is therefore pathetic. But pathos hardly reaches a reader when a diarist without any striking personality, or real intellectual perception, lifts all restraints to this extent. There are entries about her friendship with Tom Moore, her quarrel with Jane, her writing, and in 1838 she makes a lengthy self-examination which is not very interesting. She died in 1851.

ADMIRAL COCKBURN

ON his return from service in the American war, Rear-Admiral Sir George Cockburn was ordered early in 1815 to hold himself in readiness off Spithead, war having broken out again with France. In August he received orders to hoist his flag on H.M.S. *Northumberland*, and to convey General Buonaparte to St. Helena.

On this voyage Cockburn kept a daily diary which is exclusively concerned with his conversations with and the doings of the fallen Emperor. It is an example of a diary in which the special object for which it was kept entirely absorbs everything. Cockburn probably was not naturally a diary writer, but the exceptional circumstances induced him to make notes during this voyage, and these notes therefore contain none of the personal touches common to most private diaries. He writes clearly and concisely, but his position in command prevents him from extracting from his eminent prisoner such reflections and expressions of opinion as might have been elicited by some one in a position of less responsibility, nor has he sufficient literary ability to rise fully to the height of his great opportunity.

In any detailed analysis of this brief journal we should soon find ourselves discussing Napoleon and not Cockburn. The conversations are all reminiscent: the battle of Waterloo, the preparations for the invasion of England, the marriage with Marie Louise, the characters of the rulers of Europe, the murder of the Duc d'Enghien and many other episodes in the past—all quite matter of fact, no personal or philosophic rumination over the ex-Emperor's dramatic change of fate.

Buonaparte is occasionally sulky and morose, but this generally seems to be when the weather is bad. Otherwise he talks away, plays chess and cards at night, and appears to be quite cheerful.

ADMIRAL COCKBURN

We will give an entry describing a typical day :

On Aug. 19. Our weather was moderate with a pleasant breeze from the N.W. General Buonaparte since on board the *Northumberland* has kept nearly the same hours : he gets up late (between ten and eleven) : he then has his breakfast (of meat and wine) in his bedroom, and continues there in his *déshabillé* until he dresses for dinner, generally between three and four in the afternoon : he then comes out of his bed cabin and either takes a short walk on deck or plays a game of chess with one of his Generals until the dinner hour which is five o'clock. At dinner he generally eats and drinks a great deal and talks but little ; he prefers meats of all kinds highly dressed and never touches vegetables. After dinner he generally walks for about an hour or hour and a half and it is during these walks that I usually have the most free and pleasant conversations with him. About eight he quits the deck and we then make up a game of cards for him in which he seems to engage with considerable pleasure and interest until about ten when he retires to his bedroom and I believe almost immediately goes to bed. Such a life of inactivity with the quantity and description of his food makes me fear he will not retain his health through the voyage ; he however as yet does not appear to suffer any inconvenience from it.

We get a little of Cockburn himself in the following entries, which show his determination not to stand any nonsense from his distinguished passenger.

Aug. 10. It is clear he is still inclined to act the Sovereign occasionally but I cannot allow it, and the sooner therefore he becomes convinced it is not to be admitted the better.

Aug. 13. I did not see much of General Buonaparte throughout this day as owing to his appearing inclined to try to assume again improper consequence I was purposely more than usual distant with him and therefore though we exchanged common salutations and *high looks* nothing passed between us worth noticing.

Aug. 14. The General and myself were again distant and high with each other, though perfectly civil—at least he has been as much so as his nature (which is not very polished) seems capable of.

The next day is Buonaparte's birthday. The Admiral drinks his health and the civility is appreciated and relations become easier again. The last entry is dated October 22, from St. Helena, where the Admiral leaves us with a picture of the Conqueror of half Europe playing at whist with the ladies " for sugar plums."

The Admiral's secretary kept a copy of the journal. The MS. was found and printed in 1888.

LADY MALCOLM

SIR PULTENEY MALCOLM succeeded Admiral Cockburn in the naval command at St. Helena in June, 1816. He was there for a year. *A Diary of St. Helena* contains entries during that period made by his wife. The diary is written with great restraint in the third person in almost an official tone, and contains hardly any feminine touches. Moreover, interviews are described at which she herself was not present and which therefore were taken down from her husband's dictation. The acrimonious disputes between Buonaparte and Sir Hudson Lowe, the Governor, are recorded, and in one instance the whole dialogue is given in full. The writer's bias does not appear to be on the Governor's side, and this can be accounted for by the fact that Sir Hudson Lowe did not manage to be on particularly good terms even with her husband, the Admiral. There are many of the same sort of reminiscent remarks from Buonaparte as in the previous diary. He is very friendly in his intercourse with Lady Malcolm, and on her departure gives her a valuable piece of china, remarking that "Ladies had more compassionate hearts than men for an object of misfortune."

Lady Malcolm's graphic description of Buonaparte's appearance may be quoted in full:

His hair of a brown black thin on the forehead, cropped but not thin in the neck and rather a dirty look : light blue or grey eyes—a capacious forehead—high nose—short upper lip ; good white even teeth but small (he rarely shows them) round chin ; the lower part of his face very full—pale complexion—particularly short neck. Otherwise his figure appeared well proportioned but had become too fat ; a thick short hand with taper fingers and beautiful nails and a well shaped leg and foot. He was dressed in an old threadbare green coat with green velvet collar and cuffs . . . a silver star of the Legion of Honour white waistcoat and breeches ; white silk stockings and shoes with oval gold buckles. She was struck with the kindness of his expression, so contrary to the fierceness she had expected. She saw no trace of great ability, his countenance seemed rather to indicate goodness : at a second interview she remarked that it would change with his humour. The Admiral allowed that his manners were pleasing but would not agree that they were in the least graceful.

The diary, edited by Sir A. Wilson, was published in 1899.

HENRY MATTHEWS

THE *Diary of an Invalid*, published in 1819, had a considerable success and went into several editions. Byron and many other people of the time expressed their appreciation of it. Henry Matthews was a Fellow of King's College, Cambridge. He left England in 1817 on account of his health, and kept a journal of two years' travel in Portugal, Italy, Switzerland, and France—a journal, he says, " written to amuse the hours of indisposition without any idea of publication." However, on his return he was persuaded by his friends to publish it ; and though tempted at first to work it up " in a more serious and sustained style of composition," he eventually kept the journal just as he had written it with very little alteration.

In the days before Ruskin and Hare, when guide-books were no doubt dry and imperfect, one can imagine that such a book as this was welcome. It is written without method or any didactic learning and gives the daily impressions of a cultivated mind on art and nature without any sort of affectation or pose. A few little personal touches and health notes which occur naturally in diary writing add considerably to the charm of the author's simple style, and his own opinions, often very decided, never jar. Travelling in those days was still really travelling and not whirling blindly from one populous centre to another. He describes his method in Italy :

> Left Rome at sunrise—My carriage is a sort of buggy on four wheels drawn by a single horse. My bargain with my voiturier is to be taken to Florence in six days and to be fed and lodged on the road ; for which I am to give him twenty dollars. The pace is tiresome enough at first ; for the horse seldom quits his walk even for an equivocal amble ; but if you have no particular object in getting on you soon become reconciled to this. Besides it affords ample leisure for surveying the country and gratifying your curiosity at any particular point where you wish to deviate from the road ; for you may easily overtake your carriage.

On travelling alone he says :

> I doubt, all things considered, whether it be not better to travel by yourself than with a companion. It is true you may not always please yourself, but you may at least bear with your own ill humour. If you could select the very companion you would wish, it might alter the case ; though it seems fated that all travelling companions should fall out ; and history is full of instances from Paul and Barnabas down to Walpole and Gray—So I jog on, contented at least if not happy, to be alone.

His illness occasionally interferes with his enjoyment:

> My health grows worse and worse! Constant irritation—Day without rest—night without sleep ;—at least sleep without repose and rest without recreation. If life with health and wealth and all "appliances and means to boot" be nothing but vanity and vexation of spirit what is it alas! when deprived of all these embellishments?

And he sometimes falls into a philosophic vein:

> Those are the wisest and happiest who can pass through life as a play; who—without making a farce of it and turning everything into ridicule—or running into the opposite extreme of tragedy—consider the whole period from the cradle to the coffin as a well bred comedy; and maintain a cheerful smile to the very last scene. For what is happiness but a Will o' the Wisp, a delusion, a terra incognita—in pursuit of which thousands are tempted out of the harbour of tranquility to be tossed about, the sport of the winds of passion and the waves of disappointment, to be wrecked, perhaps, at last on the rocks of despair ;—unless they be provided with the sheet anchor of religion—the only anchor that will hold in all weathers.

In Rome he sees the Pope from afar only:

> Ash Wednesday. Ceremony in the Pope's Chapel—sprinkling of ashes on the heads of the cardinals—Mass as usual—I have declined being presented to His Holiness thinking with the Duke of Hamilton that when the kissing of the toe is left out the ceremony is deprived of all amusement.

The opera at Naples:

> Visited the opera for the first time. Of all the stupid things in the world a serious opera is perhaps the most stupid and the opera to-night formed no exception to this observation. The theatre is, I believe, the largest in Europe, and it is certainly too large for the singers whose voices sound like penny trumpets on Salisbury Plain.

The many descriptions of scenery, buildings, pictures, etc., of which the diary of course is chiefly composed, are never affected or laboured. He brings them in naturally as he passes, and his admirations are expressed with convincing restraint. We will just give one instance of a scene from Fiesole:

> There is something delightfully pleasant in the voluptuous languor which the soft air of an Italian landscape occasions; and then the splendour of an Italian sunset! I shall never forget the impression made on me by a particular evening. The sun had just gone down leaving the sky dyed with the richest tints of crimson—while the virgin snows on the distant mountains were suffused with blushes of "celestial rosy red"; when from an opposite quarter of the heavens there seemed to rise another sun as large as bright as glowing as that which had just departed. It was the moon at the full ;—and the illusion was so complete, that it required some minutes to convince me that I was not in Fairy Land.

He breaks off occasionally into literary criticisms and appreciations. For instance, he visits Ferney, which naturally causes him to write a good deal about Voltaire. He does not like him, and concludes his remarks as follows :

> His physiognomy, which is said to have been a combination of the eagle and the monkey was illustrative of the character of his mind. If the soaring wing and piercing eye of the eagle opened to him all the regions of knowledge it was only to collect materials for the gratification of that apish disposition which seems to have delighted in grinning with a malicious spirit of mockery at the detected weaknesses and infirmities of human nature. Though a man may often rise the wiser yet I believe none ever rose the *better* from the perusal of Voltaire.

His wanderings last from September 6, 1817, to June 10, 1819. He passes with his seeing eye from one place to another, a little weary sometimes of the constant moving and packing.

> Packing up ; this is a melancholy part of a travellers life ; to arrive and hear no welcome—to depart and hear no farewell—or if he remain stationary for a time to be called away just as he is beginning to form new connexions.

Matthews was no egotist, on the contrary he travelled to forget himself and his ailments. But a refined and charming nature can be felt behind the record. He was afterwards given a judicial appointment in Ceylon, where he died in 1828, at the age of thirty-eight.

Another nineteenth-century diary of travel may just be mentioned here by way of contrast. Edwin Rickman published *The Diary of a Solitaire* in 1835 with a long preface and copious notes. It is an account of travel in Switzerland, but his observations are very trite and commonplace. The only interest lies in the notes, which contain biographical reminiscences and an account of the Society of Friends, of which he was a member.

HENRY FYNES CLINTON

IN 1854, the Rev. Charles Fynes Clinton published a volume entitled *The Literary Remains of Henry Fynes Clinton*, which consists of part of an autobiography and of a journal kept from 1819 to 1852. In his desire to do justice to his brother's great scholarship and piety, he has eliminated so far as he could matters of a personal nature because, he says, " they would be uninteresting to the reader." He made, of course, a very great mistake. It is a glaring instance of a diary being spoilt by editorship. However much we may be amazed at the range and profundity of Henry Fynes Clinton's literary and classical studies, and however much we may admire the high moral tone of his religious views, he is removed from us and presented as somebody of an abnormal type by the unfortunate cutting of all the little humdrum and perhaps trifling incidents which are the human links which make readers conscious of the living man in a diarist. Luckily there are chinks in the shutters, and we do catch glimpses now and again of the more domestic and lighter side of the austere scholar.

His father, Dr. Fynes Clinton, rector of Cromwell, was a direct descendant of the Earl of Lincoln,[1] who died in 1616. Henry was born in 1781, and was educated at Westminster and Christ Church, Oxford. There was an idea of his taking orders, but this was abandoned, and he entered Parliament at the age of 26. He never took to political life, he was never interested in it, and he never spoke. His talents and ambitions were gradually turned into another channel, and although he remained in Parliament for nineteen years and kept up a more or less regular attendance, his absorbing interest was centred in his scholastic and literary studies. The only parliamentary references in the diary are the bare record of divisions. A few quotations may be given to show his views on this subject.

1819. My love of letters begins to revive which has been dormant or extinct for some time past and an inward alacrity and cheerfulness consequently succeeds to that spirit of despondency and dissatisfaction which I have lately felt. I perceive that I can never be a public speaker ; but I observe that those whose lives have been passed as eminent public speakers have not in general the faculty of being good writers. . . . I will not because Nature has denied me the gifts of an orator unwisely overlook or neglect the advantages and the usefulness of that literature of which I may yet be capable.

In the same year his cousin the Duke of Newcastle encourages him to endeavour to get an official post in the Treasury. But he assures the Duke that he feels himself " destitute of the gift of public speaking and of the requisites for succeeding in debate." He entirely abandons the idea.

---

[1] Sir Henry Fynes, Lord Lincoln's son, took the name of Clinton. There is a most entertaining autobiographical fragment from his pen, which unfortunately cannot be included as a diary. In it he describes his second wife as having proved " so jealous so malincholy, so angry, pevish and capsius, so proud and conseated and so full of devilish and unreformable humours " (*Gentleman's Magazine*, 1772).

As to the higher official stations I am convinced that I am not fit for them : and as to the lower offices they are not fit for me.

And when in 1826 he leaves Parliament and surveys the past, he concludes :

> All these causes concurring have contributed to render me as far as public speaking is concerned an inefficient Member of Parliament.

But he finds ample compensation in his studies, which indeed were of so profound a nature as to occupy his time and thoughts almost exclusively, so that he looked on Parliament while he was in it merely as an interruption to his work. In fact, every interval that was not filled with reading and writing he came to regard not only with regret but with dread. Here are some of his reflections on the subject :

> 1820. While I am without literary object my mind preys on itself. When shall I be able to return to those studies and literary occupations which are so necessary to the health of my faculties ?
>
> 1822. As I advance in the experience of life the more am I convinced of the importance of these literary pursuits. They are in my case a duty.
>
> 1824. Now that my researches are brought to a kind of period I fear a recurrence of desponding thoughts. I dread a cessation of employment. When unemployed my mind recoils upon itself. Any uncomfortable circumstances press upon my attention and fill me with painful apprehensions. These are forgotten while my mind is exercised with some literary object.
>
> 1830. A literary object is necessary to me for my mind's health and for my moral safety.

And in 1834, after the completion of a bit of work, he holds a long discourse with himself in which this passage occurs :

> You devoted yourself to that kind of literary labour for which you were most fitted. You have found in those labours a refuge from cares and disquietudes of life and a salutary discipline for your own mind ; a security against the dangers of an unoccupied life. You are to give God thanks for His mercies not only in calling you to this course of literary labour and service but in supporting you under it during so many years. . . . What return are you to make to God for all His mercies who has brought you to your fifty fourth year in the possession of health and leisure and of your intellectual faculties ? Are you now to cast away all diligence and rest in inaction ? Assuredly not.

And consequently he buckles to again.

And of what did his studies consist ? His diary he calls a literary journal, and it consists mainly in a minute register of the books he read and the books he was writing. The works which occupy him are entirely classical and theological. He had a perfect knowledge of Latin and Greek, as well as French. In fact, many entries in the diary are in Greek or Latin or a mixture of both. The constant lists of the books he is reading show an amazing power of mastering not only well-known classics but obscure and recondite authors. Every book is mentioned, some analysed ; the time occupied over each one noted and the actual number of pages digested carefully entered. Page after page of this sort of thing may well make most readers feel ignorant and many readers rather dizzy. The list of books he is engaged in reading in 1819 is as follows :

Plato Repub :	pp 403
Aristot. Hist. Anim :	319
Isocratis	78
Josephi Bell. Jud. 439 ⎫ ⎬ —— Vita 81 ⎭	520
Hippocratis	1482
Eusebii Praep. Ev : 1100 ⎫ ⎬ —— Hist. E : 580 ⎭	1680
Theonis Progymn :	88
Callimachus	47
Dionysius Perieget :	40
Eustachii Schol :	326
Libanii :	217
Ciceronis Orat :	913
Curtius	452
Taciti Hist :	307
	6872

And there are many daily entries mentioning one or two particular books. Here is another example of a period :

1824. May 14. Since March 4 these studies : Marbre de Choiseul, in Mem. Acad. tom XLVIII : Scholia in Euripidis. Phoeniss. ed. Matthiae = pp 400 : Zenobius, pp 112 : Diogenianus pp 56 : Boeckh. de Tragicis Græcis : Theordoreti Sermones XII = pp 327 the first 254 folio pages of Scholia in Hermogenem ed. Ald. besides collecting materials from Syncellus, Sulpicius Severus and Scaligeri Eusebius for enlarging and correcting Fast. Hell. Appendix c. 18.

Whatever may be our feelings of amazement we have no feelings of envy. However, his *Fasti Hellenici* and his *Fasti Romani*, published between 1824 and 1850, had a considerable success and went into several editions. He was also engaged on a Scripture Chronology which began :

	years	B.C.
From Adam to the Flood	2256	3157
To the birth of Abraham	1002	2155

There seems to be very little in the way of literary appreciation in the journal. He is a sort of literary statistician. He is actually engaged at one time in calculating how many letters in each page are contained in Latin and Greek authors. However arid his studies were, nevertheless his industry was astonishing.

It was a bitter disappointment to Fynes Clinton when he was passed over for the appointment of Chief Librarian at the British Museum in 1827. His great desire for the post is apparent in the diary, but he does not indulge in one word of complaint when he fails. In fact, he strove successfully throughout his life against " the indulgence of vain regrets and an unsatisfied mind " which forms the subject of his prayers. These prayers, which need not be quoted, occur in many entries, sometimes in Latin. ("*His diebus graviter vexatus curis : Deo me commendo in quo spes omnis.*")

In 1809 he married Harriott Wylde, who died in the following year. In 1812 he married Katherine Majendie, daughter of the Bishop of Bangor, who helps him with the education of his children, to which he naturally attaches great importance. He gives a full account of her lessons with them, ending : " It is just that I should give this testimony to her maternal diligence." He refers frequently to his children, and there are several entries when he is surveying his life, in which there is a good deal of humanity and atmosphere.

For instance, when he leaves his house at Welwyn he writes :

My wife and children left Welwyn for London at twelve. I remained till four. After they were gone, I passed an hour in the walk in the field occupied with many sorrowful thoughts at the remembrance of the many satisfactions which God had granted me in that place, in past years. I offered up a separate prayer for each of the children. I returned to my own room, the scene of my literary labours ; I there again prayed earnestly for my dear son, whose instruction had now for four years and a half formed a part of my daily occupation in that apartment. When I seated myself for the last time in my own chair in the place which I had been used to occupy every day at eleven o'clock, I was for a little space completely overcome.

He made an entry in his diary on October 23, 1852, the day before he died, noting that he had received the Holy Sacrament.

Although the journal is preceded by autobiographical notes, it would not appear that Fynes Clinton contemplated its publication. Some interesting observations of his on diary writing are quoted in the Introduction.

MARY BROWNE

AS a girl of 14, Mary, the daughter of William Browne, of Tallentire Hall, in Cumberland, kept a diary for one year, in 1821, in order to record the visit she paid with her family to France. It is a child's diary of an entirely natural and unsensational character, and it would be hardly worthy of any special attention were it not for the fact that it is copiously illustrated. As a writer Mary was advanced for her age; she makes no grammatical errors and hardly uses any childish expressions. As an artist she was not so advanced, but she was far more original, and the drawings of the various types she saw, a *bonne*, a fisherwoman, a priest, soldiers, market women, etc., etc., show not only a childish faithful accuracy, but an enterprising spontaneity which is quite individual.

The amusing part of the actual diary is her hatred of France and the French, and her frantic desire to come home.

> The French people do not seem to think it wrong to cheat or lie or the least disgraceful to be told they do so.

> The French women have not good figures; the old women are very fat and the others are as flat as two boards . . . the French children are old fashioned, dull, grave and ugly; like little old women in their appearance.

> They say that the French like dancing better than anything and we heard it very much admired. For my part I think it is neither graceful nor pretty nor merry.

> Although one hears so much of French politeness I do not think that the French are near so polite as the English. The men make better bows etc. but in other things there is a kind of forwardness in the manners of the people that I cannot admire.

> I cannot tell what made me dislike France so *very* much; one reason I think was that I raised my expectations too high. I had heard so much of the *fine* climate, the *excellent* fruit and the *lively* people, that I was quite disappointed at the cold weather, the bad fruit and the *dull* people.

Uncomfortable lodgings, processions, fairs, fountains and various other sights and experiences are all simply and carefully related and illustrated.

The school is well described and various masters and mistresses who taught there, including the writing master, who

> used to sit down at one end of the table and never move; he had a curious squeaking voice. I could never find out what he did except mending pens and those were so bad that we were obliged to get Madame Crosnier to mend them afterwards.

Great was her joy on returning home. The special flavour of this child's impressions of France in the early nineteenth century is lost without her amusing pictures.

The diary was published in 1905. The authoress, who became a keen naturalist, used her artistic talent in making pictures of flowers and butterflies. She died at the early age of 26.

RICHARD HURRELL FROUDE

THERE is only a short diary of two years kept by Froude, brother of the historian, friend of Newman, and one of the leaders of the Oxford Movement. He has been described as a Catholic without Popery, and a member of the Church of England without Protestantism. The diary begins in 1826, when he was 23 and a tutor at Oriel. This was before he was ordained and some time before the *Tracts for the Times* were issued, to which he contributed. There is nothing, therefore, in the diary of any public interest, but it is a revelation of character, as it is entirely introspective. It is one long chapter of self-condemnation and attempts at self-discipline with occasional prayers, and there is a certain pettiness about it which makes one almost prefer Thomas Turner's unsuccessful efforts to cure his hopeless drunkenness.

Froude was encouraged to keep a journal by reading his mother's. He thought it would help, " as I find I want keeping in order," and he appears to have enjoyed pulling himself up in very trivial lapses. It would almost seem as if people who have to combat great temptations prefer not to speak or write about them, while those who want to correct small failings make a great deal of them. He enjoyed self-condemnation and speaks of his " enthusiastic misery."

We need only give a series of instances of the morbid self-disciplinary outpourings which fill the diary:

I am in a most conceited way besides being very ill tempered and irritable.

Not a very profitable day but in some respects better, my odd feeling, I hope, is passing away as what I wrote yesterday seems nonsense and almost affectation.

To-day I have eaten beyond the bounds of moderation. I must make a vigorous stand or I shall be carried away altogether.

Looked with greediness to see if there was a goose on the table for dinner; and though what I ate was of the plainest sort and I took no variety yet even this was partly the effect of accident and I certainly rather exceeded in quantity as I was muzzy and sleepy after dinner.

As far as I have observed yet the strongholds of the evil spirit within me are inertness, disingenuousness, bullying and levity.

Was ashamed to have it known that I had no gloves. Talked about matters of morality in a way that might leave the impression that I thought myself free from some vices I censured. This was unintentional but silly.

I have a sort of vanity which aims at my own good opinion.

Pleased myself with fancying I was not common place.

Ate very little though I was very hungry but because I thought the charge unreasonable I tried to shirk the waiter—sneaking.

Disgustingly self complacent thoughts have kept continually obtruding themselves upon me on the score of my little paltry abstinences. What I give up costs me no great effort.

Was disgustingly ostentatious at dinner in asking for a china plate directly as I had finished my meat.

I am obliged to confess that in my intercourse with the Supreme Being I am become more and more sluggish.

Read affectedly in evening chapel.

I must be energetic about abstinence or I shall quickly drop back into lazy fatness.

Yet he does not think his journal gives an accurate picture of himself :

Have read my journal. I can hardly identify myself with the person it describes.

This diary was certainly never intended for publication, but his friends thought fit to include it in his "Remains." He died at the age of 33 in 1836.

W. E. GLADSTONE

IN his *Life of Gladstone,* Lord Morley tells us that amongst the vast mass of material he had at his disposal were forty-four volumes of diaries, " little books in double columns intended to do little more than record persons seen or books read or letters written as the days passed by." Gladstone himself advised one of his sons at Oxford " to keep a short journal of principal employments in each day : most valuable as an account book of the all precious gift of Time." But, as his biographer says in speaking of his social activities, " he seems to have thought that little of what passed was worth transcribing nor in truth had Mr. Gladstone ever much or any of the rare talent of the born diarist."

Throughout the *Life* a number of quotations are given from the diaries, many of them just one line or a couple of sentences. Some of these brief jottings become pregnant with meaning when they are placed side by side with other and fuller accounts of the events they record. But there is an entire absence of anything intimate or domestic—such entries, if they exist, are omitted. That they are omitted we gather from Lord Morley saying that, in using the diary, he must " beware of the sin of violating the sanctuary." There are a few reflections on life, but for the most part books, speeches, political and parliamentary activities form the subjects of his notes. And it is all strenuous, lofty and profound to an extreme degree. In fact, Gladstone's diary, or as much of it as we are allowed to see, by no means brings him down from his pedestal to the level of an ordinary mortal ; and for that reason, while our admiration may be great, our sympathy is hardly ever reached.

He began his diary when he was at Eton, and kept up the habit for practically seventy years. The school entries are brief notes chiefly of his studies. Here is one on the Eton speech day :

Feb. 27. 1827. Holiday. Dressed (knee breeches etc.) and went into school with Selwyn. Found myself not at all in a funk and went through my performance with tolerable comfort. Durnford followed me, then Selwyn who spoke well. Horrors of speaking chiefly in the name.

At Oxford records of his studies continue. We catch a reference to card playing in the following :

1830. Sep. 4. Same as yesterday. *Paradise Lost*. Dined with the Bishop. Cards at night. I like them not for they excite and keep me awake. Construing Sophocles.

In the following year his speech at the Union was so powerful and brilliant that one of his contemporaries wrote that when Gladstone sat down " we all of us felt that an epoch in our lives had occurred." But this is all we get in the diary :

Cogitations on Reform etc. Difficult to *select* for a speech, not to gather it.

Spoke at the adjourned debate for three quarters of an hour immediately after Gaskell who was preceded by Lincoln. Row afterwards and adjournment. Tea with Wordsworth.

The fact of reflecting rather than the nature of his reflections is generally what he notes.

1833. Thought for some hours on my own future destiny and took a solitary walk to and about Kensington Gardens.

. . . not too unwell to reflect.

That he should have kept a diary at all regularly during his long and arduous parliamentary career is in itself a notable fact. The brief entries show with what tremendous seriousness he undertook his public duties. Prayer, and one might almost say fasting, seemed to accompany the formation of his projects and his private deliberations, and of course an immense amount of reading.

As Gladstone's oratory was his greatest accomplishment, we may select a few references to show how he notes in his diary his performances on some of the most celebrated occasions.

His maiden speech in 1833 :

Dined early. Re-arranged my notes for the debate. Rode. House 5 to 1. Spoke my first time for 50 minutes. My leading desire was to benefit the cause of those who are now so sorely beset. The House heard me very kindly and my friends were satisfied.

It may be noted in many of the entries, only a few of which can be given here, that his impressions with regard to his powers of speaking are extraordinarily modest, not to say humble, and form a great contrast to the unlimited conceit displayed by his great rival, Disraeli, on the same subject.

In 1835, on speaking in the House of Commons, he writes :

I cannot help here recording that this matter of speaking is really my strongest religious exercise. On all occasions and to-day especially was forced upon me the humiliating sense of my inability to exercise my reason in the face of the House of Commons and of the necessity of my utterly failing unless God gave me the strength and language. It was after all a poor performance but would have been poorer had He never been in my thoughts as a present and powerful aid.

1836 :

Spoke 50 minutes kindly heard and I should thank God for being made able to speak even thus indifferently.

His Budget speech of 1860 was regarded as one of the most

extraordinary triumphs ever witnessed in the House of Commons, yet he was not well at the time.

> Spoke 5–9 without great exhaustion; aided by a great stock of egg and wine. Thank God! Home at 11. This was the most arduous operation I have ever had in parliament.

1871. His famous speech at Blackheath in the open air to several thousand people.

> My expedition to Greenwich or rather Blackheath I spoke 1 h. 50 m.; too long, yet really not long enough for a full development of my points. Physically rather an excess of effort. All went well thank God!

1877. His speech on the Eastern question was described thus by Mr. A. J. Balfour: " As a feat of parliamentary courage, parliamentary skill, parliamentary endurance and parliamentary eloquence I believe it will be unequalled."

His diary record is as follows:

> House at 4¼. For over two hours I was assaulted from every quarter except the opposition bench which was virtually silent. Such a sense of solitary struggle I never remember. At last I rose on the main question nearly in despair as to the result; but resolved at least not to fail through want of effort. I spoke 2½ hours voice lasting well. House gradually came round and at last was more than good. It was over at 9-30. Never did I feel weaker and more wormlike.

On the introduction of the Home Rule Bill in 1886:

> The message came to me this morning " Hold thou up my goings in thy path that my footsteps slip not." Settled finally my figures with Welby and Hamilton; other points with Spencer and Morley. Reflected much. Took a short drive. H. of C. 4½ to 8¼. Extraordinary scenes outside the House and in. My speech which I have sometimes thought could never end lasted nearly 3½ hours. Voice and strength and freedom were granted to me in a degree beyond what I could have hoped. But many a prayer had gone up for me and not I believe in vain.

Cabinet meetings are noted with brief entries such as:

> Cabinet 2–4½. Again stiff. But I must not lose heart.

His interviews with the Queen are also devoid of any detail or colour.

> Went to Windsor to take my leave. H.M. short but kind.

> Gave H.M. my paper with explanation which appeared to be well taken. She was altogether at ease.

On the lighter side there is very little. Occasional references to play going, such as:

Went to Drury Lane to see in Antony and Cleopatra how low our stage has fallen. Miss K. V. [Kate Vaughan] in the ballet dressed in black and gold, danced marvellously.

At 9-30 to the Gaiety, saw a miserable burlesque of which I had heard a most inviting but false account.

And of course there are references to his favourite exercise, wood cutting:

Forenoon with Bright who departed having charmed everybody by his gentleness. Began the cutting of a large beech.

Revised and sent off long letter to Lord Granville on the political situation. Axe work. . . . Tree cutting with Herbert.

Like many diarists, Gladstone takes a survey either on his birthday or at the end of the year, and these entries are rather longer.

His closing entry in 1856 begins:

It appears to me that there are few persons who are so much as I am enclosed in the invisible net of pendent steel. I have never known what tedium was, have always found time full of calls and duties, life charged with every kind of interest. But now when I look calmly around me, I see that these interests are for ever growing and grown too many and powerful and that were it to please God to call me I might answer with reluctance.

In 1861 on his birthday he writes:

Begun my fifty second year. I cannot believe it. I feel within me the rebellious unspoken word. I will not be old.

In 1864:

I am well past half a century. My life has not been inactive. But of what kind has been its activity ? Inwardly I feel it to be open to this general observation ; it seems to have been and to be a series of efforts to be and to do what is beyond my natural forces.

1873:

Sixty four years completed to-day—what have they brought me ? A weaker heart, stiffened muscles, thin hairs ; other strength still remains in my frame.

In 1886 there is a long entry, out of which the following passage may be quoted:

O for a birthday of recollection. It is long since I have had one. There is so much to say on the soul's history but bracing is necessary to say it, as it is for reading Dante. It has been a year of shock and strain. I think a year of some progress ; but of greater absorption in interests which though profoundly human, are quite off the line of an old man's direct preparation for passing the River of Death."

In his retirement at the age of 85, he resolves to break off "the commonly dry daily journal or ledger," and to note only principal events and occupations. The entries are longer. He deals with his failing eyesight, his health, and his contentment at having at last retired. "I cast no longing lingering look behind," but "I must, God knows how reluctantly, lay burdens upon others." The last entry is on his birthday in 1896, and begins:

> My long and tangled life this day concludes its 87th year.

And he makes the pregnant remark already quoted in the Introduction with regard to the practical impossibility of writing honestly on "interior matters."

The last words are:

> Lady Grosvenor gave me to-day a delightful present of a small crucifix. I am rather too independent of symbols.

Throughout the diary there are a good many health notes, and references to sleep, which he valued very highly.

Perhaps it is as well that we find no frivolous comments, no trivial jottings, no indiscreet lapses in Gladstone's diary. Some giants may remain giants, and seldom can a strenuous life have been filled with more deeply conscientious motive and more sustained religious discipline. But it was certainly not out of his diary that his biographer was able to build up the great and dramatic story of Gladstone's career.

Mrs. Gladstone kept a diary, too, a few quotations from which occur in Mrs. Drew's memoir of her. We may allow ourselves to relax into a smile for once at this entry:

> Engaged a cook after a long conversation on religious matters chiefly between her and William.

THOMAS RAIKES

AS social and semi-political diaries go, the one kept by Thomas Raikes between 1831 and 1847 is very readable. If one were more interested in the author, one would be more interested in the diary. We are told that he was "a member of fashionable clubs and mixed largely in the best society." He was, therefore, in a position to collect a great deal of tittle-tattle both in London and in Paris, where he subsequently resided. His strong political bias gives some colour to his writing. He does not disguise his mistrust of reformers: "What monsters the Radicals really are," he exclaims, and declares that "political liberty should be restrained within narrow limits." He makes disparaging remarks about Lord Grey, and dismisses Cobbett as "a bone-grabber." He is a friend of the Duke of Wellington, with whom he has several conversations. When the day gives him no material for his diary he falls back on recollections. In this way he gives pages of gossipy reminiscences of the Duke of York, Beau Brummel, and others. In France he writes very fully about the political situation and court news, and of course Talleyrand's peculiarities, including his toilet, come in for elaborate descriptions. He quotes newspaper and magazine articles—one of several pages by George Sand on Talleyrand—and gives extracts of letters from Greville and others. When he travels he puts a good deal of colour into his descriptions, and some of his many anecdotes are of the most sensational character. In his weather remarks one feels he regards the sun as a celebrity whose vagaries must be noted.

This sort of diary must be a godsend to newspaper snippet writers. As fashions revolve in cycles this comment on young ladies' clothes would be quite up to date to-day:

Les robes ressemblent à un mauvais jour d'hiver qui commence trop tard et finit trop tôt.

He hardly ever moralizes. But we find this at the end of an entry describing how one of his friends has gone mad:

Perfect happiness seems impossible; but a system of compensation appears throughout to kindly and wisely equalise our lots. No prosperity without some alloy; no adversity without some palliation. Our only course is gratitude and submission.

Once on his birthday he reflects, and it is with some surprise that we find a note of deep depression in the mood of the club man and purveyor of gossip:

1836. Oct. 3. My birthday: formerly a day of congratulation with my family and friends but now only remembered in private by myself as a point in the year which marks a continuation of misfortune and an advance to the grave. I have likewise remarked that of late years some bad news is received or some disappointment or cross event occurs upon that day, as a sort of prelude to the coming year.

But he tells us nothing whatever of his private occupations, his wife or his domestic life. Raikes published *Letters from St. Petersburg* and *Paris since 1830*. His diary was published in 1856, or rather portions of it. The whole manuscript is probably much longer and fuller.

FANNY KEMBLE (Mrs. Butler)

WE are told that Fanny Kemble had an attractive personality, and we can well believe it when we read her journal. While the little volumes which record her tour in America with her father in 1832 and 1833 of course cannot be compared to the lifelong diary of the greater Fanny, nevertheless there is a happiness of expression and freshness of presentation in her spontaneous daily entries which give her a claim to rank high among diarists.

Born in 1809, she made her first appearance on the stage at the age of 20 and became at once a popular favourite. Charles Kemble, her father, a brother of Mrs. Siddons, was an actor of some distinction, and evidently took pains with the education of his daughter, for she shows a very cultivated literary and artistic appreciation. She is always turning to her Dante, analysing her Shakespeare, and discussing poetry and literature with her friends. In later life she wrote poems, plays and reminiscences. After parting from Butler, a Southern planter, whom she married in 1834, she returned to the stage for a while, and then had a great success as a Shakespearean reader. She died in 1873.

There is in the diary a good deal of sentimental moralizing, ecstasy, tears, rather highly-coloured scenic descriptions, and rapturous apostrophizing of her native land. It is the amusing and striking little notes of her acting experiences and her adventures that form the best part of the diary.

She is never tired of laughing at the American idea of equality and American manners.

Here they were talking of their aristocracy and democracy; and I'm sure if nothing else bore testimony to the inherent love of *higher things* which I believe exists in every human creature, the way in which the lawyer dwelt upon the Duke of Montrose to whom he is allied at the distance of some miles and Lady Loughborough whom heaven knows how he got hold of, would have satisfied me that a my Lord or my Lady are just as precious in the eyes of these levellers as in those of Lord and Lady Loving John Bull himself.

Father and daughter go the round of New York, Boston, Philadelphia, Baltimore, etc., etc., having to put up with considerable discomfort very often and finding on certain occasions very inadequate companies of actors to support them. There is a Mr. Keppel who is a high trial.

> At eleven went to rehearsal. Mr. Keppel is just as nervous and imperfect as ever : what on earth will he or shall I do to-night ! . . . Mr. Keppel was frightened to death and in the very second speech was quite out ; it was in vain that I prompted him he was too nervous to take the word and made a complete mess of it.

> Poor Mr. Keppel is fairly laid on the shelf : I'm sorry for him ! What a funny passion he had by the by for going down on his knees. In Fazio at the end of the judgment scene when I was upon mine down he went upon his making the most absurd devout looking *vis-à-vis* I ever beheld ; in the last scene too when he ought to have been going off to execution down he went again upon his knees, and no power on earth could get him up again for Lord knows how long.

She describes " the fine and delicate work " in her father's acting, and tells how " there is not one sentence, line or word of his part which he has not sifted grain by grain," but she recognizes that such refinement of acting is largely lost on their audiences. But on the whole she and her father get a splendid reception wherever they go. On one occasion she is disturbed and annoyed by people talking in the audience.

> At one time their impertinent racket so bewildered me that I was all but out and this without the audience once interfering to silence them ; perhaps however that would have been an unwarrantable interference with the sacred liberties of the people. I indulged them with a very significant glance, and at one moment was most strongly tempted to request them to hold their tongues.

She is not always satisfied with their performances.

> I played like a very clever girl as I am ; but it was about as much like Lady Macbeth as the Great Mogul. My father laboured his part too much.

And more than once she describes her acting as " so-soish." At Baltimore she has a very clumsy Romeo. Here is her account of the final scene :

> In the midst of " cruel, cursed fate " his dagger fell out of his dress ; I, embracing him tenderly, crammed it back again because I knew I should want it at the end.
> *Romeo*   Tear not our heart-strings thus !
>   They crack ! they break ! Juliet, Juliet ! (dies).
> *Juliet* (*to corpse*)   Am I smothering you ?
> *Corpse* (*to Juliet*)   Not at all ; could you be so kind do you think as to put my wig on again for me ? it has fallen off.

Juliet (*to corpse*)   Where's your dagger ?
Corpse (*to Juliet*)   'Pon my soul I don't know.

She sometimes breaks into strong language with regard to the profession.

An actor shall be self convicted in five hundred. There is a ceaseless striving for effect, a straining after points in talking and a lamp and orange-peel twist in every action. How odious it is to me !

What a mass of wretched mumming mimicry acting is ! Paste-board and paint for the thick breathing orange groves of the south ; green silk and oiled parchment for the solemn splendour of her noon of night ; . . . rouge for the startled life-blood in the cheek of that young passionate woman ; an actress, a mimicker, a sham creature, me, in fact, or any other one, for that loveliest and most wonderful conception in which all that is true in nature and all that is exquisite in fancy are moulded into a living form. To *act* this ! to *act* Romeo and Juliet ! horror ! horror ! how I do loathe my most impotent and unpoetical craft.

The discomforts were sometimes very trying.

Oh bugs, fleas, flies, ants and mosquitoes great is the misery you inflict upon me. I sit slapping my own face all day and lie thumping my pillow all night ; 'tis a perfect nuisance to be devoured of creatures *before* one's in the ground ; it isn't fair.

To bed—to sleep.
To sleep ! perchance to be bitten ay—there's the scratch. And in the sleep of ours what bugs may come. Must give us pause.

There are occasional notes on her health. But only tiredness and once or twice her voice troubles her. " Now I'll to bed : my cough's enough to kill a horse," is the end of one entry.

During the day, when not rehearsing, she went for rides, she read, she sang, she embroidered, she sketched, and she learned German. In fact, she lived a very full life. " I want to do everything in the world that can be done," she says, and again : " I wish somebody would explain to me everything in the world I can't make out."

Came home at nine, tea'd and sat embroidering till twelve o'clock, industrious little me.

Finished journal, wrote to Mrs.—to my mother, read a canto of Dante and began to write a novel. Dined at five. After dinner, put out things for this evening played on the piano, mended habit skirt, dressed myself and at quarter to ten went to theatre for my father.

The diary contains a good many religious reflections, and she is a regular churchgoer, but she is not always edified, as this account of a sermon shows :

I heard about as thorough a cock and bull sermon as ever I hope to be edified withal. What shameful nonsense the man talked! and all the time pretending to tell us what God had done, what He was doing, and what He intended to do next, as if he went up into heaven and saw what was going on there every five minutes.

The successful young actress of 1922 will read with surprise and amusement the following resolution of her predecessor ninety years ago:

I promised him never to waltz again except with a woman or my brother. . . . After all t'is not fitting that a man should put his arm round one's waist whether one belongs to anyone but one's self or not. 'Tis much against what I have always thought most sacred—the dignity of a woman in her own eyes and those of others.

By and by dancing was proposed and I was much entreated to change my determination about waltzing; but I was inexorable and waltzed only with the ladies.

There are many descriptions of minor episodes and adventures of travel which are exceedingly good. An example of her rather rich style in depicting scenery may be given.

The lightning played without intermission of a second in wide sheets of purple glaring flame that trembled over the earth for nearly two or three seconds at a time; making the whole world, river, sky, trees and buildings look like a ghostly universe cut out in chalk. The light over the water which absolutely illumined the shore on the other side with the broad glare of full day was of a magnificent purple colour. The night was pitchy dark too; so that between each of these ghastly smiles of the devil the various pale steeples and buildings which seemed at every moment to leap from nothing into existence, after standing out in fearful relief against a back ground of fire were hidden like so many dreams in deep and total darkness.

A few poems are inserted here and there, and explanatory notes added by the diarist, when she published the volumes in 1835. She used to read her diary out to her father, and probably the idea of publishing it was never wholly absent from her mind. In 1863 she published another volume dealing with life on the Georgia plantation.

HENRY GREVILLE

LIKE his brother Charles, Henry Greville was practically a lifelong diarist. But in the four volumes issued by his niece (the first two in 1883, the others in 1904-5) there is nothing of special interest or importance. It is merely a social diary, pleasantly written by a diplomatist, courtier, and man about town who came in contact with many interesting people. If he wrote anything personal beyond notes about his health, that part of the diary has been cut out, so we see very little of the man himself, and beyond the fact that he was socially popular and had a marked appreciation of music and acting, he only appears like any other collector of social gossip. This sort of diary may be of passing interest to those who recollect the people mentioned in it, and the author was certainly placed in a favourable position as an observer, but the bare mention of great events and great names cannot attract any reader, and no real picture of nineteenth-century society is reflected in its pages.

Between 1835 and 1844 Henry Greville was in the diplomatic service, attached to the Embassy in Paris; after he retired he became a gentleman usher to the Queen. He wrote his diary from 1832 till shortly before his death in 1872.

He sings duets with the Duchess of Kent; he dines with the King of the Belgians; he rides with the Duke of Orleans; he goes frequently to Holland House; he is present at debates in the French Chamber and in the British Houses of Parliament; he attends courts, balls, operas, plays, concerts, drawing rooms, royal weddings and christenings, and he stays at innumerable country houses. He does not revel in it all; for after a heavy day of court functions he writes, "How I detest all this sort of thing!" But it is very seldom that he expresses any personal opinion. In addition to his great quantity of friends, such as the Granvilles, Abercorns, Hollands, Sydneys, etc., and the series of celebrities he comes across, he is closely acquainted with Fanny Kemble and her sister, and knows Ristori, Mario, Grisi and many other singers, who often perform at his own house. References to the young Lord Acton and Frederick Leighton, of whom so much was expected, would not be without interest were they not so meagre. The following reference to Gladstone is amusing:

> He has a melodious voice in speaking, but I was not prepared to hear a Chancellor of the Exchequer warble a sentimental ballad, accompanied by his wife.

There are many references to politics, and he gives long accounts of murders, crimes and trials. He notes with considerable feeling the death of his friends. He comments on the weather and occasionally on food, "a *maigre* dinner, quite excellent."

When he allows himself to record an opinion it is very much to the point. He writes after a Lord Mayor's dinner in 1855:

What a joke and what a farce it all is to hear Palmerston bespattering the Emperor of the French with praises for his noble disinterestedness in fighting for *liberty* against barbarism and despotism ! he being the greatest living despot in whose nostrils all liberty and especially that of the Press, absolutely stinks.

On what he calls " the toggery of spirit rapping " he writes in 1862 :

It would be well if anything could put a stop to this subject of conversation which has become a great bore and which seems to have taken strong hold of the minds, not only of foolish women but even of men whom one should not have supposed capable of being occupied with and deluded by such palpable humbug.

If Henry Greville had only lived in some obscure village and written equally fully, his volumes would have been of peculiar interest. But this would have required a different sort of talent.

EDWARD PEASE

NO more typical Quaker diary could be found than that kept by Edward Pease. Born in 1767, he lived to the age of 91, but his early diaries were destroyed and we only have the volumes which cover the last twenty years. Edward Pease's claim to fame rests on the fact that he was instrumental in projecting the first railway line, and was a friend of George Stephenson, who persuaded him to employ steam traction.

Diary keeping was one of the self-disciplinary exercises of Quakers, and Edward Pease was a very prominent member of the Society of Friends. The introspection is not the outcome of any natural morbidity. On the contrary, we find a self-confident and even self-complacent optimism punctuated by sincere attempts at self-correction. In this diary we get a close view of a commanding personality, pompous, prosy and rather self-satisfied, strict and simple, yet opulent; intensely domestic and religious in the sense that prayer and self-examination occupy a considerable part of many of the entries. As he kept his diary regularly, the ups and downs of his moods are very distinctly reflected.

Pease may not have contemplated publication, but he evidently thought that some day some one would read his diaries.

Their contents may never be of any value or interest to anyone but let this reader be informed that having drawn me into self examination and having been an incentive to more watchfulness so far they have not been entirely without value to me in my Christian course.

On the fly-leaf of one of the diaries is written :

Often and much alone, this book may be called my communing Companion.

One becomes rather puzzled with regard to the exact standard of self-denial of this eminent Quaker, and one is driven to the conclusion that it is a little arbitrary.

The reading of novels and travels makes him " dry empty and poor " ; the reading of a newspaper is " waste of time." He regrets in his own family " a departure from simplicity in speech, furniture and attire," and declares the Society of Friends " will wear out Quakerism " if they continue to depart from simplicity " in language, furniture, pictures and decorations." He condemns and reproaches himself for buying " some decoration to place on my lawn," and he disapproves of a flower show as " tending to increase luxury and tending to gratify the lust of the eye." The use of silver forks is a deviation from simplicity, but it appears there was not so much vanity in silver spoons. Many other instances might be given of his strait-laced and censorious attitude to objects and customs he considered vain and frivolous. On the other hand, the rare and rich fruits from his own garden were famed, and he kept a most excellent table loaded with every luxury. The silver wine labels that hung round the necks of his heavy cut-glass decanters were handed down in the family and are engraved " Port," " Lisbon," " Madeira," " British," " Bucellas," " Sherry," " Whiskey," " Rum," " Gin," " Brandy," etc. Nor does the amassment of riches appear to have caused him any great alarm :

The prospects of the family are bright and prosperous as regards colliery matters, the monthly income being very large and my own appears as if it might exceed my former year.

It is true, however, that on this point he appears to have some misgiving when he writes :

Accumulation of wealth in every family known to me in our Society carries away from the purity of our principles, adds toil and care to life, and greatly endangers the possession of heaven at last.

His religious reflections are more or less conventional. Sometimes he finds the " heavens as brass," but he often receives "drops of rich consolation." He describes his varying moods at meeting which alternate between being "lamentably heavy" and receiving "a peculiarly solid sweet feeling of peace." Here are two short descriptions of meeting:

> A drive through the Old and New Testaments without feeling or end seemed only to cover us with dust.

> My feelings much spoiled by J. Jones saying it was time to separate when we had been about one hour twenty minutes assembled and when I think religious exercise was rising.

He was of an optimistic and cheerful disposition, but even this he thought wrong. At the age of 81 he writes:

> How often in the few past days have I been in danger of my naturally cheerful spirits and been apt to be carried beyond the bounds of a pious Christian cheerfulness.

And at 84 again:

> Glad and thankful for the various checks to the natural liveliness of my disposition, and that over cheerfulness which so often causes me much Regret.

On his eighty-seventh birthday he writes:

> Surely a life so prolonged ought to have yielded more fruit.

In a patriarchal way he became the head of a large family, the members of which he constantly entertained, and he never fails to take a close interest in all their doings. His children's deaths affect him deeply, and he lived to survive many other members of his family, so records of illness and death occur very frequently. His wife died in 1833. With unfailing and devoted regularity he visits her grave every year of the twenty-five he survived her, and enters in his diary expressions of his sacred and undying grief.

When his old friend George Stephenson died, he had some misgivings about going to the funeral, as Stephenson was "an unbeliever." But he finally resolved to go:

> In the church I sat a spectacle with my hat on and not comforted by the funeral service.

He makes the following reflection on his association with Stephenson:

> When I reflect on my first acquaintance with him and the resulting consequences my mind seems almost lost in doubt as to the beneficial results—that humanity has been benefited in the diminished use of horses and by lessened cruelty to them, that much ease, safety, speed and lessened expense in travel-

ling is obtained, but as to the results and effects of all that Railways have led my dear family into being in any sense beneficial, is uncertain.

There are many comments in the diaries on the weather, on nature, on birds, and gardens. Public affairs occupy his attention more than he likes, and the Crimean War calls forth many an outburst of horror and sadness.

While from time to time he feels called upon to admonish a friend for "backsliding," he never relaxes his vigilance over himself. At the age of 89 he writes :

> Stiffness of limbs, limited powers of action and walking, more completely confirm my old age than any other senses. Sight is important, taste, touch, feeling and hearing unimpaired. Great is the longing of my soul to return to my gracious Creator, thanks and praises due.

He makes a long entry on December 31, when he is 90, dealing with nature and noting early primroses; he touches on public affairs and ends with affectionate references to his family. He lived to the end of July in the following year, 1858.

The journal, edited by Sir Alfred Pease, was published in 1907.

WILLIAM GOODALL

DIARISTS often refer incidentally to hunting and other sport. But one example must be given of a diary which is exclusively devoted to hunting. The one written by William Goodall, head huntsman of the Belvoir Hunt from 1843 to 1859, is typical, and seems the best one to choose. Goodall began life in the stables. His first master was a Member of Parliament, and Goodall had to spend many weary hours outside the House of Commons while the great debates on the Reform Bill of 1832 were going on. His heart was in the kennel rather than the stable, and in 1837 he went to Belvoir, where after serving as whipper-in he was given charge of the pack by the Duke of Rutland when the vacancy occurred. He was a remarkable character and personally popular, as well as being a great huntsman.

In his diary he not only gives vivid descriptions of the sport itself, but he makes many little comments on man, horse, and hound—especially hound. "Lucy made a famous hit at Wilsford and won her fox"; "Bell showed great superiority of nose and caught the fox "; " Willing behaved very ill, running hare most obstinately in Easton Wood "; " Knipton gave me a terrible fall jumping into a blind grip (no fault of his)."

He always gives a full account of the line of country over which they run, and then goes on in one entry :

> He crept into a rabbit hole after a tremendous run of two hours and forty five minutes, one hour and twenty minutes to change ; the first forty five minutes without more than a momentary check, the latter the same. We dug him out and killed him. A tremendous large old dog fox. A real out and out good day's sport. . . . A most beautiful hunting morning, west south west and a rising glass. I rode my good old horse Catch-me-who-can first and Prince second. Those who rode well to the hounds at the finish were [a list follows]. I never saw hounds work more beautifully and struggle through the ploughs which were for them knee deep all day ; every hound struggled through very stout indeed.

All the entries are very much the same and there is no need to quote any more. He writes for the last time on April 6, 1859, and gives as usual a description of the run, which ended in the fox being killed

> most handsomely in the open after being engaged from first finding in the morning for four hours—thus ending one of the worst seasons on record.

After giving a list of the hounds out that day, he adds :

> I rode a horse of Markwell's on trial but did not like him.

From this horse he had a severe fall and on returning home, when his wife greeted him with " Thank God, Will, I have you safe from another season," he replied, " Yes, but, mind you, I've had a rum un to-day."

He died shortly afterwards.

The original manuscript of the diary is in the possession of the Duke of Rutland. The above extracts are taken from *The History of the Belvoir Hunt.*

CARDINAL MANNING

THE publication of a large number of extracts from private diaries in Purcell's biography of Manning, which appeared in 1896, was the occasion of some controversy on the ethics of biography. Purcell states that Manning had himself handed over his diary to him, having cut out from it pages which

" he did not consider fit or expedient to be laid before the public eye."

In *Henry Edward Manning*, Mr. Shane Leslie tells the true story of how Purcell came into possession of the diaries, though by no means all of them; and it becomes clear that Manning never entrusted them to him for publication. Purcell was also guilty of many inaccuracies which Mr. Leslie exposes. But the fact remains that a large portion of Manning's genuine diary has been made public.

Quite apart from the question as to whether the diary adds to the estimate made of him in his lifetime, or whether it reveals traits in his charcter which detract from his public reputation, we find in Manning a genuine diarist who confided at the very moment to the private pages of his journal his passing thoughts and impressions and his changing views and who did not hesitate to expose himself to charges of inconsistency and to accuse himself of faults and failings which could not be to his credit, all with an apparent disregard for the verdict of posterity. Here was a man seemingly bent on the attainment of power and position, who appeared to lay great store on public regard and fame. He might have written himself up in his diary, or at any rate he might have destroyed any papers that would expose him in an unfavourable light. He did not do either, although he contemplated that his life would be written not by Purcell but by Mr. J. E. C. Bodley, whom Purcell forestalled by taking possession of the papers on the death of Cardinal Manning, while Mr. Bodley was abroad. Manning may have suffered from the curious indecision, or rather constantly deferred decision, which seems to have made so many diarists just leave their record without injunctions and without any note of their wishes. Nevertheless, Manning was not always perfectly frank even to his diary. Suddenly, on supremely important occasions, not the torn-out page, but the written page discloses an almost mysterious reticence. For instance, although he cut out many pages written at the time of Newman's conversion, when he meets Newman in Rome shortly before his own conversion he notes the fact without a single word of comment or any account of what they said to one another. Still stranger is the brief entry, " Audience to-day at Vatican " about the same time. This momentous interview with the Pope must have made a deep impression on him, yet he writes not a word of it in his diary at the time, although we get full and elaborate accounts of his doings in Italy and his talks and discussions with Father Luigi at Assissi. After his conversion also he makes no sort of record of his frequent interviews with the Pope, nor of the honours bestowed on him.

We gain some idea of his motive in keeping a diary when he writes in 1851, after having lost one of the volumes of his journal:

> Since I lost my journals I have no heart to begin again. Also keeping a journal (1) Led to self contemplation and tenderness (2) Kept alive the susceptibilities of human sorrow. Yet it was of use to me in remembering and comparing seasons and in recording marked events.

And again after another break:

> I feel my journal keeping is broken off. I am in doubt whether it is a good or bad habit. But certainly it kept alive many thoughts and convictions.

He used his diary, in fact, for careful self-examination and for searching out the inmost thoughts of his heart, though he used it also as a memorandum of his doings and often noted the wind and the weather.

The pages before 1844, when he was Vicar of Lavington and Archdeacon of Chichester, he cut out. He was at that time 37 years old, and we see at once his love of introspection and self-disparagement. And as time passes the conflict between worldly ambition and mystical idealism becomes very apparent.

> I do feel pleasure in honour, precedence, elevation, the society of great people and all this is very shameful and mean.

The offer of the post of Sub-Almoner to the Queen, which had been vacated by the Archbishop of York and was a stepping-stone to a Bishopric, produces an orgy of self-dissection and the weighing of pros and cons. He finally refuses the offer.

> To learn to say no, to disappoint myself, to choose the harder side, to deny my inclinations, to prefer to be less thought of and to have few gifts of the world; this is no mistake and is most like the cross. Only with humility.

He keeps up the argument with himself for days because from the worldly point of view he is bitterly disappointed. But he writes:

> Certainly I would rather choose to be stayed on God than to be in the thrones of the world and the Church.

He seems most anxious to note down anything discreditable:

> I came home from London last night after three weeks very illspent. My life there was irregular, indiscreet, self indulgent.

After an illness his mind turns to self-analysis with morbid intensity:

CARDINAL MANNING

If I knew that I were now to die what would I feel ?

Detailed confessions, self-denunciation, prayer and resolutions follow. The resolutions are set out in lists and marked *kept* and *kept in a measure*.

> In the course of the week I have begun again with the reckoning.
>
> Petulance twice.
>
> Want of love of my neighbours.
>
> Complacent visions.
>
> But in all these except once under the first there has been no conscious, at least *morose*, consent of the will.

Twice over he writes out a list of " God's special mercies to me," which include " the preservation of my life six times to my knowledge." In the second list each heading is introduced with one of the following words : Created ; Redeemed ; Regenerated ; Blessed ; Spared ; Restrained ; Prevented ; Converted ; Convinced ; Enlightened ; Reclaimed ; Quickened ; Chastised ; Awakened ; Bruised ; Kindled ; Softened ; Humbled.

He indulges fiercely in self-condemnation :

> For I am *capable of all evil*. Nothing but the hand of God has kept me from being the vilest creature and nothing can. I feel now that if I were within the sphere of temptation I should sin by a perpetual backsliding.

In his journeys abroad in Belgium and later in Rome he makes little pencil sketches of architectural features, and gives a daily account of conversations and visits as well as notes on political events. His growing appreciation of Roman Catholic services and ritual is demonstrated on every page, and ceremonies and processions are described in detail.

As a result of the Oxford Movement and Newman's conversion many converts were going over to Rome. Although he himself was on the same road, he makes very unsympathetic references to relations and friends who were taking this course. On the back of the actual page on which he comments unfavourably on the conversion of a lady acquaintance he writes :

> The Church of England after 300 years has failed (1) in the unity of doctrine (2) in the enforcement of discipline (3) in the training of the higher life.

" Strange thoughts visit " him, amongst others :

> I am conscious that I am further from the Church of England and nearer Rome than ever I was.

> How do I know where I may be two years hence ?
> Where was Newman five years ago ?
> May I not be in an analogous place ?

And on his birthday :

> To-day is my birthday, 38. This last year has opened a strange chapter in my life. I never thought to feel as I feel now and with my foot on the step of what I once desired.

The diary relates the momentous event very briefly.

> 1851. March 25. Executed resignation of archdeaconry and benefice.
> April 5. Went to Father Brownhill with Hope. St. George's. Cardinal.
> April 6. Passion Sunday. 9½ A.M. was received at High Mass.

After this there are a lot of pages cut, but we can gather that he has no misgivings or remorse.

> After general confession in Retreat I could hardly sleep for joy.

The entries become more irregular, but worldly ambition has still to be fought.

> I am conscious of a desire to be in such a position (1) as I had in time past (2) as my present circumstances by the act of others (3) as my friends think me fit for (4) as I feel my own faculties tend to.
> But God being my helper I will not seek it by the lifting of a finger or the speaking of a word. If it is ever to be it shall be (1) either by the invitation of superiors or (2) by the choice of others.

When he is 80 and feels the end approaching he writes :

> I have ceased all outdoor work and have not been out of the house. It is a *tempus clausum*, a slowing down into the terminus and I feel very passive and content. . . . I hope I may die on the field and in harness. But all this will settle itself or rather Our Lord will settle it for me.

The last entry is on November 9, 1890 :

> If I had not become Catholic I could never have worked for the people of England as in the last year they think I have worked for them. Anglicanism would have fettered me. The liberty of Truth and the Church has lifted me above all dependence or limitation. This seems like the latter end of Job greater than the beginning. I hope it is not the condemnation where all men speak well of me.

The publication in the biography of the diary extracts as well as autobiographical memoranda created some sensation because they revealed certain facts which were not generally known. Manning, while publicly an Anglican and dissuading others from joining the Roman Catholic Church, was found to have practically decided to take that step himself. His intrigues at the Vatican, his unfriendly relations with Newman, his intercourse with men of diverse religious or of no theological beliefs at all, while to his own clergy he exhibited a very frigid and strict demeanour—these revelations came as something of a shock to some of his warmest admirers. Nevertheless, although so few extracts can be given here from the diary itself, it affords a very good example of self-revelation. The dignified, stern, ascetic, almost saintly Cardinal is shown to be an ordinary human being, struggling sometimes successfully and sometimes unsuccessfully with the temptations and weaknesses which all flesh is heir to.

BISHOP WILBERFORCE

THE diary kept by Samuel Wilberforce covered the greater part of his life. Many extracts from it are given in the three volumes of his biography, beginning in 1830 and continuing with breaks to the end of his life in 1873. The diary is of interest because without it the inner side, which was undoubtedly the finer side, of Wilberforce's character would never have been fully known. In the public eye he was a great ecclesiastic, an eloquent preacher, a statesman and a courtier, occupied largely with questions of Church administration, discipline and ritual. He was known as the "Bishop of Society"; and the versatile facility and persuasive expediency which marked his successful career earned him the sobriquet of "Soapy Sam." Without the diary revelations the estimate of his life and character, judged only by letters and speeches, would have been very incomplete.

He writes fairly regularly, although there is a break of eight years after he was made Bishop of Oxford in 1845. In early days at Brightstone he gives brief details about his parishioners, his difficulties with them, the books he is reading, the course of preparation for each sermon and memoranda of its efficiency when delivered. He continues regularly to note his movements and sermons, with occasional comments on his health. Later on there are references to the ecclesiastical disputes, the Hampden case, Bishop Colenso's attitude, adverse criticism on *Essays and Reviews*, and his political activities. He sees a great number of people and records conversations with many statesmen, notably Peel and Gladstone, for the latter of whom he has a great admiration: "Great, earnest and honest; as unlike the tricky Disraeli as possible."

The following remarks of Gladstone, in view of subsequent events, are interesting :

Gladstone much talking how little real work any Premier had done after 60. . . .

Gladstone again talking of 60 as full age of Premier.

Dinners at Grillions, visits, court functions are all noted, but it is a diary of a very busy man and the entries are generally perfunctory and brief. He has an enormous correspondence. He notes that he has written fifty letters in the day and his incessant rounds as a Bishop take it out of him, so that he writes of his tiredness on one occasion " very much fagged," and his occasional ailments such as " a fierce toothache." Not often does he indulge in criticism of the people he meets, and of his conversations with the Queen we get nothing more than that she was " very affable." But there are one or two more critical little passages about people which may be quoted. This of Carlyle :

Then rode with Carlyle and Lowe ; on horse full of spirit round by Popham lane. Well shaken. Carlyle full of unconnected and inconsistent utterances. Full of condemnation of the present day, of its honesty etc etc praising George I, II and III for honesty and ability. A heap of discordant ideas. Yet a good deal of manhood and of looking to some better state of being. Poor man, a strange enigma ! If he did but see the True Man as his hope and deliverer how were all his sighs answered !

Napoleon III, when on a visit to Windsor :

The Emperor rather mean looking, small and a tendency to embonpoint ; a remarkable way as it were of swimming up a room with an uncertain gait ; a small grey eye, looking cunning but with an aspect of softness about it too.

His love of birds is shown by frequent notes like the following :

Walked half way to Petworth saw first swallows near the Coultershaw Mill, heard first cuckoo in woods at Burton Park.

But so far as his activities and work is concerned the diary is in no way remarkable, as the memoranda are bald and hurried. Wilberforce, however, also treated his diary as a confidant. We find passages containing prayer, self-examination and resolutions, more especially in the earlier years. He deplores his " unbridled indolence " ; he prays to be kept humble and " free from the fear of man which bringeth a snare," and he writes after talking to a lawyer :

> How very injurious it must be to the mind to have *no cooling days*. To be always *hot* and rusting with worldly cares ; no pauses ; no self examination. I ought to thank God for my lot. If as it is I find it hard to make head against sin what would it have been if I had been a successful lawyer ?

And he tabulates resolutions quite in the style of his seventeenth- and eighteenth-century predecessors. In the middle period there are fewer entries of this description, but this occurs :

> Many searchings of heart. Why so troubled ? doubtless to teach me more simplicity in serving God—less eye to success—more to His glory ; resolved and prayed.

In later years the resolutions and self-examination occur again. He surveys his life and the " wonderful advantages " he has had, and ends :

> How has God dealt and what have I *really* done—for HIM. *Miserere Domine* is all my cry.

And he resolves :

> I. to take periodic times for renewing this meditation ;
> II. to strive to live more in the sight of Death ;
> III. to commend myself more entirely a dying creature into the Hand of the only Lord of Life.

But undoubtedly the most human and touching parts of the diary are the references to his wife. The domestic side of his nature is shown by affectionate mention of his children, but the remarks about them are with one or two exceptions quite brief. Indeed, the diary as a whole, except for the self-examination above mentioned, does not enter into the more private and intimate matters. Many diarists, too, who write far more freely about their feelings than Wilberforce does, find themselves unable to write when confronted with great sorrow. But Wilberforce confides in his diary on the very day his wife dies, and on the subsequent days and on the day of the funeral. We feel a reluctance to detach these heartrending and painful reflections from their context. But the genuineness and sincerity of his affliction which he may have attempted to conceal outwardly becomes the more apparent when to the very last year of his life he continues to refer to the subject ; and he survived his wife thirty-two years. Of their married happiness there is no account. In his diary before 1841, the date of her death, he only refers to his wife casually in his short memoranda. But we find by his subsequent diary this sacred memory threading itself through his life and noted only by him to himself alone in the pages of his journal. Without quoting the passages written at the very moment, we may give a few instances of this ceaseless devotion to the memory.

> 1853. Woke early with all the events of this day 12 years as fresh as yesterday before me.
>
> 1855 [after a very busy day of Confirmations]. Full all day of thoughts of 1841. Oh, that I had profited more by that life-sorrow.
>
> 1857. On the tower a view of Hind Head. I always look from these distances at Lavington as if my Emily were there and I could find her if I went.
>
> 1860. Stood on the shore for hours watching the surf as I did when I was a boy, and thought I should meet Emily round every corner. My own, my lost one, my soul! Dearest one. I could have wept tears of blood. I could not help calling out aloud to her to come to me.
>
> 1861. Oh, if I had her but to show her how much happier I could make her than with all my love I did.
>
> 1872. They think me hurried with business. They do not know that my heart is in Lavington Church—in the house when we came back. Oh, but it is almost madness to think of it.

It is pretty certain that none of his contemporaries guessed the constant presence in the back of his mind, and some may have misjudged him.

Another sorrow in his life was the secession to Rome of his only daughter and her husband. He records the news on August 29, 1868, and it almost stuns him. He writes:

> For years I have prayed incessantly against this last act of his and now it seems denied me. It seems as if my heart would break at this insult out of my own bosom to God's truth in England's Church, and preference for the vile harlotry of the Papacy. God forgive them. I have struggled on my knees against feelings of wrath against him in a long long weeping cry to God.

And he reverts to the calamity on many subsequent days. This kind of entry stands in strong contrast to the general entries in the diary, which mostly resemble the following:

> Confirmation at Wellington College. Cold very bad; but D.G. managed to be heard. After luncheon writing and seeing, with Fosebery to Old Windsor. Dear Blunt affectionate as always. A very nice confirmation.
>
> Back to Windsor Castle and prepared sermon. Dined with the Queen. A great deal of talk with Princess Louise: clever and very agreeable. The Queen very affable. 'So sorry Mr. Gladstone started this about the Irish Church, and he is a great friend of yours, etc.'

The two widely differing kinds of entries seem to illustrate

Wilberforce's character. In the one can be seen the ecclesiastic, the courtier and the statesman, in the others the human being as few if any knew him. He was evidently one of those people who go in for cultivating a public manner which, while it becomes a habit, gives as a matter of fact a false impression of the real person. A diary alone can reveal the other side.

Bishop Wilberforce wrote an entry in his diary on July 18, 1873, in which he expressed sorrow at parting from his son, Ernest, who was bound for Lapland, and he enters as usual the doings of the day. On July 19 he was killed by a fall from his horse while riding with Lord Granville near Leatherhead.

MACAULAY

"NO kind of reading is so delightful and so fascinating as this minute history of a man's self," wrote Macaulay, after he had been reading over his old journals. "Whatever was in Macaulay's mind may be found in his diary," Sir George Trevelyan tells us. " That diary was written throughout with the unconscious candour of a man who freely and frankly notes down remarks which he expects to be read by himself alone." Macaulay was not, however, a regular writer. In 1848 he notes a lapse of more than nine years. The earlier portions of the diary, quoted in the *Life and Letters*, deal with his travels in Italy in 1838-9, and his biographer notes that Macaulay viewed the works of man and of nature with the eye of an historian, not that of an artist. " His stock of epithets applicable to mountains, seas and clouds was singularly scanty . . . when he had recorded the fact that the leaves were green, the sky blue, the plain rich and the hills clothed with wood he had said all he had to say and there was an end of it." This is not surprising when we find in his diary his own account of a walk from Malvern into the most beautiful parts of Herefordshire :

> I walked far into Herefordshire and read while walking the last five books of the Iliad with deep interest and many tears.

Reading, indeed, was his chief interest and occupation throughout his life. His diary abounds with literary judgments and the record of the enormous amount of literature he consumed. With a book or in a library he was always happy, and even in his last illness he notes :

> I read and found as I have always found that an interesting book acted as an anodyne.

Of the extraordinary rapidity with which he could devour the contents of a book many anecdotes have been related. In his diary there are several references to his astonishing memory. Crossing over to Ireland, he writes:

> I put on my great coat and sat on deck during the whole voyage. As I could not read, I used an excellent substitute for reading. I went through Paradise Lost in my head. I could still repeat half of it and that the best half. I really never enjoyed it so much.
>
> I walked in the portico and learned by heart the noble fourth act of the Merchant of Venice. There are four hundred lines of which I knew a hundred and fifty. I made myself perfect master of the whole the prose letter included in two hours.

People with abnormally good memories are like people with too much luggage. Socially Macaulay was greatly addicted to opening the contents of the many boxes of his vast store and overwhelming his auditors with the abundance of his learning. But in his writing, and this is particularly true of his diary, he exercised a restraint and wrote without any trace of pedantry or overweighted erudition. His literary opinions are very trenchantly written, often amusing and unrestrained in their violence. They occur in so many entries that it is difficult to give extracts, but his wholehearted admiration for Jane Austen's novels may perhaps be quoted:

> There are in the world no compositions which approach nearer to perfection.

After reading Dickens and Pliny:

> Read Northanger Abbey worth all Dickens and Pliny together. Yet it was the work of a girl. She was certainly not more than twenty-six. Wonderful creature!

Although most of his reading is of the classics, he occasionally indulges in a modern novel.

> I dined by myself and read an execrably stupid novel called Tylney Hall. Why do I read such stuff?

Of Bulwer Lytton's scheme for some association of literary men he writes:

> I detest all such associations. I hate the notion of gregarious authors. The less we have to do with each other the better.

Macaulay's writing, of course, occupied as prominent a place in his own record of his life as his reading. The conception, the preparation, the composition, the publication of the *History* are all recorded. The hours of arduous labour, the misgivings and the eventual striking success of his work are described in daily notes of doubt and hope. A diary alone can give us the true picture of the gradual stages of a great achievement from the point of view of its author. Some of the historian's diary jottings may be given, taken from the years he was engaged on this work :

I have thought a good deal during the last few days about my History. The great difficulty of a work of this kind is the beginning. How is it to be joined on to the preceding events ? Where am I to commence it ? I cannot plunge slap dash into the middle of events and characters.

I looked at some books about Glencoe. Then to the Athenæum and examined Scotch Acts of Parliament on the same subject. Walked a good way meditating. I see my line. Home and wrote a little but thought and prepared more.

I read a portion of my History to Hannah and Trevelyan with great effect. Hannah cried and Trevelyan kept awake.

I read my book and Thucydides's which I am sorry to say I found much better than mine.

To-morrow I shall begin to transcribe again and to polish. What trouble these few pages will have cost me ! The great object is that after all this trouble they may read as if they had been spoken off and may seem to flow as easily as table talk. We shall see.

I looked over and sent off the last twenty pages . My work is done, thank God ; and now for the result. On the whole I think that it cannot be very unfavourable.

The Duke of Wellington was enthusiastic in admiration of my book. Though I am almost callous to praise now, this praise made me happy for two minutes.

Longman called. It is necessary to reprint. This is wonderful. Twenty-six thousand, five hundred copies sold in ten weeks ! I should not wonder if I made twenty thousand pounds clear this year by literature. Pretty well, considering that 22 years ago I had just nothing when my debts were paid ; and all that I have with the exception of a small part left me by my uncle the General, has been made by myself and made easily and honestly by pursuits which were a pleasure to me and without one insinuation from any slanderer that I was not even liberal in all my pecuniary dealings.

A self-complacent tone is noticeable in several of the entries where he writes down general reflections on his birthhday :

My birthday. Forty-nine years old. I have no cause of complaint. Tolerable health ; competence ; liberty ; leisure ; very dear relations and friends ; a great, I may say a very great literary reputation.

My birthday. I am fifty. Well, I have had a happy life. I do not know that anybody whom I have seen close has had a happier. Some things I regret, but on the whole who is better off ?

My birthday. Fifty seven. I have had a not unpleasant year. My health is not good but my head is clear and my heart is warm. I receive numerous marks of the good opinion of the public . . . I have been made a peer with I think as general an approbation as I remember in the case of any man that in my time has been made a peer.

He has warnings of heart trouble which make him write in a more depressed vein from time to time.

I should like to finish William before I go. But this is like the old excuses that were made to Charon.

My strength is failing. My life will not I think be long. But I have clear faculties, warm affections, abundant sources of pleasure.

I am perfectly ready and shall never be readier. A month more of such days as I have been passing of late would make me impatient to get to my little narrow crib like a weary factory child.

Politics, of course, occupy many entries, but far less than literature. There are accounts of visits to Windsor when the Queen " insisted on my telling her some of my stories " ; and on one occasion he tactfully corrects the Queen when she refers to James II as her " ancestor."

' Not your Majesty's ancestor,' said I. ' Your Majesty's predecessor.' I hope this was not an uncourtly correction. I meant it as a compliment and she seemed to take it so.

His election for Edinburgh and other political events are described ; but it is quite apparent that politics are not his main interest. We can quote him once on food :

Ellis came to dinner at seven. I gave him lobster curry, woodcock and macaroni. I think that I will note dinners as honest Pepys did.

The historian rides.

I was pleased to find I had a good seat ; and my guide whom I had apprised of my unskilfulness professed himself quite an admirer of the way in which I trotted and cantered. His flattery pleased me more than many fine compliments which have been paid to my History.

Macaulay was a playgoer, but he had no ear for music. His recognition of " The Campbells are Coming," played at Windsor by the band which " covered the talk with a succession of sonorous tunes " as he notes in his diary, is said to be the only authentic instance on record of his having known one tune from another.

The extent of Macaulay's private generosity would never

have been known except for his diary. He gave literally hundreds away to needy authors and people in distress. His diary received his confidences to within a few days of his death in 1859. His biographer says of it : " Those who have special reason to cherish his memory may be allowed to say that proud as they are of his brilliant and elaborate compositions . . . they set a still higher value upon the careless pages of that diary which testifies how through seven years of trying and constant illness he maintained his industry, his courage, his patience, and his benevolence unimpaired and unbroken to the last."

A few extracts are given in the biography from the diary of Margaret Macaulay, his sister. They give a faithful picture of their domestic life in the earlier days. She writes of " his beaming countenance, happy affectionate smile and joyous laugh " ; and one of her entries ends with the following prophecy :

> The name which passes through this little room in the quiet gentle tones of sisterly affection is a name which will be repeated through distant generations and go down to posterity linked with eventful times and great deeds.

Among minor diaries Macaulay's must rank very high. Although he was not a regular writer, and was by no means morbidly introspective, his spontaneity is so natural and genuine that in spite of his facile pen there is never a suggestion that he was elaborating a special record for the further enhancement of his reputation.

GEORGE HOWARD (7TH EARL OF CARLISLE)

LORD CARLISLE was born in 1802. He was a Member of Parliament, Chief Secretary for Ireland under Lord Melbourne, a member of Lord John Russell's cabinet, and, with a short break, Lord-Lieutenant of Ireland from 1855 till within a few months of his death in 1864. He was a scholar and writer of verse and a speaker of some merit. He never married. The extracts from his diary, which extend from 1843 to 1864, were printed for private circulation. They show that he was a very regular diarist, but confined his record almost exclusively to his social activities. If ever he noted more domestic and personal matters they have been omitted.

A large number of diaries of this description are no doubt in existence, many of them locked up in cupboards in country houses. Not even the passage of centuries can very much enhance their value. Dinners, functions, country-house parties are duly registered, with a list of the people present. Here we have a man of cultivation in close touch with all the prominent people of the day and himself participating in the function of government, noting with regularity so many of the more trivial but impersonal events of his life with very little colour and with only occasional brief expressions of opinion. Lord Carlisle undoubtedly never intended his diary to be published, nor has it been published. His purpose evidently was not to dig down deep, but just to make superficial memoranda. Curiously enough, he comments favourably on the diary—a very different one—of another scholar politician.

Read the manuscript volume of Windham's diary. I should be for publishing, as a curious piece of psychology, the morbid nerves of a very manly and gifted mind.

Lord Carlisle reminds us of some of the earlier diarists in the unfailing way in which he notes sermons with a brief comment on the preacher. He is a great admirer of Samuel Wilberforce. He shows his interest in art and pictures and he is a great reader. He devours at once all the books of the day as they come out—Dickens, Thackeray, Kingsley, Carlyle, Macaulay, Grote, Victor Hugo, etc., but his comments are hardly worth quoting; they are mostly appreciative except in the case of Carlyle, whose "faults of style are all but intolerable; yet he does entertain and puts the scene before one."

He gives a long account of a dinner to Dickens, at which there were speeches.

Dickens replied in very good taste; he said he always found the people who were most like his characters objected to them as improbable and out of nature; a Mrs. Nickleby had talked to him in so exactly the same strain that he was thinking "Good heavens, she is going to charge me with putting her name into my book" when she began observing upon the character as utterly unnatural; so with several Pecksniffs.

Macaulay he meets very often, and occasionally records part of his conversation.

But generally it is only the bare list of names that he notes; which is tantalizing, when, as on one occasion, the following amongst others dined with him: Lady Palmerston, Sheridan, Macaulay, Prescott, and Thackeray.

Of Emerson, whom he hears lecture, he writes:

I think as I have always done there is so much of heaven in his appearance, manners, voice, mind and fancy and in all but his teaching.

On the death of Sir Robert Peel he enlarges a little more than usual on his character.

I can hardly say how immensely I think his merits preponderated over his defects; there was considerable egotism and a general want of charm; nothing very ethereal. But I believe him to have been eminently pure, truth loving, with a high ambition for his country as well as for himself, unweariedly devoted to her interests;—the prominent type of an age whose great characteristic is the love of the useful in politics.

His position as a Cabinet minister necessitated frequent visits to Windsor and Balmoral, but the only occasion on which we get anything beyond a formal report of the proceedings is an accident during the spearing of salmon at Balmoral which proceeded while the Queen was sketching on the river bank.

There was a little incident; two Highlanders went into a deep pool and could not swim out in their clothes; the Prince darted off to look after them, the Queen fancied he might go in after them and as I was standing by her pinched me very much.

He gives an account of the disturbances in London in 1848, but he abstains from touching on politics, only chronicling Cabinet dinners and making a bare mention of Parliamentary debates.

During his Lord-Lieutenancy there is only one entry which goes behind formal official and social matters.

1860. Dec. 5. They have taken to talk treason and repeal again in the country but as yet not formidably.

Railways had only just been introduced. He describes the opening of one in Yorkshire, and he always uses the expression "railed" for travelling by train. Although he describes so many functions and ceremonies he is too much accustomed to them to be very much impressed by them. An example may be given of his investiture with the Garter.

1855. Feb. 7. I railed to Windsor with Knights of the Garter actual and elect and the Ellesmere ladies. The Investiture took place in the Throne room. There was a great attendance of knights in succession—I, Lord Ellesmere and Lord Aberdeen were duly invested. The ceremony produces different effects upon minds of different mould. The Duchess of Sutherland thinks it very thrilling and very elevating. Lady Ellesmere could hardly conquer her propensity to laugh; the delivery of the old chivalrous charge by the Bishop of Oxford (Wilberforce) in his earnest pregnant accents is on

Harriet's side ; Lord Fitzwilliam, walking backwards in very long robes is on Lady Ellesmere's. The dinner was in the Waterloo chamber about fifty ; very handsome.

He likes going to the play almost as much as listening to sermons. He seldom comments on his own health, but the weather is frequently noted. Nothing could be less morbid, egotistical or introspective than Lord Carlisle's diary. For this reason perhaps we do not get in the regular formal entries much insight into his personality. The last entry is dated June 6, 1864 :

> To-day concludes the eight years of my vice-reign. I ought to think gratefully that when called upon to close it, it will not at all events be premature.

He died six months later. His *Diary in Turkish and Greek Waters* (1854) was published.

NASSAU SENIOR

THE journals published by Nassau Senior comprise journals of visits to Ireland in 1852, 1858 and 1862, journals kept in France and Italy from 1848 to 1852, and journals kept in Turkey and Greece in 1857 and 1858. None of them can be described as private diaries. Senior was a prominent economist in the early nineteenth century. He was the first to hold the chair of Political Economy at Oxford, he was a member of the Poor Law Inquiry Commission of 1832, and drew up the report of the Hand-loom Weavers Commission of 1838. On his travels his object was to make a study of political, economic and social conditions, and he presented the result of his investigations in diary form from the daily notes he made on the spot. The journals, therefore, contain serious examinations of public problems and events, relieved here and there by descriptions of scenery. To analyse them adequately would involve a comprehensive discussion of the political situation both at home and abroad and of the economic problems with which statesmen were confronted in the 'fifties. This would carry us very far beyond our present purpose.

By confining himself to a recital and consideration of purely public events Senior gave a weight and value to his books which places them in a very different category from the social diaries in which passing references to political events are found buried in social gossip. It is doubtful whether his descriptions of scenery do not interrupt rather than assist his discourse, and we are inclined to think that the diary form is not very suitable for a work of this character. But Senior has a characteristic in his writing shared only by one other diarist. Like Fanny Burney he reports conversations at length. He had so retentive a memory that he was able with the assistance of a few notes to commit to the pages of his journal with remarkable accuracy long and elaborate conversations. His object being to acquire information and having no desire to shine himself, we get very little of his own opinions; and this absence of self-assertion further accentuates the entirely impersonal character of his writing. In the journals in France and Italy more especially there are a number of these conversations, as he was in a position to come in contact with many of the leading public men of the day. The volumes on Ireland also contain a number of conversations with all sorts and conditions of people he meets, some on abstract as well as economic matters and some giving picturesque illustration of Irish characters and customs. At the time they were published these books, which dealt with subjects and situations which were matters of considerable importance at the moment, received a good deal of attention. To-day their interest is very much diminished, although they remain examples of the comprehensive and painstaking methods of investigation of their author.

COLONEL A. PONSONBY

IN all probability the larger number of diaries in existence are those which are in manuscript written by people who never reached sufficient eminence to have their biographies compiled and who were not specially prominent in any sphere. It does not follow, of course, that these are bad diaries, but no doubt a large number of them do not appear to the families who possess them to be worthy of publication. Colonel Arthur Ponsonby's diary is included here as an example, being more or less typical of this class of diary. Nevertheless, it has distinctive features which would not be commonly found in all such diaries.

To begin with, he wrote with the most scrupulous daily regularity. Hardly a break occurs throughout his life from the age of 22 in 1849, when he began, to within two days of his death in

1868. The diary fills fourteen volumes with an extra volume of early reminiscences. It was for *himself* that he kept a diary, " having found it a useful book of reference and also to myself an interesting one." Several of the volumes are fully indexed, which shows that he must have re-read them very carefully. It is seldom that he begins an entry without noting the weather, and in some volumes there are temperature and weather charts. His scores at cricket matches are entered in lists, his dinner parties, the letters he writes and his weight. On several occasions he enters his accounts, card debts, etc. The first time he does this in 1850, after a page or so of items of expenditure he leaves off and writes : " Left off here, it was such a bore and not much use." Another distinctive feature of the diary is that it is illustrated with little drawings of people, sketches of places, and caricatures, including several of himself.

Colonel Ponsonby had a by no means uneventful career. He was the second son of General Sir Frederick Ponsonby, who at the time of his son's birth was Governor of Malta. The Duke of Wellington was his godfather. He first obtained a commission in the 43rd line regiment, and was quartered in Ireland ; he served in the Kaffir war in South Africa, received a commission in the Grenadier Guards and went out to the Crimea, served on the staff in Corfu, and finally was sent to India as Lieutenant-Colonel of the 12th Regiment in 1864, where he remained till his death. Between each of these periods there were intervals in London, Ireland and other parts of the country.

As to the general character of the diary, it is a typical soldier's diary, merely recording the daily incidents of regimental life or military life on active service, with many notes about games, sport, racing, entertainments, theatricals, dinner parties, etc., etc., and very little else—a full record of doings, in fact, without any thoughts or reflections. The doings, too, are related very baldly, although sometimes he enlarges on questions of policy and strategy in war time and shows an interest in the political gossip of the day. In fact, in 1857 he unsuccessfully contested a seat in Ireland and gives an account of his canvassing and meetings. Recording his first meeting, he says :

It is not as disagreeable as I expected. But one man questioned me and one Quaker female talked bosh. All very civil—the tories also.

When he is in London he notes dinners and plays and a good deal about the opera, with criticism of the performers and great enthusiasm about the music. His accounts of dances give one a slight indication from time to time of his preference for certain of his partners. But Colonel Ponsonby had no inclination, even if he had the capacity, to note his inner feelings. In fact, one finds him deliberately avoiding it, as, for instance, when his greatest friend with whom he had been in constant companionship leaves South Africa, he writes :

> The fatal steamer had arrived which is to carry A. off. All confusion, as she only waited an hour—walked down to see him off.

And then he scores three or four blank lines with his pen as an expression of his feelings.

His elder brother, to whom he is specially devoted, he does refer to on more than one occasion with some warmth : " There cannot be a kinder brother on earth than he is," " the best brother in the world."

It is inevitable in the most matter-of-fact and coldly impersonal journal that when a man writes practically every day throughout his life he cannot avoid some comment on his deeper experiences, however much he may want to conceal his feelings even from himself. So in this diary, where there is no attempt at introspective analysis of emotions, little sentences and expressions emerge which betray his sentiments. For instance, he naturally as a daily diarist makes notes about his health. On one occasion in 1862, in India, he is more seriously ill ; he fears it is Bright's disease and writes : " Fatal ! ! ! ! well, I shan't be sorry." Those half-dozen words in a reticent writer are more eloquent than pages of groaning. So one is inclined to pass somewhat rapidly over the daily entries and the long descriptions of travel, of experiences on active service, of hunting and cricket matches, in order to try and discover more of the man. But he says practically nothing about himself except that he is shy.

Nevertheless, in the later years of the journal the story of the romance and at the same time the trouble of his life threads itself through the colourless record of his doings. One would not be justified in detaching the little sentences of affection, of hope and of despair which he cannot help jotting in his diary. The Greek young lady with whom he falls in love when in Corfu is always referred to by him with affection and pity. But from her actions which are recorded—her caprices, her flights and her childishness—something can be gathered of the trials he endured. Once there is a note of desperation, but never a syllable of complaint or regret. He never fails her, and finally marries her the day before he leaves for India. There is a brief entry :

An event of my life, went with . . . to the registry office, did the business. . . .

The diary ends in June, 1868; cholera is raging, the entries tell of its ravages. On June 14 he records a death and adds, " But no new cases since the 11th." He himself died two days later on June 16. His wife survived him for thirteen years, He had no children.

Colonel Ponsonby was known to his friends as a very amusing and unconventional man. But there is nothing in the diary which would give a reader this impression. One gathers he has a sense of humour by some of the drawings and by some witty anecdotes he writes down. But his powers of narrative and description were limited, and he makes very little out of his quite interesting experiences.

LIEUT.-GENERAL SIR CHARLES WINDHAM

IN the Crimean War, between September 1854 and September 1855, General Windham kept a diary which is little more than a military record of events.

Originally an officer in the Coldstream Guards, Windham accompanied Sir George Cathcart to the Crimea as Assistant Quartermaster-General. After his arrival he notes down the daily events of the prolonged siege of Sebastopol, his object no doubt being to keep a record for his family. He seldom refers to his own feelings except when an engagement is pending. Before the battle of the Alma he writes :

> It was my first fight and I was quite astounded at my coolness. I did not feel a bit more nervous than I should have done in Hyde Park.

And before the battle of Inkerman, in which he distinguished himself :

> This week will bring a change to many and on this corner of a small peninsula will take place events that will shake States and make families in countries far away shed many a bitter tear. May mine not be one of them is my most earnest prayer to God.

He is extremely critical, and comments frequently on the mismanagement of affairs. He says in one place that perhaps he indulges too much in " grumble and complaint." But in all probability his strictures were only too well founded, as the mismanagement of both organization and military tactics in the Crimean War is now a matter of common knowledge. The entries, written with few breaks almost daily, give the fresh impressions of the moment, and although they deal with the details of the campaign, he shows the penetration and judgment of one who can grasp the whole situation.

We will give some of the critical passages :

Oct. 18. This long range firing is all nonsense ; moreover the Russians are better at it than we are and from all I can see our present attack is an absurdity.

Dec. 12. If England and France strain every nerve and send every man I do not say but folly may ultimately be made triumphant ; without this I doubt it. How creditable to have to say that all our sick are carried to Balaclava by the French mules, our own ambulance corps being found perfectly useless, the pensioners sick or drunk, the mules used up or dead.

Feb. 8. But I must control myself even in this journal although it is unquestionably disgusting to be put under such a system and to see men rewarded as those at Headquarters have been, for casting ruin and havoc to the right and left through their ignorance or rather want of forethought and business habits.

March 23. But I will not go on growling. For my part I think everything on the part of the allies so slackly performed that I am perfectly disgusted.

April 7. I have received this night an order to prepare for an attack to-morrow and everything is ordered to be in readiness. For aught I know it may please God to prevent my seeing wife or children again in this world ; and therefore I am writing with serious feelings and with no levity. Yet I wish to record my feelings ; and I do say that the imbecility of the conduct of the allies arising from I know not what beyond pure stupidity surpasses human comprehension.

April 26. What a pity it is that we should have no real leader in either Army. The French are, I think, worse off than we are. They have as much prejudice and more conceit.

He has a great admiration for Sir George Cathcart, who fell at Inkerman, and wishes he had been appointed Commander-in-Chief. At first he has doubts about Lord Raglan.

I hope that with his " baton " he will flog matters on a little faster than he has done hitherto, but I doubt it. He has not sufficient energy and is far too old for his post.

However, at a later date he revises this judgment, and says :

He is an amiable man, the oldest soldier, and I believe, if left to himself, the best.

His comment on the charge of the Light Brigade at Balaclava is :

Captain Nolan, who took the orders to Lord Cardigan, was killed charging at the head of the Light Cavalry. Although a good fellow from all I can learn, his conduct was inexcusable. His whole object appears to have been to have a charge at the Russians at any cost, but he could not have chosen a worse time.

Windham's great exploit was the assault he led on the Redan, one of the strongest salients in the Russian fortification of Sebastopol. Although he has misgivings about the attack, he welcomes the exploit, as he is a lover of action and hates the waiting and delay in the trenches.

The day before (September 7) he writes :

> If my brigade is ordered to lead the assault against the Redan it is a hundred to one that I am killed ; but better far die so than get ignominiously hit in the trenches.

After sleeping well he makes some jottings in his diary on the morning of September 8, in which this passage occurs :

> And now my dear Pem [his wife] this journal I have ordered to be sent to you provided I am never to write in it again. It is written hurriedly and in some places violently but always honestly.

We have a short account of the assault, written on the actual evening, which is worth giving in full :

> The assault took place alone and I went over the Parallel at the head of the 41st. The Grenadiers followed me pretty well but not in the best order. I went straight at the ditch and did all that man could do to get them into the centre of the battery but it was no go. I ran out into the middle of the battery with my sword over my head, but it was useless. They would stick to their gabions and to firing and not come to the bayonet ; so after holding on to it for near an hour and having sent back Swire twice, a young officer Lieut. Young of the 19th and Colonel Eman to tell Codrington that he *must* send me the supports *in some formation* I went back myself and asked leave to have a fresh battalion.
> This was granted and I put myself at the head of the " Royals." Whilst Codrington was considering whether he would let me go on or not, the whole attacking force fell back leaving behind numbers of killed and wounded.
> If I could have got the men of the storming party to make a rush I should have carried it ; but I never could. They were all in disorder and each looking out for himself. The officers behaved well and so did the men as individuals but not collectively. Came back very hoarse. Poor Roger Swire is badly wounded.

Windham's waving sword was great. But his pen cannot do justice to the incident. The assault failed, but Windham's reputation was made. He was known afterwards as " Redan Windham." He was appointed Governor of the surrendered part of

Sebastopol, during which time he only made a few more entries in his diary. On his return to England he was received with great honour, specially in his native county of Norfolk. He was afterwards knighted. After being an M.P. for a few months he was sent out to India during the Mutiny. In 1867 he was appointed to command the forces in Canada, and he died in 1870.

Like many other soldiers, he was not a diary writer and only kept a record in time of war. The entries, though they are exclusively concerned with the military events of the moment, show us a masterful, self-confident man with a keen sense of duty and with little or no sense of humour. He sums himself up in the following paragraph :

> In fact I worked hard ; feel convinced that I did my duty like a good soldier, feeling no funk. I am sure I showed none and therefore whether I am mentioned or not in despatches is a matter of indifference.

His son, Captain Windham, published the diary in 1897, together with a number of his father's letters, which fill more colour and detail into the picture.

GEORGE ELIOT

CROSS'S *Life of George Eliot* is composed of extracts from her letters and her journal. While the whole diary is not given, and in all probability the more intimate and personal entries are omitted, we gather from George Eliot's references to her journal that she was not a regular daily writer, although at times the entries are frequent. But she acknowledges sometimes that weeks and months have elapsed without any entry being made. The first extract given is in 1855 ; but she mentions having begun the diary in 1849, and that book she finishes in 1861. She starts another book which lasts her till 1877, when she writes :

> To-day I say a final farewell to this little book which is the only record I have made of my personal life for sixteen years and more. I have often been helped in looking back on it to compare former with actual states of despondency from bad health or other apparent causes. In this way a past despondency has turned to present hopefulness. . . . I shall record no more in this book because I am going to keep a more business-like diary.

And from that date she only makes one-line occasional memoranda of engagements, etc.

George Eliot wrote for herself. The diary contains chiefly records with regard to her writing and reading, travels, and health, and several notes about concerts and her love of music. Its dryness and severity is relieved by more expansive passages in which she refers to her great devotion to George Lewes, with whom she lived from 1854 till he died, and more especially to the deep depression she passes through on account of her health. At the end of the year she often makes a sort of review of the past twelve months.

One might suppose that a learned woman of a deeply philosophic temperament would, when at the age of 38 she began publishing novels, have regarded their reception with calm, if not indifference. It comes, therefore, as a surprise, but at the same time as a pleasing testimony of the human side of her nature, to find by her diary that her excitement and elation at her success is hardly surpassed by Fanny Burney on the publication of *Evelina* when she was 25; and, like Fanny, in her first pride of secret authorship she collects and records every word of praise and commendation she receives or hears of. Entries of this description are not confined to her first book, but her subsequent successes are duly registered.

Amos Barton, the first of the " Scenes of Clerical Life," appeared in 1857, and was an immediate success. There was a good deal of mystification about the authorship. *Mr. Gilfil's Love Story* and *Janet's Repentance* followed soon after.

> Mr. John Blackwood already expressed himself with much greater warmth of admiration; and when the first part had appeared he sent me a charming letter with a cheque for fifty guineas. . . . Albert Smith sent him a letter saying he had never read anything that affected him more.
>
> Received letter from Blackwood expressing his approbation of *Mr. Gilfil's Love Story*. He writes very pleasantly, says the series is attributed by many to Bulwer and that Thackeray thinks highly of it. This was a pleasant fillip to me who am just now ready to be dispirited on the slightest pretext.
>
> The other day we had a pleasant letter from Herbert Spencer saying he had heard *Mr. Gilfil's Love Story* discussed . . . all expressing warm approval and curiosity as to the author.

Of the many letters she received, perhaps the best and the most really complimentary and gratifying was from Dickens, who was never taken in by supposing the author was a man. Dickens became a friend later on, and she notes in her diary his coming to dinner. A few extracts may be given with regard to her other books.

Adam Bede:

> Blackwood told me the first *ab extra* opinion of the book which happened to be precisely what I most desired. A cabinet maker had read the sheets and declared the writer must have been brought up to the business or at least had listened to the workmen in their workshop.

> Blackwood writes to say I am " a popular author as well as a great author." They printed 2090 of *Adam Bede* and have disposed of more than 1800 so they were thinking about a second edition. A very feeling letter from Froude this morning.

> I have left off recording the history of *Adam Bede* and the pleasant letters and words that came to me—the success has been so triumphantly beyond anything I had dreamed of that it would be tiresome to put down particulars.

To such a height had her reputation risen that she records an offer from a publisher who was ready to pay £10,000 for *Romola,* but according to an entry later on the final arrangement was to publish *Romola* in the *Cornhill Magazine* for £7,000. For *Felix Holt* she received £5,000, and of *Middlemarch* she says :

> No former book of mine has been received with more enthusiasm—not even *Adam Bede.*

And of *David Deronda :*

> The success of the work at present is greater than that of *Middlemarch* up to the corresponding point of publication.

So far as the reception of her novels was concerned she had nothing to complain of. To George Lewes she refers constantly in terms of great affection. She reads her manuscripts to him, and he encourages her. She is interested in his literary work, and they enjoy together travel, study, music and intellectual discussion. A couple of brief entries in 1858 show this :

> Jan. 24. G. came in the evening at 10 o'clock—after I had suffered a great deal in thinking of the possibilities that might prevent him from coming.

> Jan. 25. This morning I have read to G. all I have written during his absence and he approves it more than I expected.

The intellectual level was fearfully high, judging by the enormous quantity of books she notes as having been read. For *Romola,* for instance, the list of Italian works she devoured occupies a printed page. But in reading George Eliot's diary the question that presses on one is not that which has often been discussed as to whether her excessive erudition was not on the whole damaging to her genius as a writer of fiction, but the opposite one, how this abnormally learned metaphysically-minded woman could have created Mrs. Poyser, Hetty, Amos Barton, Gwendolen, etc., etc.

This sort of entry occurs frequently:

> Began Part IV of Spinoza's Ethics. Began also to read Cumming for article in the " Westminster." We are reading in the evenings now Sydney Smith's letters, Boswell, Whewell's ' History of Inductive Sciences,' the Odyssey and occasionally Heine's Reisebilder. I began the second book of the Iliad in Greek this morning.
>
> Walked with George over Primrose Hill. We talked of Plato and Aristotle.

As time goes on, in spite of success and domestic happiness, in spite of the big cheques and all the favourable opportunities for travel and intellectual pursuits, the most notable feature of the diary is the constant record of overwhelming depressions, which were caused largely by ill health. A few quotations will show that she confided to the diary, and perhaps to the diary alone, the recurrence of these moods of deep despondency.

> 1860. My want of health and strength has prevented me from working much—still worse has made me despair of ever working well again.
>
> 1861. Struggling constantly with depression. Got into a state of so much wretchedness in attempting to concentrate my thoughts on the construction of my story that I became desperate and suddenly burst my bonds, saying, I will not think of writing.
>
> 1862. Have been reading some entries in my note book of past times in which I recorded my malaise and despair. But it is impossible that I have ever been in so unpromising and despairing a state as I now feel.
>
> I am extremely spiritless, dead, and hopeless about my writing. The long state of headache has left me in depression and incapacity.
>
> 1864. Horrible scepticism about all things paralysing my mind. Shall I ever be good for anything again ? Ever do anything again ?

In the retrospect at the end of this year she only refers to bad health and repeats a tribute to George Lewes for " his perfect love."

> 1866. Ill ever since I came home so that the days seem to have made a muddy flood sweeping away all labour and all growth.

In 1868 her review of the year is more cheerful. She ends up :

> We have had no real trouble. I wish we were not in a minority of our fellow men ! I desire no added blessing for the coming year but this—that I may do some good lasting work and make both my outward and inward habits less imperfect—that is more directly tending to the best uses of life.

After this the entries in the diary are fewer. There is only one more review of the year, written on January 1, 1874. It is cheerful in tone, although at the end she says :

> I have been for a month rendered almost helpless for intellectual work by constant headaches but am getting a little more freedom. Nothing is wanting to my blessings but the uninterrupted power of work. For as to all my unchangeable imperfections I have resigned myself.

She notes in her diary, " a great gap since I last made a record," and indeed there are few other entries before she concludes the notebook in 1879 with the remark above quoted. It would seem as if she outgrew the habit of noting her moods and decided to keep only very brief memoranda of her doings. Even her marriage to Mr. Cross in 1880 is simply noted in the baldest possible way.

George Eliot's diary is definitely restricted to the progress and business connected with her writing, the books she read, notes with regard to her movements and visits abroad, and the people she meets and rather fuller confessions as to her health and spirits. But she never says one word of praise, criticism or description of the people she meets. Nor does she write in her journal any reflections on life in general. Needless to say, George Eliot makes no remarks in her diary about her food or about her domestic servants, not that she could not have been very entertaining on both these subjects. Editing has probably deprived us of much that would give us a closer knowledge of this remarkable woman.

JOHN ADDINGTON SYMONDS

MR. HORATIO BROWNE, Symonds' biographer, had, he tells us, an abundance of material at his disposal in compiling his book. In addition to thirty published volumes, notebooks, letters and memoranda, he found an autobiography and diaries. In his intention, which he carries out very skilfully and scrupulously, to make Symonds himself tell the story of his life, he quotes largely from the diaries and autobiography. But the extracts from the diaries are necessarily brief compared to the diaries themselves, though they are sufficient to show us the purposes for which he kept his diary and his manner and method of writing in it. Symonds, apart from his wonderful capacity for expression, had an almost morbid love of self-analysis and self-dissection, and the outpourings of his soul would no doubt include passages of such an intimate character that a biographer would hesitate to publish them.

Symonds was born in 1840, and he first kept a diary when he was 18. It concerns his travels, and so rapidly does he acquire the diary habit that the book, covering 233 pages, is carefully indexed at the end. In 1860, when at Balliol, he begins again, and practically never left off till the day before he died. The diary opens thus :

> It is rather adventurous to begin keeping a journal after so many failures and without the unity of subject which I thought so necessary to make the trouble endurable. Yet as I consider a diary useful as a mechanical memory and interesting personally for the future, I shall attempt to keep one. The custom of writing while abroad will make it easier to do so here and my unity of subject must be exoteric. The journey was decidedly historical and exoteric. This I will try to make more a record of what passes in myself and my more private concerns.

Later on he makes the following remark on diary writing :

> Diary good for thoughts, not for things. Ordinary log book a poor affair. Useless to eliminate what others ought not to see. Danger of overdoing emotion.

Nevertheless, his own highly-strung artistic temperament was certainly emotional, and his bad health contributed to his internal despondency. These moods of depression, however, he confided to his diary. His friends could hardly guess the presence of this inward turmoil. As Mr. Browne says, " It is possible that many who met Symonds did not surmise behind the brilliant audacious exterior, underlying the witty conversation and the keen enjoyment of life and movement about him, this central core of spiritual pain " ; and again, " all through the diary underlying his studies, underlying his affection for his friends, runs the perpetual strain of self-analysis, comparison, criticism, reproach." For Symonds a diary was a real secret confidant, nor did he shrink from its falling into the hands of his friend after he had gone.

We need hardly dwell on his constant illness, except to say that such expressions as these occur again and again : " bad depressed headache," " painful reveries," " weary dreams," " weak and melancholy," " three bad nights in succession have made me weak and nervous." " my depression is extreme."

His self-analysis is acute and merciless. A few instances may be given in the earlier years.

A man may have susceptibilities of genius without any of its creative power; but if he has any atom of talent he cannot be without practical energy.

I may rave but I shall never rend the heavens : I may sit and sing but I shall never make earth listen.

And I am not strong enough to be good—what is left ? I do not feel strong enough to be bad.

The sum of intellectual progress I hoped for has been obtained, but how much below my hopes. My character has developed but in what puny proportions, below my meanest anticipations. I do not feel a man. This book is an evidence of the yearnings without power and the brooding self-analysis without creation that afflict me. I am not a man.

His artistic appreciations are very deep and penetrating, whether for painting, architecture, music, poetry, or nature. And from a quite early age he is able to give descriptions of what he sees and hears which show, not only an exceptional power of expression, but a still more exceptional power of observation of eye and of memory. In the accounts he gives in his diary of his travels in the Alps and in Italy, there is a beauty of language which places them on a very different level from the usual descriptions which one is very apt to skip. They are, however, too long to quote, and there is a richness and exuberance about them which may not suit all tastes. We may give one of his reflections after a description of Castellamare :

The world is wide, wide, wide and what we struggle for, ten thousand happy souls in one fair bay have never dreamed of. I would give much to live and love and pass my life within the sound of these unvarying waves and in the gorgeous interchange of light and gloom which dwells for ever on the furrowed hills.

Symonds had many close friends ; it is, therefore, interesting to hear him on friendship:

It is a bad thing to base any friendship on uncommon and merely emotional sympathies. They may wear out. Friendship ought to be a matter of daylight not of gas, red lights or sky rockets.

Jowett, of Balliol, stood very high in his estimation and exercised a very sympathetic yet at the same time bracing influence over him. Jowett's laconic style and absence of emotionalism acted as some check on the unrestrained artistic luxuriance of his friend. We get many characteristic glimpses of the future Master of Balliol in the diary.

> Breakfast with Jowett. I met a stupid man called S. S. who spoiled every effort at conversation by insisting on talking about Miss Eagle and ventriloquists.
>
> We breakfast at nine. I was glad of this for it is hard to entertain Jowett. His forte is *aurea taciturnitas* and he has a habit of shutting up a subject by a single sentence. The conversation is one conducted by question and answer. I start a subject and ask a question. He makes an answer and stifles the subject.
>
> Jowett and I went to Seed's where he had his portrait taken. It was very good of him to let it be done, for he hated it. He stood so funnily—like a doll straight and stiff. The man tried to drill him into a position : he was meek but awkward. I told him to stand naturally. The man wanted him to set his necktie straight—trying to destroy personality ; but I would not let him. It took a long time and Jowett looked cross and uncomfortable.
>
> One of the reasons why he makes me shy beyond his own silent shyness is that he is so uncommunicative of himself. I feel that he is self wrapped and that he will not lift the curtain. He lives within a veil and is all in all to his own thoughts. Egotistical people are easier to get on with partly because you despise their egotism.

After taking a first in his degree at Oxford, Symonds writes :

> Certainly Oxford honours are a poor thing. The glory of them soon departs, the pleasure fleets away and we have another struggle rising up at once. Yet I can never be too thankful for having been able to give papa so great satisfaction. All the trouble I had was well compensated by his pleasure and the thought of that is my most solid gain.

The diary, as time goes on, gets filled with his artistic studies. His almost over-developed æsthetic appreciations make him pour out the most elaborate and profound analysis of what he sees and hears. So extreme is it that references to " a strained feeling in my head " come as no surprise.

He uses his diary as a sort of practice ground for his writing. After an immense entry on the Elizabethan spirit in literature, he ends :

> This diatribe, being very ill this morning, I wrote to distract my mind from its troubles, to rouse me from a clinging lethargy in which will, memory, physical force and power of thought seemed all exhausted.

In the biography we only get extracts from the diary in the earlier years. There is a great deal of other material which is drawn on for his later life up to his death.

In this period Mr. Browne tells us that speculation and analysis of abstractions become less prominent and " his artistic sensuous temperament found satisfaction in actual life."

The diary has no doubt been invaluable to his biographer,

and we can quite well gather what kind of diary Symonds kept. But we are not allowed to see sufficient of it to analyse it closely. A man who keeps a regular diary and writes also an autobiography may be condemned as an egotist. But egotism of this sort does not by any means necessarily imply conceit. If it is a fault it is a fault of temperament, not of intellect.

LIEUT.-GENERAL SIR GERALD GRAHAM

THIS distinguished soldier, who was born in 1830, saw a good deal of active service in the Crimea, where he won the Victoria Cross, and subsequently in China and in Egypt. He kept a regular business-like military diary, which, though practically exclusively concerned with his military experiences, shows in its breezy, laconic style that its author had a cheerful disposition and a sense of humour. There are no personal or subjective references in it, but curiously enough he often makes notes of the books he is reading.

I am reading daily a little of Frederick the Great.

What a wonderful knowledge of character is shown by the author of *Adam Bede*.

Reading *Adam Bede* again. This is a charming book; one seems to live in while reading. How intensely English—*rural* English—in its character. Now Miss Brontë's novels are somewhat tinged with French melodrama.

I am deeply interested in the life of Charlotte Brontë. It is a wonderful tale. She is a heroine for every Englishman to be proud of.

In the China campaign he describes being wounded:

I got shot in my leg the ball burying itself in the flesh without cutting the thick serge trousers;

but he is much more concerned about his horse being wounded, and continues to direct his men. Graham was a friend of Gordon's, having been his contemporary at the Military Academy. They come together during the China campaign in 1860.

Charlie Gordon arrived. . . . He is still brimful of energy but has sobered down into a more reflective character. He is really a remarkably fine fellow.

And in 1884, in Egypt, he has many talks with him and accompanies him as far as Assouan on his way to Khartoum. His conversations, together with a graphic description of his parting from Gordon, were eventually published in a book entitled *Last Words with Gordon*.

The diary extracts only cover comparatively brief periods in China and Egypt. Once or twice he gives rather a longer account of the events he witnesses, as, for instance, the signing of the treaty at the end of the China campaign. But for the most part the entries are in brief sentences obviously written at the moment and on the spot.

> Quaint old town—bad smells—went up to the top of the tower.
>
> Beastly place Masameh. A lot of dead bodies about. Ordered to occupy Kassassin so I moved out at 5 p.m.

And here is a description of an engagement:

> Beginning to arrange my kit as on the 28th when the Philistines are on us! Are they mad? In five minutes my dispositions are made and in twenty minutes the troops are out in line of battle. Heavy artillery fire from enemy as before but our guns advance with the Infantry and before 9 a.m. the enemy are in full retreat. . . . Posting pickets in evening. Sent telegram to dear J. [his wife] 'All right.'

The diary is quoted in the biography written by Colonel Vetch and published in 1901.

WILLIAM CORY

BIOGRAPHERS are very apt to discard all material which does not enhance the reputation of their subject, more especially if they are writing about some one whose friends and relations are still alive. It is very doubtful whether they succeed by this means in attracting the human sympathy for and appreciation of their hero or heroine in the same way as if they put in the shadows and darker parts of the picture and desisted from pedestal making. It is the man on our level we like reading about and we are likely to love the best. Abnormality and excessive righteousness fill us with awe but not with affection.

There is no biography of William Cory, the author of *Ioniac*. But in the volume published by his friends in 1897, containing his letters and extracts from his journal, he is presented as a cultivated scholar-poet with refined and correct tastes, writing, thinking, saying all the right things in the right way, and indiscretions, lapses. faults, trivialities have been carefully eliminated. There may have been good reason for doing this. But we only get part of the man, and if the diary extracts convey a rather self-complacent person expressing in well-turned phrases unexceptionable thoughts and careful judgments, and if there seems to be a noticeable absence of any rash and clumsy jottings or any of the little stupidities which rampage through the pages of many diaries, we must not misjudge Cory, but we must remember that only part of his journal is given.

William Johnson was born in 1823. He was educated at Eton and King's College, Cambridge, and served as assistant master at Eton from 1845 to 1872. During this period a number of boys who afterwards became well-known figures in public life came under his influence, and among them he made many close and devoted friends. He had the reputation of being the most brilliant Eton tutor of his day. In 1872, having inherited an estate at Halsdon, he resigned his mastership and assumed the name of Cory.

Judging by the extracts, we should say that Cory was a pretty regular diary writer. But it is only between 1863 and 1873 that sections from the journal are given. In a letter to his brother (who took the name of Furse and was afterwards archdeacon of Westminster) he says something about his motive in keeping a diary, and mentions a drawer full of them at Eton.

> I often write at considerable length leaving out all sordid and vexatious things. I wish I had written more at school ; as it is there are records of a whole fortnight and a month (last May) which may some day be valued as data for an account of Eton life. In another way I sometimes think my journals will be valuable ; they will contain some careful studies of people whose biographies will be written, if not published.

We see, therefore, that he was writing for posterity, and if he consistently avoided recording " sordid and vexatious things " we might find, were the whole of his diary available, that it contained no intimate personal reflections. Again, he says that he writes journals " for one or two friends—very garrulous sometimes." So what he wrote was to be read either immediately or later on. His diary was not a private affair, and indeed this is apparent in the polish of the writing, the self-conscious expressions of opinion and elaborate descriptions of scenery.

Staying with Lord Halifax at Hickleton (two of the sons were his pupils), he writes :

> Though ill a bit, I am revived by being here ; it makes me fancy once more that I am near the heart of my country and in some sense ennobled. I think if I write a letter from here it will be in purer English and more courteous.

This indeed seems to have been the ideal which he successfully pursued—to write in pure English and to be courteous. Nothing ever jars or is harsh. Even when he goes to the Athenæum he reads " softly."

His many descriptions of scenery, though pretty and often poetical, have a want of bite, and their delicacy sometimes becomes a little flowery, as, for instance :

> We walked on through the Abbey Grounds where nothing grows but a few sprays of tamarisk, a little grass, and samphire ; we sat close to a fallen signal post and a battered figurehead doing duty for ghost and watched the blossoms of sea weed fluttering and alighting on the little patch of turf. Then we walked on the steep slope of down to the little water-fall which ended in a little rill's life in a cleft between two promontories and was blown back like ' the wasted purpose ' in ' Lotos Eaters ' by a mighty wind from the Atlantic.

There are many accounts of travel in Scotland and the Lakes as well as abroad in Austria, Egypt, and Turkey. But by far the most natural and spontaneous entries are about his school work:

> 1864. I looked over Dalmeny's verses ; to alter them was a long delicate job as they were not commonplace *pro formâ* things but an honest attempt at turning (of his own accord) some rhymes of mine which he had read in manuscript.
>
> I had a peculiar pleasure—a letter from the father of a boy who had been in my division thanking me for making his boy's work pleasant to him : the most gratifying letter I ever had on professional matters.
>
> A splendid bit of Virgil—Evander's lament for his son—full of grammar, idiom and sentiment. I tried the patience of the boys with wanton digressions till we were getting late for school.
>
> My young boys gathered round the fire ; I read them bits of Cowper, a good passage about the wickedness of ambitious kings. . . . Told them about Cowper and Huskisson ; they filled in the dropped rhymes and were intelligent. They read to me some chapters of Nehemiah—the bit about Ezra telling the people not to weep ; and then St. Paul's parting with the elders of Ephesus. . . . I was sorry when they went, being chilly and dull ; fell asleep.
>
> Themes or rather versions—lukewarm Latin anyhow. Miscellaneous business with some brats. Shute set down to verses by himself.
>
> 1867. It seems a pity tutors generally let Sunday Private Business be a thorough bore to themselves as well as the boys ; they shirk it the first Sunday and whenever they can. The boys actually hate doing Greek Testament on Sundays ; how can it make them religious ?
>
> 1868. Expounding Tacitus and Roman history to three dozen beery, sleepy, ignorant lads. . . . forty minutes of Pharaoh in the sands, drag, drag. . . .
>
> To-day I had three stout loud emphatic fierce lectures using my voice as a horse drench or syringe.

1869. There was no time for singing before Chapel. I was with the Fourth Form an hour.

Athanasius was more horrible than usual and Church militant and Commandments more odious. At 11-20 we were off to the Beeches in a break. Ainger and Marindin were the ushers in charge, I a rover only. We sang a little on the way, first driving, then walking through the woodland. We raced about the dells and had to shout shrilly to get together. They cut sticks, climbed trees, picked ferns, combined in groups and broke up freely. We went through Dropmore with unusual vagabondary, with a dull gardener. We dined at 2-30 and enjoyed the fire, then walked up the bank to the locks, explored a brewery, looked in at a flour mill, ran races. We drove back in the dusk. At 5-30 we all came to the Mouse Trap [his house] and hanselled my German tea things finishing the Greek honey which Elliott gave me. We had songs too. This perfect party broke up at 8-30.

This may not be such pure English, but it is much more real, than the poetic prose. In fact, all the school entries when he was busy and probably wrote in a hurry are terse and vivid.

There are some good political anecdotes, and he himself makes a speech in the Windsor theatre at an election. Many literary judgments and criticisms of books are set down, and accounts of interesting conversations.

In 1878 he writes an amusing description of an imaginary wife :

If I had married as other people do, by this time my wife would be pursy, short of breath, addicted to sal volatile, unable to sing, begrimed with frugality, bent on making me write letters to people whose sons have been my pupils, to make interest for her nephews, cousins or pet clergy : fretting at my want of progress and my patient submission to all the defeats inflicted on me by younger men, feeling with cruel pain all that I feel with a mild sentimental twinge and worse than all drenching me with aphorisms about the Will of God of which she would be sure to think she knew as much as if she had been admitted to His counsels.

As a matter of fact, Cory did marry late in life, at the age of 55. He died in 1892.

As already said it would be unfair to judge the diarist by the selected and abridged sections that are published from his journal. We get very little impression of the charming man he is known to have been. In his letters, contained in the same volume, the actual personal touch with his correspondents brings out more fully and naturally some of his rare qualities.

JAMES HANNINGTON

THE last diary of an ecclesiastic in this collection differs from any of its predecessors. Hannington was a Bishop, but a very different type from Cartwright or Wilberforce. He was a missionary, but in no way does he resemble the ascetic scholar Martyn. Like the others, however, he kept a regular diary which shows him to have been a man of action, straightforward, energetic, addicted to no morbid inclinations or profound religious meditations. There is indeed a matter-of-fact conventionality in his career which is only broken by the tragic adventures which terminated it. In the early entries, which begin about 1863, his love of action, sport and travel are far more noticeable than any call to enter holy orders. At 16 he joins the volunteers, and this is noted as a red-letter day in his diary. " My first day in uniform." and later in the same year :

My father gave me a single barrel breech loader gun ; 17 guineas. My delight is great.

My seventeenth birthday. Shot eighteen brace of birds, four hares, one land rail, 5 feet 10 inches high, weight 11 stone 6 lbs.

The circumstances which led to his going into the Church were exterior, not interior. A chapel at Hurstpierpoint belonging to his father, in which Nonconformist services were held, was transferred by him to the Church of England and licensed for public worship by the Bishop of Chichester. James Hannington notes therefore :

Through the change from dissent to the Church I got to know the clergy of the parish church and college. I yearned for ordination.

Up at Oxford at St. Mary's Hall he has difficulty with his examinations. He was more interested in rowing than learning, and was full of boyish spirits :

For a bet I wheeled Captain Way up the High Street in a wheelbarrow and turned him out opposite the Angel Hotel.

Bumped Keble—Should have caught Exeter but No. 3 caught a crab instead.

Of all atrocious horrors this is the most disgusting. We have been re-bumped by Keble.

When he is in Devonshire as a curate the entries show how he was always to the fore in helping and doctoring people, and whenever there was trouble, danger, or adventure to be undertaken that was what he liked best. " I enjoy the uphill struggle path most of all." He writes very simply, without the smallest symptom of self-righteousness or pose. A very characteristic entry is the one he makes the day before his ordination at Chichester as priest in 1876.

> A day of rest. I nested in the Bishop's garden and round the belfry Tower for swifts' eggs.

In 1877 he marries. There is certainly no sentimentality about the following :

> Proposed to Blanche Hawkin-Turvin and was accepted.

But on New Year's Day, a week later, he indulges in a little reflection, which is quite exceptional with him.

> The New Year breaks in upon me. How ? How ? Under a new epoch. I am engaged to be married, I, who have always been supposed, and have supposed myself to be a confirmed bachelor, cross, crabbed, ill conditioned ! What a change in the appearance of everything does this make ! It, however, seems to fill me with the things of this world and to make me cold and dead. Lord Jesus grant that we may love Thee each succeeding hour more abundantly. Amen. Amen.

Mission work begins to interest him, and finally he writes :

> H. G. came to see me and to my surprise told me that he longed to become a missionary. I told him that I longed to be one too.

His ambition is gratified. He is appointed by the Church Missionary Society, and after farewells he undertakes his first journey to Africa in 1882. From this time onward his diary, which is kept with great regularity, is that of a traveller and explorer full of the detail of his adventures and illustrated with drawings and sketches. Owing to ill health he was obliged to return in 1883. But he was so obviously the man for the work that on his return he was consecrated as first Bishop of Eastern Equatorial Africa, and started out again in 1884. After establishing himself at Frere Town he sets out on a journey to Uganda. No obstacle or hardship daunts him. His own health he is determined shall stand the strain. " Fever threatening but I won't give way." He determines, after weighing the pros and cons, all of which considerations are noted in his diary, to go in advance of the main caravan by a new route into Uganda, and has to pass through the dangerous territory of the Masai. He and his followers are captured and imprisoned. After eight days, during which he was confined, racked by fever, in the most loathsome dirt and discomfort, he was led out to an open space, where he and the rest of his small party were speared and shot to death.

The remarkable thing, so far as his diary is concerned, is that he wrote it, though often sentence by sentence and with the greatest difficulty, right up to the very last day of his imprisonment. A few extracts must be given from these last entries:

> Up to one o'clock I have received no news whatever and I fear at least a week in this black hole in which I can barely see to write. Floor covered with rotting banana peel and leaves and lice. Men relieving nature at night on the floor; a smoking fire at which my guards cook and drink pombe; in a feverish district; fearfully shaken, scarce power to hold up a small Bible. Shall I live through it ? My God I am Thine.
>
> Going outside I fell to the ground exhausted and was helped back in a gone condition to my bed; I don't see how I can stand all this and yet I don't want to give in. . . .
>
> (Seventh day's prison.) A terrible night, first with noisy drunken guard and secondly with vermin which have found out my tent and swarm. I don't think I got one sound hour's sleep and woke with fever fast developing. O Lord, do have mercy on me and release me. I am quite broken down and brought low. Comforted by reading Psalm XXVII.
>
> In an hour or two fever developed very rapidly. My tent was so stuffy that I was obliged to go inside the filthy hut and soon was delirious. . . .
>
> (Eighth day's prison.) I can hear no news but was held up by Psalm XXX which came with great power.
>
> A hyena howled near me last night smelling a sick man but I hope it is not to have me yet.

These entries are written in a tiny handwriting in one of Letts' monthly pocket diaries. Difficult as it must have been to write at all, we can imagine that he must have derived some little solace from writing down his terrible experiences.

CAPTAIN EYRE LLOYD

FROM November 12, 1899, to October 29, 1901—that is to say, in the thick of the Boer War—Captain Lloyd kept a regular daily diary. This in itself is something of a feat, as an officer on active service has little or no leisure, and it requires a well-disciplined mind to make a daily memorandum.

The overshadowing and constant danger of warfare may encourage a man who is not naturally a diarist to note the events of each day. But as has already been pointed out, events in these conditions loom too large and the mere record of them is apt to obliterate the personality of the writer. The bare recital of movements of troops, skirmishes, casualties, battles, and intervals of waiting without the relief of personal reflections is dull reading. Captain Lloyd is a typical British officer, accepting discomfort and danger without complaint and even without comment, and noting as carefully the results of a football match, a cricket match, or a game of polo, as a brush with the enemy or even a big engagement.

Here is an instance of his laconic description of a battle:

> Nov. 28. Battle of Modder River. Called up early paraded 4 a.m. to 6-30 p.m. Personal experience in note book. Another frontal attack. Boer trenches very well made. 2nd Battalion losses 12 killed 59 wounded. When we retired the bullets came like a hailstorm and I cannot understand how any of us escaped. Acheson was hit in the foot. A. and S. Highlanders lost heavily through their kilts being so conspicuous. Lost 1 killed and 17 wounded in my company including Acheson and section commanders. A man was shot on each side of me. There were a lot of very narrow escapes. Towney Butler had a bullet through his trousers between his legs, two cut his water bottle and another his helmet. Colour Sergeant Pitt had his haversack cut off. To-day's frontal attack was very nearly a defeat. The next probably will be. We have won these battles in spite of it.

The next day he is delighted at having a bathe and his entry ends:

> There is a hotel here so I have been able to buy a tooth brush at last! I lost mine a week ago.

Quite unperturbed in the face of danger, he notes at a later date:

> In the last hour of daylight I got badly sniped by a Boer; why I was not hit I cannot imagine, he nearly hit me every time.

We get just a glimpse in the following entry of the kindness and generosity of his disposition:

> Sergeant —— was read out on parade at 10 a.m. Went to see him after parade and told him to write to me after he had done his sentence and promised to get him started in life again if I could.

There are just traces of his impatience when he says, " Seems now as if the war will last for ever ! " and in the brief entry on October 27, 1900, " Sick of Pretoria." Ceremonial fooling in the midst of the serious business of war calls forth from him the following amusing comment:

> We are to have a ceremonial parade on the 28th in honour of the King of Portugal's birthday. I don't know who cares about the King of Portugal or who was the ass who discovered his birthday.

Once or twice he notes the beauty of scenery and sees the birds, amongst them " the lovely light blue jay." But for the most part his entries are almost officially dry and colourless, and even the disagreeable duties which fell to him are executed almost callously without any sort of expression of feeling. He allows himself more than once to be critical. " I suppose this accounts for this wretched farce," is his remark at some bungling on the part of his superior officers." And again : " After fighting for nearly two years such stupidity is almost incredible " is his note on a proclamation being issued in English, which the Boers could not understand.

On October 30, 1901, Captain Lloyd was sent to lay out the camp previous to the attack of the Boers, but hearing that his Colonel was wounded and in a tight place he felt it to be his duty to leave a comparatively unimportant task and to put himself at the disposal of his chief. One account says : " He sauntered defiantly and quite upright across the open space shot at by half a thousand rifles at not more than 30 or 40 yards range." He fell before he reached his chief.

The diary is in no way remarkable, but it is thoroughly typical. It was privately printed, together with some of his letters, in 1905.

The following Diaries in this century may also be briefly noted :—
MISS BERRY

Mention may be made of the diary kept by Miss Mary Berry between 1783 and 1848. She wrote at first a diary of her travels of the ordinary guide book description. In 1807, after seeing some one else's journal, she decides to keep a regular diary of her own :

I have hitherto avoided it because I felt ashamed of the use or rather the no use I made of my time. . . . But now no future remains to me [she was 44 and lived to 89] perhaps I may be encouraged to make the most of the present by marking its rapid passage and setting before my eyes the folly of letting a day escape without endeavouring at least to make the best I can of it and above all without making impossible attempts to mend or alter anybody but myself.

Miss Berry had been in her youth a friend of Horace Walpole's, whose works she afterwards edited. She lived with her sister Agnes at Little Strawberry Hill, which had been left to them by Walpole. The diary is nothing but a social record containing all the usual elements. Royalty of course comes in. We have the Regent who " looked wretchedly, swollen up with a muddled complexion and was besides extremely tipsy—gravely and cautiously so." In 1802 she gives a very full and not uninteresting description of Buonaparte as First Consul. Her reflections she reserves for another book, but occasionally she indulges in meditations which become more melancholy in her old age. Once or twice she manages to get away from the social visits and entertainments and write about her garden.

But like so many diarists, she did not think the quiet days were worth recording.

In 1845, at the age of 82, at the end of a sad entry beginning " Life begins to be very fatiguing to me," she ends up :

> My poor sister so near my own age will I feel convinced either precede or follow me in a very few months.

This literally happened seven years later in 1852, when the lifelong companionship of the sisters was only broken for a few months. Agnes died in January ; and Mary in November.

JOSEPH HUNTER

We have here an instance of a man who in his youth intended to keep a diary, but evidently found that the increasing range of his studies made him regard diary writing as waste of time.

Joseph Hunter, born in 1783, was an eminent antiquary and voluminous writer on history and archæology. In 1806, at the age of 23, he begins on January 2 to keep a diary. He notes the lectures he attends, the people with whom he has conversations and to whom he writes letters, sermons he hears, the establishment of " a society of literary conversation " where they have a debate on a universal language ; an attack of a severe cold (" believe t'is epedemic and what is called influenza "), a tea-party where the conversation is " merest chit chat and scandal," etc. It would almost seem as if he were settling down to be a diarist when he begins describing people ; for instance, George Dyer, " a strange quizz, such a rough head of hair never was seen, but an entertaining fellow, takes snuff to wean himself from smoking." But after recording the immense lists of books he is reading he breaks into a sort of shorthand just to give the division of the day, every hour of which is occupied in the study of Greek, Hebrew, mathematics, etc., and on September 20 he leaves off for good.

The MS. of the diary is among the large collection of his papers in the British Museum.

THE MARQUIS OF HASTINGS

Lord Hastings was Governor-General and Commander-in-Chief in India. He kept a regular diary from September, 1813, to December, 1818. His term of office continued to January, 1823, but his official duties became too heavy for him to find time to keep up diary writing. The diary is occupied only with descriptions of travel, hunting expeditions and incidents connected with his official life in India. It is included because, unlike most diarists, Lord Hastings discloses very clearly in the dedication his motive in writing. He says :

> This Journal is undertaken for the sake of the Dear Little Companions of my Expedition. It will be both gratifying and useful to them in a future day to have their recollection of circumstances revived and to have many matters explained which they will be likely to have comprehended but imper-

fectly. At any rate it will convince them of the solicitude felt for them by a fond Father.

The diary was published in 1858, edited by Lady Bute, one of his daughters.

THOMAS GREY

In a little leather-bound, gilt-edged book, called *Marshall's Commercial Pocket Book* for 1826, with a print of Liverpool Town Hall as a frontispiece, Thomas Grey began to keep a diary : January 1 : " Very rainy and cold day did not go out at all." January 2 : " Staid in the house all day, went to the play in the evening which was very stupid," and so it goes on " went to Church," " went a shooting," " went to a lecture," etc., up to January 22. On March 22 he makes another attempt : · " went a hunting," " went a fishing," " had a headache," etc. But this lasted only eleven days. There is one entry in May recording his sister's marriage ; and then no more. In this very incomplete record we might gather from the handwriting and language that Thomas Grey was young, that brothers and sisters were with him, and that he sometimes had headaches. Had his parents been obscure people we should know nothing more and suspect that he belonged to the large class of diarists who begin but cannot keep up the habit. Thomas, however, was one of the younger sons of Lord Grey, the Prime Minister, and died at the age of sixteen in the very year of the diary ; hence the blank pages. The sister whose marriage he records treasured the little book, which has been handed down in her family. It is only a small broken fragment, preserved out of sentiment. The memory of the boy has vanished, but as a budding diarist his attempt survives.

SIR MOUNTSTUART GRANT-DUFF

With the exception of the first two volumes, which concern travels in India and Palestine, the fourteen volumes of diary (1851 to 1901) issued by Sir Mountstuart Grant Duff (who was a Member of Parliament and sometime Governor of Madras) hardly come under the category of a personal diary any more than Miss Wynn's *Diaries of a Lady of Quality*. Indeed, he says himself that his object is to make it " the lightest of light reading," to dwell on the less serious side of life and to avoid writing of his chief interests, which were politics and administration. The volumes consist for the most part of a vast collection of anecdotes, good stories and memorable sayings, many of which have appeared elsewhere. That he succeeded in making the books " light reading " we may venture to doubt. To flutter a page or two occasionally may help to pass the time, but to read consecutively anecdote after anecdote, epigram after epigram, joke after joke, however good some of them may be, is practically impossible. There are dinner party lists and occasional references to books, a few appreciations of scenery and gardens, but he strictly adheres to his intention of introducing nothing in the way of personal opinions, private reflections or serious matter.

Quotation, therefore, is unnecessary. Apart from anecdotes it is hardly worth while making extracts from the other passages—as, for instance, a discussion as to whether you should write Marquis or Marquess—or the literary judgment that Anatole France " contains a great deal of interesting matter but little that fixes itself in the memory." No doubt there is a considerable public for collections of anecdotes, but such books are hardly subjects for analysis as personal diaries.

JOHN EVELYN DENISON (VISCOUNT OSSINGTON)

From 1857 to 1872 Denison was Speaker of the House of Commons. During this period he kept a sort of official diary, noting carefully his rulings and the questions and points of order that came up for his decision. As a record of House of Commons procedure and a guide to the difficult problems by which a Speaker may at any moment be confronted it is a valuable book, and shows the scrupulous punctiliousness of its author. It is not, however, a personal diary. Except for a reference to an accident which prevents him from attending to his duties, and an account of a rapid excursion he took to Wollaton Park near Nottingham, there is practically no personal matter in it at all.

On taking up his office, he asked his predecessor, Lord Eversley, on whom he might rely for advice, and he was told he must rely entirely on himself. He adds :

And I found this to be very true. Sometimes a friend would hasten to the Chair and offer advice. I must say it was for the most part lucky that I did not follow the advice.

He does not describe or criticize members, or ministers except Lord Palmerston, for whom he had evidently a great admiration.

Lord Palmerston has spoken admirably well this session. It is not that the House respects a public servant who has done great service ; that they are indulgent to advanced years. It is that he can still make a better and more effective speech than any other man.

Denison seems to have taken pains to exercise judicial fairness, but he knows how to snub members, as when he tells one of them that his speech

was in every way unbecoming: that nothing could be more undignified than for a member to come to the House whining and complaining that he had not had a ticket given him for the review.

The careful way in which these notes were kept makes one suspect that Denison also kept a private diary. When he retired from the Speakership he refused any pension. He died in 1873.

The diary was first printed for private circulation, but afterward published in 1900.

TWENTIETH CENTURY

LORD BERNARD GORDON-LENNOX

EXCEPT for Barbellion's diary, there would have been no diaries to refer to in the early twentieth century, had it not been for the war. A fairly large percentage of officers kept some sort of record, and many of the diaries of fallen officers no doubt exist, treasured by their families. Not many of them, perhaps, will ever appear in print. For the most part they are probably very brief single-line notes in a pocket diary, of no particular value even to the military historian. The circumstances of modern warfare are not conducive to elaborate diary writing, and warfare and army life are hostile to originality or even the emergence of individuality. Moreover, we must repeat once more that when the subject of a diary reaches such tremendous and sensational dimensions the soldier diarists' notes appear meagre and inadequate to those who can only observe the large lines and general trend of events after the conclusion of the whole business.

No doubt a careful scrutiny of even the briefest notes would disclose characteristic features—sometimes a freedom of language or a violence of expression, but rarely anything personal. If an officer wants to record something beyond the actual military movements, he may mention where he had a bath. But the events are too overwhelmingly important at the moment, the great dangers, though seldom referred to as dangers, too constant to allow for the run of a flowing pen. In years to come some notable diaries may possibly appear as results of the war, but we are only concerned here with those of fallen officers. Even in the sketchy ones an abrupt finish has something intensely dramatic about it. Here are the last three entries from the small pocket diary of an officer:

Sept. 14. Forward. Big scrap. 4 Company Officers wounded, many others. Entrenched W of farm N of river and lay out all night.

[He was wounded in the shoulder but carried on. He does not think this worth mentioning.]

1914. Sep. 15. We were shelled all morning, miserable wet night. S.D. and M. all safe, night alarm.

Sep. 16. S. took over bridge. Blaze. [He was killed by a bullet in the head on the evening of this day.]

No doubt a conscientious search might produce a number of diaries of this sort, but there would not be sufficient variety about them to justify their being singled out for special attention.

For our purpose here we have selected a diary which is remarkable for its fullness and regularity. There are signs of its having been written up probably from notes scribbled on the day, and it presents as consecutive a story and as detailed an account of the retreat from Mons as could be furnished by an officer who was actually participating in it.

Lord Bernard Gordon-Lennox, 3rd son of the Duke of Richmond, was a Major in the 2nd Battalion Grenadier Guards. He went out with the Expeditionary Force on August 12, 1914, and marched with his battalion from Havre to the Belgian frontier, took part in the famous retreat, and after practically incessant fighting from October 21 to November 16 he was killed on November 17 of the same year during a German attack upon Ypres.

The diary begins on August 12 with the departure from Southampton and arrival at Havre. All was enthusiasm; the crews of the French boats in port cheered them.

We responded by singing the Marseillaise which caused a continual " ' eep, eep, 'ooray " in return.

On arrival at Arras about 3-30 a large crowd of people assembled around the door of the carriage in which N.D. and self were sitting and the former was presented with three enormous bouquets, the biggest I have ever seen, by the Mayor and Mayoress and the Prefect and the Town Councillors. It was most amusing. N. came up to the scratch well and in a few well chosen and felicitous phrases tendered the thanks of the Officers and the Army in general. As we were all more or less in a state of déshabillé it must have been a funny sight.

He writes daily at considerable length, giving full particulars of all the military operations; the personal element hardly enters into his record at all. Privation and discomfort are accepted at once as the ordinary routine, and the continual presence of extreme danger is noted in the same terms as the changes in the weather.

Gordon-Lennox was an officer of some years' standing. He had served in the South African War. His tone, therefore, is that of one more or less in authority, who would not think it correct to indulge in the complaints and protests which might have proceeded from a younger officer. He does, however, complain of the unnecessary secrecy.

> Owing to the absolute secrecy which pervaded everything no one knew what was going on anywhere : this has been maintained up to date and is most disheartening. No one knows what one is driving at, where anyone is, what we have got against us, or anything at all ; and what is told us generally turns out to be entirely wrong.

On August 24, the day on which the retirement began, his entry shows that he must have written in very much later the following passage :

> This began our long and tiring retirement beginning at Mons and finishing near Paris and I don't think any of us wish to go through such a trying time again. Also the British Army is not accustomed to retiring.

He always refers to the Germans as " the Dutchmen." He wastes little time in making disparaging remarks about the enemy, except to note on one or two occasions that their wounded " howl " a good deal. There is this entry about prisoners :

> We picked up a lot of Dutchmen on the way, killing, wounding, and capturing them at intervals. They were eventually given into my charge as head of Main Guard and seemed quite pleased to have a quiet time. Apparently they thought we shot all our prisoners.

There is of course hardly much chance for humour in the circumstances of modern warfare, and Gordon-Lennox was not out for collecting jokes. But now and again there is a little relief, such as the following :

> Going through Charly we saw chalked up in big letters on a door " T a n g o t a n z e in P A R I S Sept. 13." and underneath it " Yes. I don't think."

A far more gifted pen that Gordon-Lennox's would find it just as impossible as he does to convey any real impression of the scenes of devastation and destruction or the catastrophic incidents through which he continually passes. Here is his description of a shell from a howitzer—Black Maria—when he himself has a narrow escape.

> They had hardly been there a ¼ of an hour before a big 8″ came along missed the farm by inches and got the top of the quarry bank a dreadful blow. I had 103 lined up and after the explosion 44 were left all the remainder being

killed or wounded. In addition this shell killed three officers of the Oxfords and a medical officer. How it missed J–, P–, P–, and self will for ever remain a mystery. It killed and wounded people who were more under cover than we were sitting all together. It killed and wounded people to our rear, right, front, left but for some unknown reason we all escaped untouched. The trees on the bank fell down and the whole quarry was filled with dense black yellow smoke. It was truly a disastrous shot.

A few days after he has another narrow escape :

I had just taken my overcoat off and laid it on the back of the trench about a yard away when there was a tremendous explosion just above me. The man in the pit next door was badly hit by a shell. My coat had the right arm nearly taken off at the shoulder and the left sleeve cut to bits and it was only a yard off me, but I am thankful to say I was not inside the coat at the time.

The complete absence on these occasions not only of invocations to the Almighty but of even the mildest comment on his escapes, is particularly characteristic of the British officer.

There are better moments in which he shows his naturally cheerful disposition. Of his dug-out he writes on September 23 : " Our bug hutch in the trench is the envy of everyone who pays it a visit " ; and on a quieter day the only casualties are " three nice sheep," which " were borne home next morning triumphant on the cooker " and he has kidneys for breakfast. Later again fifty shells fall round them on one day, until " the field behind us was like a Gruyère cheese." The shelling becomes so incessant and continuous that he begins to write about it in an almost jocular vein. Even his " rest day " is disturbed. " No harm but beastly noise and disturbed my afternoon sleep so had a nice bath instead." On one occasion in October he is relieved by a French officer accompanied by a very inadequate number of men.

The officer was very funny and whenever I showed him my posts etc. he said " Oh, La La : je n'ai pas les hommes."

Day by day it is an unrelieved record of incessant fighting, with all the attendant misery and suffering. It is related well with typical British reticence, but with more than usual detail. A vivid imagination would be a severe handicap to any soldier in such circumstances.

The constant loss of his best friends he notes with just a passing word, which of course is not meant to convey his feelings. Once he says rather more, and this is in the last lines of what turned out to be his last entry.

We heard to-day of poor M's death—a dreadful loss and think of poor J. I suppose one gets inured to seeing all one's best friends taken away from one and can only think one is lucky enough to be here oneself—for the present.

Not many days later he had joined his friends.

ARTHUR GRAEME WEST

OF the soldiers' diaries included in this volume West's is the most modern and certainly the least typical. But it must be remembered that the Great War was fought by many more civilians than soldiers. West was not a soldier when war broke out, and had he survived he certainly would not have remained one. Among the mass of diaries which will be found in years to come to have been produced by the war it is not improbable that others of this character will be discovered. That is to say, a good many young men of reflective temperament, neither trained for nor suited to military life, were plunged into the vortex, and it is likely that some of them kept notes of their experiences which go a good deal beyond the bald military record.

The published extracts from West's diary kept between March, 1915, and November, 1916, give us a clear insight into the character and disposition of the author. Not only does he display absolute frankness in committing his thoughts to paper, but having a literary gift and a cultivated mind he is able to describe his surroundings and the incidents of modern warfare in a way which brings the atmosphere of training camp and trench before the reader with photographic sharpness. The great interest of the diary rests in the doubts and misgivings to which he became a prey in the course of his military service. He failed to get a commission owing to his defective eyesight, and in a rush of enthusiasm he enlisted from Oxford as a private in the Public Schools Battalion soon after the outbreak of war. In November, 1915, he went to the front. After four months he was sent to Scotland, where he was trained as an officer. In September, 1916, he went to France with a commission, and remained there till he was killed in April, 1917. He never became part of the machine. He retained throughout the detached point of view of an observer. Every line he writes is full of suggestion and meaning, even when he is only recording the daily routine. To detach quotations is not easy, because what we are given of the diary is all worth reading. He describes things fully and develops his arguments carefully. Extracts tear the composition and break the sequence.

We will take first the more objective entries.

In the trenches in December, 1915:

> The trenches were wet but boarded at the bottom so one did not walk in more than three or four inches of water. Our platoon was to go to the front line trenches which were not trenches at all but broken bits of trench . . . we five were together in post No. G, at the extreme left end of the line. It was a very bad place; about ten or fifteen yards of sandbags were standing but the tops had been knocked off and the things were low. There was no back to the trench at all and the water was deep; we had nothing to keep it off us but a few sticks laid across . . . at first we were quite amused and laughed at our position but soon the damp and cold and the prospect of twenty four hours' endurance of it, our isolation and exposure cooled us down and we sat still and dripped and shivered. Flares went up continually and occasional machine gun bullets whizzed over us and snipers shot.

The training in Scotland is amusingly described with passages from the speeches of the company sergeant-major. The senseless and futile restrictions and regulations and the manifest incompetence of the superior officers exasperate him and his friends, but he remarks:

> Depression is merely a passing mood with most of the men and comes rarely even so. The men with me felt indignant when told to go on a parade they did not like and for a moment after coming off it retained their resentment, but it soon passed off and depression of spirits from general greyness of outlook as an enduring attitude was unknown to them. The prospect of four days' leave made them all delirious; so did week ends or even the Wednesday half holiday. In the evening when work was done the gramophone, golf, girls, a meal at a hotel, a magazine story, a piano made them forget that they had ever had a complaint in the world or that to-morrow would begin as usual with an Adjutants' parade at 5-30.

Their contempt for their instructors knew no bounds:

> One noted first their utter inability to teach us anything because there were too many superannuated old martinets trying to do it at the same time; secondly the lack of doctrine among them all; even if they could have taught they knew nothing. The way we were taught musketry was laughable.

This on food:

> Alteration in meals. The food both degenerates and diminishes; meat baked to a dry cinder and not enough of it comes on at lunch; pudding of any sort seems to be knocked off entirely: cheese, jam etc are not provided at all as they used to be.

Here is a specimen of drill:

> This morning we had saluting drill for half an hour. It was the most pitiably comic parade I have ever seen, even here. First we were drilled in platoons: our official way of carrying the stick was outlined, and a special drill by numbers, drawn up, for tucking the stick under the arm, taking it into the hand again, and cocking it up into the air. We practised in two movements. 1 Put the stick under left arm; 2 Cut the right hand away; 1 seize stick on the under-side; 2 Bring it smartly down to the side. We were then marched up and down the road saluting by numbers imaginary officers.

In the trenches again when he returns to France in September, 1916.

> It was a smelly trench. A dead German—a big man—lay on his stomach as if he were crawling over the parades down into the trench; he had lain there some days and that corner of trench reeked even when someone took him by the legs and pulled him away out of sight though not out of smell into a shell hole.
>
> A whistle would be heard, nearer and nearer ceasing for a mere fraction of a second when the shell was falling and about to explode. Where was it coming? Men cowered and trembled. It exploded and a cloud of black ruk went up—in the communication trench again, you went down it, two men were buried perhaps more you were told, certainly two. The trench was a mere undulation of newly turned earth under it somewhere lay two men or more. You dug furiously. No sign. Perhaps you were standing on a couple of men now, pressing the life out of them, on their faces or chests. A boot, a steel helmet,—and you dig and scratch and uncover a grey dirty face, pitifully drab and ugly, the eyes closed, the whole thing limp and mean-looking; this is the devil of it that a man is not only killed, but made to look so vile and filthy in death, so futile and meaningless that you hate the sight of him.
>
> Left trenches at about 4-30 a.m. Fearfully tiring march back to C, where we lived in a kind of manhole in the trench. B—Bl—and I had one to ourselves and our valises with us. Slept and fed. Read " Scholar Gipsy " and " Thyrsis " and talked about Oxford together at night.

A few quotations may now be given showing his moods and meditations on life and death. While training he writes:

> A fearful sense of the grimness of things came over me last night which it would have been hard to express even then and of which it is hard now to recapture even the details . . . the ever increasing viciousness and malice of the Adjutant and C.S.M. towards us seemed to keep an almost personal fiend of terror hovering above our heads. The war and the army had never looked so grim. The Army is really the most anti-social body imaginable. It maintains itself on the selfishness and hostility of nations and in its own ranks holds together by a bond of fear and suspicion, all anti-social feeling. Men are taught to fear their superiors and *they* suspect the men. Hatred must be often present and only fear prevents it flaming out.
>
> I do really care less than I used to do for the fools and bullies in command

of me. They certainly do not frighten me at all as they used to. I don't care a jot for the Adjutant or the C.O. when they come and yap and make heavy speeches at me. I do not mind if I am ticked off on parade and I don't think I should be at all shamed if I were finally turned down. Mankind is perpetually puffing itself up with strange unearthly loyalties and promised rewards. Man goes out to fight for a delusion to defend what he has tricked up as his Fatherland ; he imposes all sorts of restraints and tortures on himself in the name of Virtue and Respectability, sets a fool above him to worship, crawl on his knees to and shed a blessing of " purposefulness " on his most frightful sufferings.

It was during his leave before returning to France that the scales fell from his eyes and his complete change of view with regard to the war took place. He analyses his feelings very fully, but we can only take a few passages from his entries during these days:

What midgets we all are, what brief phantoms in a dream—a dream within a dream this truly is my life and how gladly would I end it now.

If the war were to begin to-morrow and were to find me as I am now, I would not join the Army, and if I had the courage I would desert now. I have been reading and thinking fundamentally important things this last few months.

Never was the desire to desert and to commit suicide so overwhelming and had it not been that I know I would pain my people I would certainly have killed myself that night.

After much thought wrote to the Adjutant of the Battalion telling him I would not rejoin the Army nor accept any form of alternative service, that I would rather be shot than do so, and that I left my name and address with him to act as he pleased. Shortly after mid-night I went down to the post with this letter and two more one to J and one to E telling them what I had done. I stood opposite the pillar box for some minutes wondering whether I would post them—then put them in my pocket and returned home to bed.

It would certainly be much pleasanter if I could regard myself still in this rather sublime light as the man who goes into the pit for his friends ; but I cannot do so for I am beginning to think that I never ought to have gone into it at all.

I am a creature caught in a net. Most men fight, if not happily, at any rate patiently, sure of the necessity and usefulness of their work. So did I— once ! Now it all looks to me so absurd and brutal that I can only force myself to continue in a kind of dream state. I hypnotise myself to undergo it.

I feel quite clearly that I ought to have stood aside. It is these men who stand aside, these philosophers and the so called conscientious objectors who are the living force of the future ; they are full of the light that must come sooner or later ; they are sneered at now but their position is firm.

We are confronted with two sets of martyrs here ; those of the trenches and those of the tribunals and civil prison and not by any means are the former necessarily in the right.

Even be the thing as necessary as you like, be the constitution of this world really so foul and hellish that force must be met by force, yet I should have stood aside, no brutality should have led me into it. Had I stood apart I should have stood on firm logical ground ; where I was truth would have been as it is among my friends now. To defy the whole system, to refuse to be an instrument of it—this *I* should have done.

But the machine of which he had become a part was too strong for him. He returned to the front, and seven months later he fell to a sniper's bullet.

The diary is an extraordinarily faithful bit of self-revelation. He evidently writes it to clear his mind, and here and there he introduces little fragments of scene painting, notably the sight of London from the train when returning on leave. His interludes on religion show what a deeply religious nature he had, although he rejected all the orthodox beliefs. He writes when back in France :

To-night I said something about my being a respectable atheist, to which it was promptly answered that there could be no such thing ; and people said " You aren't really an atheist, are you ? " Thus we see how men cannot get out of their minds " the horrid atheist " idea—the idea that intellectual convictions of this sort must of necessity imply some fearful moral laxity. The most religious men are really the extreme Christians or mystics and the atheists—nobody can understand this. These two classes have really occupied their minds with religion.

West's mental suffering as depicted in his diary is typically twentieth century, although his misanthropy and hatred of the herd are more individual. But a diary of this kind could not have been produced in the earlier centuries.

It was published in 1920 under the title of *The Diary of a Dead Officer*, together with some poems he had written.

BARBELLION

THE concluding diary in this collection, whatever its merits or demerits may be, is very far from showing that diary writing has deteriorated into a dead art. Barbellion's diaries have provoked a great deal of discussion ; they have revived interest in diary writing, and have shown that the introspective diarist of modern days may carry psychological self-analysis into very deep recesses of human consciousness. The examination of no other diary could afford us a better opportunity for referring once again to some of the considerations about diary writing which emerge naturally in a comparison between this last modern product and the diaries of the past. In matter of comparison one might get an even more fruitful field for discussion by placing Barbellion alongside of Maurice de Guérin and Marie Bashkirtseff, for his very unusual lack of reticence is by no means British.

Barbellion's diary is a triumphant vindication of the contention made repeatedly in these pages that position and circumstances have nothing whatever to do with the production of a good diary. Barbellion's career can be given in four lines. He was the son of a provincial journalist, born at Barnstaple in 1889, he served on his father's paper until he obtained a post by examination on the staff of the Natural History Museum at South Kensington. He died in 1919. That is all. He was not connected with any exciting public events, he never met any celebrities, and he never even saw any royalty. And yet without giving it any exact place we should be justified in ranking his record very high in the long series of diaries of which we have now come to the end.

But there are some rather serious adverse criticisms to be made, and we should like to clear these out of the way to start with.

The diary was intended for publication, or at least after the first few years Barbellion's desire and indeed determination to publish becomes apparent in the entries. It is true that he refused to show it to anyone, even to his brother; nevertheless, after his boyhood had passed he was clearly bent on the journal appearing while he was alive. This in the case of a very intimate private diary unquestionably makes a difference. Indiscretions and revelations seem to become intentional, and we cannot feel quite the same sympathy for the author as we should feel for a writer of far less intellectual power who was keeping a strictly private record. Nevertheless we must remember that Greville, Haydon, and Gordon all wrote for publication, although they did not contemplate the appearance of their records during their own lifetimes.

Our next criticism concerns a more serious point. The first volume of the diaries appeared in 1919 under the title of *The Journal of a Disappointed Man*. It caused a considerable sensation. On the last page, after some rather harrowing entries, appeared the statement " Barbellion died on December 31."

The book was sufficiently remarkable to cause a good deal of speculation as to the identity of the author. When it was discovered that his name was not Barbellion but Cummings—a trifling matter of a pseudonym—and that he was not dead, then public opinion swung round to regarding the whole thing as a fake—one false entry! how many others? What is genuine and what is not? Is it all fiction? And considerable harm would have been done to, what may well be called, the authenticity of the book had it not been for the perfectly simple and straightforward explanation of all the attendant circumstances which was written by Barbellion's brother in the preface to the Last Diary.

The false entry Barbellion defended by saying, " The fact is no man dare remain alive after writing such a book," and he never expected he would be alive to see it in print. But it was a crucial fault of judgment. The device was bound to be discovered, and nothing is more damaging to a diary than the growth of suspicion as to the author's sincerity. Barbellion undoubtedly wanted a dramatic finish. Had he read Haydon's diary, we are not at all sure he would not have followed Haydon's example. In fact, there are plenty of entries such as—" thoughts of suicide—a pistol," or " I wish I could die of heart failure and at once," as well as an actual confession that he fears the end will not be dramatic. " Pray God the curtain falls at the right moment lest the play drag on into some long and tedious anticlimax."

We must accuse Barbellion, too, if not of insincerity, anyhow of posing. After the first few years, when it is clear he is writing for publication, he does a lot of attitudinising, constantly reflecting himself in a discreditable light. The self-analysis and self-revelation is searching. But we may claim Barbellion as an instance of the failure of the intense self-dissector to give an accurate picture of himself. The picture we get of him in his brother's preface corrects a good many errors which the reader of the diary may quite legitimately conceive from the written confessions. But he himself knows that his attempts to depict himself are in vain when he writes in the Last Diary :

> It is almost impossible to tell the truth. In this journal I have tried but I have not succeeded. I have *set down* a good deal but I cannot *tell* it. Truth of self has to be left by the psychology-miner at the bottom of his boring.

And right at the end, within a few months of the close, he confesses :

> In the Journal I can see now that I made myself out worse than I am or was. I even took a morbid pleasure in intimating my depravity—self mortifi-

cation. . . . I don't think on the whole my portrait of myself does myself justice.

Barbellion is one of our few literary diarists, and we can see what a snare his literary talent must have been to the conscientious fidelity of his record. He is thinking of finish, of style, of composition, of expression. With his talent, which is of a very high order, he often delights us, but we miss the blunt self-revealing indiscretion which in some diaries may make us wince, but brings the diarist's personality right before us. Again we do not get the whole diary, it has been trimmed from the artistic point of view, not by an editor, but by Barbellion himself.

Nevertheless, in spite of pose and insincerity, in spite of his instinct for publicity, we get passages so obviously, so poignantly, so intimately sincere and so intensely human that you lay down the book feeling you have been in the closest contact with a human being that is conceivably possible through the medium of a printed page. In spite of his failure to explain himself, his attempts to do it are so interesting, so ingenious, and often so amusing, that a reader finds himself eagerly beginning his own self-examination. In spite of the snares which literary talent presents to a diarist, nature and more especially animal life are depicted with a delicacy and refinement of touch which gives artistic pleasure quite apart from the psychological interest of the other parts of the diary ; and instead of the wearisome " I met Prince A, the Duke of B, and Lady C," we get portraits of lodging-house keepers, farm hands, nurses, etc., which are all gems.

People have made friends and confidants of their diaries; Barbellion's love and devotion for his was beyond all bounds : It is a " superconfidant " ; keeping a journal is " to have a secret liaison of a very sentimental kind." He begins it when he is about thirteen and continues it to make notes on natural history, in which he is deeply interested. Gradually it expands and becomes a habit, and then a passion.

> I fall back on this Journal just as some other poor devil takes to drink.

He takes the most elaborate precautions to preserve the volumes from fire or from possible Zeppelin raids, and imagines a fireman " in a brass helmet and his hatchet up at the salute " guarding them.

> These precious Journals ! Supposing I lost them I cannot imagine the anguish it would cause me. It would be the death of my real self,

and as I should take no pleasure in the perpetuation of my flabby, flaccid, anæmic, aimiable, puppet self, I should probably commit suicide.

He here makes the egotist's usual hasty conclusion that the inner self must be the real self, and the outer self that other people see counts for nothing. Nevertheless, he is quite aware that, in spite of all his efforts at meticulous recollection and detailed sifting, much is lost :

However vigilant and artful a diarist may be, plenty of things escape him.

He is not regular in his writing. After an interval of a month he writes :

Hulloa, old friend ; how are you ? I mean my Diary. I haven't written to you for ever so long and my silence as usual indicates happiness.

And there are the moments of misgiving :

Is this blessed Journal worth while ? I really don't know and that's the harassing fact of the matter.

I am tortured by two doubts—whether these MSS. (the labour and hope of many years) will survive accidental loss and whether they really are of any value. I have no faith in either.

Am busy re-writing, editing, bowdlerising my journals for publication against the time when I shall have gone the way of all flesh. . . . Reading it through again, I see what a remarkable book I have written. If only they will publish it.

His egoism is abnormal, and he cultivates it.

My egoism appals me. Likewise the extreme intensification of the consciousness of myself.

I have come to loath myself : my finicking, hypersensitive, morbid nature always thinking, talking, writing about myself for all the world as if the world beyond did not exist ! I am rings within rings, circles concentric and intersecting, a maze, a tangle ; watching myself behave or misbehave always reflecting on what impression I am making on others or what they will think of me.

My own life as it unrolls day by day is a source of constant amazement, delight and pain. I can think of no more interesting volume than a detailed intimate psychological history of my own life. I want a perfect comprehension at least of myself.

And he was ingenuous enough to think he could get it. Although at times he seems to understand that an egotist is not a good self-estimator :

I am so steeped in myself—in my moods, vapours, idiosyncracies, so self-sodden that I am unable to stand clear of the data, to marshal and classify the multitude of facts and thence draw the deduction what manner of man

I am. I should like to know—if only as a matter of curiosity. So what in God's name am I ? A fool of course to start with—but the rest of the diagnosis ?

Barbellion had ambition—high ambition. " You can search all history and fiction for an ambition more powerful than mine and not find it." He wanted to be a great naturalist, and he was remarkably well equipped for success in such a career. At the same time he was conscious of a literary gift, so that one way or another he seemed destined to make his mark. The tragedy of his life was his ill-health : at first only inconvenient, then serious, and at last he was a condemned man and he knew it. Extreme depression and morbidity were only natural. Everything he did, said, thought, or felt was coloured or rather had the colour taken out of it. His sense of proportion was dislocated. The actual tragedy of approaching death was bad enough, indeed it could hardly have been worse. But for effects' sake he begins to pile it on ; not only to welcome the " slings and arrows of outrageous fortune," but to insinuate their existence when there was no reason for it. Just as in the early entries he seems to convey that at home he had no encouragement for his naturalist studies, which his brother shows was quite untrue; so also in the later entries when he is a prisoner awaiting death he seems at times to convey that he is abandoned and deserted, if not actually neglected, by his elaborate descriptions of discomfort, draughty windows with bits of cardboard over the broken panes, etc., etc. But then again he has a way of suddenly recovering himself, as, for instance, after an entry in which he says everyone will be relieved to hear of his death, he writes the next day that this entry is " maudlin tosh—entirely foreign to my nature. I hereby cancel it." So in the ups and downs, the misrepresentations, the varieties, the shrewd observations, the yearnings and the despair, we get a very wonderful picture of a nimble brain and alert consciousness being played upon and gradually strangled by physical suffering.

In his good moods his work, nature, his father and mother, his music, and later his wife, all weave themselves naturally into his life of suffering. With the deepest compassion for him one feels conscious of his charm. In his bad moods, artificiality, sententious posing and desire to paint himself in lurid colours are sometimes sufficiently irritating to make one dislike him. We get bits of pure Bashkirtseff like the following :

Do you think I would exchange the communion with my own heart for the toy balloons of your silly conversation ? Or my curiosity for your flickering interests ? Or my despair for your comfortable Hope ? Or my present tawdry life for yours as polished and neat as a new threepenny bit ? I would not. I gather my mantle around me and I solemnly thank God that I am not as some other men are.

It is at the bottom of the page on which this occurs that the false entry of his death comes. He thought the defiant note fine and dramatic. It is all made up. Barbellion would have been all the better if he had never come across Bashkirtseff. Of course he was infatuated by her.

My father was Sir Thomas Browne and my mother Marie Bashkirtseff. See what a curious hybrid I am !

She feels as I feel. We have the same self absorption, the same vanity, and corroding ambition. She is impressionable, volatile, passionate,—ill. So am I. Her journal is my journal.

Luckily in diary writing even Marie Bashkirtseff cannot completely control and dictate the style, and the real Barbellion emerges where he is attempting least to reveal himself.

Barbellion was by no means a cynic to whom nothing was sacred. He appreciates the refined delicacy of certain human relationships as acutely as he responds to the special beauties and wonders of nature. The real drama of his opening the letter (not used by the medical officer before whom he went) which divulges to him that he is doomed, his wife's knowledge of this fact before she married him—this sort of thing is just related without a word of elaborate ornament, without a single artificial gesture.

She has known *all* from the beginning ! M— warned her not to marry me. How brave and loyal of her ! What an ass I have been. I am overwhelmed with feelings of shame and self contempt and sorrow for her. She is quite cheerful and an enormous help.

Home again with my darling. She is the most wonderful darling woman. Our love is for always. The Baby is a monster.

He writes in the same natural way when he refers to his mother :

Mother (she liked me to call her Moth. Hubbard, Lepidopterous Hubbard and she used to sign her letters Hubbard) had a pretty custom which she hated anyone to detect, of putting every letter she wrote to us when stamped, directed and sealed into her Bible for a minute or two, ostensibly to sanctify the sealing up.

And the terrible episode of his opening the letter in which his illness was described he relates quite simply :

The certificate, therefore, was not needed and coming home in the train I opened it out of curiosity. I was quite casual and thought it would be merely interesting to see what M. said.

It was.

At first he takes it calmly, not knowing by its name the horrible and obscure disease of which he was the victim. But his symptoms gradually enlighten him. One day—this is one of the most vividly realistic touches in the record—he was at work in a library where

> my eye caught the title of an enormous quarto memoir in the Transactions of the Royal Society. The Histology of —— [his disease]. I was browsing in the library at the time when this hit me like a carelessly handled gaff straight in the face. I almost ran away to my room.

The diary does not deal with regular daily doings like an ordinary diary. It is a notebook of thoughts intermingled with occasional incidents.

Some of his naturalists' notes which he continues when he is doing journalistic work may be given :

> On reviewing the past egg season, I find in all I have discovered 232 nests belonging to forty-four species. I only hope I shall be successful with the beetle season.

> A hot sultry afternoon during most of which I was stretched out on the grass beside an upturned stone where a battle royal was fought between Yellow and Black Ants. The victory went to the hardy little yellows. By the way I held a Newt by the tail to-day and it emitted a squeak ! So that the Newt has a voice after all.

> Hard at work dissecting a Dogfish. Ruridecanal Conference in the afternoon. I enjoy this double life I lead. It amuses me to be laying bare the brain of a dogfish in the morning and in the afternoon to be taking down in shorthand what the Bishop says on Mission work.

Of his early sexual experiences we expect there is a good deal more than we are allowed to see. The various kissings of girls are rather tamely vulgar. But he sums up in a terse phrase the usual position of a young man on this subject.

> For myself I never received any parental instruction. I first learned of the wonder of generation through the dirty filter of a barmaid's nasty mind.

The journals abound in beautiful descriptions of nature and animal life ; unfortunately most of them are too long to quote. He combines scientific knowledge with æsthetic appreciation which is not a common combination, and his intensest happiness is when he is just drinking in the beauties around him. Here is a summer afternoon when he is 21 :

> I waded up stream to a big slab of rock tilted at a comfortable angle. I lay flat on this with my nether extremities in water up to my knees. The sun bathed my face and dragon flies chased up and down intent on murder. But I cared not a tinker's Demetrius about Nature red in tooth and claw. I was quite satisfied with Nature under a June sun in the cool atmosphere of a Dipper stream. I lay on the slab completely relaxed and the cool water ran strongly between my toes. Surely I was never again going to be miserable. The voices of children playing in the wood made me extra happy.
> As a rule I loathe children. I am too much of a youth still. But not this morning. For these were fairy voices ringing through the enchanted wood.

There are very amusing little snatches of dialogue, notably one with a deaf old man up in an apple tree, those with his nurse in the last journal, and another with a social climber whose smile puzzles him.

> I am sorry but though I scrutinised this lick spittle and arch belly-truck rider very closely I am quite unable to say whether that smile and unwonted diffidence meant simple pleasure at the now certain knowledge that I was duly impressed or whether it was genuine confusion at the thought that he had perhaps been overdoing it.

There are wonderfully good descriptions of all sorts of trivial incidents, such as the silent workmen putting a new pile in the pier, Sunday morning in Petticoat Lane, and street scenes as he passes by. But to music he gives a very special place, his concerts and his thoughts on it are often elaborately described. It brings out the most passionate and emotional side of his character. This on Beethoven's Fifth Symphony:

> This symphony always works me up into an ecstacy; in ecstatic sympathy with its dreadfulness I could stand up in the balcony and fling myself down passionately into the arena below. Yet there were women sitting alongside me to-day—knitting. It so annoyed and irritated me that at the end of the first movement I got up and sat elsewhere. They would have sat knitting at the foot of the Cross, I suppose.

He reaches the high watermark of amusing and fantastic writing in his description of Sir Henry Wood conducting his orchestra, which unfortunately is too long for quotation and would be spoilt by extracts. The little scraps of dialogue are introduced with a very comic effect. We may give one of his brief inconsequent conversations with his nurse:

> B. (to nurse stepping on his toes) Seemingly either my feet or yours are very large.
> N. Oh, but you see it's my legs are so short I can't step across easily. It will be all right if you go to Eastbourne. Nurse —— has long legs.
> B. But what's the use of her long legs if she can't get a house?

N. Aunt Hobart's legs were so bent up that though she was six feet long her coffin was only four feet.
B. Why were Aunt Hobart's legs bent up?
N. Rheumatism. She was buried at the same time as her granddaughter.
B. But *her* legs were not bent up?
N. Oh, no. Bessie was only sixteen and died of scarlet fever.

So far as public affairs are concerned the war of course forms the background of the diary.

As he is at once rejected for military service and has to be " a compulsory spectator," it does not enter into his personal experience. Nevertheless the sombre presence of the prolonged tragedy is in keeping with his moods of depression, and he lets fly more than once in his exasperation and his gorge rises at the journalistic gloatings.

Sometimes I am swept away with admiration for all the heroism of the War or by some particularly noble self sacrifice and think it is really all worth while. Then—and more frequently—I remember that this war has let loose in the world not only barbarities, butcheries, and crimes, but lies, lies, lies— hypocrisies, deceits, ignoble desires for self aggrandizement, self preservation— such as no one ever dreamed existed in embryo in the heart of human beings.

The war is everything : it is noble, filthy, great, petty, degrading, inspiring, ridiculous, glorious, mad, bad, hopeless, yet full of hope. I don't know what to think about it.

We are like a nest of frightened ants when someone lifts the stone. That is the world just now.

And there are one or two accounts of air raid experiences which affect his heart. But on the whole and very naturally it is his own fate, the inexorable approach of death, which absorbs him. Throughout, ill health forces him into moods of depression, though sometimes he tries to take it lightly, as when he says:

Feel like a piece of drawn threadwork or an undeveloped negative or a jelly fish on stilts or a sloppy tadpole or a weevil in a nut, or a spitch cocked eel. In other words and in short—ill.

But death looms largely in his thoughts, how could it be otherwise? His attitude towards it varies; sometimes banter, sometimes petulant indignation, sometimes solemn welcome. A few entries must be given:

I cannot for the life of me rake up any excitement over my own immediate decease—an unobtrusive passing away of a rancorous disappointed morbid and self assertive entomologist in a West Kensington Boarding House—what a mean little tragedy! It is hard not to be somebody even in death.

I suppose the truth is I am at last broken in to the idea of Death. Once it terrified me and once I hated it. But now it only annoys me. Having lived with the Bogey for so long and broken bread with him so often I am used to his ugliness tho' his persistent attentions bore me. Why doesn't he do it and have done with me ? Why this deference, why does he pass me everything but the poison ? Why am I such an unconscionable time dying ?

On the Hill, this morning, felt the thrill of the news of my own Death. I mean I imagined I heard the words—
' You've heard the news about B ? '
Second voice ' No, what ? '
He's dead.
Silence.
Won't all this seem piffle if I don't die after all ! As an artist in life I *ought* to die, it is the only artistic ending—and I ought to die now or the Third Act will fizzle out in a long doctor's bill.

It is this sort of thing which makes us understand the false entry at the end of the volume.

In the *Last Diary* the prospect of death becomes more poignant, and more real, especially when he thinks of his wife.

It is cruel—cruel to her and cruel to me. There comes a time when evil circumstances squeeze you out of this world. There is no longer any room. Oh. Why did she marry me ? They ought not to have let her do it.

Lying in bed waiting, his one great excitement is the publication of the volume of the diary:

March 26. Time lures me forward. But I've dug my heels in awaiting those two old tortoises Chatto and Windus.

March 27. I've won ! This morning at 9 a.m. the book arrived. C. and W. thoughtfully left the pages to be cut, so I've been enjoying the exquisite pleasure of cutting the pages of my own book. And nothing's happened. No earthquake, no thunder and lighting, no omen in a black sky. In fact the sun is shining. Publication next week.

In the intervals he gives us terrible descriptions of the contortions of his semi-paralytic legs and details of the sick room. But the naturalist is very much alive to the end. He writes lovingly of his canary :

The jacket is put over his cage at night fall and all night he roosts on a table close to my bed. When I wake in the silence of the night, it is difficult to believe that close to me there is a little heart incessantly pumping hot red blood. I have a sense of companionship at the thought. For I too silent concealed in my bed possess a heart pumping incessantly though not so fast. I too am an animal, little bird, and we must both die.

And almost at the end :

A beautiful morning. At the bottom of my bed two French windows open out on to the garden, where a blackbird is singing me something more than well. It is a magnificent flute obligato to the tune in my heart going " thub dup " " thub dup " wildly as if I were a youth again in first love. He shouted out his song in the evening the very moment I arrived here.

What fine spirits these blackbirds are! I listen to him and my withered carcase soaks up his song with a sighing sound like a dry sponge taking up water.

There is much quotable material in Barbellion's diaries. But we must part company from our last diarist, and we do so feeling we have reached not only an end but something of a climax.

INDEX

OF ALL DIARIES AND CHRONICLES MENTIONED IN THE VOLUME

Abbot, Charles (Lord Colchester), 13, 320-1
Amiel, 10, 37
Ashmole, Elias, 14, 15, 34, 114-116
Aston, John, 119-120
Ayshcombe, William, 153

Bagot, Mary, 18
Baker, John, 13, 14, 15, 25, 212-215
Barbellion, 3, 12, 13, 14, 432-443
Bashkirtseff, Marie, 10, 43, 433, 438
Bee, Jacob, 154
Berry, Mary, 420-1
Blunt, Wilfred, viii (note)
Boswell, J., 4, 9
Brakelond, J. de, 40
Brereton, Sir William, 118-119
Brown, Nicholas, 21
Browne, Mary, 6, 25, 362-363
Browne, Mrs., 15, 29, 220-224
Brownlow, Lady, 17
Bufton, John, 155
Burney, Fanny (Madame d'Arblay), 6, 17, 21, 29, 171-183, 338
Burrell, Timothy, 14, 15, 25, 142-144
Bury, Lady Charlotte, 17, 39, 337-342
Butler, Lady Eleanor (see Ladies of Llangollen).
Butler, Mrs. (see Kemble, Fanny).
Butler, Samuel, 38
Byrom, Elizabeth, 13, 203-204
Byrom, John, 25, 200-202
Byron, Lord, 6, 11, 14, 33, 42, 264-271

Calverley, Sir Walter, 136-138
Carlisle, George Howard, 7th Earl of, 298, 393-396
Carlyle, Thomas, vii
Cartwright, Bishop, 144-147

Clinton, Henry Fynes, 6, 11, 12, 13, 19, 25, 357-361
Cobbett, William, 13, 280-287
Cockburn, Admiral, 21, 352-353
Coke, Lady Mary, 29, 233-234
Colchester, Lord (see Abbot, Charles).
Coningsby, Sir Thomas, 39, 68-70
Cook, Captain, 27
Cory, William, 412-415
Cowper, Mary Countess, 29, 193-196
Creevey, Thomas, 335-337

D'Arblay, Madame (see Burney, Fanny).
Darwin, Charles, 27-28
Dawson, John, 231-232
Dee, Dr. John, 13, 14, 15, 17, 25, 61 66
De la Pryme, Abraham, 140-142
Denison, John Evelyn (Viscount Ossington), 423
Derby, 3rd and 4th Earls of, 19
D'Ewes, Sir Simonds, 34, 71-75
Dodington, George Bubb (Lord Melcombe), 6, 17, 208-212
Dowsing, W., 20, 120-122
Dugard, T., 25, 154
Dyott, General, 34, 39, 314-318

Edward VI, 6, 55-58
Egmont, 1st Earl of (Viscount Percival), 15, 17, 18, 36, 164-170, 212
Eliot, George, 13, 14, 39, 403-407
Evelyn, John, 21, 26, 96-106
Eyre, Adam, 15, 122-125

Farington, viii (note)
Fell, Sarah, 19
Fielding, Henry, 224-227
Fiennes, Celia, 29, 148-152

Fox, Caroline, 13, 21, 30, 33, 300–305, 345
Fox, George, 2
Froude, R. H., 363–364
Fry, Elizabeth, 6, 13, 15, 16, 39, 321–326

Gale, Walter, 13, 206–208
Gladstone, Mrs., 369
Gladstone, W. E., 6, 13, 23, 39, 364–369
Goodall, William, 23, 379–380
Gordon, General, 22, 25, 306–313, 433
Gordon-Lennox, Lord Bernard, 39, 424–428
Graham, Sir Gerald, 19, 411–412
Grant-Duff, Sir M., 24, 422–423
Gray, Thomas, 236–237
Green, Thomas, 19, 249–251
Greville, Charles, 1, 5, 8, 14, 18, 21, 36, 272–279, 433
Greville, Henry, 19, 21, 374–376
Grey, Thomas, 422
Guérin, Maurice de, 433
Gyll, Thomas, 252

Hannington, James, 25, 416–418
Hastings, Marquis of, 421
Haydon, B. R., 12, 13, 33, 36, 38, 254–263, 433
Henslowe, Philip, 20
Heywood, Oliver, 12, 13, 131–133
Hobson, John, 19, 205–206
Holland, Elizabeth, Lady, 246–249
Hunter, Joseph, 421

Jackson, Sir George, 331–332
Jowett, Benjamin, 38

Kemble, Fanny (Mrs. Butler), 29, 371–374

Labouchere, H., 21
Ladies of Llangollen, 19, 20, 26, 241–246
Lake, Dr. Edward, 17, 138–140
Leeds, Thomas Osborne, Duke of, 20
Leland, 17
Lennox (*see* Gordon-Lennox).
Lloyd, Captain Eyre, 39, 418–420
Luttrell, N., 5, 152–153

Macaulay, Lord, 5, 13, 19, 389–393
Macaulay, Margaret, 393
Machyn, Henry, 58–61
Malcolm, Lady, 17, 354
Malmesbury, 1st Earl of, 5, 13, 18, 234–236
Malmesbury, 2nd Earl of, 22
Manning, Cardinal, 31, 380–385
Manningham, John, 16, 17, 24, 112–114
Marchant, Thomas, 13, 196–197
Martyn, Henry, 16, 39, 332–335
Matthews, Henry, 355–357
Melcombe, Lord (*see* Dodington, George Bubb)
Millar, W. S., 23, 39
Mitchell, J., vii
Montaigne, 76
Moore, Giles, 19, 20, 125–128
Moore, Sir John, vii
Mordaunt, Sir Charles, 23
More, John, 26, 147–8

Newcombe, Henry, 14, 15, 16, 39, 128–131
Nugent, Lady, 15, 29, 35, 328–331

Oliver, Peter, 252
Ossington, Viscount (*see* Denison, John Evelyn).

Pease, Edward, 6, 376–379
Pepys, Samuel, 6, 13, 14, 15, 17, 19, 20, 25, 34, 36, 82–95, 96, 97, 146, 202
Percival, Viscount (*see* Egmont, Earl of).
Ponsonby, Colonel A., 13, 397–400
Ponsonby, Sarah (*see* Ladies of Llangollen)
Powys, Mrs., 252–3

Raikes, Thomas, 21, 35, 369–371
Rickman, Edward, 357
Robinson, Henry Crabb, 6, 17, 21, 36, 344–349
Rooke, Admiral Sir George, 251
Rose, George, 13, 327–8
Rous, John, 24, 116–118
Rugge, T., 5, 152
Rutland, John Manners, Earl of, 154
Rutty, Dr., 6, 13, 14, 26, 215–220

INDEX

Scott, Captain, 27-28
Scott, Sir Walter, vii
Senior, Nassau, 5, 396-397
Shelley, Frances, Lady, 39, 318-320
Shelley, Mary, 15, 19, 349-352
Shelley, Percy Bysshe, 349, 350
Slingsby, Sir Henry, 15, 26, 34, 76-81
Smith, Thomas, 23
Stapley, Richard, 19, 155
Stevens, Edwin, 23
Strother, 5, 237-241
Swabey, Lieutenant, 342-344
Swift, J., vii
Symonds, J. A., 11, 14, 39, 407-411

Tennyson, Lord, 4
Teonge, Henry, 15, 39, 107-111
Thomlinson, John, 10, 197-200
Thoresby, Ralph, 13, 16, 21, 36, 134-136
Tolstoy, 10

Turner, Thomas, 5, 15, 39, 227-231

Victoria, Queen, 6, 20, 25, 29, 36, 288-299

Walsingham, Sir Francis, 66-68
Wesley, John, 13, 36, 38, 156-163
West, Sir Algernon, viii (*note*)
West, Arthur Graeme, 3, 39, 428-432
Wilberforce, Bishop, 35, 385-389
Willoughby de Broke, Lord, 23
Windham, Lieut.-General Sir Charles, 400-403
Windham, William, 6, 12, 13, 19, 31, 181, 184-192
Worthington, John, 20
Wynne, Frances, 24, 422

Yerburgh, H. B., 23
Younger, Walter, 21

THE LIBRARY
ST. MARY'S COLLEGE OF MARYLAND
ST. MARY'S CITY, MARYLAND 20686

75535

DATE DUE			
MAY 3 0 2006			